# Poetry of Contemplation

# Poetry of Contemplation

## JOHN DONNE, GEORGE HERBERT, HENRY VAUGHAN, AND THE MODERN PERIOD

ARTHUR L. CLEMENTS

State University of New York Press

Published by
State University of New York Press, Albany
©1990 State University of New York

For information, address State University of New York
Press, State University Plaza, Albany, NY 12246

**Library of Congress Cataloging-in Publication Data**

Clements, Arthur L.
  Poetry of contemplation: John Donne, George Herbert, Henry Vaughan, and the
modern period / Arthur L. Clements.
    p. cm.
  Bibliography: p.
  Includes index.
  ISBN 0-7914-0126-X. — ISBN 0-7914-0127-8 (pbk.)
    1. English poetry—Early modern, 1500–1700—History and criticism.
2. Contemplation in literature. 3. Christian poetry. English-
-History and criticism. 4. Mysticism in literature. 5. Donne,
John, 1572–1631—Criticism and interpretation. 6. Herbert, George,
1593–1633—Criticism and interpretation. 7. Vaughan, Henry,
1622–1695—Criticism and interpretation. 8. Literature,
Modern—20th century—History and criticism. I. Title.
PR545.C675C57   1990
821°.3°09384—dc19                                        88-32408
                                                              CIP

10  9  8  7  6  5  4  3  2  1

*For my children,*
*Margaret,*
*Stephen,*
*Michael,*
*and Thomas*

*And for my grandchildren,*
*Michele,*
*Phillip,*
*Rachele,*
*and Anthony*

# CONTENTS

# ACKNOWLEDGMENTS

This book has been a long time in the making. Since "gratitude is heaven itself," as William Blake remarks, it is thus a very special pleasure to express appreciation for the help and encouragement of those who contributed in various ways to its making.

I feel a particular sense of debt and gratitude to two of my teachers, W. T. Stace and R. A. Durr, who early stimulated my interest, respectively, in the philosophy of religion and in seventeenth-century poetry, and from both of whom I learned much about mysticism. I hope and believe their good influences may be apparent from the beginning to the end of this book.

Friends and colleagues made various contributions. Albert Tricomi of SUNY-Binghamton read through the manuscript and offered many thoughtful suggestions; I was able to consult with him during the development of the manuscript through earlier and later versions, and I invariably found his responses constructive and helpful. Mary Giles of California State University, Sacramento, gave much specific, useful advice not only as a reader of the manuscript but also earlier as the editor of *Studia Mystica*, in which two of my essays incorporated in this book were previously published; I am especially grateful for her advice to expand the last chapter and strengthen the case for the transformative power of contemplative poetry. Robert Boenig and Terence Hoagwood, both of Texas A&M University, also read the manuscript and provided many thoughtful and detailed comments for improvements. Norman Burns of SUNY-Binghamton read part of the manuscript. All students of seventeenth-century English literature are of course indebted to the work of Louis L. Martz of Yale University and Joseph H. Summers of the University of Rochester; I have benefitted, additionally, from their insightful read-

vii

ings of my manuscript. I am conscious of the valuable contributions made by all these readers. The shortcomings are my own.

If this book is at all gracefully written, it owes much to the help, example, and presence of the poet, Susan Hauptfleisch Clements, my wife.

My friend and colleague Philip Brady helped with the proofreading and index. Tamara Jetton, a student in my graduate seventeenth-century poetry seminar, Fall 1989, also helped with proofreading.

The National Endowment for the Humanities awarded me a fellowship which provided free time to do some of the research and writing on George Herbert. The Research Foundation of the State University of New York supported the research and writing of other parts of this book with awards of summer fellowships in 1973, 1974, and 1978. The Union of University Professionals of the State University of New York granted two Faculty Travel Awards to enable me to travel to libraries to conduct research.

The following publishers and journals kindly granted permission to reprint, usually in a much revised form, some of my previously published work.

From *The Mystical Poetry of Thomas Traherne*. Reprinted by permission of Harvard University Press.

From "Theme, Tone and Tradition in George Herbert's Poetry," *English Literary Renaissance*, 3 (1973), 264–283. Reprinted by permission of *English Literary Renaissance*.

From "Mysticism, Science, and the Task of Poetry," *Studia Mystica*, 9 (1986), 46–59, and "Meditation and Contemplation in Henry Vaughan: 'The Night,' " 10 (1987), 3–33. Reprinted by permission of *Studia Mystica*.

From "Donne's 'Holy Sonnet XIV,' " *Modern Language Notes*, 76 (1961), 484–489. Reprinted by permission of The Johns Hopkins University Press.

From "Sacramental Vision: The Poetry of Robert Penn Warren," *South Atlantic Bulletin*, 43 (1978), 47–65. Reprinted by permission of South Atlantic Modern Language Association.

From "Syntax, Structure, and Self in Galway Kinnell's Poetry," 6 (1987), 56–85. Reprinted by permission of *Cumberland Poetry Review*.

The following publishers kindly granted permission to reprint some of the work of others.

From *Mysticism* by Evelyn Underhill. Reprinted by permission of NAL Penguin, Inc.

Acknowledgments

From Robert Penn Warren's *New and Selected Poems: 1923–1985*, and *Selected Poems 1923–1975*. Copyright by Robert Penn Warren. Reprinted by permission of Random House.
From *The Complete Poems of D. H. Lawrence*, collected and edited by Vivian de Sola Pinto and F. Warren Roberts. Copyright (c) 1964, 1971 by Angelo Ravagli and C. M. Weekley, Executors of the Estate of Frieda Lawrence Ravagli. All rights reserved. Reprinted by permission of Viking Penguin, a division of Penguin Books USA, Inc.
From *The Collected Letters of D. H. Lawrence* by D. H. Lawrence. Copyright 1932 by the Estate of D. H. Lawrence. Copyright renewed (c) 1960 by the Estate of Frieda Lawrence Ravagli. All rights reserved. Reprinted by permission of Viking Penguin, a division of Penguin Books USA, Inc.
"The Bear" from *Body Rags* by Galway Kinnell. Copyright (c) 1967 by Galway Kinnell. Reprinted by permission of Houghton Mifflin Company.
"St. Francis and the Sow" and "Fergus Falling" from *Mortal Acts, Mortal Words* by Galway Kinnell. Copyright (c) 1980 by Galway Kinnell. Reprinted by permission of Houghton Mifflin Company.
"Freedom, New Hampshire" from *What a Kingdom It Was* by Galway Kinnell. Copyright (c) 1960 by Galway Kinnell. Reprinted by permission of Houghton Mifflin Company.

# PREFACE

The *Argument.* As the true method of knowledge is exper-
iment, the true faculty of knowing must be the faculty
which experiences. This faculty I treat of . . . the Poetic
Genius is the true Man.

William Blake

The desire for union with God is the basic and vital center of reli-
gious life, and this desire is the essence of mysticism. Mystical
or contemplative experience is the heart of religion in the sense that
it characterizes the divine as being present in experience. Every mys-
tic's distinction is that he or she attains to union or an aspect of it
*in this life,* and need not wait entirely until the afterlife. The mystic
is the one who, given an initial and partial realization of higher real-
ity, makes the fervent *attempt* to realize full union. Mysticism need
not and must not be set apart from orthodox faith-religion but is in
fact its most profound and essential life. The wise mystic, as Rufus
Jones notes, does not exalt his own illuminations over historical rev-
elation, but rather interprets them "in the light of the master-revela-
tions."

To understand the seventeenth-century religious poets requires
a knowledge of the central religious tradition that they themselves
would have known, lived, and dwelled in, for this tradition, through
its Bible and its writers, theologians, and Church doctors ("the light
of the master-revelations"), formulates what is most essential to
these poets: their relationship to divinity. John Donne's religious
consciousness seems in a sense more fully developed and advanced
in his secular rather than in his divine poetry. This critical percep-
tion by itself may suggest how important and permeating religious

consciousness was in everyday life during the Middle Ages and Renaissance. Perhaps the modern mind, after "the death of God" in the nineteenth century, cannot fully appreciate, at least without a radical transformation of that mind, that the religious life was as vital, integral, and nourishing to the seventeenth-century poet as earth, sun, air, and rain are to a flower. And at the center of the heart of that religious life was the passionate contemplative desire for union with divinity. Thus, a knowledge of contemplative tradition and of the nature of contemplative life is central to an understanding and appreciation of these poets. To be a Christian in the fullest sense, each one of them would thoroughly need and want to be, as this book intends the terms, a Christian *contemplative*.

Critical opinion has been vigorously and variously advanced concerning the major religious elements of meditation and contemplation (or mysticism) in the poetry of John Donne, George Herbert, and Henry Vaughan. First, there are those critics who argue ably and knowledgeably that these three are meditative poets; secondly, those who adduce considerable scholarship to establish one or another of the three poets not primarily as meditative but as mystical; and, thirdly, those who with seemingly equal skill, contend that no one of the three is at all a mystic, or who at least reject the primacy of mysticism.

One of many reasons for the critical division regarding mysticism in these poets may simply involve the matter of which poems a critic focuses upon. Some of their poems are conventionally religious and pious; some are mainly meditative; but others, usually their most distinguished and highly regarded poems, have profound and powerful mystical elements in them, sometimes alongside the pious and meditative elements. Hence critics may well be divided; and hence the answer to the question whether these poets are mystical (which some critics answer yes and others no) is yes and no—depending on which poems one is referring to, on whether one believes a few or many poems must be mystical before designating a poet mystical, and, especially, on how one understands the meaning of "mysticism."

The critical problem is of course more serious than just choosing poems, and is in part linguistic, or definitional, precisely because the vexed yet vital question of mysticism in the seventeenth-century religious poets is often answered in terms of confused, uncertain, or ambiguous usages of the word "mysticism." As the anonymous Benedictine author of *Medieval Mystical Tradition and Saint John of the Cross* remarks, "*mysticism* is one of the most abused words in all civilized languages." To say nothing of widespread popular use and misuse, various scholars, whether they regard any one of these poets as a mystic or not, may readily be found using this troublesome word and its grammatical variants in quite different and even casual, inexact ways. Oversimplified, inaccurate, and untraditional usages are misleading and in effect turn discussion of mysticism in seventeenth-century poetry essentially into rhetorical argument. Although there is no single, simple, wholly satisfactory "definition" of mysticism, there are many reliable and valuable scholarly works which should help to clarify and de-mystify the subject, and raise it from the level of rhetoric to substance. Works by such distinguished modern authors as Aldous Huxley, Thomas Merton, Sidney Spencer, W. T. Stace, D. T. Suzuki, Evelyn Underhill, and Alan Watts, to name a few, admirably describe the common and distinctive characteristics of mystical experiences.

Even if mysticism were properly understood, still another reason for the critical disputes and division is the failure to distinguish carefully the stages of the spiritual life. This failure is understandable, for such distinguishing is itself difficult and complicated; and the stages of spiritual growth through which the mystic typically passes are sometimes rendered as three or seven or five, depending on the degree of generality or particularity desired. Few travellers of the *via mystica* present them all in perfection, and in many cases some stages are blurred, not readily apparent, or even absent. Yet, even with such difficulties, the effort to distinguish, which this book shall make, must be made in order to help determine the extent to which the poetry is meditative or contemplative.

Other reasons for critical differences and difficulties arise from the notion that religious poets may have recourse to mystical terminology as a source of powerful metaphor and, more importantly, from the fact that meditation leads to and blends into contemplation and is therefore not always readily distinguishable from it. Given these circumstances, Louis Martz properly cautions against hasty and inaccurate labeling of meditative writers as mystical. He is of course aware of the presence of mystical elements in Donne, Herbert, Vaughan, and Traherne, but he believes that "the term 'meditative' seems . . . more accurate than 'mystical' when applied to English religious poetry of the seventeenth century." Although "meditative" may seem more accurate than the term "mystical" or "contemplative" when applied *in general* to English religious poetry of the seventeenth century, there still remain two important questions: (1) which term is more accurate when applied to *particular* poems and to a *particular* poet of the seventeenth century; and (2) to what extent did ancient-medieval-Renaissance contemplative litera- ture, in addition to sixteenth-century meditative literature, "influ- ence" seventeenth-century English religious poetry.

Since there is no simple, wholly satisfactory definition of mysti- cism, and since the word is emotionally charged, ambiguous, and troublesome, to say the least, a critic may, instead of using a simple or otherwise unsatisfactory definition, alternatively read widely in the primary and secondary literature of mysticism and then apply such knowledge as appropriate to the study of particular poets and poems in the hope that such efforts might be illuminating. Having recourse to mystical tradition, to the traditional distinction between meditation and contemplation, to the stages, types, and kinds of mysticism, to key contemplative ideas, and to certain lucidly de- scribed characteristics of mystical experience may help bring a de- gree of clarity and precision to this vexed subject. All of these mysti- cal matters will be discussed in Chapter One, Contemplative Tradi- tion, which thereby provides some definition of "contemplation" and "contemplative tradition." Chapters Two, Three, and Four will apply the terms and distinctions of the first chapter as necessary to, respectively, Donne, Herbert, and Vaughan, in order to determine more clearly and certainly the nature and extent of contemplation in their major poetry and thereby further to illuminate that poetry. The concluding Chapter Five will extend this study of contempla- tive poetry to some modern poets (concentrating on D. H. Lawrence, Robert Penn Warren, and Galway Kinnell) and to contemporary con- cerns, including scientific and moral matters. The primary object of this book, then, is the scholarly one of addressing the matter of mys- ticism in this major poetry. By relating this poetry to contemporary issues, the last chapter attempts to show the continuing relevance of contemplative poets to the modern reader so that, among other reasons, they, and poets in general, may acquire the larger audience that poets deserve.

In a large measure, this book is an outgrowth and continuation of my work on *The Mystical Poetry of Thomas Traherne* (Harvard). Traherne, that book shows, may best be understood by setting his poetry in the context of ancient-medieval-Renaissance contempla- tive tradition. The main question for this present book is precisely to what extent and in what particular qualified ways may Donne, Herbert, and Vaughan be thus viewed. This book intends to present the best—fullest, fairest, most accurate—reading of contemplation in the work of these poets. Although the poetry of Traherne is regarded as the least accomplished poetically of these four poets, it well may be the most spiritually, mystically, advanced. To reverse the usual progress and to proceed from the study of Traherne in the context of contemplative tradition to the study of these earlier seventeenth-century poets may thus provide a valuable perspective. As one of these poets has written,

> Some men a forward motion love,
> But I by backward steps would move.

Admittedly, forward steps may also lead to genuine progress in appreciating these poets, so, where appropriate, this book will draw, too, upon the valuable contributions to our subject made by various modern authorities, critics, and writers as well as by ancient, medieval, and Renaissance ones, so that a double perspective may bring into sharper focus, "as two eyes make one in sight," the poets of our study.

The wealth of valuable work by many critics and editors of Donne, Herbert, and Vaughan places later scholars under heavy debt. Recent scholarship has centered on the question concerning which historical contexts are most appropriate for understanding the texts of these poets, particularly on the issue of Reformation Protestantism versus medieval and counter-Reformation Catholicism, a division which in part may be a twentieth-century fabrication. The abundance of fine critical work makes citing names in this Preface impractical. Much of my indebtedness to many critics and editors will become apparent in the course of this book and in the Notes. Since various sources, influences, backgrounds, and contexts contribute significantly to informing a major poet's work, study of these various elements obviously may improve our understanding of the poetry. By considering the context of contemplative tradition both in its ancient and medieval dimensions and in its Renaissance aspects, I intend to take both telescopic and microscopic views, as it were, of Donne, Herbert, and Vaughan, to provide both a perennial and a contemporary single Catholic-Protestant tradition as illuminating context, and thereby perhaps also help bridge some of the divisions, real and apparent, between Reformation Protestantism and medieval and counter-Reformation Catholicism.

Of necessity, not all the important questions pertaining to a complex subject can be answered in a single book. For example, how generally did Anglicans and other Protestants respond to mystical tradition; how did they modify or otherwise make use of it? What is the relationship of mystical tradition to formal aspects of Anglican theology or to Calvinism? How did Perkins, Adams, Ussher, and Hall, for example, understand and define contemplation? How did Protestants in general modify medieval Catholic contemplative tradition to accord with the tenets of their faith? Do Protestant and Catholic mystical traditions differ in essential ways? Because mysticism, in its concentration on what is most essential about religion, tends to transcend sectarian and denominational boundaries, I believe Catholic and Protestant mystical traditions do not differ significantly in essential matters. But this book's primary concern is with the response of Donne, Herbert, and Vaughan (not of Anglicans or Protestants in general) to contemplative tradition and especially with the ways by which that tradition may eludicate these poets' works. While I can and do consider, directly and indirectly, some relevant sixteenth- and seventeenth-century figures, including Protestant ones, it is beyond the intention and scope of this book to study Donne, Herbert, and Vaughan exclusively (or even just more thoroughly) from the perspective of sixteenth-century Protestantism. Such a study, answering the above and other questions, should prove valuable but must be the subject of another book. Obviously, mysticism is not simply or solely a sixteenth-century phenomenon. To understand it as it probably would have presented itself to Donne, Herbert, and Vaughan necessitates adopting a large historical contemplative context from the Bible and Plato and early Church Fathers through important mystics of the Middle Ages to sixteenth- and seventeenth-century contemplatives.

The first four chapters mainly, but not exclusively, treat the poem within this broad mystical context as an object which we can determine is or is not contemplative in the precise senses delineated by this book. As indicated, for example, by the many more frequent references to "the poem" and to "the poet or speaker" rather than just to "the poet," the main focus in these chapters is on the text, not the poet, person, human being who wrote the text (such focus being all the more important because many vital biographical facts concerning Donne, Herbert, and Vaughan are unavailable). Since mysticism is essentially an experimental or experiential matter, discussing the subject necessarily involves discussing "mystical experience." But merely to say that "Donne, Herbert, and Vaughan may or may not have undergone mystical experiences" is cautiously to avoid the "naive expressive theory," according to current anti-autobiographical critical trends, and to make a true but timid, safe, and not very meaningful statement. Would we say that Donne, Herbert, and Vaughan wrote meditative poems but did not practice meditation? Should we assert that a poet wrote contemplative poems but did not experience contemplation? Of course, a poet may write one or a few "meditative" and "contemplative" poems for the sake of literary exercise or for whatever other reasons. But to suppose that a poet might compose a large body of meditative and contemplative poems with no relation to or revelation of his own spiritual life is simply silly, not genuinely scholarly. The relationship between poem and poet's life is often tenuous, complex, and difficult to determine but also usually not non-existent. That difficulty should not silence us but rather prompt us to exercise the best scholarly care and arguments in order to make informed, intelligent, reasonable statements. Besides, it is not any biographical details of the poet's life that we are here trying to determine from the poetry but, beyond our main concern with the poetry itself, whether that poetry generally suggests the poet may have been a contemplative, and, if so, in what sense. Literary criticism must be scholarly in the best senses but need not be merely insular and irrelevant. Renaissance and modern poets, including Lawrence, Warren, and Kinnell, have discussed the vital connection between their works and their own experience, especially religious experience, between poetry and the "real" world, between the moral and esthetic concerns as aspects of creative activity, and between poetry and the two selves. Scholars (as well as poets) should, at least occasionally, swim out into the deep waters, go beyond the text and attempt to use all their accumulated knowledge and wisdom to make some intelligent statements (speculations, if you prefer) about the relation of text to author, reader, and world. In the last section of Chapter Four and in Chapter Five, the question, implicit throughout the book, of contemplative poetry's redemptive and transformative power becomes most prominent, and the relevance, indeed the vital necessity, of such poetry to the "real" world and to human life, to the reader, is explicitly discussed. The poet, the reader, and the outer world, as well as the poem, all come into consideration in the hope that this book will stimulate informed dialog both about contemplation in poetry and about the value of the poetry of contemplation to our lives.

# CONTEMPLATIVE TRADITION

> One of the awful things about writing when you are a
> Christian is that for you the ultimate reality is the Incarna-
> tion, the present reality is the Incarnation, and nobody be-
> lieves in the Incarnation; that is, nobody in your audience.
> My audience are the people who think God is dead.
>
> Flannery O'Connor

In my view, the context most pertinent and enlightening for the study of Donne, Herbert, and Vaughan, as well as Traherne, is the rich and complex Christian contemplative or mystical tradition,[1] with which their own visions are most in accord. This is to imply that their most important actual or probable sources and influences, direct or indirect, are the Bible, Plato, Aristotle, Plotinus, Church Fathers, and Renaissance Humanists, and that to these one should add, either as direct sources and influences or at least as spiritual brethren, such names as Richard of St. Victor, St. Bonaventura, Meister Eckhart, Jan Ruysbroeck, the author of *The Cloud of Unknowing*, Walter Hilton, Julian of Norwich, St. John of the Cross, and Jacob Boehme, to list in chronological order but a few Christian mystics among the many contemplatives whose major ideas correspond closely to these poets' ideas and whose writings may therefore illuminate their poems.

A major assumption of this book, then, is that much of the poetry of Donne, Herbert, and Vaughan may best be understood and appreciated through the perspective and within the context of Christian contemplative tradition, including of course the effect of the Bible, Plato, Neoplatonism, and Aristotelianism on that tradition. The great speculative Christian school of mysticism, especially between Eckhart and Boehme, forms a curiously well-integrated tradition (and one which might be considered roughly equivalent to a Christian branch of the Perennial Philosophy). Renaissance and later medieval mystics were familiar with earlier Christian mystics as well as with the Church Fathers, many of whom were themselves contemplatives, and with classical writers. Even Plotinus himself, the pagan Neoplatonist who so remarkably affected Christianity, like other Neoplatonists often employs Aristotelian vocabulary, argumentation, and ideas. The numerous strands of this complex contemplative tradition are more variously and closely interwoven than might at first glance appear.[2] Even if the reader finally does not share the view that this broad yet interconnected Catholic-Protestant tradition provides the most illuminating context for the Anglican poets Donne, Herbert, and Vaughan, I trust the reader will nevertheless find that numerous poems are elucidated by this book's approach and methods and that the very confused subject of mysticism in these poets is somewhat clarified.

Drawing upon all of the authors mentioned above and other mystics, modern scholars provide an analytical overview of ancient-medieval-Renaissance contemplative tradition or, more precisely, different aspects of it as it existed in the Renaissance and was known to seventeenth-century and later writers. These aspects include the stages, types, and characteristics of mystical experience, the kinds of "vision," and some key contemplative ideas, such as regeneration and the distinctions between the two selves and between meditation and contemplation. This century has produced valuable scholarship on mysticism, and one cannot reasonably expect to improve much upon the brilliant work of distinguished authorities. Thus, availing itself of the more pertinent scholarship, this chapter presents a synthetic account of contemplative tradition, grounded in the many mystical writings of antiquity, the Middle Ages and the Renaissance, via some of the best (for our purposes) modern authorities. But as a scholar of mysticism, I hope also in other ways to make various, direct contributions to the subject. Thus, in addition to the relevant work of twentieth-century experts on mysticism, I will also, as needed, directly consider in this and later chapters contributions of the Bible, Plato, Aristotle, and numerous specifically mentioned mystics and Church Fathers. This twofold method should afford an efficient, scholarly way of providing the necessary background and concepts of a very complex subject in an orderly, clear, and accurate manner.

The anonymous Benedictine author of *Medieval Mystical Tradition and Saint John of the Cross*, who surveys the meanings of the words *meditation, prayer,* and *contemplation,* points out that in the twelfth century and later there existed the scale or order, going from lowest to highest, of *lectio divina* (prayerful reading of some portion of the Scripture), meditation, prayer, contemplation. Contemplation was understood as "an experimental union with God which no meditation can produce, but for which a soul may pray. . . . The soul is 'athirst,' 'aglow with love,' and God's answer is contemplation— obviously the 'infused contemplation' of modern spiritual theology. Since there can be no question of real 'beginners' reaching this stage, we can see how gradually, as this meaning became attached to contemplation, that word came to be synonymous with *contemplative or mystical prayer*. Meditation and contemplation came to mean an earlier and a later kind of prayer, and no longer a mere difference in degree in one and the same prayer . . . . the latter [contemplation] is a free gift of God." (9).

Although the word "meditation" was sometimes used interchangeably in the sixteenth and seventeenth centuries with the closely related words "prayer" and "contemplation," the terms did, however, also retain in those centuries the same distinct medieval meanings. As St. John of the Cross writes, "the state of beginners comprises meditation and discursive acts" (*Flame*, III, 30, in *Complete Works*, III, 68). Meditation, Louis Martz points out, "cultivates the basic, the lower levels of the spiritual life; it is not, properly speaking, a mystical activity, but a part of the duties of every man in daily life" (*The Poetry of Meditation*, 16). Even more than as a set form of prayer, meditation was understood as a lower, early, or pre-mystical stage of the spiritual life, which may very well employ certain forms of prayer. It was considered an almost indispensable preparation for the progressive realization of mystical experience or contemplation, the higher level and goal of spiritual progress. To be a meditative poet, therefore, is to be at least potentially a mystical poet, to be, in any event, in the early stages of and in progress toward the contemplative life, and we should indeed expect to find meditative poems in the body of a mystical poet's work.

In the Middle Ages and during the Renaissance, spiritual life and progress were frequently but not always charted by the threefold stages of the Purgative Way, Illuminative Way, and Unitive Way or, more simply, Purgation, Illumination, and Union. The stages of spiritual growth through which the mystic passes were sometimes rendered as more than three, depending on the degree of generality or particularity desired. As exemplified by Richard Rolle's *The Form of Perfect Living* and the anonymous *Contemplations of the Dread and Love of God*, different spiritual writers preferred different systems of stages. During the Renaissance, however, the time-honored trifold system was basic and continues so to the present day. Like the more numerous stages of other systems, the three stages, well-known to seventeenth-century writers, are, of course, to be understood as diagrammatic, as an approximate and useful map, not as the actual territory of the mystical life, with its multivaried peaks, plateaus, and valleys. It is helpful to relate this traditional threefold schema in a general way to the traditional distinction between meditation and contemplation. We may say that meditation, the early period of the spiritual life, generally corresponds to Purgation; and contemplation, advanced periods of spiritual life, corresponds to Illumination and Union. Meditation may lead to contemplation, and the early stages may lead to the later ones. To determine whether a writer is or is not a mystic is in part to make a judgment about his progress in these familiar, well-described, and traditional terms. It must be emphasized that there is no absolute disjunction but rather a continuity, interrelationship, and movement back and forth between meditation and contemplation and the stages of the mystical life. For example, "Saint John of the Cross not only says that progressives, who have begun to receive graces of mystical contemplation, should return to active meditation whenever they 'see that the soul is not occupied in repose and (mystical) knowledge.' He adds that meditation is *an ordinary means of disposing oneself* for mystical prayer. 'In order to reach this state, [the soul] will frequently need to make use of meditation, quietly and in moderation' " (Merton, 89–90). Indeed, we might well find both meditative and contemplative elements in a single poem.

The above description reveals the basic, essential way a seventeenth-century writer would regard both the *via mystica* and the significance of *meditation* and *contemplation*. Evelyn Underhill details two more stages in addition to the time-honored threefold division of Purgation, Illumination, and Union. We need not be concerned with Underhill's preliminary stage of Awakening, which precedes Purgation, for our three poets, two of them Anglican ministers, were undoubtedly awake to and believed in the reality of divinity. But the additional, *advanced* purgative stage of the Dark Night of the Soul, which follows Illumination and which Underhill bases primarily on the work of the great 16th-century contemplative, St. John of the Cross, provides a refinement that will be of particular value to the distinctions we will need to make with respect to Herbert and especially Vaughan. A large part of Underhill's classic work on *Mysticism* is devoted to describing the traditional mystic stages. For present purposes, it may suffice to quote Underhill's introductory briefer description of the stages from Purgation to Union.

The Self, aware of Divine Beauty, realizes by contrast its own finiteness and imperfection, the manifold illusions in which it is immersed, the immense distance which separates it from the One. Its attempts to eliminate by discipline and mortification all that stands in the way of its progress towards union with God constitute *Purgation*: a state of pain and effort.

When by Purgation the Self has become detached from the "things of sense," and acquired those virtues which are the "ornaments of the spiritual marriage," its joyful consciousness of the Transcendent Order returns in an enhanced form. Like the prisoners in Plato's "Cave of Illusion," it has awakened to knowledge of Reality, has struggled up the harsh and difficult path to the mouth of the cave. Now it looks upon the sun. This is *Illumination*: a state which includes in itself many of the stages of contemplation, "degrees of orison," visions and adventures of the soul described by St. Teresa and other mystical writers. These form, as it were, a way within the Way: *a moyen de parvenir*, a training devised by experts which will strengthen and assist the mounting soul. They stand, so to speak, for education; whilst the Way proper represents organic growth. Illumination is the contemplative state *par excellence*. . . . Many mystics never go beyond it; and, on the other hand, many seers and artists not usually classed amongst them, have shared, to some extent, the experiences of the illuminated state. Illumination brings a certain apprehension of the Absolute, a sense of the Divine Presence: but not true union with it. It is a state of happiness.

In the development of the great and strenuous seekers after God, this is followed—or sometimes intermittently accompanied —by the most terrible of all the experiences of the Mystic Way: the final and complete purification of the Self, which is called by some contemplatives the "mystic pain" or "mystic death," by others the Purification of the Spirit or *Dark Night of the Soul*. The consciousness which had, in Illumination, sunned itself in the sense of the Divine Presence, now suffers under an equally intense sense of the Divine Absence: learning to dissociate the personal satisfaction of mystical vision from the reality of mystical life. As in Purgation the senses were cleansed and humbled, and the energies and interests of the Self were concentrated upon transcendental things: so now the purifying process is extended to the very centre of I-hood, the will. The human instinct for personal happiness must be killed. This is the "spiritual crucifixion" so often described by the mystics: the great desolation in which the soul seems abandoned by the Divine. The Self now surrenders itself, its individuality, and its will, completely. It desires nothing, asks nothing, is utterly passive, and is thus prepared for

*Union*: the true goal of the mystic quest. In this state the Absolute

> Life is not merely perceived and enjoyed by the Self, as in Illumination: but is *one* with it. This is the end towards which all the previous oscillations of consciousness have tended. It is a state of equilibrium, of purely spiritual life; characterized by peaceful joy, by enhanced powers, by intense certitude. (169–170)

Although Christianity has been insistently monotheistic over against the polytheism of paganism, the Church does recognize what may mistakenly appear to some as a kind of pantheism. Strictly speaking, it is not pantheism but the omnipresence of the one God that is recognized. An important factor of the mystic experience is the discovery of the immanence and/or transcendence of God. To the catechism question "Where is God?" the proper response is "everywhere." To the enlightened mystic, when the veils of custom, convention and selfish solicitude are removed and the third eye opened, God appears in the features and faces of human beings and in the forms of Nature as well as being wholly transcendent. Hence, mystical experiences may be "extrovertive," aware of immanent divinity through the redeemed senses, or "introvertive," conscious of transcendent divinity beyond all the senses. In his admirable and lucid discussion of world-wide mysticism, *Mysticism and Philosophy*, W. T. Stace introduces these terms, which correspond to terminology used by Rudolf Otto and Evelyn Underhill, and he adds that both the extrovertive or outward and introvertive or inward experiences "culminate in the perception of an ultimate Unity—what Plotinus called the One—with which the perceiver realizes his own union or even identity. But the extrovertive mystic, using his physical senses, perceives the multiplicity of external material objects . . . mystically transfigured so that the One, or the Unity, shines through them. The introvertive mystic, on the contrary, seeks by deliberately shutting off the senses, by obliterating from consciousness the entire multiplicity of sensations, images, and thoughts, to plunge into the depths of his own [self]. There, in that darkness and silence, he alleges that he perceives the One—and is united with it" (61–62). By examining the detailed evidence from both Western and Eastern mysticism, Stace is able to present a list of characteristics, like lists by other writers on the subject, of both types of mystical experience.

In the extrovertive type, the primary and central point around which all other "characteristics revolve is the apprehension of a unity taken to be in some way basic to the universe," frequently though not altogether satisfactorily expressed in the formula "All is

One." "The One is . . . perceived through the physical senses, in or through the multiplicity of objects" (79). From this first characteristic, the second follows: "the more concrete apprehension of the One as an inner subjectivity, or life, in all things" (131).

In the introvertive type, the nuclear characteristic is "the Unitary Consciousness, from which all the multiplicity of sensuous or conceptual or other empirical content has been excluded, so that there remains only a void and empty unity" (110). Inevitably following from this primary point is the second characteristic of being nonspatial and nontemporal.

The remaining characteristics of both extrovertive and introvertive mystical experiences are identical for both:

3. Sense of objectivity or reality
4. Feelings of blessedness, joy, peace, happiness, etc.
5. Feeling that what is apprehended is holy, sacred, or divine
6. Paradoxicality
7. Alleged ineffability (79, 110, 131).

To this, we should add three qualifications: the extrovertive type may also exhibit the characteristic of timelessness; a serious omission from Stace's account, as R. C. Zaehner remarks, is love, which we will include along with feelings of blessedness, joy, etc.;[3] and a complex mystical experience may exhibit both extrovertive and introvertive elements. Generally, contemplative experience is distinguishable as being of one type or the other. But many mystics have both extrovertive and introvertive mystical experiences, sometimes on different occasions, sometimes on the same occasion. Often, one type of mystical experience will lead or predispose a contemplative to the other type.

Whether a mystic experiences one or the other type may depend on (or perhaps it determines) the extent of Platonism or Aristotelianism in his thinking. Plato and some but by no means all Neoplatonists almost exclusively or at least preferably incline toward introvertive mystical experience and tend not to share the extrovertive Hebraic-Christian praise of and joy in God's "very good" (Gen. 1:31) visible creation. When mystics write of not being able to apprehend ultimate reality with the bodily, fleshly, or conventional eyes or senses they are referring either to nonsensuous introvertive mysticism or to the necessity of purgation so that eventually one may sensuously perceive ultimate reality with a pure heart through cleansed senses. The idea that it is Christ who enables us to see with purified hearts in either the introvertive or extrovertive way goes back to the earliest days of the Church. St. Clement of Rome, the first-century bishop and Apostolic Father, whose *Epistle to the Corinthians* portrays an early Christianity of inwardness and the Spirit and yet simultaneously of powerful brotherhood, observes that through Christ "we see as in a mirror the spotless and excellent face of God: through him the eyes of our hearts were opened" (Bettenson, *The Early Christian Fathers*, 29). In *The City of God*, St. Augustine writes: "Thus, it was with his 'heart' that the Prophet says he saw. . . . Now just think, when God will be 'all in all,' how much greater will be this gift of vision in the hearts of all! The eyes of the body will still retain their function and will be found where they now are, and the spirit through its spiritual body will make use of the eyes" (trans. Walsh et al, 535). Redeemed vision in extrovertive experience is seeing not with the senses, but, as William Blake knew, with the heart through the cleansed senses. As opposed to seeing objects in some generalized, rationalistic, abstract way, which ultimately comes to thinking about rather than actually looking at them, contemplative extrovertive vision means Christ in us seeing, means our seeing with fully open eyes rather than with closed or indifferent eyes, seeing felicitously into the particular-universal suchness or quiddity of an object with regenerated or enlightened heart and senses rather than seeing in such a way as mentally to abstract an essence from the object, as if essence and object could ever really (that is, in fact, not just in mind) be dualistically separated. Extrovertive mystical experiences would therefore more likely give rise to (or arise out of, depending on whether or not experience precedes philosophy) an Aristotelian rather than a Platonic metaphysic, insofar as we understand Plato as asserting the separation of Forms and matter and Aristotle as insisting upon the fusing of the universal form with the particular material thing into the complete unity of the individual object. Contrariwise, introvertive mystical experiences would more likely give rise to a Platonic rather than an Aristotelian metaphysic. In other words, Plato puts emphasis on the transcendental nature of ultimate reality; Aristotle stresses its immanence.

One of the important differences, then, between Platonism and Aristotelianism on the one hand and Christian mystical theology on the other is that, whereas the former philosophers tend to regard ultimate reality as either transcendent or immanent, Christian mystics paradoxically see God as both transcendent and immanent. In this sense, Christianity represents a synthesis of the two great ancient influences on Western thought, a synthesis which is reflected in the apophatic (negative) and cataphatic (affirmative) branches of

Christian mystical theology, as discussed, for example, by Dionysius the Areopagite in Chapter 3 of his *Mystical Theology*. Apophatic theology concerns the dark, non-senuous relationship of the self and the ineffable God dwelling in Divine Darkness, concerns the self's movement upwards or, better, inwards (an idea very familiar in Augustine) to the transcendent God. Cataphatic theology concerns God's manifestation of his divinity to the redeemed senses (or, as Augustine says, to the "heart") in and through the universe, which God created and pronounced "very good." In the *Divine Names*, a work on what we can say about God, Dionysius rather succinctly sums up cataphatic and apophatic theology, epitomizes the mystic's experience of immanent divinity and of the wholly transcendent Godhead: "God is known in all things, and apart from all things" (VII.3). In a beautiful, paradoxical passage from his account of his search for God through the memory, Augustine at greater length suggests the transcendent and perhaps also the immanent discovery and love of God:

> But what is it that I love when I love You? Not the beauty of any bodily thing, nor the order of the seasons, not the brightness of light that rejoices the eye, nor the sweet melodies of all songs, nor the sweet fragrance of flowers and ointments and spices; not manna or honey, not the limbs that carnal love embraces. None of these things do I love in loving my God. Yet in a sense I do love light and melody and fragrance and food and embrace when I love my God— the light and the voice and the fragrance and the food and embrace in the soul, when the light shines upon my soul which no place can contain, that voice sounds which no time can take from me, I breathe that fragrance which no wind scatters, I eat the food which is not lessened by eating, and I lie in the embrace which satiety never comes to sunder. This it is that I love, when I love my God. (Confessions, trans., F. J. Sheed, X, vi)

From the immanence and transcendence of the omnipresent God, it follows that at any stage of the contemplative journey the "object" of the mystic may be any one of four possibilities. (The word "object" is in quotation marks because in the mystical experience the usual division between subject and object appears unreal or merely conventional; subject and object, though mentally distinguishable, are experienced as actually one or at least as inextricably interconnected.) First, if the "object" is the natural world or, more usually, some particular part(s) of it, the mystical experience is designated, to employ W. H. Auden's terminology, the Vision of Dame Kind, which medieval phrase we could render in modern terms as Mother Nature. Secondly, if the "object" is another human being with whom the mystic shares erotic love, the experience is called a Vision of Eros. (Needless to add, this does not mean that every sexual experience is a mystical one; sexuality often exists without Eros; other criteria, including the presence of at least some of the above-noted characteristics, must be satisfied as well for an experience to be designated a Vision of Eros.) Thirdly, if the "object" is other individuals toward whom the mystic feels not erotic but brotherly love, the term employed is the Vision of Philia.[4] And fourthly, if the "object" is the transcendent divinity, the experience is named the Vision of God. Auden's discussion of these four kinds of Vision, based upon consideration of Catholic-Protestant contemplative tradition as it would be known to seventeenth-century and later writers, introduces a book, *The Protestant Mystics*, which contains selections from numerous Protestant mystics, including not only the Anglican poets Donne, Herbert, Vaughan, and Traherne, but also such sixteenth- and seventeenth-century Protestant writers as Martin Luther, Jakob Boehme, Samuel Rutherford, Jeremy Taylor, Richard Baxter, and George Fox, as well as later Protestant mystics.

The first three Visions (of Dame Kind, Eros, and Philia) are primarily of the immanent or extrovertive type. The Vision of God is of the transcendent or introvertive type. Because the "object" of the Visions of Eros and Philia includes another human consciousness, these Visions often display as well some introvertive characteristics, especially the Unitary Consciousness. Although the Visions initially, as it were, differ in "object," in a strict sense ultimately they do not: for it is God that is through the redeemed senses sought in nature, the beloved, or other humans, just as it is God that is directly, inwardly, sought in the Vision of God. And although the mystical stages of Purgation, Illumination, Dark Night of the Soul, and Union usually are applied to the Vision of God, they may also profitably be applied to the other Visions. In the stages of Purgation and Dark Night of the Soul, the individual is painfully aware of the absence of the "object" of his vision. In Illumination and Union, the mystic feels the presence of or is joyfully united to the "object" of his Vision.

The end or purpose of passing through the stages of mysticism in one or another kind of Vision is to effect a radical transformation of self, called "regeneration" or "rebirth"; movement through the stages is the regenerative progress. "Regeneration," as intended here, is the heart of the contemplative experience and not just a Christian commonplace. Andrew Louth remarks that "for most of the Fathers (with only rare exceptions) the 'mystical life' is the ultimate flowering of the life of baptism, the life we receive when we share in Christ's death and risen life by being baptized in water and the Holy Spirit" (53). There are, as it were, two "baptisms," one of the letter and the other of the spirit, one of piety and the other mystical, though both are called "regeneration." Baptism of the spirit, regeneration in our sense, is not merely verbal or intellectual grasp of certain principles nor a merely superficial conversion, but rather that deeply realized, radical, and thoroughgoing change in one's mode of consciousness which is both the true beginning and center of the mystic life. This is the kind of regeneration that authoritative writers on mysticism, such as Evelyn Underhill, describe: "The true and definitely mystical life does and must open with that most actual, though indescribable phenomenon, the coming forth into consciousness of man's deeper, spiritual self, which . . . mystical writers of all ages have agreed to call Regeneration or Re-birth." Underhill points out that mystics frequently refer to this phenomenon as "the eternal Birth or Generation of the Son or Divine Word" (*Mysticism*, 122).

In the words of the fourth Evangelist: "Except a corn of wheat fall into the ground and die, it abideth alone: but if it die, it bringeth forth much fruit. He that loveth his life shall lose it; and he that hateth his life in this world shall keep it unto life eternal" (John 12:24–15).[5] This and other biblical passages are metaphors for the same transformation, the same experience of hating, giving up, the illusional, egoistic life to realize the life of the true self. This central paradox of gain through loss, of life through death, embodies a traditional distinction important to understanding so much in Donne, Herbert, and Vaughan: the distinction between the outward and inward man, Greek *psyche* and *pneuma*, Hebrew *nephesh* and *ruach*, the man "himself" and the divine, supra-individual Being. St. Paul, whose trichotomous conception of human nature includes *soma* (body), writes: "The first man Adam was made a living soul [*psyche*]; the last Adam was made a quickening spirit [*pneuma*]" (1 Cor. 15:45). Unlike their rough biblical English equivalents, soul and spirit, the terms *psyche* and *pneuma*, which we may translate into modern English as lesser life and greater life or, more strongly, as false self (ego) and true self, should not carry for the modern reader ambiguous, irrelevant, and distracting meanings after the terms are discussed in this and subsequent chapters.[6]

In a discussion of flesh, soul, and spirit that typifies the best

patristic thinking on the subject, Irenaeus follows Paul's trichoto-
mous conception of human nature and further clarifies for us the dis-
tinction between psyche (soul) and pneuma (spirit):

> There are three elements of which, as we have shown, the complete
> man is made up, flesh, soul, and spirit; one of these preserves and
> fashions the man, and this is the spirit; another is given unity and
> form by the first, and this is the flesh; the third, the soul, is midway
> between the first two, and sometimes it is subservient to the spirit
> and is raised by it: while sometimes it allies itself with the flesh
> and descends to earthly passions. . . . Soul and spirit can be con-
> stituents of man; but they certainly cannot be the whole man. The
> complete man is a mixture and union, consisting of a soul which
> takes to itself the Spirit of the Father, to which is united the flesh
> which was fashioned in the image of God . . . men are spiritual not
> by the abolition of the flesh . . . there would then be the spirit of
> man, or the Spirit of God, not a spiritual man. But when this spirit
> is mingled with soul and united with created matter, then through
> the outpouring of the Spirit the complete man is produced; this is
> man made in the image and likeness of God. A man with soul only,
> lacking spirit [?Spirit], is 'psychic'; such a man is carnal, un-
> finished, incomplete; he has, in his created body, the image of God,
> but he has not acquired the likeness to God through the spirit
> [?Spirit]. (Bettenson, *Early Christian Fathers*, 70–71)

Bettenson notes that "Irenaeus does not clearly distinguish between
'spirit of man' and 'Spirit of God' bestowed on man. It is often impos-
sible to know which he means" (70, n. 1). The ambiguity may well
be deliberate to suggest the ultimate unity of man and God, for
Irenaeus earlier writes that "God who is the totality of all these
must needs include all things in his infinite being" (65).

Traveling the *via mystica* accomplishes the most supreme act of
Self-knowledge: it is to undergo the transformation from being the
first Adam to becoming the last Adam, from psyche to pneuma, from
egohood to Selfhood. It is to make that spiritual journey whereby
man's divine image is restored. And since, as Irenaeus remarks, "first
we were made men, then, in the end, gods" (Bettenson, *Early Chris-
tian Fathers*, 69), it is to be transhumanized, in Dante's phrase, from
a human into a god. For the three Christian poets of our study it is,
in short, to become Christlike. "For since by man came death, by
man came also the resurrection of the dead. For as in Adam all die,
even so in Christ shall all be made alive" (1 Cor. 15:21–22). What it
means "to become Christlike," beyond what is said in this chapter,
is a large part of the burden of the following chapters.

Traditionally, the Bible has been regarded by Christian theologians and mystics as a definitive myth extending from Creation to Apocalypse. Its unity depends upon the series of movements related to the process of creation, fall, redemption (and apocalypse) in the coming (and second coming) of Christ. In biblical terms, this spiritual progression, successfully completed, may be spoken of as the regaining of Eden or Paradise, or the recovery of that divine, creative, and redemptive image which is hidden within man, or the restoring of divine Sonship. When Jesus was baptized, "the Holy Ghost descended in a bodily shape like a dove upon him, and a voice came from heaven, which said, Thou art my beloved Son; in thee I am well pleased" (Luke 3:22). Luke goes on to draw up the genealogy of Jesus, "being (as was supposed) the son of Joseph," continuing on back to "Adam, which was the son of God" (3:23–38). As Adam was the son of God, so is Jesus, the last Adam. Since the Fall alienated every man, Adam, from God, every man has to become again the son of God through the redemption of Christ; psyche must become pneuma, the lesser life or false self (in modern parlance) must become the greater life or true self: this is the basic meaning of the key mystical idea or overriding archetype of regeneration or rebirth. The myth of the Fall and the archetype of rebirth designate the same realities. As every seventeenth-century English poet might be expected to know, a human is an Adam, either the first or the last, and spiritual progress consists in rebirth, in the movement from one Adam to the other. Just as a Buddhist must discover his Buddha nature, a Christian must become Christ or Christlike. A Christian mystic does so in this life; that is, the mystic experimentally discovers his own divine nature or Sonship and is reunited to divinity in this life. The mystic undergoes a metaphorical death, the death of the first Adam, in order to undergo a metaphorical rebirth or resurrection as the last Adam, Christ. In a sense, we may say accurately that the mystic is precisely that person who understands and *actually* experiences the mythic, poetic meaning of God's Word. In this regard, we shall observe important differences between Donne, Herbert, and Vaughan.

Beside biblical authority, these poets had the confirming word of mystical tradition. One of mysticism's fundamental articles of faith is the doctrine, derivative in Christianity from Genesis, that man is made in God's image, that, in the words of Dean Inge, "since we can only know what is akin to ourselves, *man, in order to know God, must be a partaker of the divine nature*" (6). The idea that the true self in the depth of the particular individual is identical with or at least like unto divinity is expressed most succinctly in the

Sanskrit formula *tat tvam asi* ("that art Thou" or "you are It") and is found pervasively in worldwide mystical literature. We confine ourselves to the Christian contemplative tradition concerning the mystical stages and this central, key idea of the lesser or false and the greater or true selves.

Purgation is the means that through God's grace accomplishes the transformation of the lesser, false self (first Adam) to the greater, true self (last Adam). In that Neoplatonism adapted by the Chruch Fathers, the way whereby the self ascends to God (or to Being as designated in the *Phaedo*, to the Good in the *Republic*, to Beauty in the *Symposium* and *Phaedrus*, to the One in the *Philebus* and Plotinus' *Enneads*, for a few examples) is Plato's way of moral and intellectual purification. In the *Theaetetus*, Plato makes the point that it is only by becoming godlike that we can know God. Plotinus teaches that the self in its lapse from its original goodness falls into the "Place of Unlikeness," a phrase taken from Plato's *Statesman*, and must return to God (or the One) through its likeness to him; fallen selves become "dwellers in the Place of Unlikeness, where, fallen from all resemblance to the Divine, we lie in gloom and mud" (*Enneads* 1.8.13). Writing on Plotinus, Andrew Louth remarks, "unlikeness, difference, obscures the soul's simplicity and likeness to the divine. The 'way,' then, will be recovery of its simplicity, of its kinship to the divine. This will involve purification, both in the sense of the restoration of its own beauty, and in the cutting off of what has sullied that purity. The soul is to seek for itself, for its true self, and in doing that it is seeking for the divine, for the soul belongs to the divine, it has kinship with the divine" (42–43).

For the early Church Father Origen, who attended the school of Ammonius Saccas, the teacher of Plotinus, and whose work is permeated by Platonism, the Song of Songs, as his *Commentary* on it so clearly shows, is *the* book on the height of the mystical life, the self's union with God. Among the many ideas he develops in his interpretation of the Song, one of the most important is that of the three stages of the mystical life, subsequently called Purgation, Illumination, and Union. Origen's *On the First Principles* (of Christian theology) attempts to overcome or reconcile the classical dualism of form and matter by deriving all of reality from a single principle. Like the One of his younger contemporary, Plotinus, Origen's God is transcendent, an absolute unity beyond discursive thought. In accounting for the world of matter and change as an emanation from this transcendent principle, an intermediary is necessary, and this is the role of Christ, who is regarded as the Logos or the hypostatized Divine Wisdom of the transcendent deity.

To other mystical Fathers, like Dionysius the Areopagite and Gregory of Nyssa, God is utterly transcendent and unknowable to the rational intellect, which is at the center of the psyche. This idea of the absolute darkness of the Godhead and the Christian doctrine of creation *ex nihilo*, which (unlike Platonic and pantheistic accounts of creation) posits a greater distance between Creator and creation, increase the need for an intermediary. In other words, among other matters, the Christian doctrine of the Incarnation, for Origen and the later Fathers, reconciles the classical dualism of form and matter and the dichotomy of the transcendent and the immanent. In the words of St. Athanasius, credited with defending against the Arians at the Council of Nice the Trinitarian view that Christ was always God the Son and that when he became man as the son of Mary he remained wholly God and wholly man, "God became man that man might become God" (*De Incarnatione*, 54, iii, cited in Watts, *Behold the Spirit*, 131). While the expression is not always as memorable, the idea is of course widespread in the Fathers and others: thus, for example, Irenaeus, "Our Lord Jesus Christ, the word of God, of his boundless love, became what we are that he might make us what he himself is"; and Clement of Alexandria, "the Word, I say, of God . . . became man just that you may learn from a man how it may be that man should become God" (Bettenson, *Early Christian Fathers*, 77, 177). And in "There Is No Natural Religion," Blake directly concludes, "Therefore God becomes as we are, that we may be as he is." Christ is the way and example; the resurrection is in and of the body as well as the soul. Other persons potentially share in the Incarnation, the possibility of redemption thereby held out to them. For the Fathers generally, as for Augustine, who develops from Plotinus the idea of the *regio dissimilitudinis*, the land or place of unlikeness (*Confessions*, VII, x), the self's likeness to God has been restored in the Incarnate Word. And under the influence of Augustine, "image theology" makes its way to medieval and Renaissance Christian writers. Christ's Passion and Cruxifixion are emblems of and models for the fallen or false self's purgative way. For the Christian, the symbol of one's ultimate essential identity with divinity and the paradigm of union (and of illumination in that it is a temporary or incomplete union) is the Incarnation, the immediate and final meaning of which is the redemption or regeneration of the first Adam, the lesser, false self, and the uniting of man and God. In the words of Irenaeus, God's "Word is our Lord Jesus Christ who in these last times became man among men, that he might unite the end with the beginning, that is, Man with God" (Bettenson, *Early Christian Fathers*, 76–77).

Writing on "the fundamental dogma of mystical psychology," Abbé Bremond further clarifies and expands the meaning of "the distinction between the two selves: *Animus*, the *surface self*; *Anima*, the *deep self*; *Animus*, rational knowledge; and *Anima*, mystical or poetic knowledge . . . the I, who feeds on notions and words and enchants himself by doing so; the Me, who is united to realities." "My Me is God," St. Catherine of Genoa asserts, "nor do I recognize any other Me except my God Himself." "What is life?" Meister Eckhart asks, and boldly affirms: "God's being is my life, but if it is so, then what is God's must be mine and what is mine God's. God's is-ness is my is-ness [*istigkeit*], and neither more nor less." With direct pertinence, the great Flemish mystic Jan Ruysbroeck makes the psyche-pneuma distinction in the terms of created and uncreated nature: "all men who are exalted above their created nature into a life of contemplation are one with the Divine clarity, and they are the clarity itself. And they behold and feel and discover themselves, by means of this Divine light: they discover that they are this same single deepness, according to the manner of their uncreated nature. . . . And so contemplative men attain to that everlasting image in which they are made."[7] Quotations such as these from the contemplatives could be multiplied indefinitely. The terminology may differ, even considerably, in various writers of the contemplative tradition, but the idea remains essentially the same, as when, for example, Blake writes with his characteristic directness: "Man is all Imagination. God is Man and exists in us and we in him" ("Annotations to Berkeley's *Siris*"); and, from "the Laocoon," "The Eternal Body of Man is The Imagination, that is, God himself." Besides using "Imagination," Blake elsewhere employs the terms "the faculty which experiences," "the Poetic Genius," and "the true Man" to designate what we have here been referring to as the true self.

Purgation, then, is the process whereby the various prideful effects of the Fall (and of every person's fall) are undone and overcome so that one may regain one's Sonship or essential divinity, the process whereby one may undergo that humble ego-crucifying which conduces to the self's highest exaltation. "He that shall humble himself shall be exalted" (Matt. 23:12; see also Luke 14:11, 18:14). It should, however, be emphasized both that purification is an ongoing process and that different stages of the *via mystica* may be simultaneously present, as Underhill points out: "the purgation of the senses and of the character which they have helped to build is always placed first in order in the Mystic Way; though sporadic flashes of illumination and ecstasy may, and often do, precede and accompany it. Since spiritual no less than physical existence, as we know it, is an endless Becoming, it too has no end. In a sense the whole of the mystical experience in this life consists in a series of purifications, whereby the Finite slowly approaches the nature of its Infinite Source . . . " (*Mysticism*, 203–204). As Christ's sermon on the mount tells us, blessed are the pure in heart, for they shall see God. Purification leads to vision and enlightenment, but these latter in themselves are and help to provide a further "purification" leading to still deeper and intenser vision and enlightenment, so that one may see the divinity within as Gregory of Nyssa suggests in *From Glory to Glory* and in his sermon on the sixth Beatitude (*The Beatitudes*).

One of the reasons that purification is an ongoing process proceeds from the fact that, from a modern psychological point of view, numerous false selves exist or come into existence and must be purged away. Because the Bible and contemplative tradition generally refer to only the lesser life or false self and the greater life or true self (sometimes using various synonyms or other phrases for "life" or "self"), it suffices, for the sake of tradition and simplicity, to speak of *the* false self as representative of any one or more false selves. And, although there usually are many purgations and illuminations, as mystics regularly report, it also generally suffices simply to employ the traditional schema of Purgation, Illumination, and Union as a diagram of the *via mystica*. On occasion it will help to amplify this schema, such as in the elaboration of the Dark Night of the Soul by St. John of the Cross. Similarly, other characteristics of mystical experience in addition to those discussed by W. T. Stace will on appropriate occasion be mentioned. Nor should we expect to find every characteristic in every contemplative poem. Some are more important than others. For example, the first-listed characteristics of the Unifying Vision and the Unitary Consciousness are much more pertinent for determining whether a poem or an experience presented in a poem may be contemplative than the last-listed, alleged ineffability. Furthermore, we will not find all four Visions in each of our three poets, Donne, Herbert, Vaughan, as we do, for example, in their later contemporary, Traherne. Indeed, while each of the three sought the Vision of God, each seems to have more fully experienced a different Vision than the others, which is yet another distinguishing feature of their poetry and helps to account for some of the differences in their work. Although all of this chapter's material on mysticism will be useful and helpful in our subsequent study of seventeenth- and twentieth-century poets, not all of it is required for each poet. Where necessary and appropriate, the following chapters will avail themselves of the perspective and light provided by contemplative tradition, the master revelations, and will draw on or elaborate the preceding discussion and introduce needed refinements of it.

There is one additional refinement to be made here. A wisdom even greater than the doctrine of purgation obtains among the Christian contemplatives and helps to account for their sometimes according larger significance to the Incarnation than to the Crucifixion, even though the Crucifixion is to them so vitally important. They have the abiding and deep awareness that, in Eckhart's words, "nothing is as near to me as God is. God is nearer to me than I am to myself. My being depends on God's intimate presence."[8] Donne, Herbert, and Vaughan would have read in the Psalms that "Thou art near, O Lord" (119:151) and would have learned from St. Paul's preaching to the Athenians that God is "not far from every one of us: for in him we live, and move, and have our being; as certain also of your own poets have said, For we are also his offspring" (Acts 17:27–28). "But Thou wert more inward to me, than my most inward part," St. Augustine similarly affirms, "and higher than my highest."[9] As the self ascends to God, it discovers its essential Self. Self-knowledge and knowledge of the divine are, if not identical, at the least intimately interwoven. Recognizing the unworthiness of one's fallen nature, and all that implies, is itself prelude and key to discovering one's "more near" or "more inward" Being and ultimately to entering wholly into the state of effulgent beatitude. But only the true Self, not the fallen ego, can accept and affirm, can act. It even chooses to act as if It were fallen and in need of crucifixion. God acts and is; man, on his own, can neither act meaningfully nor be. The psyche is indeed an illusion, a fiction, however tenaciously it may foolishly persist in refusing to die and let eternal life be. By means of the Incarnation and Redemption, the psyche, would-be usurping pretender, learns and assumes its proper subordinate place; one sees through the convention, and it also becomes a blessing.

# JOHN DONNE
## *"we two being one, are it"*

This chapter will consider the contemplative dimensions of some of John Donne's best secular and divine poems in terms of the general guidelines to mystical life as set forth in the previous chapter, all in an effort to determine (as well as one might in such a delicate and complicated matter) the spiritual state of being and progression imaginatively revealed in Donne's poetry. To this end it will be helpful to classify the poems considered. That task has fortunately been largely accomplished by two of Donne's great modern editors, Sir Herbert Grierson and Dame Helen Gardner. Although under different circumstances one might wish to make certain qualifications and reservations, it is sufficient as far as our needs extend to adopt in general their classification.

In the commentary to his monumental 1912 edition of *The Poems of John Donne*, Grierson writes that "Donne's 'songs and sonets' seem to me to fall into three . . . classes, *though there is a good deal of overlapping"* (emphasis added). Using tone and theme as criteria, in the first class Grierson places poems which display cynical wit or celebrate inconstant or false love, such as "Goe and catche a falling starre," "Womans Constancy," "The Indifferent," "Loves Usury," and "Loves Diet." These and others are characteristically "anti-Petrarchan" poems in which the narrator primarily is cynical and promiscuous, mockingly illogical, probably intentionally shocking and impudent. Under his second class, Grierson subsumes poems which sing, "at times with amazing simplicity and intensity of feeling, the joys of love and the sorrow of parting." These are poems of genuine, true love, including some of Donne's best and most critically discussed poems, such as "The Good-morrow," "The Canonization," "The Exstasie," and "A Valediction: forbidding Mourning," the secular poems we will be most concerned with. In the third and smallest group, he places the complimentary, courtly poems, which either celebrate a Platonic affection for a woman or else complain that such affection is all she will give. These poems often have "the tone . . . of the Petrarchan lover whose mistress's coldness has slain him or provokes his passionate protestations," and Grierson names "The Funerall," "The Blossome," and "Twicknam Garden," among others (II, 9–10).

In *The Elegies and the Songs and Sonnets* of John Donne, Gardner uses "two objective criteria by which we can classify the Songs and Sonnets. We can group them on the basis of the kind of relation between a man and a woman that they assume, and we can group them by metrical form" (li). Using the first criterion, Gardner's classification into three main groups exhibits great similarities and some differences as compared to Grierson's. The two editors' first groups or classes seem essentially the same, Gardner characterizing her first group as follows: "By no means all the poems in the group can be called cynical, although many are. But all are untouched by the idealization of woman as the 'lady' who may command and deny as she chooses and by the sentiment of man's love as 'all made of sighs and tears.' And all, even the most tender and heartfelt, are unconcerned with the conception of love as a mystical union by which two become one" (li).

Gardner's second group consists of ten "poems of unrequited love. Here the mistress refuses. She is the lady who has the upper hand, while her lover is condemned to sigh and burn" (lii). This class is very similar, though not identical, to Grierson's third Petrarchan group, and Gardner also calls her second group Petrarchan, though with a proviso. "Wholly un-Petrarchan as they are in mood, tone, and style, they handle the classic Petrarchan situation, some fully accepting the Petrarchan concept of the lady who is 'too true to be kind' "(liii).

Finally, Gardner's third group, which is greatly though not entirely matched by Grierson's second group, "consists of poems of mutual love, in which there is no question of falseness on either side or of frustration by either lover of the other's desire. These are poems that treat of love as union, and of love as miracle, something that is outside the natural order of things" (liii).

With a few exceptions, Gardner basically confirms Grierson's classification of the Songs and Sonnets, and for convenience while discussing these poems we will use this grouping, with the following shorthand references.

*Group One*, poems of inconstant or false love, anti-Petrarchan.
*Group Two*, poems of faithful or true love.
*Group Three*, poems of Platonic love (using "Platonic" in the

popular sense, "without sexual love"); with Gardner's qualifica-
tion, also called Petrarchan, as Group One are also designated
anti-Petrarchan.[1]

Essentially corroborated by Gardner, Grierson's classification of the
poems, as interpreted by the present writer, is given in Appendix A,
the primary purpose of which is to indicate exactly which poems are
designated by this chapter's reference to each Group. (A minor pur-
pose of Appendix A is to offer some generalizations that are, because
of the difficulty of dating many Donne poems, tentative and gener-
ally acceptable.) While this chapter focuses mainly on Group Two,
those poems concerned with "the conception of love as a mystical
union by which two become one" (Gardner, li), the classification
permits easy reference to and ready comparison of large groups of
poems.

The poems of Group One, alternatively called the Ovidian or
anti-Petrarchan poems, are distinguished not only for their cynical
wit and celebration of (or persuasion to or chastisement for) incon-
stant or false love but for their relative poetic simplicity. Compared
to the poems of true love, they generally are less difficult and compli-
cated and have historically presented fewer critical problems of ex-
plication. These facts of the relative simplicity of and relative ease
in understanding the poems of Group One would seem to suggest
that these poems may have been written in Donne's more youthful
days, while most of the poems of Group Two (and also many of
Group Three) may have been written when Donne was somewhat
more mature, perhaps after he met and wooed Ann More (and, still
later, when as an impoverished husband and father, he sought the
patronage of Lucy, Countess of Bedford and other great persons and
perhaps wrote most of Group Three).

I note these interesting points but not in order to insist on a bio-
graphical interpretation of these poems. Even though the excellent
biographies of Donne by R. C. Bald and Edward LeComte, among
others, could be pressed into the argument, the strong yet too easy
temptation to such an interpretation must finally be resisted be-
cause of the limited information available on both the dating of the
poems and on the biographical facts. What most matters for the pur-
poses of this chapter are the "self" portraits that emerge from the
poems of the different groups, particularly the essential self or
pneuma of Group Two versus the false self or psyche of Group One,
whether the "selves" are wholly imaginative or literally autobio-
graphical or some combination of both; chronology and biography

*may* serve in a tentative way simply to further support the main argument concerning these selves in Donne's poetry.[2]

## II

Many of the various concerns of this chapter can be brought together in focus upon one of Donne's best and most discussed and debated poems. "The Exstasie" has long been an object of critical scrutiny and admiration: Coleridge, for example, wrote of it, "I should never find fault with metaphysical poems, were they all like this, or but half as excellent" ("Coleridgiana II," in Clements, *John Donne's Poetry*, lll). It has continued to be frequently examined, probed, admired, one of the most recent and most informed discussions being by A. J. Smith in *The Metaphysics of Love* (1985), an important study of the spiritual value accorded to love during the Renaissance. Since the amount of criticism on "The Exstasie" is so extensive, instead of attempting tediously to trace the course of critical debate on the poem it is much preferable to present a "Selected Bibliography on 'The Exstasie'" (see Appendix B) and briefly to observe here some major points of contention, before offering a discussion of the poem relevant to this book's larger concerns.

Austin Warren's statement on the division of the critics remains as good a brief synopsis as any. He points out that over the years various critics have interpreted "The Exstasie" "on the one hand, as a poem of highest spirituality expressive either of Platonic love (that is, love without sex) or of Christian love, to which both the soul and the body are requisite; on the other hand, as the supreme example of Donne's dramatism and pseudo-logic—as the seduction of a defenseless woman by sophistical rhetoric" ("Donne's 'Extasie,'" 472). In other words, to use Grierson's classification, some critics view "The Exstasie" as a seduction poem which falls into the first group; other critics regard it as a true love poem, involving both body and soul, of the second group; and still others consider it a Platonic love poem of the third group.

After Grierson's edition was published in 1912, much of the critical controversy over Donne's poetry, including "The Exstasie," stemmed, in effect, from a reductive effort to regard any one poem as exemplary of only one or another of Grierson's classes, without giving due consideration to the contradictory overlapping which Grierson mentions. It is true that Grierson's categories have been influential and useful and that many scholars have made valuable contributions to Donne studies by trying to determine the most clear, coherent, and inclusive meaning of a poem within these categories or others of their own. What needs to be emphasized, however, is that the various themes and tones which have been used to define and categorize individual "Songs and Sonnets" often exist in a single poem, as they do in "The Exstasie," not in confusion nor as an obfuscating ambiguity that diminishes meaning but in mutual support as a kind of orchestration that enhances meaning. In such multithematic and multitonal poems, one or another theme and voice at times may be in the foreground with the others clustered behind. At other times, the themes and tones may have or seem to have almost equal value in the harmony. But the total effect is a multi-leveled, enriched, and integrated poem (and at times a critical confusion, particularly when criticism attempts to reduce and oversimplify this poetic richness and complexity). Such a poem, composed of contradictory overlapping themes and tones, may be regarded as a poetic analogue to Picasso's "Woman in a Mirror," a single portrait or synthesis of various views of a woman's face. In a sense, some of Donne's Songs and Sonnets regularly deconstruct themselves, so much so at times that it is not always possible to determine or argue for an overriding voice or theme (hence my placing some poems in Group Four). The following discussion of "The Exstasie" will suggest this orchestration of themes and voices in which, nevertheless, the theme and tone of true love is dominant while the others are subordinate. Although the harmonized themes and voices discerned in "The Exstasie" will not be identical to those heard in other poems, once recognized as microcosmic of a manifold harmony, this poem may then afford a point of reference for the reading of other Songs and Sonnets in which modulated tones and themes have caused critical difficulties.[3]

In addition to these issues concerning theme and tone, other critical problems have prevailed which, I think, can only be resolved by reference to contemplative tradition since the questions pertain to mystical matters. Is one or another poem genuinely mystical or does Donne simply use mystical terminology as a source of powerful metaphor or as a high-sounding means of effecting a seduction? Secondly, and more specifically, how can a poem be mystical when its description of mystical union, while similar, clearly differs from descriptions of such union by some of the most famous and articulate contemplatives of the church, such as St. John of the Cross and St. Teresa?[4] The problems are in part in the nature of that criticism which asks for oversimplified, neatly categorized either-or answers to such intricate matters as love and mysticism, which of course transcend the merely rational and logical. The more satisfactory answer, we shall find, is often the more complex both-and. That is, not only must we take seriously into account the contradictory overlapping Grierson mentions, but we must also thoroughly understand, for a few examples, that the Vision of Eros is as genuinely mystical as the Vision of God (for all of the similarities and differences between the two), that the divine may be simultaneously immanent and transcendent, that a Renaissance poem may contain contradictory Platonic and Aristotelian elements as well as both meditative and contemplative components, that an individual may paradoxically lose and gain selfhood simultaneously, and so on. In short, we will need to apply most of the materials and principles introduced in Chapter One, Contemplative Tradition, to the following discussions. And "The Exstasie" may also afford a point of reference for the reading of other Donne poems which have contemplative elements in them.

It will be helpful to have the full text of "The Exstasie" before us with line numbers in the right margin and stanza numbers in the left margin so that in the subsequent discussion of the poem we may conveniently refer to these numbers.[5]

### The Exstasie

1    Where, like a pillow on a bed,
        A Pregnant banke swel'd up, to rest
    The violets reclining head,
        Sat we two, one anothers best;

2    Our hands were firmely cimented    5
        With a fast balme, which thence did spring,
    Our eye-beames twisted, and did thred
        Our eyes, upon one double string;

3    So to'entergraft our hands, as yet
        Was all our meanes to make us one,    10
    And pictures on our eyes to get
        Was all our propagation.

4    As 'twixt two equal Armies, Fate
        Suspends uncertaine victorie,
    Our soules, (which to advance their state,    15
        Were gone out,) hung 'twixt her, and mee.

5  And whil'st our soules negotiate there,
      Wee like sepulchrall statues lay;
   All day, the same our postures were,
      And wee said nothing, all the day.                    20

6  If any, so by love refin'd,
      That he soules language understood,
   And by good love were grown all minde,
      Within convenient distance stood,

7  He (though he knew not which soule spake,              25
      Because both meant, both spake the same)
   Might thence a new concoction take,
      And part farre purer then he came.

8  This Extasie doth unperplex
      (We said) and tell us what we love,                  30
   Wee see by this, it was not sexe,
      Wee see, we saw not what did move:

9  But as all severall soules containe
      Mixture of things, they know not what,
   Love, these mixt soules, doth mixe againe,             35
      And makes both one, each this and that.

10 A single violet transplant,
      The strength, the colour, and the size,
   (All which before was poore, and scant,)
      Redoubles still, and multiplies.                     40

11 When love, with one another so
      Interinanimates two soules,
   That abler soule, which thence doth flow,
      Defects of lonelinesse controules.

12 Wee then, who are this new soule, know,                45
      Of what we are compos'd, and made,
   For, th'Atomies of which we grow,
      Are soules, whom no change can invade.

13 But O alas, so long, so farre
      Our bodies why doe wee forbeare?                     50
   They'are ours, though they'are not wee, Wee are
      Th'intelligences, they the spheare.

14  We owe them thankes, because they thus,
        Did us, to us, at first convay,
    Yeelded their forces, sense, to us,                    55
        Nor are drosse to us, but allay.

15  On man heavens influence workes not so,
        But that it first imprints the ayre,
    Soe soule into the soule may flow,
        Though it to body first repaire.                   60

16  As our blood labours to beget
        Spirits, as like soules as it can,
    Because such fingers need to knit
        That subtile knot, which makes us man:

17  So must pure lovers soules descend                     65
        T'affections, and to faculties,
    That sense may reach and apprehend,
        Else a great Prince in prison lies.

18  To'our bodies turne wee then, that so
        Weake men on love reveal'd may looke;              70
    Loves mysteries in soules doe grow,
        But yet the body is his booke.

19  And if some lover, such as wee,
        Have heard this dialogue of one,
    Let him still marke us, he shall see                   75
        Small change, when we'are to bodies gone.

"The Exstasie" begins with a description of the setting and of
the lovers' physical and spiritual state, continues with an analysis of
the significance of "This Extasie," of the effect of love, and of the
nature of the soul, and then concludes with a plea and argument that
the lovers return to their bodies, as it were, and turn from their
spiritual union to physical union. Although the whole poem may be
regarded as a colloquy or, more precisely, a "dialogue of one," it is
helpful to adopt Martz's outline of the meditative structure and to
observe that the poem falls into three distinguishable parts, which
might usefully be designated composition, analysis, and colloquy,
corresponding to the acts of memory, understanding, and will.
Donne uses a meditative structure in "The Exstasie" to formalize
his description of a contemplative experience, a Vision of Eros, much

as Vaughan employs meditative structure in "The Night" to frame and help express the contemplative Vision of God. Although these poems may be said to use meditative structure, we shall see in detail that they go far beyond meditation into contemplation. Stanzas 1 to 7 of "The Exstasie" compose the scene, describing the passive physical and active spiritual state of the lovers. Stanzas 6 to 7 may alternatively be viewed as the transition to the analysis of stanzas 8 to 12, which consider ecstasy, love, and souls or "this new soule." And, finally, stanzas 13 to 19 argue for a completion of love by means of return to "Our bodies" and physical union, much as a colloquy is ordinarily used by the devout supplicant as a plea for mystical union with God.

This same threefold division also corresponds, interestingly, to Grierson's classification. The first division or the composition is rather similar in theme and tone to some of the Platonic poems. Here spiritual activity obtains, with little or no physical activity. The second part of "The Exstasie" parallels various poems in Grierson's second group, which celebrate and anatomize true love's paradoxical union of two souls in one. And in the concluding section, one may hear something of the tone of the seductive lover of Group One. But overall, in my view, the voices and themes do not have equal value in the harmony; rather, as shall be argued, all is subordinate to the concerns of true love, as the opening description of setting foreshadows and signifies.

Uncharacteristically set outdoors, the poem nevertheless manages in its very first line to suggest a bedroom-like setting (the more typical Donnean setting) for the two lovers, "one anothers best," who are actually sitting on a bank beside "The violets reclining head." The attitude itself of the violet, its "reclining head," helps to convey its significance. In Christian art, the violet, which appears again importantly in the middle of the poem, traditionally symbolizes humility, as George Ferguson's *Signs and Symbols In Christian Art* points out (40). It also more particularly signifies the humility of the Second Person of God in assuming human or bodily form (in other words, pneuma or the last Adam, which the redeemed or resurrected self becomes). The color violet symbolizes truth and love (Ferguson, 152). And since the flower exists in a single and a double form, it also provides a subsequent symbol for "That abler soule," the new soul that the lovers through Love become. Thus, with an initial image in the first stanza, Donne graphically and brilliantly sketches and anticipates major concerns of the poem: humility, incarnation, the paradox of two-in-one, and truth and love or true love.

Physically, the lovers are simply holding hands and gazing into one another's eyes, but in specially united ways. For the sweat of their palms serves as a "fast balme," a steadfast or fastening moisture which "firmely cimented" their hands. And though the issue was in general unsettled in Donne's day, whether his own theory of perception was extramission (beams from the eye striking the object) or intramission (beams from the object imprinting an image on the eye) the result would in this instance be the same: "Our eye-beames twisted, and did thred / Our eyes, upon one double string." What is different, must be different, is the sense of connection with external reality which the Renaissance consciousness and sensibility must have had as compared with modern consciousness and sensibility. In the very act of seeing, a Renaissance man believed and felt that he was literally in touch with the object of his perception by means of real, physical, if invisible, beams. Such an epistemological theory would have profound metaphysical and cosmological consequences. Not only would a meaningful correspondence obtain between microcosm and macrocosm, an idea familiar and frequent in Donne, but man and his universe would be intellectually regarded and emotionally felt to be in actual continuous connection, a unitive rather than a divided consciousness: man as a part of, not apart from, the world.[6] At the head of creation, God's special creature, man, in the Renaissance view, was a part of and yet also the fruition of creation as an apple is a part of and the fruit of the tree. Renaissance man could feel at home in and at touch with the well-ordered universe, the celestial spheres governed by angels or intelligences, just as modern man, as has often been observed, feels isolated and alienated in a universe without much order or purpose, a world feared, conquered, and polluted to the point of ecological suicide. If the whole life-effort of man is, as D. H. Lawrence has said, to get his life in direct contact with the elemental life of the cosmos, then perhaps Renaissance man, given his theory of perception, would have had considerable advantage over modern man, anxious and anguished from being out of touch. Donne's wit and fondness for paradox (or *aporia*, as is said nowadays) are marks of an inclusive, supra-rational or poetic mode of apprehending the world rather than of an exclusive, simply logical, discursive consciousness; they are marks of his use of the right brain, as is also said nowadays, as well as the left. Some modern thinkers, including D. H. Lawrence and the Nobel physicist Wolfgang Pauli, have observed how modern man has become increasingly "rational" (the quotation marks signal the principle that to become increasingly rational without simultaneously becoming increas-

ingly supra-rational paradoxically results in enormous irrational-
ity—witness the history of the twentieth century) and thus needs to
embrace or re-embrace both the mystical and the rational, to be dis-
cussed more fully in Chapter Five.

The lovers, at any rate, in Donne's poem are very much in touch,
by hands and eyes, even as they are in spiritual ecstasy. But given
that their experience is so far primarily spiritual and their ecstasy as
yet not physical, this first section seems rather like the Platonic
"The Relique":

> Coming and going, wee
> Perchance might kisse, but not between those meales;
> Our hands ne'r toucht the seales
> Which nature, injur'd by late law, sets free.

The title, the word "ecstasy," means in one of its senses the exalted
rapture of the mystic united to God or engaged in the contemplation
of divine things. Literally, etymologically, "ecstasy" means "to
stand or place outside of" and conveys the meaning "to drive out of
one's wits" in the sense of being transported, in rapture. To be in
ecstasy is to go out of the "ordinary" state of mind governed by the
rational intellect and psyche in clock time to the "extraordinary"
state of being graced by pneuma, the essential self, in timelessness.
This movement is the precise meaning of humility and precisely the
progress from meditation to contemplation. While the lovers' souls
have "gone out," their bodies are passive, as St. John of the Cross rec-
ommends, "like sepulchrall statues lay; / All Day, the same our post-
ures were, / And wee said nothing, all the day." To remain physically
in the same posture and to be silent *all the day* (the repetition in the
poem underscores the phrase) are signs of an exceptional state and
emphasize the timeless, non- or supra-intellectual mode of this ec-
static spiritual love. The "humble" or empty condition of minimal
bodily state and nonintellectual mode is precisely the most recep-
tive mystical condition, for they who humble themselves shall be
exalted. It is, furthermore, as if the lovers are in eternity or the eter-
nal now-moment, at least in the sense of being outside of time and
ordinary time-consciousness. Silence is the mode of ecstatic eter-
nity, and achieving it, as Eckhart says, "must be done by means of
forgetting and losing self-consciousness. It is in the stillness, in the
silence, that the word of God is to be heard. There is no better avenue
of approach to the Word than through stillness, through silence. . . .
[St. Paul's] spirit had so far withdrawn all its agents that the body

was forgotten. Neither memory nor intellect functioned, nor the senses . . . a man should diminish his senses and introvert his faculties until he achieves forgetfulness of things and self. . . . Once we get beyond tme and temporal things, we are free and joyous and then comes the 'fulness of time' when the Son of God is born" (*Meister Eckhart*, Blakney, 107, 99, 152). In St. Paul's terms, body and intellect, soma and psyche, should be diminished so that the essential self, pneuma, may come fully and ecstatically into being, and it is exactly this state that the first section of the poem describes.

In a sense, a sense consistent with Donne's characteristically self-conscious poetry, each reader may be or become the hypothetical observer introduced in stanzas 6 and 7, if the circumstances are right, as described in these stanzas. Then the reader may "part farre purer then he came." An experience of contemplative illumination or union, as the mystics report, not only acts to enlighten and unify but also may serve as a further purification. Usually, it is the same individual or (in the Visions of Eros and Philia) individuals who experience contemplation who also find a further purgation of self in that ecstatic contemplative experience. Putting an added twist on the matter, Donne's poem seems to suggest that, insofar as the hypothetical observer is understood as a reader, contemplative poetry itself may have some power to purify, enlighten, and possibly effect a radical transformation of self, a topic to be explicitly considered at the end of Chapter 4 and particularly in Chapter 5. These remarks, as intended, of course raise interesting, complex questions about the poetic text, especially the contemplative poem, and what it supposedly describes or refers to beyond itself.

As much as is possible for a Renaissance man to do, Donne exalts the lovers throughout the poem not only overtly and obviously by asserted denotations but also subtly through the poetic medium. For example, after stanzas 6 and 7 introduce the hypothetical observer, the next few stanzas, the analysis, poetically present mystical meanings and characteristics (such as timelessness, ecstasy, joy, unitary consciousness, peace, and so on) by aural, rhythmical, syntactic, as well as semantic means. To focus on timelessness as a particular instance, we note that the middle part of the poem is actually slowed down in the reading aloud, thereby engendering an expanded sense of time, a kind of otherworldly eternity and immortality, specifically by means of repeated alliteration and assonance (especially recurrent sounds signalled by *s*, *t*, *w*, *m*, and *o*), incantatory rhythms, complex syntax, and abstract language and ideas. Both the music and the meaning of the poem in stanzas 8 to 14 especially, but also to a lesser extent in the rest of the poem, by a variety of means require a longer period of reading aloud. The clusters of consonants, the repetition of certain words, and the various quatrain rhymes with their frequent internal echoes both give phonetic continuity to the poem and in the slowing of the reading suggest a protracted time process. Stanza 8, for a more specific example, in addition to its *abab* rhyme scheme, repeats *we* five times and the rhyming *see* twice, and contains a variety of other resonant or echoic sounds. Three of the four iambic tetrameter lines in this stanza consist of eight single-syllable words rather than fewer multisyllabic words; and the metrical foot is often a heavier spondaic rather than iambic foot: for example, *we* occurs all five times in the initial normally unstressed position in the iambic foot, but actually receives a heavier than normal stress in each occurrence. Such spondaic or heavier-than-normal iambic stress characterizes the whole poem and, by slowing the reading aloud, contributes significantly to the feeling that time is suspended or altered into a sense of timelessness.

The richness of the poetic medium is matched and in a sense necessitated by the complexity, density, profundity of the meaning. The most abstract part of Donne's poem (the analysis of the middle stanzas, 8–12) is the most musical part of it, as if Donne were compensating for the abstraction, a kind of spirituality, by the added musical sensuousness, giving "body" to his poem as if in anticipation of the concluding stanzas' plea to turn to the body. The abstract analysis of the significance of "This Extasie" combined with the musical sensuousness is a poetic example and model of the very reconciliation or union of soul and body that Donne's great poem centrally concerns.

In tone and theme this analysis bears similarities to other Group Two poems. The tone is somewhat academic, pedantic, like the tone of "A Lecture Upon the Shadow," which begins

> Stand still, and I will read to thee
> A Lecture, Love, in loves philosophy.

These lines characterize the middle stanzas of "The Exstasie," a lecture on love, ecstasy, and united souls. The lovers of "The Exstasie" have been quiet, passive, and still "all the day." The lovers of "A Lecture Upon the Shadow" have been "Walking here" for "three houres," and now they are to be still, inner stillness being an essential pre-condition for unitive experience. The lovers in what is perhaps the best *carpe diem* poem in the English language, Andrew

Marvell's "To His Coy Mistress," "cannot make our Sun / Stand still"; and so the poem concludes, "yet we will make him run." Donne's lovers, if they remain true and firm in their love, evidently can make their sun stand still, for

> Love is a growing, or full constant light;
> And his first minute, after noone, is night.

When lovers are in ecstasy, time stands still. Since *carpe diem* poems are not primarily so much about love as they are about death (specifically, the fear of death), Group Two poems are further distinguished in that the ecstatic death of the lovers' psyches or egos (the human center of fear and trembling) and the ecstatic rebirth of their true self, "That abler soule," releases the lovers from such fear and elevates them to that mode of being which is peaceful, unitive, timeless, sacred, joyful, blessed, and wholly real or divine. Love's mysteries are such that true lovers can make the sun stand still. "Then comes," as Eckhart writes, "the fullness of time when the Son of God is born" (Blakney, 152).

Their psyches or false selves having been transcended in their ecstasy which "doth unperplex," the lovers now see that they did not previously understand what was the cause and source of their love. "Wee see, we saw not what did move." They are like the lovers of "A Valediction: forbidding Mourning," who are "by'a love, so much refin'd, / That our selves know not what it is." "Love, these mixt soules, doth mixe againe, / And makes both one, each this and that." "Love," in this Aristotelian and Neoplatonic poem, may refer both to their embodied feelings for one another and to God, who is Love. For, as Ficino observes, "the passion of a lover is not quenched by the mere touch or sight of a body, for it does not desire this or that body, but desires the splendour of the divine light shining through bodies, and is amazed and awed by it. For this reason lovers never know what it is they desire or seek, for they do not know God Himself" (*Commentary*, 140).

Lovers desire or seek, by implication, God Himself, but the Godhead is unknowable to the psyche and rational intellect, an idea which abounds in Christian contemplative literature. St. Augustine, St. Bonaventure, and Nicholas Cusanus, for example, all know that images of God must be abandoned, for if one is to go beyond metaphor, they hold, one can only speak of God in negative terms, a concept Donne uses in "Negative Love." St. Thomas Aquinas expresses the idea succinctly and precisely: "in matters of Divinity, negative statements are to be preferred to positive, on account of our insufficiency, as Dionysius says" (*Summa Theologica*, II, 122, 2, 1).

> Wee see by this, it was not sexe,
> Wee see, we saw not what did move.

The Vision of Eros, though it differs in "object" and may differ in intensity and effect, is a matter of divinity as much as the Vision of God is, and the experience Donne describes would, in Auden's terms, be designated a Vision of Eros: "All accounts of the experience agree on essentials. Like the Vision of Dame Kind, the Vision of Eros is a revelation of creaturely glory, but whereas in the former it is the glory of a multiplicity of non-human creatures which is revealed, in the latter it is the glory of a single human being. Again, while in the vision of Nature, conscious sexuality is never present, in the erotic vision it always is" (*The Protestant Mystics*, 19).[7]

The very mention of "sexe" as not being the prime mover is indication that conscious sexuality is present. More importantly, the revelation of creaturely glory, the revelation through ecstasy of the essential self, is the profound discovery of one's own Godlikeness. Contemplative tradition makes it clear that though ecstasy is neither a necessary nor sufficient condition of mystical experience it frequently accompanies or even serves as a vehicle for the self's discovery of its Godlikeness. Near the beginning of Plato's *Symposium*, Socrates is described as being in a mystical rapture, "having taken up his position in a neighbor's front porch . . . deaf to all the servant's entreaties to come in." It is explained that "it's a way he has. He goes apart sometimes and stands still wherever he happens to be" (Hamilton, tr., 37). In other words, Plato early provides an instance of the ecstatic mystical experience which Diotima later describes: "The man who has been guided thus far in the mysteries of love . . . will suddenly have revealed to him . . . a beauty whose nature is marvellous indeed, the final goal . . ." (93). Similarly, after discussing the process of purification which "has The Good for goal," Plotinus describes the sudden ecstatic experience when "the quester holds all knowledge still of the ground he rests on, but, suddenly, swept beyond it all by the very crest of the wave of Intellect surging beneath, he is lifted and sees, never knowing how; the vision floods the eyes with light but it is not a light showing some other object, the light itself is the vision. No longer is there thing seen and light to show it . . . . With this he himself becomes identical, with that radiance . . . (*Enneads*, VI.7.36). Plotinus himself evidently had numerous experiences of such ecstatic, unitive rapture, flights of the alone to the Alone. "Many times it has happened: lifted out of the body into myself; becoming external to all other things and self-centered; beholding a marvellous beauty . . . acquiring identity with the divine" (IV.8.1).

The Platonic view of ecstasy continues in the Church Fathers, such as Gregory of Nyssa, Dionysius the Areopagite, and Augustine. In his chapter on "Nicene Orthodoxy," Andrew Louth describes Gregory of Nyssa's conception of ecstasy in terms which apply as well to Donne's lovers. "If there is properly an ecstatic element in Gregory's doctrine, it is in the ecstatic nature of love, which continually seeks to draw the soul out of itself to union with God as He is in Himself. Gregory uses both *eros* and *agape* to describe this love, a love which is essentially a desire for union with the beloved. . . . The longing that stretches the soul out towards God as He is in Himself, this *ecstatic* longing, is *eros*; and *eros* is the *ecstatic* aspect of *agape*." Louth cites Gregory's *Commentary on the Song of Songs*: "The bride then puts the veil from her eyes and with pure vision sees the ineffable beauty of her Spouse. And thus she is wounded by a spiritual and fiery dart of *eros*. For *agape* that is strained to intensity is called eros. And no one should be ashamed of this, whenever the arrow comes from God and not from the flesh" (96). Dionysius similarly describes an ecstatic *eros* by which the self goes out of itself and is united with the Divine. He also writes of God's own ecstasy (175, 176). In a sense, this idea follows from the union of self and God, from the primary characteristic of introvertive mystical experience, the Unitary Consciousness. Since the beloved in Donne's poem is a godlike consciousness and in ecstasy is united with the lover, the Vision of Eros exhibits the introvertive characteristic of the unitary consciousness, revealed in such terms as "That abler soule," "this new soule," "dialogue of one."

Augustine's famous account in his *Confessions* of an ecstatic experience he shared with his mother Monica bears upon Donne's poem in several interesting and pertinent ways.

> And our conversation had brought us to this point, that any pleasure whatsoever of the bodily senses, in any brightness whatsoever of corporeal light, seemed to us not worthy of comparison with the pleasure of that eternal Light, not worthy even of mention. Rising as our love flamed upward towards that Selfsame, we passed in review the various levels of bodily things, up to the heavens themselves, whence sun and moon and stars shine upon this earth. And higher still we soared, thinking in our minds and speaking and marvelling at Your works: and so we came to our own souls, and went

beyond them to come at last to that region of richness unending, where You feed Israel forever with the food of truth: and there life is that Wisdom by which all things are made, both the things that have been and the things that are yet to be. But this Wisdom itself is not made: it is as it has ever been, and so it shall be forever: indeed "has ever been" and "shall be forever" have no place in it, but it simply is, for it is eternal: whereas "to have been" and "to be going to be" are not eternal. And while we were thus talking of His Wisdom and panting for it, with all the effort of our heart we did for one instant attain to touch it; then sighing, and leaving the first fruits of our spirit bound to it, we returned to the sound of our own tongue, in which a word has both beginning and ending. For what is like to your Word, Our Lord, who abides in Himself forever, yet grows not old and makes all things new!

So we said: If to any man the tumult of the flesh grew silent, silent the images of earth and sea and air: and if the heavens grew silent, the very soul grew silent to herself and by not thinking of self mounted beyond self: if all dreams and imagined visions grew silent, and every tongue and every sign and whatsoever is transient—for indeed if any man could hear them, he should hear them saying with one voice: We did not make ourselves, but He made us who abides forever: but if, having uttered this and so set us to listening to Him who made them, they all grew silent, and in their silence He alone spoke to us, not by them but by Himself: so that we shoud hear His word, not by any tongue of flesh nor the voice of an angel nor the sound of thunder nor in the darkness of a parable, but that we should hear Himself and not them: just as we two had but now reached forth and in a flash of the mind attained to touch the eternal Wisdom which abides over all: and if this could continue, and all other visions so different be quite taken away, and this one should so ravish and absorb and wrap the beholder in inward joys that his life should eternally be such as that one moment of understanding for which we had been sighing—would not this be: *Enter Thou into the joy of Thy Lord*? But when shall it be? Shall it be when we shall all rise again and *shall not all be changed*? (Bk. IX, x; Sheed, trans., 164–165)

As in Donne's poem, there are two persons who ecstatically rise above or outside of the body, but in a Vision of Philia (with perhaps also elements of the Visions of Dame Kind and God) rather than in a Vision of Eros. They evidently attain to silent eternal Wisdom, godlikeness, "for one instant" or "in a flash of the mind" before they return "to the sound of our tongue, in which a word has both a beginning and ending," so that at least for that eternal (that is, timeless) instant they may well have engaged in a dialogue of one. And the passage is sufficiently ambiguous to suggest that their talk may have been, like Donne's lovers, soul's language, so as to be otherwise silent for longer periods of time as well. As in Donne's poem, there is a kind of hypothetical observer, "if any man could hear them," hear everything that has grown silent—the characteristic contemplative profound silence that conduces to hearing God's Word. For Augustine, if the ecstatic contemplative experience were to continue, it would evidently be indistinguishable from the beatific vision that is to follow actual death. We may wonder whether this Augustinian passage served as a partial Christian-Neoplatonic model and influence on the first two sections of "The Exstasie," while we note Donne's characteristic poetic boldness in the suggestion of the final section that the lovers be bodily united as well, so that finally it is clear that whereas Augustine describes a Vision of Philia, wherein two Platonically seek out God in each other's presence, Donne presents a Vision of Eros.

As remarked earlier, the idea that the true self in the depth of the particular individual is identical with or at least like unto the Divinity is found pervasively in mystical literature. We recall here briefly some of the relevant observations made in Chapter One. In the *Theaetetus*, Plato makes the point that it is only by becoming godlike that we can know God. Plotinus, in a manner reminiscent of the myth of the Fortunate Fall, teaches that the self in its lapse from its original goodness falls into the Place of Unlikeness and must return to God through its likeness to him. For Augustine, who develops from Plotinus this idea of the region of unlikeness, the soul's likeness to God has been restored in the Incarnate Word. And under the influence of Augustine, "image theology" makes its way to the many Christian mystics of the Middle Ages and Renaissance. In the words of St. Athanasius, "God became man that man might become God."[8] For Christian mystics and the Church Fathers, generally, the Incarnation reconciles the dichotomies of form and matter and of the transcendent and the immanent, and it most vividly symbolizes the fallen self's potential for regeneration and union with God. And it is the Incarnation, God's willing, loving descent into the body and physical universe, a high mark of profound humility, that clearly distinguishes the Church Fathers, even of course the Neoplatonic ones, from the non-Christian Platonists. Christ, pneuma, is the way and the example; the Resurrection is in and of the body as well as the soul. "The Exstasie" is, among other things, a description of contemplative tradition's central amazing rediscovery (through ecstatic, transformative, human love) of the lovers' Godlikeness.

Commenting on St. John's "Spiritual Canticle," which in image and intent closely resembles the biblical Song of Songs, Mary Giles gathers together and illuminates a number of points relevant to Donne's poem:

> Ecstasy pointed the way to transformation in breaking down old modes of knowing and revealing a knowing whereby we see ourselves as one yet two, or two yet one, and even more deeply as a unity beyond all logic. Mystic lovers may experience ecstasy not once but several or many times prior to the definitive event we here call transformation; and ecstasy will leave them at once exhilarated and depressed, longing for an habitual seeing that transcends all hint of dichotomy. When transformation is experienced, it culminates but does not close off the process of ecstasy; it crowns and celebrates the simplicity of gazing; it consummately clarifies our God-bound path; it enables us to see unerringly the greater vocation of loverhood.
>
> When human lovers are ecstasized out of themselves in sexual union, they experience a radical change of perspective whereby they are enabled to see from within the consciousness of the partner. They realize in this intensely humbling yet ennobling moment that they have received a gift of immeasurable beauty for which no amount of self-sacrifice has made them worthy. When this momentary perspective is transformed into the condition of a changed perspective, it is possible that a transforming is being wrought whose effects are similar, if not the same, as the spiritual event John celebrates in these stanzas. (116–117)

Donne's lovers are not yet by the end of the poem "ecstacized out of themselves in sexual union," their bodies not yet resurrected from being "like sepulchrall statues." But in their souls' ecstasy they have already experienced "a radical change of perspective whereby they are enabled to see from within the consciousness of the partner," as Donne indicates throughout the poem, particulary in stanzas 7, 11, 12, and 19 and in such phrases as "both spake the same," "That abler soule," "this new soule," and "dialogue of one." And because they have already spiritually experienced that "radical change of perspective . . . ," the hypothetical observing lover at the end of the poem "shall see / Small change, when we'are to bodies gone." That is, in sexual ecstasy and union as in spiritual ecstasy and union the lovers will experience the same radical change of perspective and (in Stace's terms) unifying vision or unitary consciousness. Because the Vision of Eros may have both sensuous and non-sensuous aspects and because it includes another human consciousness, it may well display both the extrovertive characteristic of the unifying vision and the introvertive characteristic of the unitary consciousness. It (like the Vision of Philia) stands in a middle ground between the more purely extrovertive Vision of Dame Kind and the introvertive Vision of God. In any case, whether the lovers are in the spiritual or sexual mode (strictly, these two modes are distinguishable but not finally divisible in the Vision of Eros), it culminates "in the perception of an ultimate Unity—what Plotinus called the One—with which the perceiver realizes his own union or even identity" (Stace, *Mysticism and Philosophy*, 61). As Giles' last sentence indicates, it is possible that in the Vision of Eros (in both its spiritual and sexual aspects) "a transforming is being wrought whose effects are similar, if not the same, as the spiritual event" St. John of the Cross celebrates in the "Spiritual Canticle," that event being mystical union in the more usual sense, the Vision of God. Donne's poem in effect informs us that one may discover (or, better, re-discover) one's own Godlikeness through unitive knowledge of the immanent divinty of one's human beloved as well as through unitive knowledge of the transcendent divinity of God.

The lovers' love (which, according to Neoplatonic philosophy, participates in the Form of Love) has the same transformative power as God (Love) does: miraculously to make one of two, to make something that is pure, simple, and thereby immortal (especially in the sense of not governed by time-consciousness), something "no change can invade." Such is the extraordinary power of love. "That abler soule, which thence doth flow," is divine or is like divinity, and has divine knowledge, knowing "Of what we are compos'd, and made." Having managed to break out of the closed ego, the lovers now know the truth about their essential selves, have essential self-knowledge, and all of this is accomplished by true love and spiritual ecstasy.

In the midst of poetically and musically rendered abstract philosophical and theological ideas, which also slow the reading and thereby suggest timelessness, Donne wisely re-presents an image of "A single violet transplant," which "Redoubles still, and multiplies," as the symbol of the lovers' new soul transformed by love:

> When love, with one another so
>   Interinanimates two soules,
> That abler soule, which thence doth flow
>   Defects of lonelinesse controules.

38

Whether we take "interinanimates" to mean either mutually breathes life into, or mutually removes the (ordinary) consciousness of, or both (since both do apply), the lovers' love and thereby the lovers are again in this way presented as Godlike. The image of the violet, which symbolizes true love and the paradox of two-in-one, also especially signifies the humility of the Second Person in assuming human or bodily form. To become like Christ, the last Adam, one must give up the psyche or the first Adam (becoming humble or empty) in order to realize pneuma, one's essential spiritual self. The lovers in Donne's poem, as indicated by the first two sections, have already realized through ecstatic love their true self, "That abler soule" or "this new soule." In order to be still more Godlike and Christlike, the lovers must like Christ undergo an incarnation, incorporate soma, turn or descend from the transcendent world of spirit and their spiritual ecstasy to their bodies, as the third section of the poem urges, for Donne's writings clearly indicate that we exist not as a soul or a body but as a union of soul and body.

This unifying or unitive rather than dualistic and divisive view of human nature (precisely compatible with the mystical passion for unity and union, and with the mystical way of seeing, knowing, and being) is exemplified throughout Donne's prose as well as his poetic works.[9] As Donne writes in *Pseudo-Martyr*, "It is intire man that God hath care of, and not the soul alone; therefore his first worke was the body, and the last work shall bee the glorification thereof" (17). Stanzas 13 to 19 may be regarded as a kind of symbolic poetic concentration of the life of Christ in that Donne seems to have both incarnation and resurrection[10] in mind. (Such a conflation of biblical texts in a Donne poem is not unusual, as the conflation of Creation, Flood, and Apocalypse in the second stanza of "A Valediction: of Weeping" testifies.) The lovers' bodies, which "like sepulchrall statues lay," will be resurrected, glorified when "pure lovers soules descend / T'affections, and to faculties." The ideal is for humans through love to die and be reborn, to realize fully their Christlike nature, to become perfect. In *Biathanatos*, Donne writes "let us follow the truth in love, and in all things grow up into him, which is the head, that is Christ, till we are all met together, unto a perfect man. By which we receive the honour to be one body with Christ our head" (178–79).

Not only are these early prose works, written perhaps in the general period of "The Exstasie" and other secular poems celebrating true love, consistent with this poetry, but so also is the later prose. As A. J. Smith rightly observes in *The Metaphysics of Love*, the reversals of Donne's career did not alter certain of his intellectual attitudes. "The understanding of love which he opened in 'The Ecstacy' needed no drastic renunciation when he took holy orders. On the contrary, a series of sermons which span his preaching ministry, many of them delivered on Easter Day, affirm the mutual dependence of soul and body as it is assured by Christ's taking flesh for pure love, and by the indivisibility of the human and the divine elements in Christ's own manhood. In this conviction Donne never wavered" (213). Smith then cites Donne's sermon for Easter, 1623:

> Never therefore dispute against thine own happiness; never say, God asks the heart, that is, the soule, and therefore rewards the soule, or punishes the soule, and hath no respect to the body. . . . Never go about to separate the thoughts of the heart, from the colledge, from the fellowship of the body. . . . All that the soule does, it does in, and with, and by the body. . . . The body is washed in baptisme, but it is that the soule might be made cleane. . . . In all unctions, whether that which was then in use in Baptisme, or that which was in use at our transmigration, and passage out of this world, the body was anointed, that the soule might be consecrated. . . . The body is signed with the Crosse, that the soule might be armed against tentations. . . . My body received the body of Christ, that my soule might partake of his merits. . . . These two, Body, and Soule, cannot be separated for ever, which, whilst they are together, concurre in all that either of them doe. Never thinke it presumption . . . To hope for that in thy selfe, which God admitted, when he tooke thy nature upon him. And God hath made it . . . more easie then so, for thee, to beleeve it, because not onely did Christ himselfe, but such men, as thou art, did rise at the Resurrection of Christ. And therefore when our bodies are dissolved and liquefied in the Sea, putrified in the earth, resolv'd to ashes in the fire, macerated in the ayre, . . . take account that all the world is Gods cabinet, and water, and earth, and fire, and ayre, are the proper boxes, in which God laies up our bodies, for the Resurrection. (*Sermons*, IV, 14, 358–59)

In another sermon, using the metaphor of marriage that is prominent in St. John of the Cross and Henry Vaughan, among others, Donne indicates, as Smith points out, that "Christ's mixed nature effectively seals the marriage of our flesh to divine being" (215):

> As our flesh is in him, by his participation thereof, so his flesh is in us, by our communication thereof; and so is his divinity in us, by making us partakers of his divine nature, and by making us one spirit with himself . . . for this is an union, in which Christ in his

purpose hath married himself to our souls, inseparably, and *Sine solutione vinculi,* Without any intention of divorce on his part. (*Sermons,* IX, 10, 248)

As we read in a favorite mystical test, "ye shall know that I *am* in my Father, ye in me, and I in you" (John 14:20).

In the poem, Donne exerts considerable figurative effort to explain the nature of humans as a union of soul and body. The lovers are identified with or likened to the celestial spheres (their bodies) that in the Middle Ages and Renaissance were thought to be governed by angels or intelligences (their souls). Their bodies are compared to a strengthening alloy rather than to dross, the weakening impurity discarded in the process of refining a metal. In stanza 15, Donne uses one or both of two analogies to elucidate further the relation of soul and body: first, astrology held that the stars influence humans through their effect on the air; secondly, theology held that God's messengers, the angels, assumed bodies of air in order to appear to humans, a notion also employed in "Aire and Angels." Stanzas 16 and 17 are an extended analogy using the idea of spirits as a *tertium quid* bonding body and soul, spirits being the vapors produced by the blood to form a link between body and soul. "Such fingers," the spirits, are needed "to knit / That subtile knot, which makes us man." Similarly, as Donne explains in a sermon and as also cited by Smith (214), "In the constitution and making of a natural man, the body is not the man, nor the soul is not the man, but the union of these two makes up the man; the spirits in a man which are the thin and active part of the blood, and so are of a kind of middle nature, between soul and body, those spirits are able to doe, and they doe the office, to unite and apply the faculties of the soul to the organs of the body, and so there is a man" (*Sermons,* II, 12, 261).

Donne's argument in the poem is that just as humans are a knot of soul and body so must pure lovers' imitate the Second Person by becoming incarnate, by descending to their bodies, "Else a great Prince in prison lies." Various critical interpretations of this line have been put forth, and various suggestions made for the meaning of "Prince," including love, a child, or third soul, and the "abler soule" or "new soule" of the lovers. I prefer the last suggestion, though it seems to involve a contradiction: how can Donne urge that if the abler or new soul of the lovers does not descend to their bodies then a great Prince (that soul) lies in prison, the body? I believe a passage from one of Donne's sermons answers this problem by indicating that in the Resurrection the body united to the soul is no longer its prison but its temple, its means of vision, part of its very essential self: "such a gladnesse shall my soul have, that this flesh, (which she will no longer call her prison, nor her tempter, but her friend, her companion, her wife) that this flesh, that is, I, in the re-union, and reintegration of both parts, shall see God; for then, one principall clause in her rejoycing, and acclamation, shall be, that this flesh is her flesh; *In carne mea, in my flesh I shall see God"* (*Sermons*, III, 3, 112). As observed in Chapter One, Irenaeus writes that "men are spiritual not by the abolition of the flesh. . . . But when this spirit is mingled with soul and united with created matter, then through the outpouring of the spirit the complete man is produced; this is the man made in the image and likeness of God" (Bettenson, *The Early Christian Fathers*, 71). Just as in the final Resurrection the re-united self joyfully in the flesh sees God, so the poem signifies that the lovers, who have through ecstatic spiritual love been reborn a new soul, will in turning to their bodies undergo little or no change, will also ecstatically in the body see God or, to put it more precisely, enjoy the Vision of Eros, see and enjoy the immanent divinity within themselves.

Critics continue even in recent years to feel uncertain about which Group to place "The Exstasie" in. Graham Parry, for example, writes that "whether 'The Exstasie' is one of Donne's most solemn poems of love or is really a platonic shaggy dog story whose purpose is an invitation to love or a 'persuasion to enjoy,' distinguished by all manner of specious intellectual promises, one cannot with certainty say" (59). Since stanzas 13 to 19 in theme and tone have appeared to some readers like poems in Group One, some critics, in the effort to disprove that "The Exstasie" is a seduction poem of the Group One variety, have raised the question whether the poem has sexual love in mind at all as the end of its main argument; and they thereby push the poem in the direction of Group Three. Whether the final plea that the lovers turn to their bodies is to be understood as a persuasion to actual sexual union or is to be taken only as a suggestion "that the lovers' souls should return from their ecstatic communion to reanimate their bodies," as Gardner, for example, argues (*The Elegies and The Songs and Sonnets*, 260), is also an issue which some critics feel cannot with certainty be finally decided in this poem. I would point out, however, that it is not cogent to argue that the presence of the observer referred to in stanzas 6, 7, and 19 militates against the plea being taken as one for sexual union, because the observer is strictly hypothetical ("If any" and "if some lover") and serves largely as a device for communicating the lovers' wordless communion, their "soules language."[11] Furthermore, since mystical ecstasies are usually of short duration as measured by clock time, may be of long duration as in Donne's poem ("all the day"), but in any case are in this life not permanent, the lovers will naturally and inevitably turn to their bodies in the sense of simply reanimating them; thus, a plea to do so seems unnecessary and pointless. Finally, if the plea is taken as one for sexual union, then the title and poem are considerably more meaningful, referring both on the spiritual level to the ecstatic union of the lovers' souls and on the physical level to the ecstatic experience of sexual congress, with the implication that while the two experiences are distinguishable they are not actually or permanently divisible in true love, just as soul and body are distinguishable but not finally divisible in Donne's view. In other words, whereas Group One may be said to neglect the soul and Group Three slight the body, the ecstatic union of the lovers' bodies and souls which characterizes Group Two is most consistent with Donne's dominant and mature thinking in his poetry and prose.

In their argument that the poem concerns true love of both soul and body, some critics downplay the idealist elements of the poem's first part, de-emphasizing the tonalities and themes of Group Three. While affirming the Aristotelian and Thomistic elements, especially that union of soul and body which denies the body is mere dross, A. J. Smith, for example, rightly observes that " 'The Ecstasy' is far from urging lovers toward a pure contemplative stasis. . . . In the end the ecstatic revelation justified their bodily union by the union of souls itself" (*The Metaphysics of Love*, 193, 194). But the final plea for bodily union should not be regarded as a denial or undercutting of "contemplative stasis" or Platonic ecstasy (Smith writes, "the poems show [Donne] consciously formalizing his experience in a precise scholastic way which undercuts idealist thinking," 195), but rather as a continuation of contemplative ecstasy in the vital domain of the body. "The Exstasie" is a thoroughly contemplative poem from Platonic or introvertive beginning to Aristotelian or extrovertive end. To downplay the poem's opening Platonism risks pushing it in the direction of Group One, risks giving support to those who wish to misconstrue the poem as a cynical seduction or "platonic shaggy dog story whose purpose is . . . a 'persuasion to enjoy' " (Parry, 59). It's a delicate balance: one must neither overemphasize (Gardner) nor merely undercut (Smith) the poem's Platonism. One must take the Platonism (like the Aristotelianism) seriously, but not exclusively so. Donne wittily has it both ways in his poems of true love:

(1) even though the lovers engage not in the Plotinian flight of the alone to the Alone but in the flight of a communal two to all one, they nevertheless may spiritually enjoy ecstatic non-temporal, non-spatial contemplation of the Platonic sort (and so, as in some valediction poems, not be apart even when one lover must physically depart); and (2) just as certain Church Fathers transcend their own Platonism through the doctrine of the Incarnation, this idealist contemplation may, should, continue in Aristotelian or extrovertive terms in the bodily realm, for ideal Forms may paradoxically become even more fully realized in physical being.

However one chooses to take the final plea of "The Exstasie," what should now be clear is that if we are wholly aware of Donne's deeply felt and long-held high estimation of human beings as a union of body and soul ideally and incarnationally realizing their Christlikeness and Godlikeness in that union, and if we understand that sexuality is present in the mystical Vision of Eros, and if we take fully into account the significance of both overlapping in Grierson's grouping and the syncretic presence of Platonism and Aristotelianism in many of Donne's poems, we shall not misread "The Exstasie" and other poems like it as merely seductive poems or simply idealistic poems rather than as true love poems which are also genuinely mystical, spiritually and physically. Furthermore, if we understand that the Vision of Eros, though it is distinguishable from the Vision of God and therefore different from as well as similar to it, is nevertheless also a real mystical experience, we will not make the common critical error of supposing that Donne only uses mystical terminology as a source of powerful language but without any real mystical meaning.

In a special sense, it is relations between subjects and objects rather than subjects or objects per se that are real for mystics. Subjects and objects, creatures and things, the "I" and the world, have their meaning, value, and being not just in isolation from but especially in relation to one another. This vivid experience and consequent profound transfiguring realization have in all cultures always been the root and flower of mysticism and of much great poetry. It has been a major error to consider or try to treat "The Exstasie" and certain other secular poems as if they were mystical in the sense in which that elusive term is applied to certain religious poetry (the poetry of St. John of the Cross, for example) as a special unitive experience between the individual soul and God. "The Exstasie" and certain other of Donne's secular poems are indeed mystical, but as Visions of Eros (not as Visions of God) in the sense of a special unitive, immanently divine experience, including sacred bodily union, between two lovers (not between the soul and the transcendent God). Both the Vision of Eros and the Vision of God are mystical experiences but they are different kinds and are therefore not fully comparable. The first Vision may be said to be an experience of divinity through the mediation of the Godlike beloved "object," and the second a more direct experience of divinity. If one changes the immediate object, then naturally and inevitably the subject-object relationship is at least initially if not ultimately altered. In the sense of Visions of Eros, Donne's poems of true love are genuinely mystical and so appropriately expressed in genuinely mystical language.

### III

Whatever one decides about the nature of the plea in "The Exstasie," there is no question that "The Canonization" concerns sexual love, and not only because of the Renaissance pun on "die," slang for sexual consummation. Just as the lovers in "The Exstasie" are to become more fully Christlike by turning to their bodies, their ecstatic souls becoming incarnate and then their bodies becoming ecstatically united too, so the lovers in "The Canonization" are Christlike (continuing to understand Christ or the last Adam in the mythic sense of "essential self") by giving up the sorry-go-round world of getting and spending, and by dying for love. There are actually two worlds, corresponding to the two selves, and thereby the seeming contradiction of condemning and enjoying the world is resolved. The two worlds are the perfect, natural world, including creatures and objects, and eternally created by the Second Person of God and by the Second Person in the redeemed individual—indeed, in Traherne's words, the "visible World is the Body of God" (*Centuries*, II, 21)—a glorious world for which, in Hebraic-Christian tradition, one renders joyful praise; and the fallen world fabricated by man's conceptualizing ego—an artificial, prideful, and ultimately illusory world, of which one should be contemptuous (the familiar but often misinterpreted theme of *contemptus mundi*). It is the first, perfect and glorious world, or a part of it, that is appreciated in the Vision of Eros or the Vision of Dame Kind. In his secular poetry, Donne concerns himself only with the former and not the latter; Vaughan's poetry, as we shall see, does engage the Vision of Dame Kind. And whereas Gerard Manley Hopkins, influenced by Duns Scotus, discovered the "individually-distinctive beauty" or "inscape" of the natural world in both the non-human and human, in Visions of Dame Kind and of Philia, Donne's discovery seems limited to the human beloved only in Visions of Eros. So while Hopkins would say that "the just man" particularly (and each person potentially), Donne might only say that the beloved

> Acts in God's eye what in God's eye he [or she] is—
> Christ—for Christ plays in ten thousand places,
> Lovely in limbs, and lovely in eyes not his
> To the Father through the features of . . . faces.
> ("As kingfishers catch fire," ll. 11–14)

The idea that "the just man" or essential self "is Christ" and the idea embodied in the line "Christ plays in ten thousand places" are wholly consistent, as the priests Hopkins and Donne may be expected to have known, with biblical and patristic views. Wisdom, as it were, playing before the throne of God. Justin and Clement of Alexandria, for example, develop the Johannine theme that the indwelling Logos is the source of all spiritual and intellectual enlightenment (see, for example, Bettenson's Introduction to *The Early Christian Fathers*). Donne's frequent microcosm-macrocosm distinction and comparison should be understood in these terms. The psyche's larger fallen world may well be given up for pneuma's perception and realization of the beloved's Christlikeness.

Even though we need not fully explicate Donne's much-discussed poems (precisely because of excellent previous discussions) and even though we are analyzing his poems only to the extent that such scrutiny is pertinent to the major concerns of this book, it is useful to have the full text of "The Canonization" before us:

### The Canonization

For Godsake hold your tongue, and let me love,
   Or chide my palsie, or my gout,
My five gray haires, or ruin'd fortune flout,
With wealth your state, your minde with Arts improve,
   Take you a course, get you a place,          5
   Observe his honour, or his grace,
And the Kings reall, or his stamped face
Contemplate; what you will, approve,
   So you will let me love.

Alas, alas, who's injur'd by my love?                                          10
   What merchants ships have my sighs drown'd?
Who saies my teares have overflow'd his ground?
When did my colds a forward spring remove?
   When did the heats which my veines fill
   Adde one man to the plaguie Bill?                                 15
Soldiers finde warres, and Lawyers finde out still
   Litigious men, which quarrels move,
      Though she and I do love.


Call us what you will, wee'are made such by love;
   Call her one, mee another flye,                                   20
We'are Tapers too, and at our owne cost die,
And wee in us finde the'Eagle and the Dove;
   The Phoenix ridle hath more wit
   By us, we two being one, are it,
So, to one neutrall thing both sexes fit.                                      25
   Wee dye and rise the same, and prove
      Mysterious by this love.


Wee can dye by it, if not live by love,
   And if unfit for tombes or hearse
Our legend bee, it will be fit for verse;                                      30
And if no peece of Chronicle wee prove,
   We'll build in sonnets pretty roomes;
   As well a well wrought urne becomes
The greatest ashes, as halfe-acre tombes,
   And by these hymnes, all shall approve                             35
      Us *Canoniz'd* for Love.


And thus invoke us; You whom reverend love
   Made one anothers hermitage;
You, to whom love was peace, that now is rage;
Who did the whole worlds soule extract, and drove                              40
   Into the glasses of your eyes,
   So made such mirrors, and such spies,
That they did all to you epitomize,
   Countries, Townes, Courts: Beg from above
      A patterne of your love!                                    45


In celebrating the theme that the world, the fallen world, is well lost for love, "The Canonization," after the false-lead opening of the first two stanzas, effects a radical transformation of self that paradoxically is both merely witty and playful and yet wholly serious. It may very well be that the combination of witty levity and seriousness was, if not the only, one of the very few ways Donne could in his day express his views on human love as both erotic and divine. The first two stanzas basically are catalogs, that poetic form which Renaissance books of rhetoric advised novice poets to practice, though of course the catalog device would continue to be of use to the mature poet. Form here follows content: both stanzas are skillfully accomplished but elementary compared to the third stanza. The speaker brilliantly but simply lists, in the first stanza, alternative castigatings or courses that his audience (presumably, a well-meaning friend) might practice rather than prevent the speaker's loving. The second stanza is mainly an imagistically anti-Petrarchan series of rhetorical questions designed to establish the lovers' innocence and innocuousness: the world continues its routine, businesslike, often quarrelsome and militant way even "Though she and I do love." Stylistically, but not thematically, these two stanzas are like the poems of Group One; such poems as "Womans Constancy" and "The Indifferent" consist wholly or in large part of catalogs and anti-Petrarchan images. Thematically, and to some extent tonally, these two stanzas are like the poems of Group Three, seemingly Platonic in the insisted innocuousness and innocence of the lovers.

While the reader of the poem is initially led falsely to believe that the lovers' love is without significant consequences for the world, the central, fulcrum third stanza begins to turn that misbelief all around, as it begins to present its transformation of the lovers' selves. The rhetorical tactic of the false-lead opening of the first two stanzas has been that of concession. Stylistically, symbolically, and semantically much more complex than the first two stanzas, the third stanza begins in the same mode of concession and listing; the speaker-lover in the first two lines of this stanza, lines 19–20, enjoins his audience-friend to call the lovers what he will, and even provides the disparaging labels or epithets—provides the ammunition, so to speak. Lines 19–20, like stanza one, are in the imperative mood; stanza two, except for its last three lines, is in the interrogative mood; but with the instructive declarative mood of the rest of stanza three, lines 21–27, and of all of stanza four, Donne turns the false-lead opening completely around to a thorough exaltation of the lovers. This achievement and the wit of the marvelous third stanza obtain not only in the abruptness yet consistency of a rich, compressed imagery and symbolism, but also in the rapid traversing (by means of this same imagery) of the Renaissance chain of being, a metaphor which expresses the plenitude, order, and unity of God's creation. This chain, as E. M. W. Tillyard points out (though his views are now contested), in the Elizabethan world view stretches from the base of God's throne to the lowest of inanimate objects and includes every entity and aspect of creation as a link in the chain (23). Donne's poem moves from the lowest link to nearly the highest in the chain of being, from the inanimate taper to the glorified saints, sitting below the angels next to God. Using imagery derived from Petrarch, the third stanza enjoins the friend to call the lovers flies, general symbols of the ephemeral and lustful as well as a Christian symbol of sin (Ferguson, 18), frequently associated with the devil; and, as if to be even more outrageous, this stanza then declares the lovers are also tapers, which are even lower than flies and are self-consuming, "at our owne cost die." At this point it becomes certain because of the pun on die that the protestations of innocence in the second stanza do not include sexual innocence. The lovers die at their own cost because, according to Renaissance medical belief, sexual activity reduced one's life span.

In anticipation of the symbolism of the rest of the stanza, lines 20–21 indirectly refer to a moth or taper-fly which burns itself to death by approaching a flame and which was considered "hermaphroditic and resurrectable" (A. B. Chambers, "The Fly in Donne's 'Canonization'," 255). Continuing the imagery of flight and fire, Donne moves quickly to "Eagle" and "Dove" and "Phoenix," which, as well as being advancing steps in the alchemical process ("flying eagle" and "Diane's doves") leading to the philosopher's stone ("phoenix"), are complex Christian symbols of higher realities, especially associated with Christ and the Resurrection. On a secondary level, the dove appropriately also functions "as the bird of Venus and as a symbol of conjugal love" (Chambers, 253).

Associated with biblical stories of purification (Luke 2:22,24) and the Flood (Genesis 8), the dove in Christian art represents purity and peace (see line 39), but it is most significantly representative of the Holy Spirit, this symbolism first appearing in the story of Christ's baptism (John 1:32). The highest order of bird in the chain of being, the eagle, which similarly also signalizes new life begun at baptism, usually sumbolizes the Resurrection and Christ both because of the belief that the eagle periodically renewed its plumage and youth by flying toward the sun and then plunging into water and because of the belief that it could gaze into the dazzling noon sun. A particular symbol of St. John the Evangelist, the eagle also stands more generally for those who are just and for the virtue of contemplation (Ferguson, 15–17). As Gardner points out, the dove and eagle together are emblematic "of strength and gentleness. Joined, they symbolize the perfection of masculine and feminine qualities; compare Crashaw's address to St. Teresa, 'By all the Eagle in thee, all the Dove' " (*The Elegies And The Songs and Sonnets*, 204). The phoenix, the unique mythological bird that is consumed by its own funeral fire yet rises reborn from the ashes, is also, like the eagle, symbolic of the Resurrection of Christ.

So the lovers, made one by love, are consumed in their fire of passion but revive, undergo a death and resurrection. With Donne playing upon the slang meaning of "die" as consummating the sexual act, the lovers imitate Christ: they "dye and rise the same." By this mystery and miracle, by giving up the materialistic fallen world, by dying for love (as, in another sense, saints and martyrs do), the lovers are "*Canoniz'd* for Love." Dante says of Beatrice that she went straight to heaven after her death without spending any time in purgatory, the prerogative of a saint. Through the greater consciousness bestowed upon him through his love, Dante performed, as it were, his own act of canonization. So Donne performs the same for his lovers, who die and are resurrected in this life, the mark of contemplatives. Though some might possibly hear the tones and themes of Group One in the background, "The Canonization" is not merely a clever rationalization and justification of the speaker's love (or lust, his friend might say) that cynically uses mystical terminology. Rather, it is a poem about the extraordinary power of love to transmute the least into the greatest, to exalt the lowest on the chain of being into the highest, to transfigure tapers, flies, and sinners mysteriously into saints seated next to the throne of God. It is indeed for God's sake that the friend should hold his tongue and let the lovers love.

As the last stanza in the imperative mood shows, these lover-saints ("to whome love was peace" and blessedness, among other mystical characteristics) can then be invoked by the faithful, in the Roman Catholic fashion, to intercede with God on behalf of the faithful. The lovers give up the macrocosm, which is actually the lesser world of the commonwealth, the world of wealth, power, and earthly glory, and by that loss they paradoxically gain the greater world of the microcosm, the perfect and truly glorious world of their essential, Christlike selves. The humbled lovers of the first half of the poem (lines 1–21) are in the second half exalted as highly as human beings may possible by exalted. But why?

In his brilliant and detailed study of "The Canonization," to which all subsequent discussions of the poem have been indebted, Cleanth Brooks observed that Donne "daringly treats profane love as if it is divine love," and he further remarked that "the poem then is a parody of Christian sainthood; but it is an intensely serious parody of a sort that modern man, habituated as he is to an easy yes or no, can hardly understand." Whereas, according to Brooks, modern man thinks that Donne either does not take love seriously or does not take sainthood seriously, and so thinks the poet is either simply sharpening his wit as an exercise or "merely indulging in a cynical and bawdy parody, . . . a reading of the poem will show that Donne takes both love and religion seriously" (in Clements, ed., *John Donne's Poetry*, 179). Brooks' reading of the poem admirably succeeds in demonstrating this thesis.[12]

I have tried to go a step further than Brooks in order to show not only that Donne takes both love and religion seriously but also that he daringly treats "profane" love as if it were divine love because it is: that is why the lovers are glorified as highly as possible. More precisely, Group One poems (sexuality without Eros) treat profane love as profane love; Group Two poems treat seemingly profane love as divine love. There are various characteristics (or the absence of such) by which we can distinguish between the two groups, the primary one being the presence or absence of the unitary consciousness or unifying vision by which the two lovers are or are seen as one. In "The Canonization," the primary characteristic finds expression in the central lines:

> The Phoenix ridle hath more wit
> By us, we two being one, are it,
> So, to one neutrall thing both sexes fit.
> Wee dye and rise the same, and prove
> Mysterious by this love.

The appropriate biblical text for these lines is Galatians 3:28: "There is neither Jew nor Greek, there is neither bond nor free, there is neither male nor female: for ye are all one in Christ Jesus." The Gospel of Thomas, which Donne probably did not directly know, reads "Jesus said to them, 'When you make the two into one, when you make the inner like the outer and the outer like the inner, and the upper like the lower, when you make male and female into a single one, so that the male will not be male and the female will not be female . . . then you will enter the kingdom," (Meyer, 24). Gregory of Nyssa understands St. Paul to mean in I Corinthians 15 that "the resurrection is nothing other than the reconstitution of our nature to its pristine state" (Bettenson, *Later Christian Fathers*, 164). By their death and resurrection, imitating Christ, the two lovers over-come the effects of the Fall and become one again, become an an-drogynous or hermaphroditic being, "one neutrall thing" (not sex-less, but containing "both sexes"), not only like the phoenix (which symbolizes the last Adam) but also like the unfallen first Adam be-fore Eve was created out of his rib. For, as Augustine suggests, the significance of the story of Eve's creation is that the unfallen Adam contained both sexes so that the whole human race might be derived from a single unified being (*The City of God*, XII, 21). Thus the real meaning of the mystery of sexual intercourse is that it is a prefigur-ing realization as well as a symbolic representation of that mystical body of which we are all members, according to Paul's Epistle to the Ephesians 5:28–32:

> So ought men to love their wives as their own bodies. He that loveth his wife loveth himself.
> For no man ever yet hated his own flesh; but nourisheth and cherisheth it, even as the Lord the church.
> For we are members of his body, of his flesh, and of his bones.
> For this cause shall a man leave his father and mother, and shall be joined unto his wife, and they two shall be one flesh.
> This is a great mystery: but I speak concerning Christ and the church.

We may further distinguish between Group One and Group Two poems by observing that sexual love in the former is partial, genital, and therefore fallen (divided, $2 = 2$), whereas in the latter it is poly-morphously erotic and thereby redeemed (united, $2 = 1$). A text from Donne's great later contemporary, John Milton, will help to explain. In *Paradise Lost*, Adam, observing the angel Raphael eat with relish, wonders in his healthy curiosity whether and how angels also make love, "for Love thou say'st / leads up to Heav'n, is both the way and guide." As if in a cherubic blush, Raphael answers affirmatively "with a smile that glow'd / Celestial rosy red":

> Let it suffice thee that thou know'st
> Us happy, and without Love no happiness.
> Whatever pure thou in the body enjoy'st
> (And pure thou wert created) we enjoy
> In eminence, and obstacle find none
> Of membrane, joint, or limb, exclusive bars:
> Easier than Air with Air, if Spirits embrace,

Total they mix, Union of Pure with Pure
Desiring; nor restrain'd conveyance need
As Flesh to mix with Flesh, or Soul with Soul.

(VIII, 611f.)

This total mixing or union, which is a perfect hermaphroditic image for polymorphous eroticism, presumably will become Adam's and Eve's mode of loving when they ascend to Heaven, just as their reason (as Raphael tells them in Book V) in time may like angelic reason become more intuitive and less discursive. In any case, this image may serve to render more plain, vivid, and meaningful Donne's various expressions in the Group Two poems of the paradox of two-in-one. This paradox may at least in part grow out of feelings, actual physical sensations, of flowing together, of being bodily united during sexual intercourse in all parts and pores of the lovers' bodies as, conceivably, only angels could be. "So, to one neutrall thing both sexes fit." All the feelings and profound significance of the unitive polymorphously erotic love of the Vision of Eros may be symbolically suggested by the angelic love described by Raphael. In such love and Vision, the lovers mix totally "nor restrain'd conveyance need / As Flesh to mix with Flesh, or Soul with Soul" because, as Donne repeatedly makes efforts to explain, in some deeply meaningful (and actually felt and sensed) way their flesh and souls mysteriously but truly are One.

What has been said about "The Exstasie" and "The Canonization" is generally true of Group Two poems. Without belaboring it, we may illustrate the point that these poems display many of the distinctive characteristics of contemplative experience as a Vision of Eros. Some additional instances of the unitary consciousness and unifying vision, or of the typical Donnean paradox of two-in-one, follow:

Here you see me, and I am you.
   "A Valediction: of my Name in the Window"

Our two soules therefore, which are one.
   "A Valediction: forbidding Mourning"

But wee will have a way more liberall,
Then changing hearts, to joyne them, so we shall
   Be one, and one anothers All.
      "Love Infiniteness"

> What ever dyes, was not mixt equally;
> If Our two loves be one, or, thou and I
> Love so alike, that none doe slacken, none can die.
> "The Good-morrow"

The true lovers realize their essential nature, pneuma, by becoming one, and this unitive transformation, transcending (at least in the eternal now-moment) time, decay, and death, helps to make the microcosm that is the lovers greater than the temporal, multiple or disunified, and mortal macrocosm, especially as this macrocosm is understood as the fallen world of the psyche. In the Vision of Dame Kind, which does not figure in Donne's work, the natural macrocosm as apprehended by redeemed senses is at one with or at least inextricably connected to the enlightened perceiver. Critics have shown the importance of "correspondence" in Metaphysical poetry.[13] For Donne, the "identity" of the lovers overrides the significance of the microcosm-macrocosm correspondence. In Donne's Vision of Eros the lovers, having realized their true self, are in that sense greater and more real than the outer world:

> She'is all States, and all Princes, I,
>     Nothing else is.
> Princes doe but play us; compar'd to this,
> All honor's mimique; All wealth alchimie.
>     Thou sunne art halfe as happy'as wee,
>     In that the world's contracted thus;
>     Thine age askes ease, and since thy duties bee
>     To warme the world, that's done in warming us.
> Shine here to us, and thou art every where;
> This bed thy center is, these walls, thy spheare.
> "The Sunne Rising"

Commenting on these lines, Brian Vickers makes the important point that "the hyperbole 'asserts the incredible in order to arrive at the credible': it is as Sir Thomas Browne might have said, 'not only figuratively, but literally true' that—and by decoding the message I risk a banality which Donne transcended—the universe *does* revolve around them; their bed *is* the centre; nothing else *is*; love *is* 'infinitely delightful . . . infinitely high . . . infinitely great in all extremes'" ("The 'Songs and Sonnets' and the Rhetoric of Hyperbole, in Smith, ed., *Essays in Celebration*, 155). Such a "message," though different, than say, Herbert's "Thy word is all, if we could spell," also precisely describes the contemplative experience that God—or, in

54

Donne's Group Two poems, the realized Christlike natures of the lovers—is all that truly is.

"The Sunne Rising" gives voice to the non-spatial characteristic of some contemplative experiences. At the least, it tends to de-spatialize the world, reduce the macrocosm to the microcosm, the redeemed latter being in any event of greater value and significance than the fallen macrocosm. This poem and others express, too, the contemplative characteristic of timelessness and, hence, of eternity:

> Love, all alike, no season knowes, nor clyme,
> Nor houres, dayes, months, which are the rags of time.
>> "The Sunne Rising"

> All other things, to their destruction draw,
>   Only our love hath no decay;
> This, no tomorrow hath, nor yesterday,
> Running it never runs from us away,
> But truly keepes his first, last, everlasting day.
>> "The Anniversarie"

Group Two poems exhibit the sense of objectivity or reality associated with both extrovertive and introvertive mystical experiences:

> 'Twas so; But this, all pleasures fancies bee.
> If ever any beauty I did see,
> Which I desir'd, and got, 'twas but a dreame of thee.

> And now good morrow to our waking soules.
>> "The Good-morrow"

The mystical characteristics of joy, peace, blessedness, love, etc., abound in Group Two, as various Valedictions, for example, exemplify.

Contrariwise, the common and distinctive characteristics of contemplative experience are absent from Group One poems. In general, these poems are devoid of "spiritual" qualities. As "Loves Usury" reads, "let my body raigne." There is only a partial and temporary "loving," at best, and giving of the self, versus the total genuine loving and self-giving of Group Two. Additionally, instead of the fidelity, tenderness, and blessed, joyous union of the latter, Group One exhibits inconstancy, anger, bitterness, spite, scorn, contempt, revenge, loathing, jealousy, hostility, and a desperate or agitated pleasure. Such a listing does not of course do justice to the quality of these poems as poetry nor to readers' responses to them. A. J. Smith's insightful remarks restore some balance to the mere cataloging of mostly "negative" emotions: "One responds to [the world represented in Group One] for the positive qualities it has: the life, the gusto, the sense of Rabelaisian relish for experience which expresses itself in this spirit of comic extravagance and hyperbole. This is a zest, indeed, which is so far from coarseness that it manifests itself in conduct in a marked elegance of style—a bland and jaunty insouciance, a gay self-reliance. Moreover, we are in the real world, even if it is a partial picture of it that we get" (*John Donne: The Songs and Sonnets*, 48).

This partialness deserves emphasis. Women are not regarded in their totality or fullness of real being. As Smith rightly observes, "this is a young man's world, in which women are mere objects, to be tried, enjoyed, and lightheartedly discarded" (47). We are much aware of a pose, a mask, an attitude, often misogynous. It is apparently a persona, not the poet, who in "Song: 'Goe and catche a falling starre'" believes that "No where / Lives a woman true, and faire." At the end of the witty "The Curse," which heaps up anathemas upon "Who ever guesses, thinks, or dreams he knowes / Who is my mistris," there appears the gratuitous joke or punch-line "For if it be a shee / Nature before hand hath out-cursed mee." Similarly, the concluding couplet of "Loves Alchymie" suggests in a bitter punch-line manner, among other meanings, that even the sweetest and wittiest women are merely dead flesh possessed or animated by an evil demon; or are, when a man possesses them, merely bodies without minds:

> Hope not for minde in women; at their best
> Sweetnesse and wit, they'are but *Mummy*, possest.

These are poems of a divided and anxious psyche in a fallen world, driven (with great wit to be sure, but ultimately out of fear of one's own death) to seize the day and seek a desperate pleasure before fragile flesh decays. These separative poems present a failure of realized vision, not seeing the beloved at her best, as she truly is, but content to take her and discard her, only as soma. By contrast, Group Two, with the awareness that it is the relation between subject and object that is ultimately real and that therefore the two lovers are one and blessedly unafraid and peaceful in the eternal now-moment, presents unitive poems of the resurrected self, reconciling and exalting the lovers' bodies and souls through the unifying Vision of Eros, seeing the beloved for all that he or she is, divine, Christlike, one's very own essential being.

The possibility that by far most of Group One poems were written before 1599 and that by far most of Group Two poems were written during or after 1599 would suggest that Donne may indeed have gone through the equivalent of a "conversion" experience, a radical transformative realization of the true self by means of the Vision of Eros. The evidence of the poems points to the likelihood, if not the certainty, of such a realization. The date must remain uncertain, though probability would suggest sometime shortly before, during, or shortly after 1600. We know that Donne and Anne More throughout 1599 were at York House, Sir Thomas Egerton's official residence, that Sir George More removed his daughter from there sometime in 1600 with much haste, as Walton says, "to his own house" (27), and that the lovers met again in the Fall 1601 and were married in either December 1601 or January 1602.[14] A profound, life-changing experience such as a Vision of Eros might help to explain why Donne committed so seemingly rash an act as to marry Ann More. Whatever practical reasons there may have been for marrying, including the possibility that Ann was pregnant,[15] a Vision of Eros would be compelling reason enough for lovers to wish to be together for all time. About the love between John and Ann Donne, Edward Le Comte concludes, "I do not doubt it was mutual and true and lasting unto the grave and beyond. Ann, as well as God, was to be thanked for delivering Jack 'from the Egypt of lust, by confining my affections' . . . he continued to find her, or they each other, irresistible, even when he was 45 [in 1617, the year Ann died], which in those days was the threshold of old age" ("Jack Donne: From Rake to Husband" in *Just So Much Honor*, 22–23).[16]

It seems reasonable to suppose that Donne's relation with Ann More may account for the fact that, roughly speaking, at approximately sometime during and after 1600 he started to write poems of true love. Yet regardless of the biographical construction one may put or not put upon the poems, the single major difference between Groups One and Three on the one hand and Group Two on the other is the absence from the former and the presence in the latter of the Vison of Eros and all that that entails. The poems of true love are precisely those which have received the most critical attention, and rightly so, since, as many would agree, they are Donne's best. At some particular time, Donne—a brilliant poet in any case as the early Elegies and Group One poems attest—found form, style, and expression for the extraordinary contemplative Vision of Eros and thereby produced the great love lyrics of Group Two. Even if no biographical or chronological significance is attached to them, they remain the best poetic expression of the Vision of Eros in the English language.

## IV

There are of course other great poetic expressions of the Vision of Eros, and in languages other than English, some available to Donne. Beyond what has already been discussed we must now consider contemplative tradition in some of its various historical, philosophical and theological as well as literary aspects and sources as they are pertinent (and may have contributed) to Donne's view and presentation of the lovers in Group Two. We will also briefly consider the relevant modern theology of Eros.

Christian thinking about Christ's redemptive work follows three main channels of interpretation, concerning which Gustaf Aulén provides a detailed discussion in his *Christus Victor: An Historical Study of the Three Main Types of the Idea of Atonement*. The classic idea of Atonement, "Christ as Hero," is the typical view of the New Testament and the Fathers. The so-called Latin view of Atonement, "Christ as Ransom," did not gain force until Anselm's *Cur Deus Homo*. The "subjective" or exemplarist view, which arose to challenge the Latin view, far from returning to the classic idea, diverged from it still further, and concentrated attention on the psychological process of man's reformation. As Aulén argues, the classic idea, developed by Irenaeus, recurs repeatedly in both the later Greek and Western Fathers, such as Origen, Athanasius, Gregory of Nyssa, John Chrysostom, Ambrose, Augustine, Leo the Great, and Gregory the Great, and it was powerfully revived by Luther. (It is truly evangelical and truly catholic, and as such offers hope of the reunion of Catholic and Protestant.) "Its central theme is the idea of the Atonement as a Divine conflict and victory; Christ—Christus Victor—fights against and triumphs over the evil powers of the world . . . under which mankind is in bondage and suffering, and in Him God reconciles the world to Himself . . . . it represents the work of Atonement or reconciliation as from first to last a work of God Himself, a *continuous* Divine work" (Aulén, 4, 5).

Most importantly for our concerns, the Incarnation, which has its basis in divine love, and the Atonement belong inseparably together. As Aulén observes, "the organic connection of the idea of the Incarnation with that of the Atonement is the leading characteristic of the doctrine of the redemption in the early church" (42), and he discusses the development of this central thought especially in Irenaeus, Athanasius, Augustine, and Gregory of Nyssa. The famous statement of Athanasius remains a most insightful, forceful, and succinct expression of this vital thought: "God became man that man might become God." While some of the Church Fathers occasionally speak of the redemption according to more than one main type, sometimes trying to combine them, the idea of the identity or likeness between Christ and humankind remains dominant. Although Gregory of Nyssa, for example, also discusses the redemption in terms of "ransom," he writes mainly about the restoration of man through identification with the Incarnate and the sharing of the victory of the last Adam, which cancelled the defeat of the first. Writing on Christ's Immanence and Incarnation, Gregory observes:

> The birth of godhead in our nature should not reasonably present itself as a strange novelty to those whose notions are not too limited. For who, surveying the whole scheme of things, is so childish as not to believe that there is divinity in everything, clothed in it, embracing it, residing in it? For everything that is depends on Him-Who-Is, nor can there be anything which has not its being in Him-Who-Is. Then if all things are in the divinity, and the divinity is in all things, why are men embarrassed at the divine plan displayed in the revelation which tells us of the birth of God in humanity, since we believe that God is not outside mankind even now? (Bettenson, The *Later Christian Fathers*, 134)

"If all things are in the divinity, and the divinity is in all things" and "God is not outside mankind even now," then it ought to be possible to discover the presence of immanent divinity (Christ) in the human beloved. And that discovery is what "The Exstasie" and "The Canonization," among other Group Two poems, are about. "The Exstasie" certainly concerns that discovery at the level of the lover's souls, and may well contain a plea that the lovers make the discovery also in the domain of the body. "The Canonization" certainly concerns that discovery at the level of the lovers' bodies and very probably also in the realm of their souls. Indeed, just as Christ signifies the union of divinity and humanity, so Donne in many of the Group Two poems labors to show that body and soul are and should be, though mentally distinguishable, indivisibly united. It is true, as Vaughan's "The Night" tells us, that the *historical* Christ can no longer be seen or known in the flesh, as "Wise Nicodemus . . . did at mid-night speak with the Sun." But the immanent Christ is realizable in the bodies and souls of the lovers, Donne seems to be saying, in ways which simply "extend" Church doctrine and which therefore appropriately employ religious and mystical expression.

To counter that the Church (or parts of it) in Donne's day (and in the present day, too) might vehemently object to Donne's "extension" of Church doctrine is no cogent argument against such a view of Donne's but rather a testimony to his genius (and perhaps also a comment on the nature of his own experiences of the Vision of Eros). Modern theologians, especially feminist ones, like Donne before them, are doing much to re-integrate sexuality and spirituality, which have often been dichotomized by branches of institutional Christianity.[17] Dorothy Donnelly, for example, writing in *The Feminist Mystic* on "The Sexual Mystic: Embodied Spirituality," points out that the historical categorization of love into eros, agape, philia, and libido, which has continued even until recent times, not only overlooks or slights the integrating power of love, but also is variously flawed in other serious ways.

The separation of God's love (*agape* as sacrificial love), the asserted model of Christian love, from human love or sexual passion (*eros*), such as is found in Anders Nygren's influential work, has "little support in the Scriptures or in the historical development of the use of these terms; it is based on Platonic dualism, Stoic approaches to virtue as absence of passion and the work of Christian theologians who were influenced by both. . . . *Agape* in relation to eros is part of the process of expressing . . . love in a human way to God and to others. *Eros* and *agape* are not separate loving, one sexual and the other spiritual; they are merely labels, now outdated, but once convenient for discerning the nuances of the thrust to wholeness which is manifested in our yearning for human or divine lover" ("Sexual Mystic," 129). In her book *Radical Love: An Approach to Sexual Spirituality*, Donnelly adds that "*Agape* never need exclude sexual love; indeed it incorporates it validly into spirituality" (35). Her call for a theology of Eros based on human experience and the fact that we do experience unity in our embodied selves, a call for a theory of sexual love that accepts bodiliness as a valid part of holiness, is in effect exactly what Donne was doing indirectly, and perhaps in the only way possible for him in his age, in his secular poems of true love. Our post-Freudian age presumably enables us to understand and express more explicitly than our predecessors of the Middle Ages and Renaissance that "everything we do is sexual because the body is necessarily and beautifully involved in the doing. Sexuality, then, is also the greater intercourse we enjoy with the world in and through its Creator" ("Sexual Mystic," 129). If holiness were not divorced from sexuality in our culture and time, as in Donne's (though the Protestant Reformation may have helped to shape Donne's attitude toward reconciling sexuality and spirituality), it would be less likely that "The Exstasie" could ever be considered a cynical seduction poem or, "Like *The Canonization* . . . also a satiric comedy which makes fun of lovers who deceive themselves into believing that their profane love is not profane" (N. J. C. Andreasen, *John Donne, Conservative Revolutionary*, 168). No doubt, profane love can be profane, sexual love can be inconstant, cynical, and exploitive, as the Group One poems so wittily demonstrate. But ideally, as Daniel Day Williams writes, "Christianity does not look upon sex as something which belongs to the lowest part of human nature, but as a power which leads to one of the highest forms of communication" (239). And Donne seems to have known in his century, as D. H. Lawrence knew in ours, that sexual love which springs from tenderness has an intrinsically redemptive power.

In her *The Poetics of Love: Meditations with John of the Cross*, Mary Giles, another feminist theologian of mysticism, raises the important question whether it is appropriate to speak of being transformed through encounters with a human beloved (the Vision of Eros) or with some part of the physical universe (the Vision of Dame Kind) "in the same breath with consummation of the spiritual marriage of soul and God" (the Vision of God). The thoughtful answer she offers lies in the two considerations of degree of intensity and effect. "Sexual lovers . . . may not perceive their God-destiny as clearly as do the mystics so that their loving may lack the directness and intensity of the mystics. They may not see as finely as do the mystics that the transforming process and event are divine gifts. But the lesser intensity is not to say that non-mystics (in the strict sense of the word) do not bow before the immensity of what is happening to them and in their own way trace the word 'God' in dust at their feet. Nor is it to say that in living they do not give as ample and appealing form to tracing as does the mystic to the fullness of God's marriage embrace" (119–120).

Donne's lovers often do seem to experience the intensity that the mystics (in the strictest sense) express in their writings. The long-term effect of human sexual loving Donne has himself characterized in Holy Sonnet 1 (XVII), which begins with a reference probably to the death of his wife, Anne More Donne, who died on August 15, 1617, the seventh day after the birth of their twelfth child:

> Here the admyring her my mind did whett
> To seeke thee God; so streames do shew the head.

Remarking upon these lines, R. A. Durr writes, "we are reminded perhaps of Dante and Petrarch, or yet of Augustine, passionate lovers, and consider the voice to have spoken truth that inspired Yeats to record in *A Vision* that 'the love the Saint brings to God at this twenty-seventh phase was found in some past life upon a woman's breast'" ("Donne's 'The Primrose'" in Clements, ed., *John Donne's Poetry*, 216).

Nor is it merely anachronistic to consider here the views of these modern feminist theologians, for they are attempting to recover what would have variously been available to Donne. The essence of humanism, which spread out of Italy to the whole of Europe, the primary meaning of the Renaissance itself, according to some scholars, is the rebirth of man in the likeness of God. Pico Della Mirandola and his fellow humanists declared that man, a creature capable of descending into the depths, also had the power to become godlike. Speaking to Adam, God, according to Pico, says "We have made you a creature neither of heaven nor of earth, neither mortal nor immortal, in order that you may, as the free and proud shaper of your own being, fashion yourself in the form you may prefer. It will be in your power to descend to the lower, brutish forms of life; you will be able, through your own decision, to be reborn into the higher forms which are divine" (7–8). Further, in language particularly pertinent to Donne's lovers, Pico writes "Whoever is a Seraph, that is a lover, is in God and God is in him; even, it may be said, God and he are one" (14). It is as if in his poems of true love Donne substitutes the beloved (or, more precisely, God in the beloved) for God and then applies Pico's words: "And at last, smitten by the ineffable love as by a sting, and, like the Seraphim born outside ourselves, filled with the godhead, we shall be, no longer ourselves, but the very One who made us" (27).[18]

With similar kinds of subsitution the language of St. John of the Cross applies to Donne's Group Two poems. Writing on St. John's conception of union, Truman Dicken remarks that "the soul itself is said to be 'transformed in God by love'. . . . The human soul when thus transformed is, in fact, 'deiform' . . . and, in the saint's characteristic phrase, has become God by participation. . . . It has been totally transformed, as we said, into the beloved" (358). There are some passages in St. John which, though he is talking about the soul and God, may be read as applying directly to Donne's lovers. The following passages on the loftiest states of union, for example, from St. John's sublime *Spiritual Canticle* appear, with the possible exception of the third, directly applicable to Donne's lovers.

1. It should therefore be known that love never attains perfection until those who love so far match each other that the one is transfigured into the other, and then love is altogether complete.

2. In the transformation of those who love, love causes such likeness that it may be said that each is the other, and that the two are one. The reason is that in the union and transformation of love one gives himself into the possession of the other, and each surrenders to and exchanges himself for the other; so each lives in the other, and the one is the other, and both are one by transformation of love.

3. In accordance with this likness of transformation, we can say the the life of the soul and the life of Christ are all one life by union of love.

4. This bond of love both joins them and transforms them and makes them one by love. (cited in Dicken, 359)

As well as having his own experience and the various testimony of contemplative tradition, shaped by his poetic interpretation and expression of both experience and tradition, Donne would have had available several distinguished literary models, some of which may have provided him with pattern and "authority." In addition to the Song of Songs and Shakespeare's sonnets (some of which sonnets Donne may have read in manuscript), Donne had available "the two most serious attempts to analyze the Vision of Eros and give it a theological significance," Plato's *Symposium* and Dante's *La Vita Nuova*, to quote Auden's words. "Both agree on three points: (a) the experience is a genuine relevation, not a delusion; (b) the erotic mode of the vision prefigures a kind of love in which the sexual element is transformed and transcended; (c) he who has once seen the glory of the Uncreated revealed indirectly in the glory of a creature can henceforth never be fully satisfied with anything less than a direct encounter with the former" (22). Donne's own poetry agrees on all three points with Plato and Dante. Some critics may wish to argue that the poems really should be read as ironic and that the lovers' unitive experience is thus delusional, but the speaker at least in Donne's Group Two poems does not present it as such. We have already noted Donne's own words in Holy Sonnet 1 (XVII) that the love of a woman did whet his mind to seek the love of God. And Donne's long, passionate quest in the divine poems, to be discussed shortly, for the Vision of God may well have grown out of earlier visions of Uncreated glory revealed indirectly in the glory of a beloved creature. In other respects, Donne is much closer to Dante than to Plato.

For Plato and for Neoplatonists, the form of the Good is the highest form, at one with the beautiful and true, and subsuming all other forms. Contemplation of it is the goal of the lover in *The Sym-*

*posium*, a goal attained, if attained at all, only after years of effort, intellectual training, and devotion. In this book, Plato's Diotima defines love as the desire for the perpetual enjoyment of the good. She describes a lengthy progression of vision that proceeds from love of one particular beautiful person to love of all physical beauty to love of the soul's beauty to love of moral beauty to love of absolute beauty, this last being identical with the form of the Good. The lover is to contemplate absolute beauty and be in constant union with it. The progression from sense perception to spiritual and moral understanding to direct intuitive apprehension ordinarily takes many years, with sensuous contemplative experience appearing as the lowest rung on a very tall ladder. This is one reason for the apparent Platonic depreciation of the physical universe and of sensuous, extrovertive mystical experience. But, as Auden points out, "The Vision of Eros is not, according to Dante, the first rung of a long ladder: there is only one step to take, from the personal creature who can love and be loved to the personal Creator who is Love. And in this final vision, Eros is transfigured but not annihilated. On earth we rank 'love' higher than either sexual desire or sexless friendship because it involves the whole of our being, not, like them, only a part of it. Whatever else is asserted by the doctrine of the resurrection of the body, it asserts the sacred importance of the body. As Silesius says, we have one advantage over the angels: only we can each become the bride of God. And Juliana of Norwich: 'In the self-same point that our Soul is made sensual, in the self-same point is the City of God ordained to him from without beginning' " (25–26). We should indeed expect Donne to be closer to Dante than to Plato. For, unlike Plato (who was of course Aristotle's teacher), Dante and Donne are both Christians, who believe in the Incarnation and in the vital doctrine of the resurrection of the body, and students of Aristotle and scholastic philosophy, as well as heirs to literary and other sources not available to Plato.

Just as Dante elevates Beatrice in *La Vita Nuova* into an image of Christ, so Donne characteristically elevates the lovers and especially the beloved in many of the Songs and Sonnets. Both Beatrice and Donne's lovers are beyond the reach of ordinary reason.[19] Both Donne and Dante had training in scholastic philosophy, which was intent on reconciling Aristotle's teachings with those of the Church Fathers, many of whom were Neoplatonists. The whole of *La Vita Nuova* maintains a tension between Neoplatonism and Aristotelianism, as do Donne's poems of Group Two. Specifically, we have observed that the first section of "The Exstasie," the so-called composition, displays various mystical characteristics (most importantly, the unitary consciousness) of introvertive contemplative experience, the non-sensuous kind favored by Plato and many Neoplatonists, especially non-Christian ones. And we remarked that this section is in theme and tone most like the Platonic poems of Group Three. The third section of "The Exstasie" is a plea for the lovers more fully to enjoy the sensuous extrovertive Vision of Eros. In other words, the poem reconciles or balances both Platonism and Aristotelianism in its concern for both types of mystical experience.[20]

Aristotle, we recall, was restored to the west through the works of Moslem scholars, who had a wide-ranging influence on various scholastic philosophers, and Dante possessed an extraordinary familiarity with Moslem culture. Discussing parallels between Dante and the Sufi poet Ibn Arabi, William Anderson remarks in his Introduction to Dante's *The New Life* that "there is no other known source in European literature for this revolutionizing idea of sexual love sublimated into the means of salvation itself, and when we know that Ibn Arabi asserted that it is God who appears to every lover in the image of his beloved, we may be nearer to understanding how Dante was able to stress the Christlike nature of Beatrice" (26). Whatever Donne's direct or indirect literary sources, when we know there is a literary tradition according to which God appears to the lover in the image of his beloved, we may well be nearer to understanding how Donne was able to stress the Godlike or Christlike nature of the lover and especially the beloved. I wish to emphasize, however, that though the philosophical, theological, and literary aspects of contemplative tradition may provide sources, context and direction for a poet like Donne, I do not believe that Donne's poetry is merely conventional; rather, I believe that the Group Two poems are more meaningful because they grew out of his own mystical experiences, which poems in part were given shape and voice by contemplative tradition, by the master revelations. Furthermore, even if one does not hold this belief concerning the relation of Donne's poetry and experience, the text of the poetry is nevertheless still illuminated by the context of the tradition.

## V

Perhaps written during a decade of Donne's mature life, the Holy Sonnets are fairly representative of his divine poems with regard to the question of meditation and contemplation. In his *Bishop Joseph*

*Hall and Protestant Meditation in Seventeenth-Century England,* Frank Huntley provides a full account of a Protestant mode of meditation. He writes that "Protestant and Catholic meditation have much in common, since they are both Christian; and yet, as Protestant meditation came to be more and more opposed [after the beginning of the seventeenth century] to the *Spiritual Exercises* of the Jesuits, it may be recognized by five major characteristics" (4), which Huntley then goes on to discuss. Other books by such critics as William Halewood, Barbara Lewalski, and Andrew Weiner (see Works Cited) have argued for one or another Protestant poetics as an influence on certain English religious poetry. Challenging this view in a very recent and cogent essay, "Donne's Holy Sonnets and the Theology of Grace," R. V. Young contends, as Summers and Pebworth succinctly point out, "that the view of the Holy Sonnets as doctrinally and aesthetically Protestant results from a simplistic understanding of the theological issues of Donne's time and from an attempt to force the Holy Sonnets into an inappropriate doctrinal frame." Young himself more generally observes that "the English devotional poets of the seventeenth century, . . . though generally Protestant, are not, *in their poetry,* so much militant proponents of the Reformation as Christians confronting God. These poets bring to their poetic encounter with God varied experiences and draw upon a number of Christian resources—Catholic and Protestant, Medieval and Renaissance" (in *"Bright Shootes of Everlastingnesse,"* ed. Summers and Pebworth, xii, 38). Once again, the inclusive both-and, rather than the exclusive either-or, seems the more accurate and appropriate approach. More particularly, the end of meditation is always contemplation, realized or not. Regardless of the means used in moving toward it, contemplation exhibits essentially the same characteristics. While it is useful and interesting to know whether meditative or other elements in a poem are Catholic or Protestant or some combination (a question on which more critical work will have to be done), it is finally more important, and determinable, critically, to ascertain whether and to what extent a poem is meditative or contemplative or contains elements of both. And it is this latter question with regard to Donne's (and, later, Herbert's and Vaughan's) religious poetry that constitutes a central concern of this book.

The Holy Sonnets are filled with a deep sense of sin and with profound angst, fear and trembling, sorrow and grief, near despair, and repeated insistent pleas for salvation.[21] The speaker addresses God and laments "Oh I shall soone despaire" (1 [II]), fearful that "my sinnes . . . would presse me, to hell" (3 [VI]).[22]

Despaire behind, and death before doth cast
Such terrour, and my feebled flesh doth waste
By sinne in it, which it t'wards hell doth weigh.

(1 [I])

He begs his Lord to "Teach mee how to repent" (4 [VII]) and to forget and forgive his many sins (5 [IX]), which are as black as his soul (2 [IV]), "For I have sinn'd, and sinn'd" (7 [XI]). And, just as he is weaker and worse than the sinless animals (8 [XII]), so his sins are also worse than

the Jewes impiety:
They kill'd once an inglorious man, but I
Crucifie him daily, being now glorified.

(7[XI])

He wishes that the vain sighs and tears previously spent in idolatrous service of profane love would return to him so that he now might mourn fruitfully in his present "holy discontent," but he concludes that no ease is allowed to him,

for, long, yet vehement griefe hath beene
Th'effect and cause, the punishment and sinne.

(3 [III])

This 1635 sonnet and the preceding (2[V]), "I am a little world made cunningly," especially invite general comparison with the Songs and Sonnets:

I am a little world made cunningly
Of Elements, and an Angelike spright,
But black sinne hath betraid to endlesse night
My worlds both parts, and (oh) both parts must die.
You which beyond that heaven which was most high
Have found new sphears, and of new lands can write,
Powre new seas in mine eyes, that so I might
Drowne my world with my weeping earnestly,
Or wash it, if it must be drown'd no more:
But oh it must be burnt; alas the fire
Of lust and envie'have burnt it heretofore,
And made it fouler; Let their flames retire,
And burne me ô Lord, with a fiery zeale
Of thee'and thy house, which doth in eating heale.

If we compare "A Valediction: of Weeping" with this sonnet and with "A Hymne to Christ," usually dated 1619–20 and also filled with flood and drowning imagery, we find that the secular poem appears more vivid, concrete, sensuous, fully imaged. Although one or another Holy Sonnet or divine poem may be highly imaged and vivid, the divine poems in general tend noticeably toward relatively more abstraction than the Songs and Sonnets do, and they are marked by more general words like terror, despair, death, beauty, pity, sin, lust, envy, foulness, etc., used in less specific senses. Nor perhaps should this be surprising. For all of Donne's "metaphysical" qualities, he remains a very physical poet, especially in his secular poetry, with his senses focused on one or more particular physical object. The body and the senses figure in his love poetry as very real and powerful. The Vision of Eros is, among other things, a sensuous experience of a physical being, the human beloved, whereas the Vision of God is a non-sensuous experience of a transcendent being that cannot be physically perceived. (That Herbert and Vaughan write more vividly and concretely about the Vision of God in itself indicates that they more fully and successfully than Donne realized such Vision.) These observations may help to explain some of the differences in language between the secular and divine poems as well as suggest why Donne appears more readily to have found union and godlikeness in the secular poems which celebrate extrovertive mystical experience than in the divine poems that seek introvertive mystical experience.

As other scholars have done, Martz rightly observes and cautions that in Donne's love poetry "the religious aspects are frequently so strong that they seem to overwhelm the fainter religious themes of Petrarchan poetry; while in six of the Holy Sonnets (3, 13, 14, 17, 18, 19, [in Grierson's numbering]) the memories and images of profane love are deliberately used in love-sonnets of sacred parody. One must observe, then, the greatest possible caution in considering the relation between the 'profane' and the 'religious' in Donne's work: individual poems will not fall easily into such categories: nor can the poems be safely dated by assumptions about the more religious, and the less religious, periods of his life" (*The Poetry of Meditation*, 216). I should like to go a step further and suggest that the assumptions about which are Donne's more religious and less religious periods must be questioned. Given uncertainty about dating, if it is true, as I think most scholars agree, that Donne wrote most of his "religious" poems *after* he wrote most of his "profane" (or secular) love lyrics, it does not follow that the "more religious" period came after the "less religious" period. I believe the reverse is true. Setting uncertain dating aside and putting it another way, the Group Two poems display more advanced spiritual states of being, understood in terms of contemplative progress, than the divine poems. We have already discussed Group Two and closely examined "The Exstasie" and "The Canonization." A close examination of "Batter my heart" (10 [XIV]), a fairly representative Holy Sonnet with regard to the question of mystical stages, will give detailed insight into the characteristic spiritual state and stance of the Holy Sonnets and of the divine poems in general[23] and will subsequently enable us to compare and contrast this sonnet with Herbert's "Artillerie" and Vaughan's "The Night," poems extensively discussed in Chapters Three and Four and, like Donne's sonnet, filled with biblical allusion and organized by the central mystical paradox.

> Batter my heart, three person'd God; for, you
> As yet but knocke, breathe, shine, and seeke to mend;
> That I may rise, and stand, o'erthrow mee,'and bend
> Your force, to breake, blowe, burn and make me new.
> I, like an usurpt towne, to'another due,      5
> Labour to'admit you, but Oh, to no end,
> Reason your viceroy in mee, mee should defend,
> But is captiv'd, and proves weake or untrue,
> Yet dearely'I love you, and would be lov'd faine,
> But am betroth'd unto your enemie,      10
> Divorce mee,'untie, or breake that knot againe,
> Take mee to you, imprison mee, for I
> Except you'enthrall mee, never shall be free,
> Nor ever chast, except you ravish mee.

Several critics have commented that the three persons of the "three-person'd God" are to operate separately: God the Father is to break instead of merely knocking; God the Holy Ghost is to blow instead of merely breathing; and God the Son (Sun) is to burn instead of merely shining.[24] Certainly *three-person'd God* of the first line occasions such an expectation, and it seems both natural and inevitable that Donne should draw upon the traditional emphasis of the symbolism of the Three Persons—the Father as Power, the Son as Light, and the Holy Ghost as Breath. Correct in so far as it goes, this view of the poem tends, however, to overlook certain rich biblical values and associations of *knocke, breathe, shine,* associations of which Donne would not have been ignorant. (The very order of *knocke, breathe, shine* and of Donne's translation of these to the vio-

lent *breake, blowe, burn* suggests the inaccuracy of exclusively as-
signing each word respectively to the Father, the Holy Ghost, and the
Son: to reflect the traditional order of Father, Son, and Holy Ghost,
Donne could instead have written "knocke, shine, breathe" and
"breake, burn, blowe.") An examination of several biblical uses of
*knocke, breathe, shine* indicates, at least for the purposes of the
poem, that each of the other Persons is "involved" in the activity of
any one; in other words, the paradox of three-in-one is truly and pro-
foundly a paradox and is operative as such in the poem. In turn,
Donne's treatment of the trinitarian paradox and of the organizing
paradox of death and rebirth yields insight into the unitive experi-
ence, or lack of it, in this sonnet and the divine poems.

Traditionally the courting of man by God, the knocking at his
heart, is associated with Christ, not the Father. The bridegroom of
the Song of Songs is usually taken to symbolize Christ; the heart of
man is the Bridegroom's, the Saviour's, Chamber, but the heart is
hardened with sin, and the Bridegroom, standing outside, must
knock to gain entrance. "I sleep, but my heart waketh: it is the voice
of my beloved that knocketh, saying, Open to me . . ." (Song of Songs
5:2). In the New Testament, Revelation 3:20 follows this tradition:
"Behold, I stand at the door and knocke: if any man hear my voice
and open the door, I will come in to him, and will sup with him, and
he with me."[25] Christ's knocking is, I think, definitely germane to
the poem's theme of love and courtship, even though this theme has
been characteristically transformed by Donne to a violent love and
courtship. With his translation of *knocke* to *breake*, Donne is not
only calling on the power of the Father but he is also imploring
Christ to court him not in Christ's usual role and manner of mild
Lamb but rather as battering, overpowering Ram.[26] Moreover, since
Donne is seeking God's courtship and love—"Yet dearely I love you,
and would be lov'd faine"—and since traditionally, the Holy Ghost
infuses love into the hearts of men—"the love of God is shed abroad
in our hearts by the Holy Ghost" (Romans 5:5)—there seems to be
no necessity for reading the poem as excluding the Comforter from
the activity of courting or knocking.

*Breathe* is traditionally associated with the Holy Ghost's infu-
sion of grace into the heart of man, yet is also linked, biblically,
inevitably, with activities of both the Father and the Son. From
Genesis on, the Father is referred to as the giver of life to man by
breathing into his nostrils the breath of life.[27] This is at least rel-
evant to the sonnet since Donne is asking for new, innocent life, as
was given Adam before the Fall: "make me new." After His resurrec-

tion Christ appeared to his disciples, and "he breathed on them, and saith unto them, Receive ye the Holy Ghost" (John 20:22). Grace may be infused into man's heart not by the activity of the Third Person alone but by the activity of the Son as well. The possible objection that New Testament theology took the breath of life to be the Spirit of God, that is, the Holy Spirit or Ghost, and that *breathed* in the verse just quoted is a signal of the Third Person merely emphasizes, in effect, the ultimate identity of the Three Persons and thus their actually united trinitarian actions in the poem, for, as St. John of the Cross says, "the Holy Spirit Who is love, is also compared to air in the Divine Scripture, since he is the breath of the Father and the Son."[28]

There can be no disputing about the relation between the Son and *shine*. In "A Hymne to God the Father," Donne writes "Sweare by thy selfe, that at my death thy Sunne / Shall shine as it shines now . . ."; the Son-sun pun is familiar enough. And the many biblical references to Christ as the Light or the bringer of light, most notably in John, need no quoting. But, in some ways, the First and Third Persons are also associated with light and shining. The Father is, to begin with, the creator of light, and many verses link light and the word *shine* with God the Father or with just God without distinction made as to person: 2 Corinthians 4:6, for example, reads, "God, who commanded the light to shine out of darkness hath shined in our hearts."[29] Especially because the poem refers to "Reason your viceroy in mee," the activity and efficacy of the Third Person, who shines upon and rectifies the weak and unfaithful reason or understanding, may also be designated, though perhaps less obviously than the Father and Son, by the word *shine*. The Holy Ghost, who is truth, descended in "tongues like as of fire" upon the apostles, enabling them to shed the light, the word of God, abroad in many tongues; as Christ promised, "the Comforter, which is the Holy Ghost . . . shall teach you all things . . . will guide you into all truth."[30] When Christ absents himself to go to the Father, the Holy Ghost will bring the truth or light to men, that is, will shine in their hearts. There seems, then, to be no justification in the sonnet, and no need, for ignoring the association of the First and Third Persons with light and *shine*.

May we not grant that Donne is exploiting both the traditional distinctions among the Three Persons (Father-Power, Son-Light, Holy Ghost-Breath) and also the traditional biblical values and associations of *knocke, breathe, shine*? His undoubted familiarity with all these biblical passages would not, I think, have permitted the oversimplifying division of powers along the lines suggested by the critics, a division which tends to rationalize and diminish the paradox of the Trinity. Profound paradox and the consequent greater complexity of the poem are characteristic of Donne, who in this sonnet is asking *three person'd God* to break (not just the Father alone), to blow (not just the Holy Ghost alone), to burn (not just the Son alone) and make him new. It is as if all the triple strength of the Three Persons acting as one, with true trinitarian force, is required to raise Donne from his deeply sinful life and hence to effect his salvation.

A consequence of recognizing the full implications of *knocke, breathe, shine* is that the sonnet's structure cannot then be viewed as the development of three quatrains each separately assigned primarily to each of the the Three Persons.[31] Rather, I believe the organizing principle of the poem is, with Donne's qualification of it, the paradox of death and rebirth, which (as previously noted) is the central paradox of mysticism and of Christianity: "Except a corn of wheat fall into the ground and die, it abideth alone: but if it die, it bringeth forth much fruit. He that loveth his life shall lose it; and he that hateth his life in this world shall keep it unto life eternal" (John 12:24–25). To enter the kingdom of God man must die and be born again. Donne knows he must give up his unregenerate sinful life, but he feels his heart and will are so black and obdurate, his sense of sin so great, that (the thought is almost blasphemous) the "ordinary" means of God's mercy and grace, His knocking, breathing, shining, will not suffice. God must forcefully overpower and overwhelm him, must batter and overthrow him in order that he may rise reborn.[32] To the familiar biblical paradox Donne has added his own peculiar meaning; it is in his characteristic manner that Donne insists, because of his deep and adamant sinfulness, on the necessity of God's forceful overpowering. Such insisting underscores the lack of union or even of illumination and maps the vast distance between Donne and God.

This paradox of dividing in order to unite, destroying in order to revive, throwing down in order to raise, determines the choice of and finds expression in the poem's figurative language, which is of two kinds; one kind is warlike, military, destructive, dividing; the other is marital, sexual, or uniting. Each kind of figurative language operates *throughout* the sonnet, in the first two quatrains and in the sestet. Looking at words and phrases, we can recognize the military and destructive kind in *Batter, o'erthrow, bend Your force, breake, blowe, burn* of the first quatrain; most obviously in the besieged, usurped town imagery of the second quatrain; and in *enemie, divorce, untie, breake, imprison, enthrall,* and *ravish* of the sestet. The marital, regenerating or uniting kind can be observed in *heart, knocke, breathe, shine, rise, stand, make me new* of the first quatrain; *untrue* in the second quatrain; all of line 9, *bethroth'd, divorce, Take mee to you, enthrall, chast, ravish* in the sestet. The first quatrain, as we have seen, using traditional biblical terms and Donne's translation of these into new and violent metaphors, calls on the triune God to destroy the sinful old man and remake, regenerate him.[33] The terms *Batter, o'erthrow, bend your force* and *breake, blowe, burn* prepare for and serve as a transition to the besieged, usurped town imagery of the second quatrain, if they do not actually participate in that metaphor. Through the development of military metaphors, the heart is compared to a town wrongfully appropriated and helplessly possessed by God's "enemie." Briefly, in the second quatrain, Donne *implies* what the first quatrain states, that God must act for him, must batter down and overthrow his sinful heart in order to raise it purified since his reason is captive and he cannot help himself.

The word *untrue* (in the sense of "unfaithful" it is a marital kind of metaphor) serves as a transition to the sestet, which develops overtly, on the level of violence and rape, the theme of love and courtship implicit in lines 1 and 2, particularly in *heart* and *knocke.* The heart is now metaphorically construed as a woman. In line 9 and 10, Donne says explicitly that his sinful heart still loves and would be loved by God but is willfully bound to satanic powers. *Enemie,* at the end of line 10, is a return to military metaphor and provides the transition to the rough and irresistible love of lines 11 and 12, exceptionally heavy-stressed lines, and of lines 13 and 14, the paradoxical, explanatory couplet. Again, Donne implies, so great is his sense of sin and helplessness, that God must forcefully sever his sinful bonds, must release him from the prison of sin to bind and imprison him in the triune personality of God and thereby, paradoxically, free him. He will never be essentially free unless God enthralls him and never chaste, that is pure, innocent, whole, holy, unless God ravishes him.

Throughout the sonnet there has been this paradox of destroying in order to make whole, of throwing down in order to raise, expressed by the two basic kinds of figurative language. Significantly, the words *divorce, enthrall, ravish* in lines 11, 13, 14 partake of both kinds of metaphor: a divorce is a dividing, yet the word is associated with marriage; to enthrall is both to subjugate and to captivate or enamor; ravishing is both sexual and violent. In lines 11 to 14, then, the organizing paradox, having been argued throughout the poem in Donne's characteristic intellectual mode, even though the poem is highly emotional and personal, is enhanced and compounded in force not just by a juxtaposition but now by a fusing or uniting of the two kinds of metaphor; it is as if the metaphors are made to achieve between themselves what Donne wishes to achieve with God.

And that is the major point to be emphasized about Holy Sonnet 10 [XIV], which, as the above analysis should suggest, is with regard to the mystical stages fairly representative of not only most of Donne's Holy Sonnets but also many of his other divine poems: Donne wishes to achieve union with God, but the poem just powerfully expresses the desire, not the actual realization of union, not even partially or temporarily at the stage of Illumination. In this and other regards, "Batter my Heart" may fruitfully be compared to and contrasted with Vaughan's "The Night," another extraordinary poem organized by paradox and filled with biblical allusion. Vaughan's great contemplative poem, as we shall see, clearly concerns both Illumination and the Dark Night of the Soul. Donne's poem does not get beyond Purgation. The speaker actively insists upon God's taking a much more active role in his salvation. Illumination and the Dark Night of the Soul (or the Passive Night of the Spirit, as St. John of the Cross describes this advanced stage of purification) are totally absent from "Batter my Heart," as generally from Donne's divine poems.

"Illumination brings a certain apprehension of the Absolute, a sense of Divine Presence: but not true union with it. It is a state of happiness" (Underhill, *Mysticism*, 169). This characterization of the stage of Illumination does not apply to "Batter my Heart" nor to any of the other Holy Sonnets, filled as they are with sorrow and grief, fear and trembling, and a profound sense of alienating sin. In the Dark Night of the Soul "the Self now surrenders itself, its individuality, and its will, completely. It desires nothing, asks nothing, is utterly passive" (Underhill, *Mysticism*, 170). Again, such a characterization does not accord with the Holy Sonnets, which actively and willfully demand that God, with triune effort, "breake, blowe, burn and make me new." Donne has to learn, as in the next chapter we shall see that Herbert learned, that he has free will in order to will his self-will out of existence, even when the will is bent toward a good end, including Illumination or Union. Donne uses biblical allusion for meditative ends, whereas, as we shall see, Herbert and Vaughan (including the latter's allusions to the Song of Songs in "The Night") employ biblical allusion for contemplative ends.

Our close analysis of the fairly representative Holy Sonnet 10 [XIV] also shows that this poem has almost none of the distinctive characteristics of mystical experience as they were discussed in Chapter One, and in this respect 10 [XIV] is again fairly representative of all the Holy Sonnets and divine poems. Since these divine poems have God as their "object," if they were contemplative we could reasonably expect to find some of the common characteristics of introvertive or transcendental mystical experiences: the unitary consciousness; nonspatial and/or nontemporal aspects; sense of the objectivity or reality of the direct experience of divinity; feelings of the presence of the holy, sacred, or divine; and blessedness, peace, etc. The feelings of the Holy Sonnets and the divine poems generally involve the absence or remoteness of the divine; and the experiences of these poems revolve around the sense of the reality of sin, fear, grief.

It is true that "Batter my Heart" contains paradoxes, as the divine poems generally do. But the paradox of the trinity is not in and of itself a mystical paradox, though, given different uses and context than this sonnet, it could be. The paradox of death and rebirth is, as observed, both the organizing principle of Holy Sonnet 10 [XIV] and the central paradox of mysticism and therefore of Christianity; but the transformation from psyche to pneuma that is the meaning of this paradox is prayed for, not realized. The profoundly inextricable unity of the trinity (a three-in-one somewhat reminiscent of the true lovers totally unified two-in-one) contrasts sharply with the eagerly sought but unrealized union between Donne and God. The more Donne insists, as he characteristically does throughout the divine poems, on the blackness of his obdurate heart, the abysmal depths of his sins, and the necessity of all the triple strength of the Three Persons to raise him into the Light, the clearer it becomes that these poems describe earlier rather than later stages of spiritual progress; and it becomes clearer yet when Herbert and Vaughan are compared with Donne. We will see, for example, in Chapter Three that Herbert also uses marital and martial metaphors to express the central mystical paradox of death and rebirth, as Donne does in 10 [XIV], but in ways which signal more advanced spiritual states than those found in Donne's divine poems. These poems contrast, too, with Vaughan's "The Night," wherein the many suggested illuminations indicate, as argued in Chapter Four, that the unitive transformation from willful psyche to affirming pneuma has in Vaughan at least been temporarily realized.

Underhill's brief description of the stage of Purgation, cited in Chapter One, seems generally characteristic of Donne's divine poems: the individual "realizes by contrast [with divinity] its own finiteness and imperfection, the manifold illusions in which it is immersed, the immense distance which separates it from the One. Its attempts to eliminate by discipline and mortification all that stands in the way of its progress towards union with God constitute *Purgation*: a state of pain and effort" (Mysticism, 169). Following Grierson, many critics have agreed that in Donne's religious poetry "effort is the note which predominates" (II, li). To look at the Holy Sonnets and divine poems from the perspective of ancient-medieval-Renaissance contemplative tradition and to conclude that they do not advance beyond the stage of Purgation means, in other words, that they are meditative rather than contemplative. This conclusion confirms the view of critics who have regarded the Holy Sonnets from the perspective of sixteenth-century meditative practice.[34] This confirmation may be all the more significant because no such full and clear-cut critical agreement obtains when the poems of Herbert and Vaughan are studied from both perspectives. In our study of Donne, we do not need to consider, for example, the refinements regarding purification provided by St. John of the Cross or Evelyn Underhill at the advanced stage of the Dark Night, as we must in our study of Herbert and Vaughan.

Louis Martz has shown that "La Corona" "is an adaptation of the popular practice of meditation, according to the Corona" (*The Poetry of Meditation*, 107). This sequence is a devout, pious meditation on Christ, not at all contemplative poetry. Similarly, Martz has discussed the meditative structure of one of the best of the divine poems, a poem that has been dated from its title, "Goodfriday, 1613. Riding Westward." (54–56).[35] The colloquy concludes with a clear request for purification:

> O Saviour, as thou hang'st upon the tree;
> I turne my back to thee, but to receive
> Corrections, till thy mercies bid thee leave.
> O thinke mee worth thine anger, punish mee,
> Burne off my rusts, and my deformity,
> Restore thine Image, so much, by thy grace,
> That thou may'st know mee, and I'll turne my face.

And in "A Hymne to God the Father," throughout which Donne puns on his name, the speaker lists his various sins, saving the "sinne of feare" for last, and insists in the final stanza that God the Father give assurances he will be saved by "thy Sunne." We are again in the world of the Holy Sonnets, where Donne's genuine, deep, and repeated consciousness of sin may begin at times to seem almost like a perverse boast.

Whether we study "La Corona," Donne's earliest important divine poem,[36] or the Holy Sonnets, usually dated at least from 1609 to perhaps 1620, or "Goodfriday, 1613. Riding Westward," or "A Hymne to God the Father," which Walton says Donne wrote in his illness of 1623, or any of the other divine poems, the conclusion must be the same: these are meditative rather than contemplative poems; they are purgative rather than illuminative or unitive; they are pre-mystical rather than precisely mystical; they exhibit few or none of the distinctive characteristics of contemplation; they do not at all display the necessary first characteristic of unitary consciousness or unifying vision; they do not show the true self breaking through the barriers of the false self. Many of the divine poems do contain paradoxes, but in general these tend to be verbal rather than substantial; when they are substantial, they are usually not mystical paradoxes; and as in Holy Sonnet 10 [XIV], when the paradox is the central, mystical one of death and rebirth, it is desired, not realized in either illumination or union. The "object" of Donne's divine poems is of course God, and the end of them is the Vision of God. Unlike Group Two of the Songs and Sonnets, the end of which is the Vision of Eros, Donne's divine poems do not attain their end, not even temporarily or partially, and are not, strictly speaking, mystical poems.

It is true in what may be Donne's last divine poem,[37] the brilliant "Hymne to God my God, in my sicknesse," the speaker expresses considerable joy at the prospect of his imminent death, the whole weight of the preceding dependent stanza coming down in emphasis on the main clause that begins stanza three: "I joy." And it is true that both Adams are alluded to in the penultimate stanza's concluding couplet:

> As the first *Adams* sweat surrounds my face,
> May the last *Adams* blood my soule embrace.

We may be tempted to invoke here the great fourteenth-century English mystic, Julian of Norwich, who in her *Revelations of Divine Love* writes that "the good Lord showed his own Son and Adam are one man" and "by *Adam* I always understand *Everyman*" (148). But the poem, unlike Julian, reveals not so much a present discovery and assertion of identity with divinity, or even of Christlikeness; it rather more expresses a plea for salvation and union in the afterlife. True, the eloquent plea in this poem seems more hopeful and joyful, yet, as in Donne's other divine poems, it is a request for, not a realization of, union, nor even of illumination. As in what may be his earliest important divine poem, "La Corona," so in the Hymn which may be his last divine poem: the two Adams, death, the Incarnation and Resurrection are understood more in the literal and historical senses than in the metaphorical or mythic sense of the poems of true love among the Songs and Sonnets. And this fact points to an essential difference between Donne's secular and divine poems. Whatever the reasons, we discover in the Group Two poems a much more mythic and metaphorical imagination than appears in the divine poems. One of the reasons may well be that some of the experiences behind some of the secular poems are illuminative and unitive, whereas the experiences behind the divine poems are essentially purgative. Although the secular poems of true love, the divine poems, and the earlier and later prose works[38] are all of a piece in their desire for union, variously expressed, the mystical life does not necessarily nor even usually proceed in any predictable, well-ordered, straight-line fashion. To use a paradox he could himself have appreciated, Donne appears, on the evidence of his poetry, to have been more religious when he was less religious.

Since it is unlikely that Donne could have explicitly written of the godlikeness of human lovers, perhaps the only means and vocabulary possible for expressing the unitive experiences of human love were his own distinctive poetry. Though the developing new theology of Eros could profit today from studying this poetry, there was no such theology of Eros in his day for him to draw upon. And there was no "confessional" poetry in his time, as there is in ours. In "The Fury of Cocks," Anne Sexton writes

> When they fuck they are God.
> When they break away they are God.
> When they snore they are God.
> In the morning they butter the toast.
> They don't say much.
> They are still God.
> All the cocks of the world are God,

blooming, blooming, blooming
into the sweet blood of woman.

Though these lines *generally* express some ideas found in Donne's poetry, Donne of course could not and would not write in this plain, explicit, and, I must add, somewhat crude manner, to say nothing of the fact that his poetry is graced by great wit, skill, and verbal felicity, which brilliantly and subtly transmute and significantly enhance basic meanings. The subject matter of modern confessional poetry often concerns intimate experiences of the poet's life rendered with unabashed candor and in shocking or clinical detail. Although that is not the way we would characterize Donne's poetic style, we may ask, though there may never be certain answers, to what extent is his poetry based on his own intimate experiences. One answer is that just as Cartesianism developed out of ancient Sophistical Skepticism and Platonic and Stoic dualism, so Donne's poems of true love may be regarded as a still poetically admirable response to those prevailing philosophies and to the centuries-old institutionalized attitude that holiness relates only to celibacy and certainly not to sexuality, in spite of the sacrament of marriage—a skillful and brilliant response, based perhaps on his own experiences in human loving.

# 3

# GEORGE HERBERT
## *"Was ever grief like mine?"*

Though he seems on occasion to wish for Visions of Dame Kind and Philia, and possibly briefly to experience the latter, Herbert fully enjoys only the Vision of God, not at all the Vision of Eros.[1] And he is one of the best examples of contemplatives expressing their vision in "the light of the master revelations," the Bible and the Church Fathers and doctrines.[2] *The Temple's* richness and complexity, deriving largely from the major technique of its structure and ordering, both enrich and complicate critical study. Herbert himself reveals his own biblical hermeneutics and provides an important reading clue and insight into its major technique when he writes about the Bible in "The H. Scriptures, II":

> Oh that I knew how all thy lights combine,
> And the configuration of their glorie!
> Seeing not onely how each verse doth shine,
> But all the constellations of the storie.
> This verse marks that, and both do make a motion
> Unto a third, that ten leaves off doth lie.[3]

This sense of and passion for interconnections and unity in the microcosm of verse (as well as in the macrocosmic universe and, particularly for Herbert, in the relation between God and human being) is yet another characteristic of contemplative consciousness, and that may help to explain why, while others also write in groupings, mystics so often express themselves in sequences, usually complex and subtle ones because the religious life does not fall into facile patterns.

In his *George Herbert*, T. S. Eliot rightly considers *The Temple* "a coherent sequence of poems setting down the fluctuations of emotion between despair and bliss, between agitation and serenity, and the discipline of suffering which leads to peace of spirit"; he recommends that "we must study *The Temple* as a whole" (21, 15). In

"Herbert's Sequential Imagery: 'The Temper,'" Fredson Bowers observes that "the order of the poems in George Herbert's *Temple* is planned according to developing sequences that work out major themes" and that "within these sequential poems Herbert develops clusters of images that are appropriate not only for the poem in which they appear but also—in some sense—exist coincidentally with the individual poems and apply independently to the great central theme of the section and then of *The Temple*" (Essential Articles, ed. J. Roberts, 231). While many critics have tried to determine the principles behind the unity, order and sequences of Herbert's book, Amy Charles may be right in her important article "The Williams Manuscript and *The Temple*" to "doubt that anyone can now discern the precise reasons for the order of the poems in *The Temple* because, for one thing, they were not precise, but personal, intuitive, and allusive." But even she adds: "The general concept is clear"; "it is beyond question that the same basic order prevails in W [MS. Jones B 62 in Dr. Williams Library] and in B [Bodleian MS. Tanner 307, from which the edition of 1633 was probably printed] and that in both volumes the soul moves haltingly but surely to the final triumph of joy in 'Love'"; and "what Herbert perhaps learned during the years between the preparation of the two manuscripts is that the Christian's road is not one of immediate achievement, of unexceptional joy, or even of steady progress: eventual achievement, ultimate joy, yes—the final comprehension" (*Essential Articles*, 417, 422). Keeping all of these critical remarks in mind is vital to the study of Herbert because, as Blake knew, there are many paths to the Palace of Wisdom and most of them, like Herbert's, are long, steep, arduous ones, winding back and forth and up and down. Such is the usual progress from meditation to contemplation, and studying the rich complexity of "*The Temple* as a whole" or, particularly, of "The Church" as a whole reveals this progress.[4]

Although scholarship on George Herbert has contributed significantly to our knowledge of the religious elements in the poetry of "The Church," various critics are divided on the vexed matter of contemplation in Herbert. Some, like George H. Palmer, Margaret Bottrall, Mary Ellen Rickey, Helen Vendler, and Barbara Lewalski think that he is not a mystic. Others, like Helen White, Itrat Husain, Aldous Huxley, Anthony Low, and Robert Boenig contend that he is. Still others, like Joseph Summers, hold that he is not a mystic in the sense of one who practices the "negative way" to union with God, but that he might be considered a mystic of the *via positiva*.[5]

It is just possible that in some sense all of these critics speak a part of the truth in that Herbert's poetry expresses a wide range of spiritual experiences and in that a number of critics attribute a variety of meanings to "mysticism." As Anthony Low writes, "*The Temple's* devotional mixture corresponds to a full, typical spiritual life, which is seldom pure vocal prayer, song, meditation, or contemplation, but a combination of them all. In breadth of devotion and truth to experience, Herbert is unsurpassed" (114). Many of Herbert's poems are not mystical in themselves though they contribute as part of a sequence to contemplative ends. Some poems, including the most highly regarded, are brilliantly contemplative. Thus, some of the vital questions to ask about any study or denial of mysticism in Herbert are: which poems does it focus upon; does it consider the work as a whole and the direction of its sequences; in what sense does it use the abused and confusing term "mysticism"; and does it distinguish adequately between meditation and contemplation, between the earlier and later stages of religious life and spiritual progress?

Louis Martz's chapter on "The Unity of *The Temple*" in *The Poetry of Meditation* and his trifold division of "The Church" into "Sacramental Introduction," "Body of Conflicts," and "Plateau of Assurance" remain a strong foundation upon which other critics may construct their own interpretation of Herbert's work. In my view, however, "The Church" begins in meditation or an early stage of the spiritual life and ends in contemplation, the advanced stage of religious life. As previously noted, although "meditative" may seem more accurate than the term "mystical" when applied *in general* to English poetry of the seventeenth century, there still remain two important questions: (1) which term is more accurate when applied to *particular* poems and to a *particular* seventeenth-century poet; (2) to what extent did ancient-medieval-Renaissance contemplative literature in addition to sixteenth-century meditative literature "influence" seventeenth-century English religious poetry? Undoubtedly, as Martz has shown, Herbert was conversant with meditative patterns of writing and ways of thinking as found in such meditative writers as St. Francis de Sales and Lorenzo Scupoli. But to what extent may Herbert also have availed himself, as Vaughan and Traherne did, of contemplative modes of writing and thinking as found in many of the Church Fathers and other contemplatives such as Meister Eckhart, Walter Hilton, and Julian of Norwich? I believe that we may come to a fuller and more exact understanding of Herbert's poetry by studying it, especially neglected aspects of it, against the background of the complex contemplative tradition in the terms of Chapter One, and that the division of the critics on Herbert's mysticism necessitates re-thinking and re-evaluation along these lines. As a contribution toward these ends, this chapter shall first present a reading of Herbert's, "Artillerie," and then, by focusing on the sequential, meditative-to-contemplative progress of "The Church," relate this and other Herbert poems to the great tradition of Christian mysticism, especially to its basic contemplative doctrine of the two selves, which is but another way of expressing submission to God's will.

## II

Careful studies by David Novarr and Amy Charles rightly question the reliability of Izaak Walton. Having cautiously noted that much, we may further observe that given the title, theme, and major imagery of "Artillerie," special pertinence to this representative poem obtains in the famous description of *The Temple* which Herbert himself, according to Izaak Walton, is said to have written when he sent his book to Nicholas Ferrar: "a picture of the many Spiritual Conflicts that have past betwixt God and my Soul, before I could subject mine to the will of Jesus my Master: in whose service I have now found perfect freedom." "Artillerie" is a picture of one of the many spiritual conflicts between God and Herbert's soul; and it ends on that dominant theme in Herbert's poetry: submission of his will to God's. Like Donne, Herbert is often "at war" with God in his religious poetry, but unlike Donne, who characteristically remains at the battlement demanding still that God batter his heart, Herbert, in "Artillerie," as in many of his poems, finally lays down his weapons, crosses over into God's camp, and surrenders unconditionally. An overview of "Artillerie" indicates that its dialectical structure underscores the unqualified completeness of the submission of Herbert's will: the first stanza establishes the conflict of wills; the second achieves a temporary, incomplete submission; the third ironically qualifies this surrender, which in effect continues the conflict; the fourth resolves the tension of wills through Herbert's absolute submission. This dialectical structure not only reflects Herbert's description of *The Temple*, as we might expect, but also is a structure that Herbert re-employs with or without modification in a number of other poems. The final submission is not a disillusioned resignation but a thoroughly deliberated acceptance of his limitations in the face of God, and, paradoxically, through this acceptance a greater enhancement and awareness of his own true value. The poem's rest and serenity, those high desiderata in Herbert, result not from any easy optimism but from a courageous and complete acceptance or, rather, affirmation of God's will. The tension of contrary wills is resolved and peace follows.

The first two lines of "Artillerie" have a striking and arresting quality often observed in the opening lines of "metaphysical" poets: "As I one ev'ning sat before my cell, / Me thoughts a starre did shoot into my lap." Throughout "The Church," there are several voices (including the voice of Christ) and it is sometimes though not always possible to distinguish between the voice of the speaker of any one poem and that of Herbert. It seems to the speaker of this poem, as perhaps also to Herbert, that as he sat, no doubt meditatively, before his chamber in a state of apparent restfulness a star shot into his lap, "lap" here having, as later lines confirm, the seventeenth-century generalized meaning of "breast" (O.E.D.). This is an extraordinary and fantastic occurrence, yet the tone is calm, composed, almost casual and complacent. From the beginning of the poem, Herbert establishes an essentially assured, quiet, nearly playful tone that reflects an attitude underlying and pervading the whole poem; with his turning to God in the third line of stanza two, Herbert will permit his reasoning intellect also to operate, though never solemnly, and with the intellect's collapse, so to speak, into the final paradox of stanza four the reader will see there has never been a real contest or battle. It is as if the poet uses logic to confute and destroy logic itself and thereby lead us to overwhelming paradox. Herbert's common sense, his logic, dictates his shaking the flaming star away from his clothes, an action which is immediately practical but ultimately misguided. "I rose, and shook my clothes, as knowing well, / That from small fires comes oft no small mishap." The simple rising, rather than anxious jumping or leaping up, to shake off the fire and the studied understatement of the last quoted line (1. 4) indicate equanimity and good-humored irony, as indeed does the subsequent advice:

> When suddenly I heard one say,
> *Do as thou usest, disobey,*
> *Expell good motions from thy breast,*
> *Which have the face of fire, but end in rest.*
> *(II. 5–8)*

This advice of lines 6–8 apparently is spoken by an inner voice in a dialogue of self or by some heavenly voice. (The poem's conclusion suggests that the inner self may finally be one with the divine self.) Ironically, the advice is intended to have an effect opposite to what it states: do *not*, as is your habit, expel good motions (that is, shooting stars, impulses, workings of God or his ministers in your soul) from your heart, for they will purify you so that you will finally rest with God. Acceptance of one's sufferings, purification by fire, is the way that leads to rest with God. By pointing to customary or habitual opposition and by describing a particular instance of it, the first stanza, then, presents the conflict between Herbert's will and God's will.

The second stanza arrives at an initial but incomplete and temporary submission:

> I, who had heard of musick in the spheres,
> But not of speech in starres, began to muse:
> But turning to my God, whose ministers
> The starres and all things are; If I refuse,
>> Dread Lord, said I, so oft my good;
>> Then I refuse not ev'n with bloud
>> To wash away my stubborn thought:
> For I will do or suffer what I ought.
>
> (ll. 9–16)

In lines 9–10, a personal tone of jestful conversation obtains; Herbert humorously makes a slight joke. The phrase "But turning to my God" marks the somewhat more serious turn which the poem now takes for the remainder of this stanza. Herbert knows there can be no genuine war between his will and God's, for the line "whose ministers / The starres and all things are" implies the orderliness of the universe, implies at least one central aspect of the Renaissance concept of the great chain of being.[6] All things, properly ordered and functioning, including stars, are God' ministers, that is, not only his agents or representatives, but also his attendants and servants; all things are subordinate to God, "who maketh his angels spirits; his ministers a flaming fire" (Ps. 104:4). Herbert would have a particular consciousness of his own special humble place as ordained minister and servant to the "Dread Lord."

The fuller meanings of *star*, a key word in the poem, now become clearer. All created things testify to God, but stars traditionally have assumed distinct roles in Christian belief. Literally guiding lights for sailors, they are in Christian thought beacons which lead to God. The pagan belief that the souls of illustrious persons after death appear as new stars find its Christian parallel in the idea of the stars as God's saints, most notably in the well-known verses of Daniel 12: 3: "And they that be wise shall shine as the brightness of the firmament; and they that turn many to righteousness as the stars for ever and ever." In "Joy of my life," a poem thought to be written in memory of his first wife, Henry Vaughan tells us that "Stars are of mighty use," for "God's Saints are shining lights." Thus the astrological notion, widely held during the Renaissance, that the stars influence human affairs, sway destinies, and mold temperaments undergoes, in Herbert's poem, as in Vaughan's, its Christian transformation: the enlightened holy ones, shining like stars in the sky, set the example and provide guidance for those who are lost and wandering in search of divine truth. Herbert's flaming, speaking star inevitably suggests Acts 2:3: "And there appeared unto them cloven tongues like as a fire," enabling the apostles to preach the truth to all men. Revelation 8 and 9 are also germane: after the third and fifth angels sound their trumpets a star falls from heaven and great affliction upon mankind follows, all of which will be finally concluded by Christ's ultimate triumph. One of the signs of Christ's coming is that ". . . the stars shall fall from heaven." (Matt. 24: 29). In "Artillerie" there is the coming, the acceptance of Christ, preceded and "effected" by a falling star, into the heart of a specific individual.

With the full significance of lines 11–12 evident to him, Herbert cannot ignore the central message of the New Testament: "For this is my blood of the new testament, which is shed for many for the remission of sins" (Matt. 26–28). He cannot refuse to wash away his stubborn thought with Christ's blood. Since Christ made a total sacrifice of himself, Herbert must accept the ironic advice of the first stanza, which, in effect, he does in the conclusive line, "For I will do or suffer what I ought." He submits his will and yields to the dangerous and disturbing motions which eventually end in rest; he follows the example of Christ and the saints in accepting redemptive suffering. Thus stanza two ends in Herbert's submission.[7]

This acquiescence, however, is only temporary, for stanza three, employing reversal strategy, a device favored by Donne also, qualifies it and hence continues the conflict of wills; if the divine advice of stanza one is ironic, then indeed so may Herbert's response be playfully ironic.

> But I have also starres and shooters too,
> Born where thy servants both artilleries use.
> My tears and prayers night and day do wooe,

And work up to thee; yet thou dost refuse.
  Not but I am (I must say still)
  Much more oblig'd to do thy will,
  Then thou to grant mine: but because
Thy promise now hath ev'n set thee thy laws.
(11. 17–24)

The effect of such qualification will be to make possible a profounder and more permanent submission—that of stanza four. For the brief time being, however, Herbert, by parodying several traditions or conventions, further exploits the dominant martial metaphor and expands the love metaphor that has been adumbrated by the tone of familiar conversation between lovers. We shall subsequently discuss sixteenth-century spiritual exercises, particularly Lorenzo Scupoli's *Spiritual Combat*. A second parodied convention is the Petrarchan. Throughout his poetry, Herbert boldly borrowed Petrarchan imagery, especially the complicated imagery of the heart. In stanza three of "Artillerie," he parodies the courtly lover unsuccessfully wooing his lady. Whereas Donne inverts the Petrarchan convention in some of his secular poems, Herbert uses it to woo God.

The stars and shooters born in Herbert's heart are his tears and prayers; these are his artilleries, his arrows,[8] which "night and day do wooe, / And work up to thee." The emblem tradition which itself exploits courtly and Petrarchan conventions and biblical tradition, particularly the Psalms, underlies this idea. In Francis Quarles' *Emblems* there is a print of a devout suppliant kneeling, with an arrow from his breast pointing upward; above him arrows bearing banners of prayers and sighs ascend upward to God's eye and ears; beneath him is a reference to Psalm 38: 9 and the words: "On Thee, O Lord, is fixed my whole Desire / To Thee my Groans ascend, my Prayers aspire." The accompanying poem in its most relevant lines reads:

  . . . In prayer and patience, find Him out again:
  Make Heav'n thy mistress; let no change remove
  Thy loyal heart,—be fond, be sick of love:
  What if he stop his ear, or knit his brow?
  At length he'll be as fond, as sick as thou:
  Dart up thy soul in groans; . . .
  Shoot up the bosom shafts of thy desire,
  Feather'd with faith, and double-fork'd with fire;
  And they will hit: fear not, where Heaven bids come;
  Heav'n's never deaf, but when man's heart is dumb.[9]

Like many of Herbert's titles, the title of our poem is emblem-atic; "Artillerie" is the poetic equivalent of an emblem, symbolizing the spiritual combat between God and Herbert. Herbert, however, deviates from the emblem and Petrarchan "traditions" in that his God still refuses him, as the God addressed in emblem poetry will not, indeed seemingly cannot refuse, and in that Herbert's language is playful and bantering (note the parenthetical "I must say still"), whereas the traditions he draws upon and parodies tend to be more solemn. True, the final consequence is the same in all cases: com-plete capitulation to God, and ultimate joy. But though and because Herbert knows all the time that "I am . . . / Much more oblig'd to do thy will, / Then thou to grant mine," he can ironically insist in his own contrary way that God is bound to obey His own promise, for hasn't He promised to wash away all man's sins and sufferings with His own blood? Herbert the poet, as distinguished from the speaker, has known all along that "There is no articling with thee" (1. 31); there is no need for it. He can be casual and playful in tone precisely because he sees so clearly that *ultimately* there is no real possibility of deviating from the will of God (to do so is to become unreal). His casualness is an aspect of the nature of children—innocent, spon-taneous, unselfconscious inheritors of Eden who, as Henry Vaughan writes in "Childe-hood," "by meer playing go to Heaven." Ironic qualification (a mode of playfulness) of his compliance to God's will renders possible and more meaningful and vividly emphasizes the utter submission of stanza four.

> Then we are shooters both, and thou dost deigne
> To enter combate with us, and contest
> With thine own clay. But I would parley fain:
> Shunne not my arrows, and behold my breast.
>    Yet if thou shunnest, I am thine:
>    I must be so, if I am mine.
>    There is no articling with thee:
>    I am but finite, yet thine infinitely.
> 
>                 (11. 25–32)

This last stanza, a "fireworks" of reflexive phrases and lines wherein the metaphors of war and love merge, as in Donne's Holy Sonnet 10 [XIV], summarizes and resolves the preceding three stanzas. On the basis of what Herbert has said in stanzas one and three he can con-clude in line 25, "Then we are shooters both." And his constant awareness of God's supremacy enables him to recognize and write of

God's condescension when "thou dost deigne / To enter combate with us, and contest / With thine own clay." Knowing he is no match for his divine opponent, Herbert seeks a truce and mutual surrender. The "arrows," which he asks God not to shun, are both weapons against the Almighty and darts of love; the merging of war and love metaphors unites the conventions Herbert has been parodying, and, like the Psalmist, emblemist, and the courtly lover, Herbert pleads "behold my breast." The last four lines, using both military language and the language of lovers, emphatically reaffirm the conclusion of stanza two and assert with earned finality the paradox that Herbert's true being lies in giving up his finite ego in infinite submission to God. As Richard Strier remarks, " 'I am but finite, yet thine infinitely' expresses the profound feeling of creaturehood, of ontological distance and moral obligation, which Rudolf Otto took as central to the human experience of the holy" (104). Yet the lines in context also express the sense of one's larger true identity and the bridging of the ontological distance, for whether or not God shuns "my arrows" "I am thine" and "thine infinitely." As other poems like "The Flower," "The Invitation," "The Banquet," "The Elixir," and "Love" (III) suggest (as we will see), to have true being at all is to participate in divinity.

Whereas Donne's divine poetry is characterized by fear and trembling and uncertainty, Herbert's poetry frequently comes after conflict to assurance about salvation. It is not that the anxiety, restlessness, and passionate desire for union, ever present in Donne, are absent from Herbert. Rather they are interspersed and modified by periods of rest and assurance, which paradoxically are brought about partly by the initial or intermediate or subsequent anxiety and restlessness. At the very beginning of his *Confessions*, Augustine provides us with the guiding principle of his mystical theology: "Thou hast made us for Thyself and our hearts are restless till they rest in Thee" (Sheed trans., I, 1). Irenaeus offers a key when he observes, "Submission to God is eternal rest" (Bettenson, *The Early Christian Fathers*, 72). And great wisdom obtains in "The Pulley," that poem so explicitly about rest and restlessness, the latter being the pulley that tosses man to God and true rest:

> If goodnesse leade him not, yet wearinesse
> May tosse him to my breast.

As Blake says, "if the fool will persist in his folly, he will become wise." Even more pertinently, out of the same passionate desire for union apparent in Donne and Herbert, Julian of Norwich writes "until I am essentially united with him I can never have full rest or real happiness; in other words, until I am so joined to him that there is absolutely nothing between my God and me." In the same passage, Julian goes on to distinguish between Nature or "creation" and the uncreated God in much the same way that Herbert does in the penultimate stanza of "The Pulley." "We have got to realize the littleness of creation and to see it for the nothing that it is before we can love and possess God who is uncreated. This is the reason why we have no ease of heart or soul, for we are seeking our rest in trivial things which cannot satisfy, and not seeking to know God, almighty, all-wise, all-good. He is true rest. It is his will that we should know him, and his pleasure that we should rest in him" (68). Evidently, in Herbert's view, God in wisdom and goodness gives man restlessness in order that he may thereby paradoxically come to true rest.

The contrast between Donne's anxiety about and Herbert's assurance of salvation is critically familiar, though more recently some critics stress the conflict and restlessness in Herbert.[10] Rather than insist on only one or the other aspect of Herbert's work, I believe both should be emphasized. To do so in traditional terms, while placing Donne of the Divine poems at the stage of Purgation, means regarding the "two Herberts," the restlessness and the rest, the conflicts and accords, as marking Herbert's progress from meditation to contemplation through the stages of Purgation, Illumination, the Dark Night of the Soul, and Union. To be more particular and precise, we should talk of many purgations, illuminations, dark nights, unitive experiences, and alternations back and forth between them. Underhill points out that in a sense "purification is a perpetual process" (204) and that the spiritual life consists of "a series of oscillations" (381). Purification leads to insight, enlightenment and rest, but these latter in themselves, along with the alternating restlessness, help to provide a further purification leading to still deeper vision and enlightenment and truer rest. The dialectical structure of "Artillerie," its alternations between conflict and submission or accord, not only reflects Herbert's description of *The Temple* and the structure of many poems in it but also characterizes the whole alternating progress of "The Church."

### III

I have previously alluded to Scupoli's *Spiritual Combat*, a book which, considering Herbert's use of the term "Spiritual Conflicts" in his own description of *The Temple*, is perhaps of some direct significance especially in that one English edition of Scupoli's book was entitled *Spiritual Conflict*. I wish now briefly to consider Scupoli's work in relation to Herbert, and then, while affirming the pertinence of sixteenth-century spiritual exercises as one of several "traditions" Herbert drew upon, to go on to suggest the relevance of ancient-medieval-Renaissance contemplative tradition, and particularly its basic doctrine or idea of the two selves, to Herbert's "Artillerie" and other poems.

*Spiritual Combat*, according to Louis Martz, is "the second great landmark in the development of spiritual exercises during the sixteenth century . . . a book which may hold some significance for English literature of the seventeenth century and especially for . . . Herbert." (*The Poetry of Meditation*, 125–26). The martial metaphor implied in the title of the book is pervasive in the book itself, and it is quite possible that "Artillerie" and similar poems, allowing for the transformation effected by Herbert's originality, were influenced and nourished by the book's major metaphor. "The center of the book is self-analysis, the prime weapon in the spiritual combat":

> . . . you must wage continual warfare against yourself and employ your entire strength in demolishing each vicious inclination, however trivial. . . .
> The first thing to do when you awake is to open the windows of your soul. Consider yourself as on the field of battle, facing the enemy and bound by the iron-clad law—either fight or die. . . . Begin to fight immediately in the name of the Lord, armed with distrust of yourself, with confidence in God, [with] prayer, and with the correct use of the faculties of your soul. With these weapons, attack the enemy. . . .[11]

There can hardly be any question that Herbert was very aware of and knowledgeable about the central ideas and imagery of *Spiritual Combat*, if not the book itself. In his prose work *A Priest to the Temple, or, the Countrey Parson*, Herbert discusses the "double state of a Christian even in this Life, the one military, the other peaceable."

> The military is, when we are assaulted with temptations either from within or from without. The Peaceable is, when the Divell for a time leaves us, as he did our Saviour, and the Angels minister to us their owne food, even joy, and peace; and comfort in the holy Ghost. These two states were in our Saviour, not only in the beginning of his preaching, but afterwards also, as *Mat.* 22, 35. He was

tempted: And *Luke* 10.21. He rejoyced in Spirit: And they must be likewise in all that are his. (280)

The military state here described (similar in language, tone, and other qualities to *Spiritual Combat*) doubtlessly derives ultimately from the basic and well-known idea of St. Paul that the Christian life is like a battle and the Christian like a soldier. St. Paul describes the discipline to which the Christian is subject, his armor and his weapons of offense, and the enemies, internal and external, against whom he has to fight. The Pauline military metaphor is given continuous and varied expression in the earliest apostolic records, such as the *Epistle to the Corinthians* by Clemens Romanus (see, e.g., Bettenson, *The Early Christian Fathers*, 31), as well as in the later patristic writings.

As Rosemond Tuve in her *A Reading of George Herbert* and other critics have shown, Herbert characteristically employs in his poetry a traditional central invention; he explores and labors within it to discover new veins of meaning and nuance. (It may be, of course, that considering Herbert's historical time and place, his selection and usage of military language also has at some level of consciousness an ideological significance, a political or historical specificity.) What is for our purposes especially remarkable is the significant difference in tone between "Artillerie" and the typical passages quoted from Scupoli. Although the imagery of both is martial and derivative from that most important companion volume to the reading of Herbert's poetry, the Bible, the deadly serious tone of *Spiritual Combat* is quite unlike the familiarity and playfulness of "Artillerie." The difference in tone between Scupoli's and Herbert's work signals the spiritual distance or progress between the early or meditative stages of the religious life and Herbert's own attainment of more advanced or contemplative stages, as evidenced in "Artillerie" and a number of his other poems. Considering Herbert's use of other conventions and traditions in the poem, "Artillerie," in tone at least, would seem to be a particular result of one of Herbert's poetic practices, a kind of gentle parody of *Spiritual Combat*.[12] Herbert the poet, as distinguished from the speaker, appears to be in fuller control. He seems to know in this poem what the conclusion, both in and outside the poem, is going to be, and thus he can adopt a less somber and more assured tone than that of *Spiritual Combat*. Indeed, the merging of the metaphors of war and love in the last stanza suggests that the poem is not the intense, passionate "warfare" of the spiritual exercises but, rather, simply a lovers' quarrel, a quarrel between the two "selves" of the poem. And, in general, the differences between Herbert and Scupoli are similar to important differences between Herbert and Donne's divine poetry. To help account for these differences, particularly the differences in tone and theme, between Herbert and Scupoli, one should look more closely at the conception of the two selves found in *The Temple*. Since this conception itself develops out of biblical, contemplative tradition, about which Herbert, the country parson, was knowledgeable, one should, in other words, look to the tradition constituted by the Bible and "the Fathers also, and the Schoolmen, and the later Writers, or a good proportion of all."[13]

As observed in Chapter One, the contemplative tradition's fundamental conception of man's twofold self derives, naturally enough, from the Bible. The Old Testament provides important scriptural authority in well-known verses such as "So God created man in his own image, in the image of God created he him" (Gen. 1: 27). The New Testament sometimes expresses the idea of man's dichotomous nature directly, as in "The first man Adam was made a living soul; the last Adam was made a quickening spirit" (1 Cor: 15.45), and in "though our outward man perish, yet the inward man is renewed day by day" (2 Cor. 4: 16; see also Heb. 4: 12, Rom. 7:22, Eph. 3: 16, Col. 3: 9). Sometimes the twofold distinction is embodied in the crucial paradox of gain through loss or of life through death, as in the famous passage of John 12: 24–25, previously quoted (see also Luke 9:24–25). All these and many other biblical passages pertain to the central conversion experience of hating and giving up the corrupt egoistic life of the old Adam or outward man to realize the life of the true Spirit, inward man, or last Adam.

The contemplatives, that is a good proportion of "the Fathers . . . and the Schoolmen, and the later Writers," variously articulate the biblical idea that man is made in God's image, that when the fallen outward man is purged away the real Self in the depth of the particular individual may be seen as identical with or at least like unto the Divinity, for which widespread idea citations from the Fathers and other mystics were given in Chapters One and Two. Largely under the influence of Augustine, "image theology" made its way to late-medieval writers who expressed the essential spiritual unity of man and God in such terms as the apex of the soul, the ground, the spark, anima, the interior castle, the two Adams, created and uncreated nature, and so on. Julian of Norwich, an

English mystic with a religious sensibility not unlike Herbert's, writes that "the good Lord showed his own Son and Adam as one man," and "by *Adam* I always understand *Everyman*" (148). Still another English mystic, Walter Hilton, who freely translated the very popular medieval spiritual classic *Stimulus Amoris*, declares in a chapter entitled "How good it is to a man for to be turned into God," that "yet mickle more wonder and more delightable and without comparison, more ought to be coveted the gracious turning and the glorious changing [of a man] into God. . . . This turning is here, in his life through grace" (*The Goad of Love*, 144).

The basic contemplative doctrine, then, is that man has two selves: the phenomenal or finite ego, of which he is mainly conscious and which he tends mistakenly to regard as his true self, and an infinite and hence not wholly definable self, the inward man or image of divinity in him, which is in reality his true Self. It is important to emphasize that this idea does not mean that "therefore, I am God Almighty!" For the "I" or ego is one's conception of oneself, the known created object, not the knowing creative actuality. It is a prideful sense of separate and independent existence, the role one assumes and is assigned to play, a somewhat abstract and conventional self. In order to know God fully and be united to Him, man's will and entire being must come into full accord with God's will and being. The isolated and isolating ego, the fallen Adam, must itself die or be transformed so that a process of infinite expansion may occur, so that inner unity may be attained.

*The Temple* may very well be regarded as a various record of many spiritual conflicts, griefs, and joys, coordinated and made more coherent by the central theme of submission to God's will, particularly if this submission is understood as the major means of effecting the glorious changing of the fallen Adam into the Son of God. Indeed, this transformation of a man and this submission to divine will are but two ways of speaking of the same event, as, for example, "The Crosse" makes perfectly clear. Throughout "The Church," Herbert frequently voices the idea of the two selves in each man through the distinction expressed in the words *mine* and *thine*, the most crucial words in the last stanza of "Artillerie." "The Altar," at the beginning of "The Church," concludes with this petition:

> That, if I chance to hold my peace,
> These stones to praise thee may not cease.
> O let thy blessed SACRIFICE be mine,
> And sanctifie this ALTAR to be thine.

If the speaker comes to peace and silence, rather than being enchanted by notions and words, his poems paradoxically will endlessly praise God (for Herbert believed that only certain appropriate spiritual states and attitudes could produce immortal divine poetry). In the last two lines, the speaker prays to become Christ-like, to have the altar which is his heart ("A broken ALTAR, Lord, thy servant reares, / Made of a heart") become Christ's own. The word *Sacrifice* in the penultimate line is gathered up in the title of the next poem, "The Sacrifice," which treats Christ's Passion in the first person voice of Christ and which contains the refrain "Was ever grief like mine?" The "I" of "The Altar" (the very shape of the poem is not only an altar but also an I) is a fallen Adam, and the "I" of "The Sacrifice" is Christ or the Last Adam. The record throughout *The Temple* of Herbert's own afflictions, sufferings, and many spiritual conflicts is, then, a way of indicating the speaker's complex movement toward Christlikeness, from meditation to contemplation, the two Adams or "I"s becoming one, a movement which is completed in "Love" (III), the last poem in "The Church."

## IV

"The Church" begins at an altar and ends at a table, another name for an altar. It begins with meditations on Christ's bloody sacrifice and ends with a celebration of his bloodless sacrifice in a contemplative Eucharistic feast. Herbert's "broken Altar . . . Made of a heart," which "No workman's tool hath touch'd," corresponds exactly to the altar described by the Church Father Gregory of Nazianzus:

> I know of another altar, of which the present visible altars are merely types; an altar to which no axe or hand went up, nor was the noise of iron heard, nor any work of craftsman or skilful artist. It is all the work of the mind, and the ascent is by contemplation. It is at this altar that I will stand, and on it I will sacrifice acceptable offerings . . . (Bettenson, *The Later Christian Fathers*, 123)

Herbert's contemplative ascent by heart or mind is essentially a eucharistic one.[14] Various critics have remarked upon the pervasiveness and centrality of eucharistic words, images, and themes in Herbert's poetry. The Eucharist even figures as an organizing, structural principle. In his fine edition of *The English Poems of George Herbert*, C. A. Patrides rightly observes that diverse strands in *The Tem-*

*ple* "merge in Herbert's thought because they depend on a singular reality, the immanence of God in history through the sacrament of the Lord's Supper, the Eucharist. The Eucharist is the marrow of Herbert's sensibility. . . . If *The Temple* is indeed a 'structure' [as T. S. Eliot wrote], it is an eucharistic one" (17, 18).

To understand the full significance of the Eucharist for Herbert in the structure and progress of "The Church" we must know the full significance of the Eucharist in the Bible and in the contemplatives, that is, in "the master revelations" or, in Herbert's words, "the holy Scriptures . . . the Fathers . . . and the Schoolmen, and the later Writers," whom "the Countrey Parson hath read" (*A Priest to the Temple*, 228–229). Writing on the Eucharist and citing key passages from the Gospel of John, Hilary of Poitiers explains how by it Christ "remains in us" and we "advance to unity with the Father":

> If the Word was truly made flesh, and we truly take the Word-flesh by means of the Lord's food; surely we must think that he naturally remains in us, seeing that by being born as man he assumed the nature of our flesh as now inseparable from himself, and has mingled the nature of his flesh with the nature of eternity under the sacrament of the flesh which is to be communicated to us.
>
> Christ himself gives evidence of the nature of our life in him through the sacrament of the flesh and blood imparted to us, when he says . . . "Since I live, you also will live; since I am in my Father, and you are in me, and I am in you." If he means a unity merely of will, why did he describe a kind of order of ascent in the establishment of that unity? His purpose surely was that we should believe that he was in the Father by nature, as being divine; whereas we are in him in virtue of his birth in the flesh, and he is in us through the mystery of the sacraments: and that thus we should have a doctrine of a unity consummated through the Mediator, since, while we abide in him, he would abide in the Father, and, thus abiding, should abide in us; and thus we should advance to unity with the Father. . . .
>
> Christ also gives evidence of this natural unity in us: "He who eats my flesh, and drinks my blood, dwells in me, and I dwell in him." For no one will be in Christ, unless Christ is in him, unless he has taken into himself the flesh of Christ, who took man's flesh. . . . He lives "through the Father": and as he lives through the Father, so we live through his flesh. . . .
>
> The mystery of the real and natural unity is to be proclaimed in terms of the honor granted to us by the Son, and the Son's dwelling in us through his flesh, while we are united to him bodily and inseparably. (Bettenson, *The Later Christian Fathers*, 57–58)

Also writing on the Eucharist, Gregory of Nyssa explains how the devout communicant "may be deified":

> The God who was manifested mingled himself with the nature that was doomed to death, in order that by communion with the divinity human nature may be deified together with him. It is for this purpose that by the divine plan of his grace he plants himself in the believers by means of that flesh, composed of bread and wine, blending himself with the bodies of believers, so that man also may share in immortality by union with the immortal. He bestows those gifts by the virtue of the blessing, "transelementing" the nature of the visible things into the immortal body (Bettenson, *The Later Christian Fathers*, 163).

"The Church" reveals that Herbert's Vision of God, by which he is "deified" and "advance(s) to unity with the Father," is effected through the eucharistic means of being "united to [the Son] bodily and inseparably."

"The Church" may be regarded as a poetic record of Herbert's sacrifices, divine acts, whereby he "may be united with God," if we understand these matters as St. Augustine does:

> A true sacrifice is every act which is performed so that we may be united with God in holy fellowship; directed, that is, towards the achievement of our true good, which alone can bring us true happiness. . . . Although this sacrifice is made or offered by man, still the sacrifice is a divine act . . . we ourselves are the whole sacrifice. . . . This is the sacrifice of Christians; the "many who are one body in Christ." This sacrifice the Church celebrates in the sacrament of the altar, which the faithful know well, where it is shown to her that in this thing which she offers she herself is offered (*The City of God*, 10. 5, 6).

So Herbert properly begins "The Church" with "The Altar" and "The Sacrifice." "The Sacrifice," in Christ's voice, concludes

> Onely let others say, when I am dead
> Never was grief like mine.

This is the answer to Christ's recurrent refrain "Was ever grief like mine?" Appropriately and importantly, Christ does not here say (as he does at line 216) but recommends that others say, "Never was grief like mine." For Christ not to say thus at the conclusion of "The Sacrifice" is in keeping with his own humility. For Christ to encour-

age others to say thus is to teach humility. And for others repeatedly
to say thus is to come eventually to say the contrary. In other words,
through the beginning and long middle sections of "The Church,"
Herbert's sense of sin and unworthiness is so great that his answer
to Christ's refrain must be "no, never was grief like Christ's." But by
the end of "The Church," with its record of Herbert's many griefs
and spiritual conflicts and afflictions, as well as joys, all coordinated
and rendered more meaningful by the central theme of submission
to God's will, which submission is necessary to partake of the
Eucharist, Herbert is in effect able to answer also "yes, my grief is
like Christ's." And by such means the fallen, afflicted first Adam be-
comes Christlike, is gloriously changed into the last Adam, is
"deified," "united with God."

Following immediately upon "The Sacrifice," "The Thanksgiv-
ing" begins with a rhetorical question which in effect has Herbert
already saying, in accord with Christ's final instruction in "The Sac-
rifice," "Never was grief like mine" (that is, of course, "thine"):

> Oh king of grief! . . .
>     how shall I grieve for thee,
> Who in all grief preventest me?

The word "preventest" not only means, as Hutchinson notes (487),
"dost come before, excel," but also may have for Herbert its archaic
theological sense, so that the line means not only that Christ's grief
precedes and is greater than "my" grief but also that Christ and his
grace goes before with spiritual guidance and help in anticipation of
("my") human need (O.E.D.). With this theological meaning and the
ordinary meaning of "prevent," current in Herbert's day as it is today,
the lines have the subtle mythic sense, which will occur repeatedly
throughout "The Church" but which the speaker (as distinguished
from Herbert) does not yet understand, that Christ's sacrifice by its
spiritual help and grace has already prevented (precluded, stopped)
all grief, has for all time effected human salvation, particularly if the
fallen psyche could fully realize all of this through eucharistic sub-
mission to God's will.

In the midst of wondering "how shall I grieve for thee," the
speaker remarks,

> *My God, my God, why dost thou part from me?*
> Was such a grief as cannot be.

Depending upon who is the intended speaker of the first line, which is from Matthew 27:46 and uttered by Jesus on the cross shortly before he dies, this couplet conveys a variety of meanings. First, if, as is most likely, the first line quotes Christ, then the couplet signifies, among other meanings, that Christ's grief was so enormous as to be (or at least to seem) impossible. Throughout "The Church," Herbert expresses the feeling that God has parted from him; so, secondly, the first line may be spoken by this poem's speaker in the midst of his wonderings, as it is in effect spoken by the speaker of many subsequent poems. In any case, whoever the speaker of the first line, the couplet wisely suggests that it is not possible in the ultimate sense for anyone to feel grief (or even simply to *be*) without God, Who is, after all, *Being*. The speaker more fully understands and expresses later throughout the sequence that God is in his grief as well as in his joy and that the great grief of being parted from God is in a real sense impossible. As shall be more clearly seen, to the extent that one has being at all, one is with and in God.

"The Thanksgiving" concludes:

> My musick shall finde thee, and ev'ry string
> Shall have his attribute to sing;
> That all together may accord in thee,
> And prove one God, one harmonie.
> If thou shalt give me wit, it shall appeare,
> If thou hast giv'n it me, 'tis here.
> Nay, I will read thy book, and never move
> Till I have found therein thy love,
> Thy art of love, which I'le turn back on thee:
> O my deare Saviour, Victorie!
> Then for thy passion—I will do for that—
> Alas, my God, I know not what.

"My musick" refers of course as well to "my poetry," "The Church," *The Temple*. In the line "And prove one God, one harmonie" "prove" not only has its current transitive sense ("to establish as true; to demonstrate the truth of by evidence or argument"), but also carries its Middle English meaning: "to find out, learn, or know by experience; to experience, 'go through,' suffer"; and, most imporantly, both "to find by experience (a person or thing), to be (something)" and "to come to be, become." Herbert's book or structure of poems will find God, especially by the experience of his sacrifice of suffering, and the church or temple which is himself ("Know ye not that ye are the temple of God, and that the Spirit of God dwelleth in you?" 1 Cor. 3:16) will be harmoniously at one with God. The phrase " 'tis here" refers not only, as Hutchinson notes, to "this book of poems," but also perhaps to the heart (which is the speaker's altar, tabernacle, temple), imagining the speaker to point there. In any case "the temple" is both the book of poems and the heart or true self. The references to "love" at the end of "The Thanksgiving" look forward and alert us to the many appearances of that word in Herbert's poetry and especially to "Love" I, II, and III.

A number of critics have remarked upon the obvious connections, which we need not repeat, between the end of "The Thanksgiving" and the beginning of the next poem, "The Reprisall" (titled "the Second Thanksgiving" in the Williams Ms.). The martial metaphors of its concluding stanza, to be echoed in such poems as "Artillerie," foreshadow and underscore continuing "spiritual conflict" throughout the book in terms of both the historical and mythic first and last Adams. The "love" of "The Thanksgiving" and the "Sinnes" of "The Reprisal" are then developed in the "Sinne and Love" of "The Agonie," which devotes its second stanza to "Sinne," vividly conveyed by the vehicle of "Mount Olivet," and its third stanza to "Love," graphically conveyed by the vehicle of the crucifixion, in eucharistic terms that conclude:

> Love is that liquour sweet and most divine,
> Which my God feels as bloud; but I, as wine.

Obviously, by such means, the first five poems of "The Church" ("The Altar," "The Sacrifice," "The Thanksgiving," "The Reprisall," and "The Agonie") are sequentially interconnected. Less obviously, by such means, these poems and others throughout "The Church," such as the eucharistic "The H. Communion," "Love-Joy," "The Bunch of Grapes," "The Invitation," "The Banquet," "The Altar," and indeed all those poems concerning sin and suffering, love and joy, among other clusters and sequences of images and themes, discussed and as yet undiscussed, are profoundly and cunningly interwoven throughout Herbert's work, whose thus multiplied meanings in subtlety as well as number seem to approach infinity, all as a consequence of the biblical method of composing poetry that he himself describes in "The H. Scriptures" II:

> This verse marks that, and both do make a motion
> Unto a third, that ten leaves off doth lie.

No wonder that so much good criticism has been written about Herbert's work, without exhausting or fully appreciating it, and so much remains to be written. To describe Infinity and become one with it (or, as Herbert puts it in "Superliminare" to "approach, and taste / The churches mysticall repast"), one needs an appropriate means. Herbert's form and content are precisely suited to one another. Under such circumstances, criticism that proceeds by rational and linear rather than in poetic and mythic ways can only hope to be helpfully suggestive rather than wholly satisfactory and complete, mapping out certain high points in Herbert's poetry rather than fully surveying and exploring all its terrain of rich, varied, and complex meanings.

Except for its first-person last line, "The Agonie" is written in the third person. By its title and its first person speaker, "The Sinner" continues "Agonie" and its theme of "Sinne." Both agony or grief and sin frequently recur throughout what Martz aptly calls the Sacramental Introduction and the Body of Conflicts, the beginning and the large middle sections of "The Church." By their titles, the poems which follow "The Sinner" ("Good Friday," "Redemption," "Sepulchre," "Easter," and "Easter-wings") indicate that Herbert continues his meditations on the historical Sacrifice, the Passion and Crucifixion of Jesus Christ, but these poems, moving readily between the historical past and the present, exhibit mythic meanings as well. The sonnet "Redemption," for example, seems to be a story about a "tenant" who seeks out his "rich Lord" in order to obtain a new lease, a story that could happen at any time, but the end of the poem locates it at the scene of the Crucifixion on Good Friday, and so the rich Lord's response "Your suit is granted" (given even before the tenant's request is made) is true for all time. Although the speaker seems not to know, the poet must know that in some sense his suit is granted, he is already redeemed. Similarly, as the last stanza of "Easter" suggested, Easter Sunday, the day of redemption, is now, today, the only real time being the timelessness of the eternal now-moment:

> Can there be any day but this,
> Though many sunnes to shine endeavour?
> We count three hundred, but we misse:
> There is but one, and that one ever.

The first stanza of the famous pattern poem "Easter-wings," which concerns both history and the eternal moment, begins in direct address to "Lord, who createdest man," presumably Adam, referred to in the third person, turns to first person as the lines of the stanza grow longer, and concludes with "Then shall the fall further the flight in me." This line, expressing the archetype of the Fortunate Fall, calls to mind the last line of Donne's "Hymne to God, my God, in my sickness": "Therefore that he may raise the Lord throws down." But whereas Donne's poem seems primarily concerned with resurrection in the afterlife, "Easter-wings" concludes with a request for union in this life, "this day," when the first and last Adam may be one, and with the important recurrent themes and imagery of affliction and flight:

> With thee
> Let me combine
> And feel this day thy victorie:
> For, if I imp my wing on thine,
> Affliction shall advance the flight in me.

In addition to sequences in which the poems immediately follow one after the other, such as "The Altar" to "H. Baptisme" (II), "Antiphon" (I) to "Praise" (I), "The Search" to "The Flower," and "The Invitation" to "Love" (III), many of Herbert's poems form groups or "constellations" at a distance in the sense that verses may "make a motion / Unto a third, that ten leaves," or thirty or forty, "off doth lie." In "H. Baptisme" (II), for example, Herbert pleads "O let me still / Write thee great God, and me a childe" and concludes, in contrast to the "sicknesses" of "Easter-wings," "Childhood is health." Many leaves hence in "Longing," a poem that ends with echoes of "Artillerie," we read the bitter lines of the tenth stanza:

> Thou tarriest, while I die,
> And fall to nothing: thou dost reigne,
> And rule on high
> While I remain
> In bitter grief: yet am I stil'd
> Thy childe.

A few leaves later, as if in continuing responses to this "bitter grief," the speaker of "The Collar" raves and rants and threatens,

> But as I rav'd and grew more fierce and wilde
> At every word,

> Me thought I heard one calling, *Child*!
> And I replied, *My Lord*.

Although the theme of childhood, of being born again and becoming like unto a child in order to enter the kingdom of heaven, does not have in Herbert and Vaughan the central importance it has in Traherne, it does on occasion serve as a variation on the archetype of that regeneration or rebirth which is the heart of the mystical experience and not just a Christian commonplace. As remarked in Chapter One, baptism of the spirit, regeneration in our sense, is not a merely verbal or intellectual grasp of certain religious principles nor a merely superficial conversion, but rather that deeply realized, radical, and thoroughgoing change in one's mode of consciousness which is both the beginning and center of the contemplative life.

This archetype of mystical regeneration finds various expression throughout "The Church," as, for example, in the aforementioned themes and imagery of affliction or grief and flight. Among the five poems entitled "Affliction," the first begins a few leaves off from the last line of "Easter-wings," "Affliction shall advance the flight in me." Like "Easter-wings" and many other poems, "Affliction" (III) reveals a dialectical pattern similar to the alternating falling and rising pattern so frequent in Herbert's poetry:

> My heart did heave, and there came forth, *O God*!
> By that I knew that thou wast in the grief,
> To guide and govern it to my relief,
>     Making a scepter of the rod:
>       Hadst thou not had thy part,
> Sure the unruly sigh had broke my heart.
>
> But since thy breath gave me both life and shape,
> Thou knowst my tallies; and when there's assign'd
> So much breath to a sigh, what's then behinde?
>     Or if some yeares with it escape,
>       The sigh then onely is
> A gale to bring me sooner to my blisse.
>
> Thy life on earth was grief, and thou art still
> Constant unto it, making it to be ˙
> A point of honour, now to grieve in me,
>     And in thy members suffer ill.
>       They who lament one crosse,
> Thou dying dayly, praise thee to thy losse.

Just as "The Thanksgiving" reveals that it is not possible for anyone to feel grief (or even simply to *be*) without God, so the first stanza above indicates that God is in Herbert's or the speaker's grief and, the last stanza indicates, that God grieves in Herbert. Perhaps Paul's mystical conception of Christ and human beings, particularly Church members, best explains the poem: "For as the body is one, and hath many members, and all the members of that one body, being many, are one body: so also is Christ. . . . And whether one member suffer, all the members suffer with it; or one member be honoured, all the members rejoice with it. Now ye are the body of Christ, and members in particular" (1 Cor. 12:12–13, 26–27). Discussing the Eucharist and referring to Paul's words, St. Augustine, in sermon 272, sheds light not only on this and other poems of affliction but also on the many eucharistic and joyful poems, expecially "Love" (III): "If you wish to understand the body of Christ, listen to the apostle's words: 'You are the body and the members of Christ.' If you are the body and members of Christ, it is your mystery which is placed on the Lord's table; it is your mystery you receive" (Bettenson, *The Later Christian Fathers*, 244). "Thou dying dayly" expresses the timeless, mythic view of Christ over against a simply historical, literal view. That Christ grieves "in me, / And in thy members" means that the answer to the question "Was ever grief like mine," which was "no," is becoming through the middle section of "The Church" "no and yes" and will by the end of "The Church," when the speaker and Christ are one, be "yes." In language reminiscent of the opening of "Affliction" (III), and especially "Easter-wings," we read in "Sion":

> grones are quick, and full of wings,
> And all their motions upward be;
> And ever as they mount, like larks they sing;
> The note is sad, yet musick for a King.

The joyful paradox is that the deeper Herbert sinks in agony, groans, and grief, the higher he soars, because the way down and the way up are one and the same, because the more he suffers the more he is Christlike and the more the answer to the question "Was ever grief like mine?" is yes.[15]

## V

The contemplative process of becoming Christlike, "deified," undergoing the transformation from the first Adam to the last Adam, is significantly expressed throughout "The Church," especially in the large middle section, by the repeated mine-thine distinction. Evidently, Herbert, like Donne and various contemplatives, believed that we may participate in and be partakers of the divine nature. As we saw in the previous chapter, Donne writes, "As our flesh is in him, by his participation thereof, so his flesh is in us, by our communication thereof; and so is his divinity in us, by making us partakers of his divine nature . . ." (*Sermons* IX, 248). We also saw that according to the conception of union found in St. John of the Cross, for one example among many contemplatives, "the soul itself is said to be 'transformed in God by love.' . . . The human soul when thus transformed is in fact 'deiform' . . . and, in the saint's characteristic phrase, has become God by participation" (Dicken, 358). "All may of thee partake," Herbert writes in "The Elixir," and it may be that he regularly uses the mine-thine distinction to express the contemplative progress toward Christlikeness because he, like other contemplatives, believed humans may participate in or partake of divine union rather than become one in substance with God.

Some of the more important recurrences of the *mine-thine* distinction which appear between "The Altar" and "Love" (III) confirm the centrality of the contemplative conception of the two selves in Herbert's poetry. An obvious and prominent example is "Clasping of hands," a poem that is a constant, quite serious playing upon the repeated *mine* and *thine*. At least one and often both of these words occur in eighteen of the poem's twenty lines. The metaphysical convolutions or shifts in meaning and identity consequent upon the poem's playful variations may be difficult to follow closely, but the conclusion is plainly a prayer for union:

> LORD, thou art mine, and I am thine,
> If mine I am: and thine much more,
> Then I or ought, or can be mine.
> Yet to be thine, doth me restore;
> So that again I now am mine,
> And with advantage mine the more,
> Since this being mine, brings with it thine,
> And thou with me dost thee restore.
>    If I without thee would be mine,
>    I neither should be mine nor thine.
>
> Lord, I am thine, and thou art mine:
> So mine thou art, that something more
> I may presume thee mine, then thine.

For thou didst suffer to restore
Not thee, but me, and to be mine,
And with advantage mine the more,
Since thou in death wast none of thine,
Yet then as mine didst me restore.
O be mine still! still make me thine!
Or rather make no Thine and Mine!

The second stanza of "Clasping of hands" shows that the "Lord" being addressed is the Second Person of the Trinity, the Son of God or Christ. It is usually, but not always, the case in *The Temple* that Herbert employs the terms *mine* and *thine* to designate specifically the first and last Adams. Among various biblical passages, Herbert may have had in mind Jesus' prayer to the Father in Chapter 17 of John, which includes the lines "And all mine are thine, and thine are mine; and I am gloried in them" (17:10).

"Judgement," which appears near the end of "The Church" and appropriately has an eschatological theme, similarly involves the last Adam whose sacrifice included the bearing of blame for man's sins. The speaker of the poem considers that time when each man's book of his life shall be called for to be examined, and he concludes:

But I resolve, when thou shalt call for mine,
That to decline,
And thrust a Testament into thy hand:
Let that be scann'd.
There thou shalt finde my faults are thine.

(The phrase "a Testament" refers of course to the New Testament, but it may also refer to *The Temple*, another kind of testament, at the end of which in "Love" III we read, echoing the last line quoted above, "And know you not, sayes Love, who bore the blame?") On the other hand, "The Quip," a poem in the allegorical mode, does not make distinctions clearly with respect to divine Person. In successive stanzas, Beautie, Money, Glory, and Wit and Conversation are presented with their respective temptations, and each stanza ends with the refrain "*But thou shalt answer, Lord, for me.*" The final stanza reads:

Yet when the houre of thy designe
To answer these fine things shall come;
Speak not at large; say, I am thine:
And then they will have their answer home.

The interesting point about the penultimate line is its ambiguity. That is, not only may it mean, in indirect quotation, that the speaker's being is the Lord's, but it may also be understood in direct quotation that the Lord's being is the speaker's, that the Lord is to say "I am thine."[16] Taken in the second sense, the speaker's own answer is the best answer or quip because it is the shortest possible answer. It is no answer of his own. He has chanced to hold his peace, as "The Altar" petitions, and the end result is, so the speaker hopes, that the Lord shall answer for him and shall answer in terms which suggest the ultimate identity or union of the individual suppliant with God. The recurrent uses of *mine* and *thine*, then, point significantly to the centrality in and pervasiveness throughout *The Temple* of the contemplative tradition's basic idea of the two selves which are to be one, temporarily in illumination and permanently in final union.

The widely noted alternation in state of mood, mind, and soul in *The Temple*, sometimes from poem to poem and at other times even within the same poem, not only parallels the stanzaic alternation (in poems such as "Artillerie" and "Dialogue") between conflict and accord but also, more importantly, reflects the self within the speaker (or Herbert) which is predominant at any one time. These alternating states of affliction and joy, of spiritual conflict and perfect freedom, that obtain throughout Herbert's work find a correspondence in the fifteenth chapter of Dame Julian's *Revelations of Divine Love*. This chapter concerns "the recurring experience of delight and depression." Like Herbert, Julian writes "then I felt the pain again; then the joy and pleasure; now it was one, and now the other, many times." She understands, as Herbert comes to understand, "that it was for their own good that some souls should have this sort of experience: sometimes to be consoled; sometimes to be bereft and left to themselves. The will of God is that we should know he keeps us safely, alike 'in weal or woe.' . . . Both are equally his love" (86–87). "My wo, mans weal," Christ says in "The Sacrifice." While many of Herbert's poems might here be cited, "The Temper" (I) best expresses and embodies the ideas in Julian's fifteenth chapter:

> How should I praise thee, Lord! how should my rymes
>   Gladly engrave thy love in steel,
> If what my soul doth feel sometimes,
>   My soul might ever feel!
>
> Although there were some fourtie heav'ns, or more,

Sometimes I peere above them all;
Sometimes I hardly reach a score,
    Sometimes to hell I fall.

O rack me not to such a vast extent;
Those distances belong to thee:
The world's too little for thy tent,
    A grave too big for me.

Wilt thou meet arms with man, that thou dost stretch
A crumme of dust from heav'n to hell?
Will great God measure with a wretch?
    Shall he thy stature spell?

O let me, when thy roof my soul hath hid,
O let me roost and nestle there:
Then of a sinner thou art rid,
    And I of hope and fear.

Yet take thy way; for sure thy way is best:
Stretch or contract me, thy poore debter:
This is but tuning of my breast,
    To make the musick better.

Whether I flie with angels, fall with dust,
Thy hands made both, and I am there:
Thy power and love, my love and trust
    Make one place ev'ry where.

Presumably, it is the "Immortal Heat" of God, addressed in "Love" (II), immediately preceding "The Temper" (I), which will purge, refine, and temper the steel-like, stony-hard heart of the old Adam by means of alternate stretching and contracting from heaven to hell, thereby initiating his transformation into the new Adam. The poem works subtly. The speaker's plea in stanza three, though understandable enough, is at a deeper level a contesting of God's will and ways, and hence it is a form of egoistic willfulness. In asking not to be racked, the speaker is in effect, if unwittingly, refusing to follow Christ and the model he provides through his own racking, his willing self-sacrifice and suffering in the crucifixion. The fourth stanza, in terms not unlike "Artillerie," spells out the battle of wills between God and man. The questions asked are: will God meet arms with man, as in a duel, a meeting of swords, or will God measure with, that is compete with or try his strength against (O.E.D.), wretched man? (Of course, as indicated by l. 16, "measure" may also retain its usual meaning, and "meet" may be a pun on "mete.") In stanzas six and seven, again as in "Artillerie," there is finally a turning toward and affirmation of God's will. The stretching and contracting, the alternate joy and affliction or rising to heaven and falling to hell, are at last seen as a tempering or tuning of the heart. Both weal and woe, delight and depression, ascent and descent, are equally God's love. In other words, through God's power and love and man's love and trust, the way down and the way up are one and the same; man's willingness to affirm God's will and even to accept the burden of suffering, "for sure thy way is best," makes him Christ-like and consequently ultimately gives him joy. Notably, if we take *The Temple* as a body of poems which are in some sense sequential, the opening lines of "The Temper" (II), following immediately after (I), reveal that the joy just attained is soon lost, and affliction and conflict return:

> It cannot be. Where is that mightie joy,
>    Which just now took up all my heart?
>    Lord, if thou must needs use thy dart,
> Save that, and me; or sin for both destroy.

A pattern similar to the alternate grief and joy, or spiritual darkness and illumination, of "The Temper" poems is observable in the four-poem sequence of "The Search," "Grief," "The Crosse," and "The Flower."[17] These four poems suggest, however, that the narrator is past the purgative and illuminative stages and is experiencing the dark night of the soul and then contemplative joy. They represent a steady progression of the soul, which by descending ascends. The speaker's "shrivel'd heart . . . was gone / Quite under ground" ("The Flower"). Although the speaker has a sense of sin, at least of past sins (see, for example, "The Search," 1. 28 and "The Flower," 1. 28), he has not abandoned God but feels, mistakenly, that God has abandoned him: "Whither, O, whither art thou fled, / My Lord, my Love," "The Search" begins. He is plunged deeper into the depths of grief, a repeated word throughout the four poems, by the sense that he has relapsed to a lower spiritual level after having attained illuminative joys and even that he is now farther away than when he first undertook his ascent to the Divine Center. All that the speaker feels—the absence of God, the sense of sin, the loss of the self's former peace and joy, the profound depths of grief and suffering, the apparent relapse to a lower spiritual level—are characteristics, according to Evelyn Underhill, of the dark night of the soul (*Mysticism*, 395). We recall Underhill's description of this dark night: "As in Purgation the senses were cleansed and humbled, and the energies and interests of the Self were concentrated upon transcendental things: so now the purifying process is extended to the very centre of I-hood, the will. The human instinct for personal happiness must be killed. This is the 'spiritual crucifixion' so often described by the mystics: the great desolation in which the soul seems abandoned by the Divine. The Self now surrenders itself, its individuality, and its will, completely. It desires nothing, asks nothing, is utterly passive, and is thus prepared for Union" (170). That purgation which St. John of the Cross calls the "passive night of the spirit" is an exceedingly painful process because the purging goes on against the will. The individual, like Herbert or his speaker, has progressed far along the *via mystica* and may assume he can on his own act to speed himself along in the presumably "right" direction. But still he feels frustrated of his final goal, and so there is an enormous and painful struggle—until he realizes that all his efforts, even the "good" ones, are in vain, which "good" efforts he must make in order to come to realize that all his efforts are in vain. And then, as Underhill says, "the purifying process is extended to the very centre of I-hood, the will." And then the self "surrenders itself, its individuality, and its will, completely . . . and is thus prepared for Union."

The speaker's griefs, as the poet knows, have the redemptive value of teaching him on his pulses the utter futility of the old Adam's willfulness, even when the will is bent toward a good end but presumes or acts "as if heav'n were mine own" ("The Flower"). This difficult lesson seems to necessitate much anguish in the learning. Indeed, the speaker's grief as recorded throughout *The Temple* and particularly in "The Search," "Grief," and "The Crosse" is cumulatively equivalent to the grief of the speaker of "The Sacrifice" and constitutes an affirmative response to Christ's refrain "Was ever grief like mine?" as the brilliant last stanza of "The Crosse" indicates:

> Ah my deare Father, ease my smart!
> These contrarieties crush me: these crosse actions
> Doe winde a rope about, and cut my heart:
> And yet since these thy contradictions
> Are properly a crosse felt by thy Sonne,
> With but foure words, my words, *Thy will be done.*

As in "Artillerie," when after stanzaic alternations between conflict and submission the speaker finally concedes "there is no articling with thee," and as in "The Temper" (I), when after averring that "sure thy way is best," he begins to understand that both grief and joy are somehow paradoxically equally God's love, so in "The Crosse," after affirming God's will Herbert experiences a spiritual renewal, confirmed in "The Flower." The ambiguity and wordplay of the last stanza of "The Crosse" are similar to the double sense of "I am thine" in "The Quip." The grievous "Crosse actions" felt by Herbert are indeed "properly a crosse felt by thy Sonne." By following Christ's example and making his words *"Thy will be done"* "my words," Herbert spiritually and actually realizes with Dame Julian in serious playfulness that God's Son and Adam, who is Everyman, are one man. By these means, the first Adam becomes the last Adam. Herbert could say with Walter Hilton that "it is a wonderful changing of a sinful wretch to be God's son made, through the right hand of him that is highest" (*The Goad of Love*, 144).

Coming shortly after the last stanza of "The Crosse," the third stanza of the much-discussed and deservedly-praised "The Flower," a poem revelatory of the correspondence between natural cyclical life and human spiritual life, is especially notable:

> These are thy wonders, Lord of Power,
> Killing and quickning, bringing down to hell
> And up to heaven in an houre;
> Making a chiming of a passing-bell.
> We say amisse,
> This or that is:
> Thy word is all, if we could spell.[18]

While the first half of the stanza echoes "The Temper" (I), the last three lines, as profound a mystical statement as one might find, have more than a single meaning. First, like Milton's Christ in *Paradise Regained*, whose preference for Hebraic over classical literature has critically been regarded as springing from a hierarchy of values which embodies an intense thirst for the beatific vision, Herbert believes that if one could read and comprehend by study God's word, the Bible, or scan and consider it intently (all various meanings of *spell* according to the O.E.D., which cites Herbert's "Shall he thy stature spell?") that would suffice for spiritual knowledge or "true wisdome." Secondly, the mystical sense seems to be that God's word as he is described in John 1, the Word that in the beginning was God, made all things, and was the true light and life of men, is all, at least to those who, truly understanding, receive him and become sons of

God (John 1: 11). When rightly apprehended, all else ("this or that") is egoistic illusion, and God's word, as sacred words (including especially *Thy will be done*) and as the Son of God, is all that really is.[19] Either human beings ("we") exist as Sons of God, last Adams, or we do not truly, fully, meaningfully exist at all.

Theologically and philosophically understood, the last three lines of the third stanza refer to the primary characteristic of either extrovertive or introvertive mystical experience, or they may refer to both. In the sensuous extrovertive type, the primary and central point around which all other characteristics revolve is, as noted in Chapter One, the apprehension of a unity taken to be in some way basic to the universe, frequently though not algotether satisfactorily expressed in formulas such as "All is One." Another such "formula," Herbert's own, might be "Thy word is all." The apprehension of a basic unity obtains in the Vision of Dame Kind. In the non-sensuous, introvertive type, the nuclear characteristic is "the Unitary Consciousness, from which all the multiplicity of sensuous or conceptual or other empirical content has been excluded, so that there remains only a void and empty unity" (Stace, *Mysticism and Philosophy*, 110). The voiding of the sensuous or "created" universe from the consciousness of the mystic for the sake of union with its uncreated essence obtains in the Vision of God. Is Herbert an extrovertive or introvertive mystic or both? Did he enjoy the Vision of Dame Kind or the Vision of God? While I do not wish to be unfair to Herbert and while I believe "Thy word is all" *may* be another formula for "All is One," I do not believe that Herbert is an extrovertive mystic or that he enjoyed the Vision of Dame Kind. Herbert may have wanted to believe and may well have believed that God is in everything, as any number of contemplatives know and have so experienced. But his poetry simply does not testify, as the poetry of Vaughan and Traherne and, for that matter, of Whitman and Lawrence and others in different ways does, to actual Visions of Dame Kind. His lines "Teach me, my God and King, / In all things thee to see" express a request, not a realization. Herbert is primarily an introvertive mystic, enjoying the Vision of God.

The idea and experience of God's omnipresence is so pervasive in the contemplatives, in the writings, to use Herbert's words, of the "Commenters and Fathers . . . and the Schoolmen, and the later Writers," whom "the Countrey Parson hath read," that it would be odd to contend that Herbert never read about the idea. We may recall that the orthodox Gregory of Nyssa writes, "The birth of godhead in our nature should not reasonably present itself as a strange novelty to those whose notions are not too limited. For who surveying the whole scheme of things is so childish as not to believe that there is divinity in everything, clothed in it, embracing it, residing in it?" Who, indeed? Gregory continues, "For everything that is depends on Him-Who-Is, nor can there be anything which has not its being in Him-Who-Is." In other words, "We say amisse, / This or that is: / Thy word is all, if we could spell." And Gregory concludes, "Then if all things are in the divinity, and the divinity is in all things, why are men embarrassed at the divine plan displayed in the revelation which tells us of the birth of God in humanity, since we believe that God is not outside mankind even now?" (Bettenson, *The Later Christian Fathers*, 134).[20] Herbert must have known, as his poetry indicates, of the idea of God's omnipresence, but his poetry suggests that he rather more believed in it intellectually than he actually saw it in a Vision of Dame Kind.

Herbert, like Donne and Vaughan, also believed in and no doubt witnessed the reality of good and evil. In Chapter Eleven of *Revelations of Divine Love*, the orthodox Julian of Norwich expresses the characteristic contemplative idea that "God does everything except sin" (80), holding that sin and evil *non est substantia*, as Augustine and Aquinas do. Theirs is essentially a monistic theory of substance and goodness as interchangeable, evil being understood as a privation of good, as nonbeing, which helps to explain why evil is so real and destructive, and distinguishable (though not always readily) from good. "God in fact does everything," Julian writes, and "Hence it follows that we must admit that everything that is done is well done, for it is our Lord God who does it. . . . There is no doer but he" (80, 81).[21] This doer is the Second Person of the Trinity, the Son, Logos, or Word. Richard E. Hughes points out that "In whatever body of philosophy the Logos or Word appears, it is always the principle of Order. It was left to the Church Fathers, most especially Origen and Clement, to emphasize the Johannine identification of the Logos with Christ and thus with the Incarnation. . . . The Incarnate Christ is Logos, Word, Order, Music, Intelligibility: this is the tradition lying behind Herbert's celebration of the Incarnations, the doctrine in which 'all thy sweets are packt up.' . . . For the Incarnation, as we have seen it defined, envisions a series of conflicts and triumphs: form overcoming inchoate matter, reason overcoming incomprehensibility. In such terms as these the Incarnation is both a theological and an artistic concern. What Incarnate Christ as Logos has done, so too the poet must do, bring order out of disorder and bestow divinity on raw matter" ("George Herbert and the Incarnation" in Roberts, ed., *Essential Articles*, 56, 58, 59). The Word does everything, according to the contemplatives. "Thy word is all," Herbert writes in a poem in which he also writes

> And now in age I bud again,
> After so many deaths I live and write;
> I once more smell the dew and rain,
> And relish versing: O my onely light,
>   It cannot be
>   That I am he
> On whom thy tempests fell all night.

And, of course, it is *not* "he / On whom thy tempests fell all night" who also does the writing, bringing order out of disorder. After "so many deaths," the first Adam at last gives up the ghost and the "I" as last Adam or Word can "live and write," for "I live and write, yet not I but Christ in me," to paraphrase a favorite mystical text. "Nothing is our own," Herbert writes in "The Holdfast," a poem which precedes "The Flower" by some twenty leaves and concludes:

> That all things were more ours by being his.
>  What Adam had, and forfeited for all,
> Christ keepeth now, who cannot fail or fall.

Herbert may not have actually perceived in a Vision of Dame Kind, as apparently Hopkins did, that Christ is everywhere, playing in ten thousand places, though he seems to have understood and expressed the idea intellectually and poetically. In a variation of the mine-thine distinction, he also delightfully understood the wonderful paradox "that all things were more ours by being his." And his fundamentally and pervasively eucharistic poetry, especially certain poems following "The Flower," reveals that through the mediation of the Word in communion he repeatedly experienced the rebirth of the godhead in his own nature, experienced the Word as the real inward doer within himself, enjoyed in this sense the introvertive Vision of God.

In "The Flower," Herbert is not "Fast in thy Paradise, where no flower can wither"; he is not "past changing" in final union, as he might be at the end of "The Church" in "Love" (III). Although he has not reached the tenth and last rung in the ladder of love described by St. John of the Cross, he has perhaps reached the eighth rung, which is characterized by knowing God at intervals and at least for short and intense periods. Even so, this should be recognized as a considerable achievement. Some of the critical confusion on Herbert's mysticism is owing to the failure to make sufficient and clear distinctions between process and result, between meditation and achieved (if temporarily) contemplation, between "the many Spiritual Conflicts" and the attained "perfect freedom." "The Flower," like a number of other poems in *The Temple*, points to such attainment:

> These are thy wonders, Lord of love,
> To make us see we are but flowers that glide:
> Which when we once can finde and prove,
> Thou hast a garden for us, where to bide.
> Who would be more,
> Swelling through store,
> Forfeit their Paradise by their pride.

Just as the corn of wheat that falls into the ground and dies brings forth much fruit, so the poet who undergoes "many deaths" blooms again in Paradise. Seeing that "we are but flowers that glide" is essentially equivalent to not clinging to the prideful life of the outward man and so finding life eternal as the Son of God.

"The Flower" is notably followed by, among other poems, poems on flowers and on poetry (weaving "A wreathed garland of deserved praise") and on eucharistic and eschatological themes. One of the eucharistic poems, "The Invitation," reads in its last stanza:

> Lord I have invited all,
> And I shall
> Still invite, still call to thee:
> For it seems but just and right
> In my sight,
> Where is All, there All should be.

All of the stanzas of "The Invitation" begin in the imperative mood, "Come ye hither all," except this quoted, last stanza. To whom might "thee" refer? Perhaps to the reader, more certainly to the "Lord" and/or the "all" of the last stanza's first line, but the very ambiguity of this pronominal reference implies, as the final line confirms, that All and All are or should be One, that the true self and Christ are essentially the same. In any case, here, perhaps, Herbert briefly comes close to the Vision of Philia more fully expressed in

Traherne's "Goodnesse" and other works, wherein the individual self is joined by other selves to form a single choir or Communion of Saints united in praise of God, like Dante's hymn of all Paradise, to realize the Mystical Body of Christ, to become him. The word play of the last line, "Where is All, there All should be," recalls "The Flower's" "Thy word is all." Tom Harpur writes that the Sacrament of Holy Communion "confirms the Jungian insight that deep down all humans are connected, one, and then lifts that communal perception to join in still deeper oneness with the source of all our beings, God" (42). *Sub specie aeternitatis*, God is all that truly is, and therefore, "The Invitation" suggests, all individuals in their true, unitive aspect, as pneuma or the last Adam, should be mystically united with God through the Anglican eucharistic feast. And the greater number of poems with eschatological themes at the end of "The Church" makes clearer the whole sequence's progress from time and meditation to eternity and contemplation.

But in the next poem, "The Banquet," also eucharistic, the focus turns again to the "I"-speaker, as it does in almost all the poems of "The Church," rather than being on all the other members of Christ's mystical body (though, of course, the "I" may represent all others). For, Herbert's main concern throughout continues to be on the I-Thou relationship of the Vision of God, rather than on the I-Others relationship of the Vision of Philia. This poem clearly concerns the eucharistic contemplative experience, if we take Herbert at his word in, for example, the second stanza:

> O what sweetnesse from the bowl
> > Fills my soul,
> Such as is, and makes divine!
> Is some starre (fled from the sphere)
> > Melted there
> As we sugar melt in wine?

As in "Artillerie," the "starre," often generally associated with saints, signals Christ's coming. While Herbert could not use "divine" in the modern, informal sense of "extremely good, unusually lovely" and while he *might* imply the late medieval and Renaissance sense of "excellent in a superhuman degree," he surely means "divine" as "pertaining to God" and as "partaking of the nature of God; godlike," and *perhaps* also "beatified" (the O.E.D. gives 1632 as the terminal year for the now obsolete meaning, "beatified"). In the words of the contemplative Church Fathers, by means of the eucharistic banquet, Herbert or the speaker or the devout communicant "may be deified," "united to [the Son] bodily and inseparably," and "advance[d] to unity with the Father." Recalling the timeless, mythic "There is but one" day of "Easter" and the flight motif of "Easter-wings" and other poems, Herbert writes in "The Banquet" "Wine becomes a wing at last,"

> For with it alone I flie
> To the skie:
> Where I wipe mine eyes, and see
> What I seek, for what I sue;
> Him I view,
> Who hath done so much for me.

With their eucharistic mysticism, these lines suggest that the Vision of God is in part a matter of right apprehension, that, as "The Flower" instructs, we see amiss this or that is; thy Word is all if we could see with wiped, cleansed, opened eyes. Herbert's flight to Heaven and the sight of God is a eucharistic one. With such purified vision, Herbert can say "Him I view."

Two leaves hence, Herbert begins "The Elixir":

> Teach me, my God and King,
> In all things thee to see.

For, as Julian writes, "the fullness of joy is to see God in all things" (114). Although Herbert uses alchemical language as Donne does in "The Canonization" and although "all things" *could* include the human beloved, we may be reasonably confident that Herbert is not here referring to a Vision of Eros. Unlike Donne, Herbert left no such poems, but he wrote poems, like the sonnets sent to his mother from Cambridge, that repudiated such poetry. Perhaps the alchemical imagery of "The Elixir" is turned against some of that poetry. The opening lines could reasonably be read as a plea for a Vision of Dame Kind and perhaps also for a Vision of Philia, such visions as we find in Vaughan and Traherne. The speaker does plainly ask in these lines to be taught to see God in all things. Having had Visions of God as actual experiences and apparently having the belief and intellectual understanding that "all things are in the divinity, and the divinity is in all things," Herbert might well be asking for Visions of Dame Kind and perhaps also Visions of Philia. The line "All may of thee partake" not only may refer to Holy Communion but also seems to confirm that Herbert understood, as contemplatives generally do, that all creatures and things may partake of or participate in God, though not be of God's substance. The elixir, "the famous stone / That turneth all to gold" and "makes drudgerie divine," is the wise man's "tincture," which is the words "for thy sake"; and the "all" may include the self. Every deed, event, or word may be turned into a meditation (an "extemporal" rather than a "deliberate" meditation, to use Bishop Joseph Hall's terminology—see Huntley, 21) by the phrase "for thy sake," which is but another way of saying "not my will but thy will be done." As St. John of the Cross advises, when the self is not caught up in the bliss of contemplation, then it ought to return to meditation. When the hunger for ultimate reality, God, is profound enough, then every moment of one's life through the elixir may become a meditation, a prayer for union. And union may be realized directly, inwardly, introvertively, in a Vision of God, the vision Herbert usually seeks and sometimes finds; or since, as Julian writes, "God is in man, and God is in everything" (75), union may be realized indirectly through God's book, "in all things," people, creatures, objects, in kinds of visions Herbert (or the speaker) apparently prayed for.

The eschatological poems, "Death," "Dooms-day," "Judgement," and "Heaven," which precede "Love" (III), help to move "The Church" out of time into eternity and return us to "The Altar" both in the sense that these poems lead to the Lord's table of "Love" (III) and in the sense that they also help to move "The Church" toward silence. "The Altar" concluded

> That, if I chance to hold my peace,
> These stones to praise thee may not cease.
> O let thy blessed SACRIFICE be mine,
> and sanctifie this ALTAR to be thine.

In Herbert's beginning is his end. The ideal is silence, "to hold my peace," for "it is in the stillness, in the silence, that the word of God is to be heard. There is no better avenue of approach to this Word than through stillness, through silence" (*Meister Eckhart*, trans. Blakney, 107). In "The Church" Herbert begins writing, singing, with the hope of holding his peace (meaning both coming to peace and to silence) and of paradoxically thereby forever praising God, "these stones" being, among other things, the poems of "The Church." How can Herbert be silent and praise God? The answer lies, as so much else does, in the two selves. In other words, the answer is "Thy word is all, if we could spell." If the first Adam will hold his peace, the last Adam will write the poetry. The Word is Logos, Order, Music. The life of poetry, always regarded as inspiration from the gods, and the life of the Spirit are one, after all; this must be so if "I am thine" and "Thy word is all." Imagination and Love are inextricably interconnected synthesizing faculties. After "Judgement," wherein the speaker thrusts a Testament into God's hand and says "There thou shalt finde my faults are thine," Herbert comes to "Heaven," which, like "Paradise," in the interest of moving toward silence employs the echo technique. The answer is in the question:

> O Who will show me those delights on high?
> *Echo.*     I.
> Thou Echo, thou are mortall, all men know.
> *Echo.*     No.
> Wert thou not born among the trees and leaves?
> *Echo.*     Leaves.
> And are there any leaves, that still abide?
> *Echo.*     Bide.
> What leaves are they? impart the matter wholly.
> *Echo.*     Holy.
> Are holy leaves the Echo then of blisse?
> *Echo.*     Yes.
> Then tell me, what is that supreme delight?
> *Echo.*     Light.
> Light to the minde: what shall the will enjoy?
> *Echo.*     Joy.
> But are there cares and businesse with the pleasure?
> *Echo.*     Leisure.
> Light, joy, and leisure; but shall they perserver?
> *Echo.*     Ever.

The very technique of the poem, in the echoic answers of its two voices, shows the two "I"s or Adams coming much closer together, if not yet quite identical. The answer is in the question, and thereby Herbert is holding his peace. As in "The Quip," *"thou shalt answer, Lord, for me"*; "Speak not at large; say, I am thine." The Echo of "Heaven" is not mortal and was born among the "Leaves," the leaves of the good book, surely, and also the leaves of *The Temple.* Indeed, here as everywhere, "Thy word is all," and the Word is the doer, the speaker, the writer. In alternating lines, God rimes with Herbert, so to speak. Like the poetic and spiritual life, Herbert and God are at one through the mediation of the Word throughout and especially at the end of "The Church" in "Love" (III).

But before we speak at large about the last poem let us briefly note that "Heaven," like "The Church" generally, is filled with unitary consciousness, holiness, bliss, light, joy, and eternity or timelessness. These distinctive contemplative characteristics, discussed by Stace, echo the "Softnesse, and peace, and joy, and love, and blisse" of "Prayer" (I), the language of which in turn is echoed throughout "The Church" in ways too numerous to detail.

While I find Stanley Fish's fine work on Herbert to be generally insightful and consistent with some of my own views, I must take exception and offer a different emphasis in regard to a few points, particularly as they relate to "Love" (III). In his reading of "Love" (III), Fish writes that the speaker loses the contest of courtesy: "(he never had a chance) and with it his independent will. This, of course, is the goal of the Christian life ('In him we live and move and have our being'), but in this poem Herbert chooses to emphasize the price we pay for it, the price of knowing that it has been paid for by another. Vendler says that 'during the actual progress of the poem,' the distance between God and the soul 'shrinks' (p. 274). In a way this is true, but the process is less comfortably benevolent than she implies because what shrinks or is shrunk is the speaker's self. He has been killed with kindness." And Fish concludes: "It is easy to see why many readers (including this one) would like it otherwise, would like to reach a 'plateau of assurance' and feel some measure of personal satisfaction at having attained it (along with the speaker) after so many false starts and defeated expectations. This is not to say that 'Love III' communicates no sense of closure, but that it is a closure which, rather than being earned, is imposed. Insofar as we know that and know too that this tasting of 'the churches mysticall repast' is only preliminary to another siege of doubts and questions, we will have been driven to another deep and dark point of religion" (*The Living Temple*, 135, 136).

While he attends adequately and insightfully to the shrinking or diminishing or destruction of the self, what Fish neglects or insufficiently emphasizes is the simultaneous, paradoxical expanding or exaltation or re-creation of the self.[22] In traditional terms, he attends to the death of the first Adam but tends to overlook or slight the rebirth of the last Adam. Indeed, it would be more accurate to speak of the shrinking, diminishing, or destruction of the non-self for the sake of the full emergence of the essential self. Familiarity with contemplative tradition should help avoid the oversight Fish makes. This overlooking is understandable in that what is, appropriately, most apparent throughout "The Church" is the sense of unworthiness and the self-abnegating, which contributes to (but does not on its own) achieve worthiness and self-exaltation. Fish is quite right to say the speaker's self (better, non-self) has been killed with kindness, but he should add the vital other half of the truth: the real self is reborn with that ego-killing kindness. The whole progress from discursive meditation to loving-imaginative contemplation, the whole oscillating process of spiritual death and rebirth may indeed be initially and repeatedly painful (the ego dies hard, or, as Fish writes, "there is nothing easy about the 'letting go'" *Self-Consuming*, 157), but the whole process is essentially benevolent and loving. Weal or woe, both are equally God's love, particularly insofar as the woe arises out of the ego's refusal to let go. To paraphrase Blake, if the ego will persist in its folly, which causes the self (and others) pain, it will become wise, and in that transformation the self enters bliss. Other ways of saying this is that suffering is redemptive or that the Fall, every fall, is ultimately fortunate, a very basic Christian doctrine.

Fish reads the line "You must sit down, sayes Love, and taste my meat" as a polite covering for a naked command, "as if your hostess were to entreat you for the fifth of sixth time . . .'you must try some of my cheese-puffs'" (*The Living Temple*, 134). However, Love, Christ, the Host, is not offering cheese-puffs to some other person but meat, his own bloody and bloodless self-sacrifices, which nourishing food gives life, rest, peace, holiness, joy, blessedness, and so on, to his other self. The closure of "Love" (III) is not imposed but earned and granted as in "Redemption's" *Your suit is granted*. Who earns it? As noted in Chapter One, meditation and contemplation refer to an earlier and a later kind of prayer, and contemplation was further understood as a union with God which discursive meditation cannot produce. As also noted, there is no absolute disjunction but rather a continuity, interrelationship, and movement back and forth between meditation and contemplation and the stages of the mystical life. Many of the alternations in Herbert's poetry may be accounted for in these traditional terms. Saint John of the Cross, for example, recommends that progressives, who have begun to receive graces of mystical contemplation, should return to active meditation whenever they observe that the soul is not occupied in mystical repose and knowledge, and he adds that meditation is the ordinary and frequent means of disposing oneself for contemplation. The first

Adam does not earn mystical repose but may dispose himself for it. By bloody and bloodless sacrifice, the last Adam earns and grants mystical union. To whom? Why, of course, to himself, his true self, who was or seemed to be "the other" before union. Expressed another way, by suffering and unitive eucharistic partaking, as recorded in "The Church," the self realizes its true nature. As *Saint* Catherine of Genoa reveals, "My Me is God, nor do I recognize any other Me except my God Himself"; and *Saint* Bernard asserts, "In those respects in which the soul is unlike God, it is also unlike itself" (cited in Huxley, *The Perennial Philosophy*, 18).

Meditation is the effort that is not earning. And while the suppliant is always on his own unworthy, that same suppliant is paradoxically worthy when Love says "Your suit is granted" or "You shall be he." He must be worthy (if he cannot be worthy on his own, and the first Adam cannot be, then it must be by the last Adam deeming him worthy); otherwise, he remains profane ("Avoid, Profanenesse; come not here"— "Superliminare") and the sitting down and eating becomes gross sacrilege rather than eucharistic feast. To see and think in contemplative terms is to see through "the contradiction that exists at [the] heart" of Herbert's poetry, "the contradiction between the injunction to do work . . . and the realization, everywhere insisted upon, that the work has already been done" (Fish, *The Living Temple*, 169)—to see through the contradiction as a seeming contradiction only, as the paradox that the work to do in time (and it remains to do in time) is the work that has already been done in eternity (and it continues to be done for all eternity).

This paradox and others permeate "Love" (III), which presents time and tense complexly:

*Love (III)*

Love bade me welcome: yet my soul drew back,
    Guiltie of dust and sinne.
But quick-ey'd Love, observing me grow slack
    From my first entrance in,
Drew nearer to me, sweetly questioning,    5
    If I lack'd any thing.

A guest, I answer'd, worthy to be here:
    Love said, You shall be he.
I the unkinde, ungratefull? Ah my deare,
    I cannot look on thee.    10
Love took my hand, and smiling did reply,

Who made the eyes but I?

Truth Lord, but I have marr'd them: let my shame
Go where it doth deserve.
And know you not, sayes Love, who bore the blame?     15
My deare, then I will serve.
You must sit down, sayes Love, and taste my meat:
So I did sit and eat.

The Lord's table or altar is where this poem takes place. The back and forth movement of the poem, especially its opening, recapitulates the alternating movement of "The Church," repeated spiraling alternations being signals of advanced spiritual stages. The first two stanzas are in the past tense. The first two lines of the third stanza may be a present statement in the dialogue about past and future actions, but in any case provide a transition to the present tense of line 15: "And know you not, sayes Love, who bore the blame?" Whereas the action of Love in the first two stanzas is described in past tense verbs ("bade," "Drew," "said," "did reply"), Love now speaks in the present ("sayes") about the past-but-eternal act of a self "who bore the blame" by sacrifice and death so that for all time and eternity all may live. (Two earlier leaves off doth lie "Judgement," which concludes in future tense that in the Word "thou shalt finde my faults are thine.") Presumably, it is the invited guest who then says "My deare, then I will serve," indicating a reformed disposition of the will for his future behavior certainly, but perhaps also for the *immediate* future which is the present. Who is this guest who would willingly be a servant? A pertinent text from the Good Word sheds light: "Blessed are those servants whom the lord when he cometh shall find watching: verily I say unto you, that he shall gird himself, and make them to sit down to meat, and will come forth and serve them" (Luke 12:37). Love comes forth as the host and servant who "sayes" to the guest who would willingly be a servant "You must sit down . . . and taste my meat." Clearly, the guest, the served, the servant, the host (also meaning the eucharist), and Love paradoxically are one in mystical union, "The churches mystical repast." Like, but also unlike, Donne's "The Exstasie," "Love" (III) is a "dialogue of one." The guest's saying (the unattributed line) "My deare, then I will serve" (said in the present for all of the future) anticipates and leads to Love's becoming the servant. In the real sense that it is and can only be the last Adam who submissively (willingly negating ego-will) speaks line 16, and in so speaking effects self-transformation, both guest and Love say "My deare, then I will serve." As "the world" and "we" in "Man" may "both thy servants be," so both speakers in "Love" (III) become servants, and are thereby one, a single unitary consciousness uttering the same words, as in "my words, *Thy will be done.*" He who humbles himself shall be exalted. (The "I" being representative, all are invited, as in the eucharistic "The Invitation," "Where is All, there All should be.") "So I did sit and eat." "Not only ought we to see the Lord," John Chrysostom, writing on the Eucharist, advises, "we ought to take him in our hands, eat him, put our teeth into his flesh, and unite ourselves with him in the closest union" (Bettenson, *The Later Christian Fathers*, 175). Citing John 6:41, "I am the living bread who came down from heaven," the Church Father Ambrose asks "How, then, did bread come down from heaven—and bread that is 'living bread'?" He answers, "Because our Lord Jesus Christ shares both in divinity and in body: and you, who receive the flesh, partake of his divine substance in that food" (Bettenson, *The Later Christian Fathers*, 185). "Whoso eateth my flesh, and drinketh my blood, hath eternal life; and I will raise him up at the last day. For my flesh is meat indeed, and by blood is drink indeed. He that eateth my flesh, and drinketh my blood, dwelleth in me, and I in him" (John 6:54–56).

These texts may also help illuminate the tense of the last line, "So I did sit and eat." Why after the present tense of lines 15 to 17 does Herbert conclude with past tense? First, the auxillary verb "did" lends emphasis to the main verbs "sit and eat." Secondly, since "Love" (III) recapitulates "The Church," the last line refers back to the many eucharistic eternal now-moments of "The Church." Thirdly, just as in line 15 Love speaks in the present ("sayes") about the past but timeless, eternal act of the self "who bore the blame" by sacrificial death so that for all time and eternity all may live, so in the last line the "I," who is all the "I"s of "The Church" and who is the guest, served, servant, Lord, host, and Love, by the past (and perhaps present) but timeless, eternal acts of eating is raised up and reborn to eternal life (every timeless now-moment is an apocalyptic last day), partaking in the closest union of the divine substance in that food. More simply, every (past) eucharistic union paradoxically occurs in time and in timelessness.

The punning line "Who made the eyes but I?" which precedes the tense-shifting last stanza confirms the idea that the "I"s or speaker(s) of "The Church" are many yet one and that there is no doer but Love. The only truly real "I" is the Love which made the eyes ("I"s) and "turns the sun and other stars," as Dante says. Also, the "I" at the end of line 12 is a pun on the eye which is a traditional image of God. "The eye by which I see God," as Eckhart expresses it, "is the same as the eye by which God sees me. My eye and God's eye are one and the same—one in seeing, one in knowing, and one in loving" (*Meister Eckhart*, trans. Blakney, 206). A eucharistic feast at the allegorical level, "Love" (III) is, anagogically, a description of the soul's perfection in union with Christ.[23] The first and last Adams, the guest, the served, the servant, the host, and Love become one in communion, that is, in the temporal bloodless re-enactment of Christ's sacrifice which is timeless union.

With "The Altar," "The Sacrifice," and following poems, "The Church" begins in meditation with the need for purgation and with a deep awareness of the Passion and Crucifixion, emblems of purgation; it proceeds through many purgative afflictions, dark nights, and temporary illuminations, as well illustrated, for example, in the sequence of poems from "The Search" through "The Flower"; and in order to, as Chrysostom says, "unite ourselves with him in the closest union" (Bettenson, *The Later Christian Fathers*, 175), it culminates contemplatively with the meaning of the Incarnation, union, through a final celebration among many of the bloodless re-enactment of the Passion and Crucifixion, a holy communion, "the churches mysticall repast." It is one complex, perfect model of the *via mystica*. Its rich alternating and spiraling complexity reveals how much easier it is to utter the lovely Athanasian aphorism and ideal, "God became man that man might become God," than to realize it. Typically, in Herbert's poems the self is to be at once obliterated and exalted; that is, the willful, combative, self-seeking, fallen Adam must die, and the new Adam must arise reborn, atoned, and united to God. After many griefs, Herbert sees the absurdity of opposing, even in presumably good causes, the finite, illusory ego against the infinite real Self; he knows he has free will in order to will his self-will out of existence and so eventually come to live continuously in a state of atonement, "at-one-ment." He thinks of the Incarnation as a constantly renewed fact of experience. As the three Magi were led, historically, by a star to the place of the Incarnation, so Herbert throughout "The Church," as in "Artillerie," is led, imaginatively, by a star to an understanding of the Incarnation in its full sacramental meaning, to the paradoxical and profound realization of his being in God or God's being in him. In Meister Eckhart's words, "God's being is my life, but if it is so, then what is God's must be mine and what is mine God's. God's is-ness [*istigkeit*] is my is-ness, and neither more nor less" (trans. Blakney, 180). Herbert's mode of articulating this central contemplative idea throughout

"The Church" is less abstract and philosophical but no less precise. "Your suit is granted." "I am thine." "I am but finite, yet thine infinitely." "Thy word is all." "So I did sit and eat." For in God's "Providence," "all things have their will, yet none but thine." On his final note of holding his peace and totally affirming divine will, Herbert's infinitely enhanced true Self may "end in rest."

# 4

# HENRY VAUGHAN
## *"I saw Eternity the other night"*

What was generally observed earlier about critical views on mysticism in seventeenth-century poetry applies also specifically to Vaughan. As with Donne's and Herbert's poetry, critical opinion concerning meditation and contemplation in Henry Vaughan's poetry is strongly divided. First, there are those critics, most notably Louis Martz, who argue ably and knowledgeably that Vaughan is a meditative poet; secondly, those, like Helen White, Itrat Husain, R. A. Durr, Cleanth Brooks, H. J. Oliver, and Anthony Low, who adduce considerable scholarship to establish Vaughan not primarily as a meditative but as a mystical poet; and, thirdly, those, such as E. L. Marilla, James Simmonds, Frank Kermode, and Jonathan Post, who with seemingly equal skill contend that he is not at all a mystic or who at least reject the primacy of mysticism.[1]

One reason for the critical division regarding Vaughan's mysticism simply involves the matter of which poems a critic focuses upon. Some of Vaughan's poems, like "Peace," are conventionally religious and pious; some, like "The Search," are mainly meditative; but others, usually Vaughan's most distinguished and highly regarded poems, have profound and powerful mystical elements in them, sometimes alongside the pious and meditative elements. Hence critics may well be divided and hence the answer to the question is Vaughan a mystical poet (which some critics answer yes and others no) is yes and no—depending on which Vaughan one has in mind, which of his poems one is referring to, whether one believes a few or many poems must be mystical before designating a poet mystical, and, especially, how one understands the meaning of "mysticism." Some critics, for example, apparently take "mysticism" in diminished, trivial, or vague senses, as a visionary exaltation or "sudden visitation" (Marilla, 165) or a kind of "otherworldliness" (Brooks, 5). Another critic argues that Vaughan's poetic subjects are devotional or meditative but that "he is in no sense at all a mystic" (Kermode, 225), as if these terms were mutually exclusive rather than interconnected and conducive one to the other. Still another scholar seems to associate "mystical vision" with "emotional rapture, ecstasy, or excitement of one kind or another" (Simmonds, 20).[2]

As with Donne's and Herbert's poetry, critical confusion concerning mysticism in Vaughan's poetry also arises from the failure carefully to distinguish the stages of the spiritual life, the differences between meditation and contemplation, and the different kinds of mystical Visions. In an effort to clarify the question of mysticism in Vaughan's poetry and to illustrate the kind of study of individual poems necessary for determining the nature and extent of Vaughan's mysticism, section II of this chapter will first, through a detailed analysis, observe some of the meditative, contemplative, and biblical elements in a familiar and famous poem of Vaughan's, "The Night," a poem much discussed by critics and variously regarded as Metaphysical, Hermetic, meditative, or mystical; section III will then discuss "The Night" and its mystical elements in the illuminating context of ancient-medieval-Renaissance contemplative tradition (with special focus on St. John of the Cross) and of the stages and common characteristics of mysticism; and section IV, touching upon the important matter of sequences, will discuss the archetype of death and rebirth and the Visions of Dame Kind and of God in a number of Vaughan's other poems. Finally, as a transition to Chapter Five's discussion of the modern period and in a partial recapitulation of some of the important points of this and previous chapters, section V will offer some comparisons of Donne, Herbert, and Vaughan.

## II

My view, in essence, is that "The Night" is a paradoxical prayer in which Vaughan draws mainly on the Bible as source; its structure is that of a modified meditation; it is pervaded by a number of the distinctive characteristics of mysticism; it indicates the realization of the mystical stages of Illumination and the Dark Night of the Soul; and its intention and goal are infused contemplation or mystical Union in a Vision of God. "The Night" is a mystical poem, let me emphasize, not because it may contain allusions to Dionysius or St. John, as it does to the Bible, but because it exhibits unmistakable signs of mystical consciousness and experience.[3]

Vaughan's reference to John 2:3, heading "The Night," should read John 3:2. The Fourth Gospel is, according to Dean Inge, the charter of Christian mysticism, and Jesus' conversation with Nicodemus in chapter 3 is among those Johannine passages most valued by mystics (see Happold, 164, 166). John 3:2 tells of the Pharisee, Nicodemus, a ruler of the Jews, who "came to Jesus by night, and said unto him, Rabbi, we know that thou art a teacher come from God: for no man can do these miracles that thou doest, except God be with him." Jesus answers in paradox, the language of mystical religion, that "Except a man be born again . . . of water and *of* the spirit, he cannot enter into the Kingdom of God" (John 3:3, 5). This paradox of rebirth, then, is the essential text for Vaughan's poem. Employing the image of the night, it is extended throughout the poem: just as Nicodemus "did at midnight speak with the Sun" so Vaughan prays for the mystical experience whereby he might be reborn and "enter into the Kingdom of God," "where I in him," the "deep, but dazling darkness," "Might live invisible and dim."

Of course, not all paradox is mystical, but mystical consciousness and experience, in plain contradiction of the laws of logic, are radically and distinctively paradoxical. As noted, W. T. Stace includes paradoxicality among the common characteristics of both extrovertive and introvertive mystical experiences (*Mysticism and Philosophy*, 131 *et passim*), and he also lists and discusses some of the major paradoxes of mysticism (253 *et passim*). These paradoxes are not the merely verbal and witty kinds but those having to do with the discovery of hidden affinities or identities between disparate phenomena and with the consequent compelling deduction that some aspects of reality are inconsistent with certain logical patterns of human thinking and therefore that some thinking has to be modified, made more imaginative and realistic. The fundamental and most important mystical paradox, as we observed in Chapter One, is that of the dual and contradictory nature of human beings, who have, as it were, two selves: an ego or false self and a true Self, this latter being identical with divinity (or, at the least, made in the divine image): "I in him / Might live invisible and dim." Many biblical passages are metaphors for the essential transformation or experience of giving up the illusional, egoistic life to realize the life of the true Self. As noted, this central paradox of gain through loss, of life through death, embodies the traditional distinction between the outward and the inward man, between the first Adam who is a living soul and the last Adam who is a quickening spirit (1. Cor. 15:45). And, as also observed, traveling the *via mystica* is the highest act of self-knowledge: it is to make that spiritual journey, often begun in prayer, whereby one is transformed from egohood to selfhood; it is to be transhumanized, in Dante's phrase, from man into a god.

Significantly, stanzas 5 and 6 of "The Night" specifically concern meditation and contemplation, or prayer, as the preparation for the desired "infused contemplation" of stanza 9. Adopting Martz's outline of the meditative structure, we find that "The Night," like Donne's "The Exstasie," falls into three distinguishable parts: composition, analysis, and colloquy; these parts correspond to the acts of memory, understanding, and will. Although there are actually no hard and fast lines, we might profitably view the stanzas of the poem as corresponding to the above division in this manner: stanzas 1 and 2, the composition, set the scene in discussing Nicodemus' finding of God during a time of literal and spiritual darkness; stanzas 3 to 6, the analysis, raise the question how one is to know God during the present age, which is also a time of spiritual darkness, and give the partial and temporary answer that during literal darkness, the night, one may come closer to God through prayer and love; stanzas 7 to 9, the colloquy, consider the inevitable coming of daylight with its evils and conclude therefore with the wish for mystical union with the "deep, but dazling darkness," such union being the full and final permanent answer.[4]

> Through that pure *Virgin-shrine*,
> That sacred vail drawn o'r thy glorious noon
> That men might look and live as Glo-worms shine,
> And face the Moon:
> Wise *Nicodemus* saw such light
> As made him know his God by night. 6

> Most blest believer he!
> Who in that land of darkness and blinde eyes
> Thy long expected healing wings could see,
> When thou didst rise,
> And what can never more be done,
> Did at mid-night speak with the Sun! 12

Although the phrase "that pure *Virgin-shrine*" may refer to the mother of Christ, the Virgin Mary, who was conceived immaculately and with whom "the Moon" is traditionally associated, it refers primarily to the stainless temple of Christ's mortal body; for, ultimately, both "pure *Virgin-shrine*" and "sacred vail" mean the flesh which is the veil that dims the divine glory of Christ in order that men, Nicodemus here in particular, might see the veiled Son whose unveiled light, "thy glorious noon," would be too bright for ordinary men. The conventional, poetic Son-Sun pun is involved in the complex analogical metaphor of stanza 1: as the moon dimly reflects the sun, so the mortal Christ (who was given flesh by a woman traditionally associated with the moon) is a dimmed divinity; moreover, as glowworms may shine only in the relatively dim light of the moon, so mortal men may see only a dimmed divinity, a veiled or fleshly son, for they cannot gaze with the naked physical eye upon the unveiled, divine brightness of the Son (Exodus 33:20). Paradoxically, then, divinity is veiled in order that it may be revealed.

That Vaughan drew heavily on biblical sources becomes more and more evident on examination. The main source of Vaughan's symbol of the veil is, as M. M. Mahood observes, the Bible, "where St. Paul had already achieved a fusion between different symbolistic uses of the word 'veil'. For the Apostle, Isaiah's prophecy, 'And he will destroy in this mountaine the face of the covering cast over all people, and the vail that is spread over all nations,' [Isa. 25:7] was fulfilled when the rent veil of the Temple disclosed 'a new and living way, which he hath consecrated for us, through the vail, that is to say, his flesh' [Hebrews 10:20]." Vaughan uses the word *veil* variously to stand for "*the Old Law, time, the body,* and *the limits of the physical world*: four barriers between the soul and God which were penetrated in [the Incarnation and] the first Resurrection and which are to be destroyed at the last" (263, 264). Although the "vail" as Christ's body is the dominant meaning, some of these other meanings of *veil* may be implicit in line 2. Moreover, because all created things point to the creator and are symbols by which he may be partially known, the night itself is also a "vail." Thus line 6 is profoundly rich: Nicodemus knew "his god by night," that is, during the literal night time, in the flesh, and perhaps through created things, though Nicodemus' distinction of course is that he knew his God directly as Jesus Christ. Part of the great accomplishment of "The Night" resides in the ways that Vaughan, largely though not entirely through biblical allusion, confers a rich multisignificance upon words like *vail, night, darkness,* and *light.*

Several verses in *John* underlie stanza 2. To the skeptical Jews, Jesus says "I am the light of the world: he that followeth me shall not walk in darkness, but shall have the light of life" (John 8:12). The first chapter of *John* is of course full of comment relevant to these lines: "And the light shineth in darkness; and the darkness comprehended it not. . . . He was in the world, and the world was made by him, and the world knew him not. He came unto his own, and his own received him not" (John 1:5, 10, 11). And finally, "this is the condemnation, that light is come into the world, and men loved darkness rather than light, because their deeds were evil" (John 3:19). The "land of darkness and blinde eyes" is Israel in the time of Christ; the darkness here is evil, the sin and ignorance of the non-believers, who are blind to God, though He stood veiled in flesh before their eyes. Nicodemus is the exceptional man; before the Pharisees in the temple he defends Christ (John 7:50ff). Lines 9 and 10 have their source in Malachi 4:2. "But unto you that fear my name shall the Sun of righteousness arise with healing in his wings;" and in *The Mount of Olives* Vaughan writes: "Thou Sun of righteousness with healing under thy wings arise in my heart" (Martin, 151). In the poem, "Sun" is of course a play on the "Son" who is Christ; thus the ambiguous "rise," which inevitably implies the resurrection of Christ, is more forcefully felt. Though it is not essential, possibly Vaughan also assumes that Nicodemus was among the disciples to whom Christ appeared after His resurrection (John 20:19ff.). It is more certain, however, that "mid-night" in line 12 and therefore "by night" in line 6 are used both literally and figuratively to mean the night as the dark part of the diurnal cycle and the night or darkness as an era or period of sin and ignorance in Israel.

The transition to the personalized stanza 3, which begins the analysis, is more smoothly felt when one considers that seventeenth century England, like the Israel of Christ's time, was a land of religious as well as political strife, as Vaughan well knew.[5]

<blockquote>

O who will tell me, where
He found thee at that dead and silent hour!
What hallow'd solitary ground did bear
    So rare a flower,
Within whose sacred leafs did lie
The fulness of the Deity.                   18

   No mercy-seat of gold,
No dead and dusty *Cherub*, nor carv'd stone,
But his own living works did my Lord hold
    And lodge alone;
Where *trees* and *herbs* did watch and peep
And wonder, while the *Jews* did sleep.       24

  Dear night! this worlds defeat;
The stop to busie fools; cares check and curb;
The day of Spirits; my souls calm retreat
    Which none disturb!

</blockquote>

*Christs* progress, and his prayer time;
The hours to which high Heaven doth chime.                    30

Gods silent, searching flight:
When my Lords head is fill'd with dew, and all
His locks are wet with the clear drops of night;
His still, soft call;
His knocking time; The souls dumb watch,
When Spirits their fair kindred catch.                        36

The analysis starts with a sense of the absence of God, specifi-
cally with the realization that men and particularly the I-narrator
can no longer speak with Christ in Israel at night nor, for that mat-
ter, anywhere on earth, day or night—not, that is, in the literal sense
as Nicodemus did. But stanzas 3 and 4 not only carry over the literal
neutral significance and the figurative pejorative significance of
"night," but also continue to suggest and begin to explore an hon-
orific significance which attaches to "night," this last meaning
being most explicitly developed in stanzas 5 and 6. Stanza 3, which
is dominated by important garden and flower imagery, an imagery as-
sociated with one of the three major contemplative metaphors (see
Durr, 29–78), begins with Vaughan's wish that he might repeat
Nicodemus' experience of finding God "by night." This stanza's first
two lines could carry all three meanings of "by night" just dis-
cussed: during the literal night time, in the flesh, and through
created things. Because the first two meanings of "night" are no
longer available as ways of finding Christ, the next few stanzas, as
we shall see, propose still another way, that of prayer at night. The
paradox of Light veiled in a land of darkness is in stanza 3 restated
in terms of flower imagery and symbolism: the flower presents only
its outer appearance, but hidden within is the total divinity;
paradoxically, it took root in a sunless garden, the land of Israel. This
suggests that the calcified heart may yet be regenerated. Subsequent
stanzas develop this suggestion and continue the garden imagery in
mystically significant terms.

Understood as "the golden covering placed upon the Ark of
the Covenant and regarded as the resting-place of God" (O.E.D.),
"mercy-seat" alludes to Exodus 25:17ff.: "And thou shalt make a
mercy seat of pure gold . . . And thou shalt make two cherubins of
gold . . . in the two ends of the mercy seat . . . and thou shalt put
the mercy seat above upon the ark; and in the ark thou shalt put the
testimony that I shall give thee." Christ's coming replaces or supple-
ments the old law, as is symbolized by the rending of the temple veil.

"But Christ being come an high priest of good things to come, by a greater and more perfect tabernacle [his body and blood], not made with hands, that is to say, not of this building" (Hebrews 9:11). Thus, we read lines 19–22 as: it was not the mercy seat, not mere dead stone but his own living works which did hold the Lord and lodge him alone. "Living works" may refer to Christ's deeds, his miracles, and to his true followers, both of which or whom testify to his divinity, and indeed may refer to the human body and blood born of the Virgin Mary. But given the context of stanzas 3 and 4 and especially the dominant garden and flower imagery, it is clear that "living works" particularly refers to the physical creation (theologically understood to be created by the Second Person) and specifically to watching, wakeful, plant nature, the *trees* and *herbs* which are alive to Christ, while "the *Jews*," human nature with a heart of stone, in the night indifferently close their eyes to Him. Stanza 4, especially its last two lines, is also reminiscent of the garden of Gethsemane (Matthew 26:39ff.), where Christ's followers slept after he had asked them to watch and pray with him. Vaughan often writes of plant nature being in sympathy with and testifying to God; a plant's growing and striving upward makes it an apt and natural symbol for such sympathy and testimony. Throughout his poetry he frequently uses "a stone" as the symbol of the unregenerate heart. The ultimate source for the central image of *Silex Scintillans*, the flint and stone (heart-shaped in the 1650 title page) which must be struck before it can emit a fire, is, again, the Old Testament; and, notably, Ezekiel 36 addresses sinful Israel, promising to cleanse and deliver it "into your own land," the promised Edenic Garden: "A new heart also will I give you, and a new spirit will I put within you: and I will take away the stony heart out of your flesh and I will give you an heart of flesh" (36:26). Thus stanza 4 suggests, as subsequent stanzas bear out, that in order to hold and lodge the Lord, the stony heart must be refined and regenerated; the heart must become pure as a flower, like the "trees and herbs" alert to Christ, watered by the dew of his blood. (Concerning Christ in the Garden of Gethsemane, Luke 22:44 reads: "and his sweat was as it were great drops of blood falling down to the ground.") The way of the flowers which held commerce with Christ at night is, so to speak, the way still available for men to speak with the Son. How do men's heart's become pure, living, and watchful as flowers, watered by dew? The next stanzas show that the night, the time of meditation and contemplation, or prayer, can make the heart another Virgin-shrine for Christ to enter.

In many of Vaughan's poems, "night" and "darkness" have disvalues (or, at best, less positive values than "light" and "day") and symbolize sin, error, ignorance, the flesh, the old law, ceremonies, and so on, as in "The World," "Rules and Lessons," "Ascension Day," "Faith," and "Repentence," among many poems. In other poems it is the stars as guiding lights that are valued, not the night, as for example in "Midnight," "Joy of my life," and "The Constellation." Of the few poems in which "night" or "darkness" has multiple and contradictory values, "The Night" is Vaughan's clearest expression. Like Herbert, but unlike Traherne, Vaughan is a poet who seldom travels the *via negativa* to contemplative union.

In the appositive lines 25–36, which bear structural similarity to Herbert's sonnet "Prayer,"[6] Vaughan now develops the positive values of night, which till now have mainly been only implicit. If sleep in the metaphorical sense of indifferently closing one's eyes and heart to Christ has disvalue, then sleep at night in the literal sense of physical inactivity has the value of preventing the "busie fools," non-believers and unregenerate hearts from committing further evil. "The day of Spirits" is a rich figure: first, night traditionally is a spiritual time of various kinds; second, as the body is inactive at night, the spirit may be active; third, as the poem has shown, night acts as a veil to spiritual reality, paradoxically giving man access to that reality by dimming it; fourth, because of the preceding reasons, it is a time of renewed innocence, as "my souls calm retreat" suggests. This last phrase also suggests, as subsequent lines make explicit, the inner pilgrimage, the soul's night journey through a land of darkness, in which the soul is alienated from God, to Light and reconciliation or union with God. To line 29 Vaughan gives these textual references: "And in the morning, rising up a great while before day, he went out, and departed into a solitary place, and there prayed" (Mark 1:35); "And in the day time he was teaching in the temple; and at night he went out, and abode in the mount that is called the mount of Olives." (Luke 21:37).[7] The line, then, echoes back to the preceding stanza. With the word *progress* being used in its now rare sense, "Christs progress" is a journey at night to and of prayer.

Biblical allusion continues in the next stanza to enrich the poem. In line 31, the metaphor of "flight," a term of Falconry meaning the "pursuit of game, etc., by a hawk" (O.E.D.), would seem to be a reasonable alternative to the "fisher-of-men" metaphor of the Gospels. God pursues men at night and through the night. Lines 32–33 are adopted by Vaughan from The Song of Solomon 5:2: "I sleep but my heart waketh: *it is* the voice of my beloved that knocketh, *saying,* Open to me, my sister, my love, my dove, my undefiled: for my head is filled with dew, and my locks with the drops of the night.*"* With regard to "His knocking time," Revelation 3:20 reads "Behold, I stand at the door, and knock: if any man hear my voice, and open the door, I will come in to him, and will sup with him, and he with me." The Gospel of John, which Vaughan cited at the beginning of his poem, also contains a verse relevant to these lines: "Jesus answered [to the question how will he manifest himself] and said unto him, If a man love me, he will keep my words: and my Father will love him, and he will come unto him, and make our abode with him" (John 14:23).

It is not by random choice that lines 25–36 are structurally similar to Herbert's "Prayer"; for the content of these lines is prayer. Working within the traditions of meditation and contemplation, Vaughan, variously influenced by Herbert, uses the structure of "Prayer" for that part of his poem's content pertaining directly to prayer, a word closely associated with meditation and contemplation. Such a practice indicates a highly conscious and deliberate craftsmanship, and, for the reader, the integration of structure and content yields an added pleasure. In stanzas 5 and 6, Vaughan employs a poetic device, apposition (many terms with a single referent), that is precisely suited to the subject of mystical Union, the many in the one. Without main finite verbs and therefore in a sense timeless and beyond the sequential, reasoning intellect, stanzas 5 and 6 modify the conventional analysis of meditative structure and mark the transition between meditation and contemplation, an essential point to be developed along with the significance of the rich biblical allusions, in section III's fuller discussion of these most important stanzas.

> Were all my loud, evil days
> Calm and unhaunted as is thy dark Tent,
> Whose peace but by some *Angels* wing or voice
> Is seldom rent;
> Then I in Heaven all the long year
> Would keep, and never wander here.          42
>
> But living where the Sun
> Doth all things wake, and where all mix and tyre
> Themselves and others, I consent and run
> To ev'ry myre,
> And by this worlds ill-guiding light,
> Erre more then I can do by night.          48

> There is in God (some say)
> A deep, but dazling darkness; As men here
> Say it is late and dusky, because they
> See not all clear;
> O for that night! where I in him
> Might live invisible and dim.            54

These stanzas (which at least begin as a colloquy; note line 38) logically and emotionally extend the preceding stanzas. Night must pass into day, and night's meditation and contemplation must end. Stanzas 7 and 8 develop the idea of the day as evil and by contrast praise the night. The poem has paradoxically reversed the significance of light and dark imagery by subtle equivocation, by gradually shifting the denotations and connotations of light or day and night or dark. By the last stanza, the poem in this progressive manner earns maximum value for night as an aspect of divinity.

"Thy dark Tent" is of course the night which houses Christ. But there is a further subtlety involved here too. "Tent" also means "tabernacle," and in Jewish history the tabernacle was "the curtained tent, containing the Ark of the Covenant and other sacred appointments, which served as the portable sanctuary of the Israelites during their wandering in the wilderness and afterwards till the building of the temple" (O.E.D.). Numbers 10:15 reads "And on the day that the tabernacle was reared up the cloud covered the tabernacle, *namely*, the tent of the testimony . . ." We have seen (stanza 4) that no mercy-seat or carved stone or tabernacle held and lodged Christ. It is rather the night in its various meanings which is his dwelling-place, his tabernacle or tent—the night which, encouraging prayer, can purify and enliven the heart in order that Christ may enter. Lines 39 and 40 refer to various angelic events which are recorded in the Bible and which are accordingly evoked by the lines.[8] The word "wander" in line 42 involves the major contemplative metaphor of the quest as well as wandering as *straying*, losing the Way: "I . . . would . . . never wander here" because the quest would be over. Union would be achieved if all the days were like the nights.

However, stanza 8 says this is not the case, for "I" live where the Sun and not the Son wakes all things, and so paradoxically "I" wander more "by this worlds ill-guiding light . . . then I can do by night." That the "Sun" in line 43 (as opposed to the multi-significant "Sun" of line 12) refers only to the sun of the phenomenal world is a clear instance of Vaughan's reversing of the significance of light and dark in particular preparation for the final paradox of stanza 9.

Since "night" in the sense of stanzas 5 and 6, night as the time of meditation leading to contemplation, cannot continue perpetually but must give way to the day of stanzas 7 and 8 and its evils, Vaughan prays in stanza 9 for that permanent night of the "deep but dazling darkness"—i.e. for the mystic experience of the Divine Darkness or Negative Divinity, an idea pervasive in Christian mysticism. Various commentators have suggested that the source for lines 49–50 may be Dionysius the Areopagite's *Mystic Theology*. "The Divine dark is nought else but that inaccessible light wherein the Lord is said to dwell. Although it is invisible because of its dazzling splendours and unsearchable because of the abundance of its supernatural brightness, nevertheless, whosoever deserves to see and know God rests therein; and, by the very fact that he neither sees nor knows, is truly *in* that which surpasses all truth and all knowledge."[9] Dionysius the Areopagite, like Gregory of Nyssa, Augustine, and others, preached the method of negation, which consists in denying all predicates of God, because the Godhead is beyond the pale of the rational intellect and predicating conceptualization. Interpreting the trumpets that Moses heard on his first ascent of Mount Sinai, Gregory describes in his *Life of Moses* a kind of Platonic ascent from contemplation of the universe, a Vision of Dame Kind, to contemplation of the invisible and incomprehensible divine darkness, a Vision of God: "When the hearing of the heart has been purified, then will a man hear this sound—that is, the contemplation of the universe from which we derive our knowledge of the divine omnipotence—and by this he is led in spirit to penetrate to the realm where God exists. This realm the Scriptures call a dark cloud (*gnophos*). And by this is meant the invisibility and incomprehensibility of God. It is in this darkness that he sees the tabernacle not made by human hands" (cited in Louth, 85–86). Other mystics who follow the example of Gregory or Dionysius might be included in Vaughan's parenthetical "some say"; the phrase indicates that Vaughan himself did not achieve, at least as far as this poem is concerned, the final stage of mystical union but that he is with appropriate humility referring to the experience of other mystics, while earnestly desiring union for himself.

This desire for union is the essence of mysticism, as of religion generally, and Vaughan's distinction, as every mystic's distinction, is that he attains to such union or an aspect of it (even if only initially, incompletely, and temporarily at earlier stages of spiritual progress, such as Illumination) *in this life*, and need not wait entirely until the afterlife.

## III

As previously remarked, we might well find both meditative and contemplative elements in a single poem. In fact, in one form or another, *lectio divina*, meditation, prayer, and contemplation all appear in "The Night." And where we find clear evidence of, say, the stage of Illumination, rather than just Purgation, we may be confident that the poem or certain parts of it are contemplative rather than just meditative. While "The Night" clearly indicates that the speaker had not attained final Union at that point, it also unmistakably reveals, I believe, that he had realized not only Illumination, a remarkable realization in itself, but also the Dark Night of the Soul if this term is fully and correctly understood in the Renaissance formulation given by the great contemplative St. John of the Cross.

Even more so than Dionysius the Areopagite or St. Gregory of Nyssa, St. John of the Cross is regarded by some scholars as "the leader of the 'apophatic' theologians, the teachers of the 'dark' knowledge of God. He completes and fulfills the tradition of the greatest contemplatives among the Greek Fathers" (Merton, 17). In the *Ascent of Mount Carmel* and *Dark Night of the Soul*, companion volumes which outline the scale of perfection in one of its most influential Renaissance forms, St. John actually distinguishes several dark nights.[10] First, there is the night of the sense and the night of the spirit. In St. John's words: "This night, which, as we say, is contemplation, produces in spiritual persons two kinds of darkness or purgation, corresponding to the two parts of man's nature—namely, the sensual and the spiritual. And thus the one night or purgation will be sensual . . . and the other is a night or purgation which is spiritual, wherein the soul is . . . made ready for the union of love with God. The night of sense is common and comes to many. . . . The night of the spirit is the portion of very few, and these are they that are already practiced and proficient . . ." (*Dark Night*, I, viii, 1). Secondly, St. John distinguishes active and passive modes, also called the active and passive nights. His earlier work treats the active night of sense and spirit and *Dark Night of the Soul* treats the passive night of sense and spirit. "Active" refers to the soul's own purging of itself, and "passive" pertains to the soul's being purged by God. In other words, in the active night the mystical aspirant may purify himself with the ordinary help of grace in order to prepare his senses and spirit for union with God. In the passive night, with more abundant grace than before, while the individual soul is passive, God does the purifying of the senses and spirit for the same ultimate purpose of union. This passive night also obtains in Vaughan's poem, as I shall shortly demonstrate. What does not obtain in the poem for the speaker is the final vision of God as "dark night to the soul" (Ascent I, ii, 1), God as the "dazling darkness" that is incomprehensible to man's reasoning intellect.[11]

Since purification is an ongoing process, different stages may be simultaneously present. "In a sense the whole of the mystical experience in this life consists in a series of purifications, whereby the Finite slowly approaches the nature of its Infinite Source" (Underhill, Mysticism, 204). As Christ's sermon on the mount tells us, blessed are the pure in heart, for they shall see God. "For cleanness of heart is nothing less than the love and grace of God" (Dark Night, II, xii, 1). As previously noted, purification leads to vision and enlightenment, but these latter in themselves are and help to provide a further purification leading to still deeper vision and enlightenment. At the risk of oversimplifying, it may be said that contemplative life consists of increasing purification and enlightenment, or the nada y todo of St. John: everything that is not divine is to be negated or purified away so that with intensifying illuminations the mystic may eventually be wholly united with the divine All.

For St. John of the Cross, the traditional via mystica (Purgation, Illumination, Union) "provides the basic framework of his whole teaching on spiritual progress" (Dicken, 136). Because purification is an ongoing process, the following comparative table helpfully amplifies and refines the traditional threefold way in a manner which distinguishes between different degrees of purification:

| | |
|---|---|
| Active Night of the Senses | Purgation |
| Passive Night of the Senses | Transition to Illumination |
| | |
| Active Night of the Spirit | Illumination |
| Passive Night of the Spirit | Transition to Union[12] |

The stage of Union is just beyond the passive night of the spirit. Understanding St. John's commentary within this traditional framework should help to provide clearer insight into the mystical aspects of "The Night."

In general, stanzas 5 through 9 of the poem suggest the speaker realized Illumination, as well as Purgation, and indicate that he dwelled in the nights of the senses and spirit. As observed, "The Night" is a modified meditative poem. Stanzas 5 and 6, similar in structure to Herbert's "Prayer," reveal that there must have been many "illuminations" enjoyed by Vaughan or the speaker and suggest that Vaughan or the speaker progressed to the dark nights of the senses and spirit. With Christ no longer on earth, prayer at night is the way now for man "at mid-night [to] speak with the Sun!" " 'What is prayer?' asks Meister Eckhart, and answers in the words of Dionysius the Areopagite: 'The mind's ascent to God, that is what prayer means' " (cited in Durr, *On the Mystical Poetry*, xi). These appositive stanzas, stylistically implying the many in the one and marking the transition from multiplicity to unity, have no independent finite verbs (verbs appear only in subordinate modifying clauses) and are thus in a sense eternal or timeless, existing in the eternal now-moment: "The hours to which high Heaven doth chime." Anthony Low's critical comment on these stanzas is insightful: "The poem moves insensibly from the historical-material world of the meditating imagination into a spiritual world of mystical contemplation. . . . The tense also changes. Up to this point, the past perfect of completed action was used, and Vaughan even asserted that the experience of Nicodemus, meeting with God at midnight, cannot be repeated. The poem now belies that assertion. What Vaughan describes seems like something presently happening. Grammatically, the two stanzas are an extended apostrophe to Night that have no tense because they lack a main verb. They are in the timeless rather than the simple present . . ." (203–204).

A passage from St. John of the Cross is also in various ways illuminating of stanzas 5 and 6: "in this state of contemplation, which the soul enters when it forsakes meditation for the state of the proficient, it is God Who is now working in the soul; He binds its interior faculties, and allows it not to cling to the understanding, nor to have delight in the will, nor to reason with the memory. . . . God now begins to communicate Himself to it, no longer through sense, as he did aforetime, by means of reflections which joined and sundered its knowledge, but by pure spirit, into which consecutive reflections enter not; but He communicates Himself to it by an act of simple contemplation . . ." (*Dark Night*, I, ix, 7, 8).

The night as the dark part of the diurnal cycle effectively shuts off the sense of sight, the dominant mode of perception among the five senses, accounting for the great majority of all our perceptual data. But stanzas 5 and 6 (and 7 as well) also emphasize the turning off to the outside world of the sense of hearing, humans' second most important sense, thereby providing silence and stillness. To be quiet and receptive seems a necessary condition for contemplative communication or communion with divinity. "It is in the stillness, in the silence, that the word of God is to be heard. There is no better avenue of approach to this Word than through stillness, through silence" (Eckhart, tr. Blakney, 107). In Vaughan's quiet night, "God now begins to communicate Himself to [the soul] no longer through sense": "Gods silent, searching flight . . . His still, soft call . . . The souls dumb watch." These phrases plainly reveal that the soul is passive and God active, that in the nights (in the sense of dark periods of the day) referred to in these stanzas Vaughan expresses his passing through the passive night: "it is God Who is now working in the soul." And God communicates himself "by pure spirit into which consecutive reflections enter not . . . by an act of simple contemplation." The night is "The day of Spirits . . . When Spirits their fair kindred catch."

Beyond the senses and the temporal, reasoning intellect (with its "consecutive reflections") and marking the mind's ascent to God, the mode and meaning of the appositive stanzas modify the conventional analysis of meditative structure and move the poem from meditation to contemplation, from the lower stages of mystical or pre-mystical activity to the higher mystical stage of Illumination and then, subsequently, to the passive night of the spirit. In time, on different nocturnal occasions, Vaughan or the speaker apparently experienced the night as Purgation and as a night of the senses and spirit. Because Vaughan or the speaker is or was in a night of the senses, he experiences the illuminations of stanzas 5 and 6 and he moves toward the night of the spirit, as also indicated elsewhere in the poem. During the period of "the aridities of this night of sense," God draws "forth the soul from the life of sense into that of the spirit— that is, from meditation to contemplation. . . . The way in which they are to conduct themselves in the night of sense is to devote themselves not at all to reasoning and meditation . . . but to allow the soul to remain in peace and quietness . . . and persevere in prayer without making any effort" (Dark Night, I, x, 1, 4). These timeless stanzas 5 and 6 portray the night in which the soul finds "the most serene and loving contemplation and spiritual sweetness without the labor of meditation" (Dark Night, II, i, 1). In their timelessness, they apparently refer to many nights of Illumination and various past dark nights, which may have occurred on numerous separate, timeless nocturnal occasions but which are by the poet inductively collapsed into a detailed, generalized description of "Dear night," profoundly rendering its meaning as if it were nevertheless a single night. One imagines that the night of these stanzas may very well include among its many occasions the one referred to in those brilliant opening lines of "The World":

> I saw Eternity the other night
> Like a great *Ring* of pure and endless light,
> All calm, as it was bright.

The vital difference between meditation and contemplation is precisely the vital difference between the rational intellect and Love[13] (there is not a better word unless one uses Greek terms like the Platonic *noesis* or the biblical *pneuma*). Just as the absence of main verbs stylistically and structurally signal that the meditating mind has no place in the eternal now-moment, so the relevance of the previously noted biblical passages on love reveal that stanzas 5 and 6 are in the mode of contemplation. Like Dante's Virgil, the meditating intellect may help guide one through the Inferno and up Mount Purgatory, but it is Love that leads into the Garden of Eden and Paradise. Just as Stanley Stewart, in his study of the imagery of the Song of Songs, has demonstrated with respect to Vaughan's "Regeneration" and Marvell's "The Garden," the full context of "The Night," so rich in biblical allusions, also includes the Song of Songs with its themes and imagery of love, timelessness, and the garden. In his commentary on his own *Spiritual Canticle*, which is also a commentary on Solomon's Song, St. John of the Cross holds, as did Origen and Gregory of Nyssa in their Commentaries on the Song of Songs, that the true subject of the biblical Song is the wonder of the mystical state. The interpretation by Origen and St. Gregory of the Canticles, rich in garden imagery, as representing the union of love between God and the soul has generally been accepted by all subsequent mystical theologians.

The imagery of the garden in which Christ was wont to pray at night runs through and unites stanzas 3, 4, 5, and 6 of Vaughan's poem. The night is the time of prayer; Christ prayed in the garden at night. "God's silent, searching flight" is his night prayers, by which he seeks out humankind. Lines 32–33, adopted from The Song of Songs, with its references to love, echo the flower imagery of stanza 3: Christ is a rare and sacred flower, his head "filled with dew." The symbol of dew in Vaughan's poetry is invariably to be interpreted as having a healing and saving power. Dew is a symbol of regeneration, the symbol of God's grace and Christ's blood. (Expecially because of the reference to the mount of Olives in Luke 21:37, noted by

Vaughan, lines 29–33 also suggest Christ in Gethsemane, its dark night of agonizing purification and "bloody sweat.") In *I Sleep and My Heart Wakes*, a title of course taken from the same passage in the Song of Songs that Vaughan alludes to, the English mystic and poet Richard Rolle distinguishes three degrees of love by which man comes to be united to God. One particular passage in Rolle's discussion of the second degree, which involves the love of Jesus Christ and "meditating upon His Passion," seems especially pertinent to the middle stanzas of "The Night": "and when your heart is completely disposed to the service of God, and when all worldly thoughts are expelled from it, then you will wish to steal away and be alone to think of Christ and to spend much time in prayer" (*The Mediaeval Mystics of England*, 148). This is similar to St. John's third sign of positive attraction for solitary contemplative prayer, the most important of the three signs for indicating that the soul is ready to leave behind meditation and to dwell in passive contemplation (see *Ascent*, II, xiii, 4).

We have also seen the relevance of The Song of Songs 5:2 and Revelation 3:20 to "His knocking time." "As we read in Mrs. Sutcliff's *Meditations of Man's Mortalitie* (1634), the only cure for the sickness of the Spouse, expressed in the complaint in the Song of Songs, is the Second Coming, described by St. John in the Apocalypse . . . . There was a sense, then, in which the Song of Songs was understood as an apocalyptic prayer" (Stanley Steward, 132, 134). The marriage metaphor obtains in the poem largely through biblical allusion. This metaphor, fundamental and vital in the writing also of St. John of the Cross, is one of the three basic contemplative figures in Vaughan's poetry, as R. A. Durr has shown, figures which symbolically transform archetypal mystical experience and embody the theme of regeneration or rebirth. The heart is the Bridegroom's, the Lord's chamber; but the heart ordinarily is calcified, is like the "carv'd stone," and the Bridegroom must stand outside and knock. Two things are working in "busy commerce" for the desired union of man with God. One is, metaphorically, God's "prayer," that is, his suffering, crucifixion, resurrection, the grace of his redeeming dew or blood. The Lord knocks, but the heart must be prepared and answer if there is to be mystical union. The prayer of man is the other force working for union. Night stops the busy day; it permits, indeed, it *is* "the souls dumb watch," its silent prayer. By the Lord's knocking and "the souls dumb watch," apocalyptic Union in this life, or at least temporary Illuminations, may be achieved, "Spirits [may] their fair kindred catch." ("Kindred," of course, means "relationship by blood, sometimes by marriage.") Man's love and prayer and Christ's love and "prayer," or redeeming dew, soften the heart, open the door, and permit the Bridegroom to enter. Mythically understood, such apocalyptic entering is both sacramental marriage and rebirth. "Except a man be born again . . . of water [dew] and *of the Spirit, he cannot enter into the Kingdom of God"* (*John* 3:3, 5). Love and prayer or contemplation at night, then, are the way for man "at mid-night [to] speak with the Sun!"

In her chapter on "The Dark Night of the Soul," Evelyn Underhill points out that in its movement toward transcendent reality "the self experiences a series of oscillations between 'states of pleasure' and 'states of pain' . . . oscillations between a joyous and a painful consciousness seem to occur most often at the beginning of a new period of the Mystic Way. . . . Mystics call such oscillations the 'Game of Love' in which God plays, as it were, 'hide and seek' with the questing soul" (*Mysticism*, 381, 383). The centrally important stanzas 5 and 6 suggest that Vaughan or the speaker enjoyed through love and prayer timeless illuminations and that he had passed through nights of sense and passive nights. But the quiet night (as the dark part of the day) of contemplative prayer and love ends with daylight and swings over to "loud, evil days." Stanzas 7 through 9 especially show clearly the oscillation from Illumination to St. John's passive night of the spirit or, in a modern formulation, to "The Dark Night of the Soul" exactly as Underhill describes that Night.[14]

Stanzas 7 through 9 are a modified colloquy in that they begin with the speaker addressing God (as signaled by the second person "thy" in line 38) but then by the last stanza move on to regarding God in the third person (as signalled especially, though not only, by "him" in the penultimate line). This shift from second to third person reveals and underscores the fact, fully developed in stanza 9, that, although the poet or speaker after the illuminations of stanzas 5 and 6 feels close enough to God for direct address in the following stanza, he still does not yet enjoy Union. His address to God in stanza 7 subjunctively observes that "Were all my loud, evil days / Calm and unhaunted as in thy dark Tent," then he would in effect enjoy permanent Union "here" in this life: "Then I in Heaven all the long year / Would keep, and never wander here." Like the non-temporal stanzas 5 and 6, these lines express the peculiar non-temporal and perhaps also non-spatial characteristics of mystical experience, as noted by Stace (*Mysticism and Philosophy*, 131) and other distinguished commentators on mysticism. That is, more precisely, he would paradoxically be both in and out of ordinary space and time, enjoying Heaven eternally while still here on earth, though never again wandering, "all the long year."

A major aspect of the poem, however, is exactly that the speaker does not at this point dwell in permanent Union but rather suffers a Dark Night of the Soul. Such Union "is the 'perfection' toward which the beginner aspires when he undertakes the active mortification ('night') of the senses, and which the progressive approaches in the 'passive nights' of the senses and of the spirit. Neither beginners nor progressives have attained this 'Divine Union.' It is the reward of the 'perfect.' Yet progressives are already contemplatives, which is to say, in Saint John of the Cross's language, mystics" (Merton, 75). The fact that the speaker so fervently wishes for the unitive dwelling in the "deep, but dazling darkness" is in itself a likely sign that he has passed through the various stages following Purgation and preceding Union, but there is abundant other evidence for such passage, for his being a "progressive" or mystic. The sense of the present absence of God pervades much of the whole poem. The sense of sin appears particularly in lines 37 and 45 to 48. The former peace, joy, and blessedness, all characteristics of mystical experience (Stace, *Mysticism and Philosophy*, 131) and indicated by stanzas 5 and 6, are revealed as lost in stanzas 7 and 8, which along with stanza 3, especially mark the grief and suffering. And all of this that Vaughan or the speaker feels— the absence of God, the sense of sin, the loss of former peace and joy and blessedness, the grief and suffering, the apparent relapse to a lower spiritual level—are "types of darkness," "forms" or characteristics of the Dark Night of the Soul (Underhill, *Mysticism*, 389–395). The Dark Night of the Soul "is the completion of that ordering of disordered loves, that transvaluation of values, which the Way of Purgation began" (Underhill, 395). It is the full and final humbling of the false self so that the true self may eventually be exalted in full and final Union; it is that total self-simplification and emptying which leads paradoxically to a fullness of effulgent beatitude. In St. John's words, "although this happy night brings darkness to the spirit, it does so only to give it light in everything; . . . although it humbles it and makes it miserable, it does so only to exalt it and to raise it up; and although it impoverishes and empties it of all natural affection and attachment, it does so only that it may enable it to stretch forward, divinely, and thus to have fruition and experience of all things. . . . In this way, being empty, it is able indeed to be poor in spirit and freed from the old man, in order to live that new and blessed life which is attained by means of this night, and which is the state of union with God" (*Dark Night*, II, ix, 1, 4). This night is St. John's passive night of the spirit; and "The Night" manifests this advanced degree of mystic consciousness.

The last stanza, which has elicited much comment, has puzzled critics unfamiliar with mystical tradition. John Pollock, for example, thinks that the final line contains an inconsistency which reveals Vaughan's "divided consciousness." "The last line is not, however, simply a straightforward cry for mystical union with God, for Vaughan—to put the matter bluntly—is contradicting himself: to be dim is not to be invisible. This contradiction suggests that Vaughan actually has drawn back from an ultimate commitment to invisibility, that is to the total renunciation of self that invisibility implies. It is as if his mind were divided against itself, for at the very moment he asks to be taken into the Divine Nothingness, part of him hesitates and so he totters on the brink, afraid to lose himself entirely" (422–423).

Such a view of the poem thoroughly violates its whole progress, meaning, and integrity. Of course, "to be dim is not to be invisible," but Vaughan is not contradicting himself, nor is he drawing back from a full commitment. Here is a clear instance of serious confusion owing to the critical failure to understand mystical tradition and Vaughan's place in it, specifically to understand "the essential paradoxicality of the mystical consciousness" and to realize that "the paradox of the dissolution of individuality, in which dissolution the 'I' both disappears and persists, is reported in all ages and cultures by countless independent witnesses" (Stace, *Mysticism and Philosophy*, 253, 259–260). In other words, in accord with the central paradox of rebirth or of life through death, Vaughan or the speaker prays for the ego or false self to be annihilated, made "invisible," and for the regenerated true Self to be exalted and united to God, whose "dazling" nature makes that Self appear "dim." His is not a divided consciousness but rather one deeply desirous of Union with the Highest Consciousness or with what Stace in the same book designates the "Unitary Consciousness" (131). Like Dionysius, Vaughan unhesitatingly says "Unto this Darkness which is beyond Light, we pray that we may come" (*Divine Names and the Mystical Theology*, 194). A modified meditation employing the meditative structure, the poem has steadily moved us toward contemplation and the ultimate object of contemplation, the "deep, but dazling darkness." The alliteration in this phrase serves to emphasize the paradoxical nature of God and to focus attention on the climatic word, "dim," which also involves that paradox. (It should also be noted that contemplation of the Dionysian "Divine Dark" is traditionally referred to as "dim contemplation," as in St. John's *Dark Night of the Soul*.) While the first four lines of the last stanza emphasize the negative, mysterious nature of God, the concluding couplet intensely sums up, in terms of the marriage metaphor, Vaughan's prayer for union with God, "that night," in which his false individuality would be abolished, dissolved (the point of "invisible") and in which by losing his life he would gain it (a large part of the point of "dim"), so that his true "individuality" would be realized. That is, the poem takes us back full circle to the first stanza: the speaker, like Nicodemus, wishes "to know his God by night," to become Christlike, to be exactly the dimmed divinity that Christ is at the beginning of the poem. And in this highly accomplished way, Vaughan brilliantly brings together the two main streams of Christo-mysticism and God-mysticism, the originating founts of which are the Johannine and Pauline writings and the Christian Neoplatonism of Dionysius (see Happold, 164–166). As we read in a favorite mystical text, "ye shall know that I *am* in my Father, and ye in me, and I in you" (John 14:20).

## IV

The three kinds of contemplation that appear in varying degrees in "The Night" were typically described by medieval and Renaissance mystics in the terms used by St. Edmund Rich, a Dionysian theologian whose *The Mirror of Holy Church* achieved wide circulation in both Latin and English. "The first is contemplation of created beings, the second of the Scriptures, the third of God Himself and His nature. Contemplation is nothing else than looking at God: and His creatures can look at Him in this way" (in *The Medieval Mystics of England*, 129). The first two forms of contemplation are an acquired contemplation—of created beings and of the Scriptures. The Scriptures included the Bible and the Fathers, and Vaughan practically treats Herbert as if he were a Church Father, alluding to his work only a little less frequently than to the Bible. The third kind of contemplation, of God Himself and His nature, is an infused contemplation, often leading inwardly along the *via negativa*, as in "The Night," and often referred to as "the Book of the Soul," so that there are "three books." A single poem may of course refer to several kinds of both meditation and contemplation. "The Night," as we have seen, touches upon and hints of past contemplative experiences of created things that many other poems dwell upon more explicitly and fully. Whereas "The Night" primarily presents Vaughan's desire for a Vision of God through the *via negativa,* in many of his other poems, as we shall be discussing, Vaughan reads the book of nature and the book of Scriptures and looks both outside of and within himself to find God.

Although it was a medieval and Renaissance commonplace to regard nature as a book, Vaughan's poems portray his contemplation of created things as so special, distinctive, and charged with numinous significance that these portraits, while they are common or frequent in his work, are never commonplace. Nor should such contemplation be confused with abstract, discursive reasoning from the existence of a creation to a Creator, in the manner of scholastic rational argument. Rather, many of Vaughan's poems concern the unmediated sights or actual direct experience of divinity in created things. For all of the important pervasive presence of Herbert in Vaughan's work, this kind of contemplation distinguishes Vaughan's poetry and moves him away from both Herbert and Donne and closer to his later contemporary, Traherne. Like Herbert, Vaughan places a series of eschatological poems near the end of *Silex Scintillans* (Part II). Unlike Herbert, who follows his eschatological poems and concludes "The Church" with the eucharistic and unitive "Love" (III), Vaughan concludes his book with "The Book" and "To the Holy Bible" (preceding his "L'Envoy"). Biblical allusion and meditation on or contemplation of the Scriptures of course figure prominently in both Herbert and Vaughan. But, although they are significant in Vaughan, eucharistic imagery and themes do not in his work have the central and pervasive importance that they do in "The Church." Vaughan's poems on the contemplation of created things make the difference. Vaughan is led to mystical experience more by book (one or the other) than by Eucharist. His "To the Holy Bible" contains a catalog of some distinctive contemplative characteristics, including "union." Remarking upon the commonplace of seeing the world of nature as a book, Alan Rudrum rightly observes about "The Book" that "Vaughan's originality is to see the world of nature *in* a book" (*Henry Vaughan: The Complete Poems,* 641). With the mystic's passion for seeing things as interrelated and unified, Vaughan describes how various created, natural objects go into the making of a book, no doubt the Good Book (but possibly also *Silex Scintillans?*), suggesting that God's books are interconnected. "The Book" Concludes:

> O knowing, glorious spirit! when
> Thou shalt restore trees, beasts and men,
> When thou shalt make all new again,

> Destroying onely death and pain,
> Give him amongst thy works a place
> Who in them lov'd and sought thy face!

Coming in a crucial position near the end of *Silex Scintillans*, "The Book" summarizes and emphasizes with all the weight of Vaughan's book what many of Vaughan's poems individually reveal: Vaughan loved, searched for and sometimes found God not only in Scriptures and inwardly in the Book of the Soul but also outwardly in nature, "amongst thy works," for now we see through a glass darkly, but then, when the veil of custom, convention, and selfish solicitude drops away, shall we see face to face, in the extrovertive Vision of Dame Kind, to use W. H. Auden's phrase. Auden describes this Vision in the following manner: "The basic experience is an overwhelming conviction that the objects confronting [the mystic] have a numinous significance and importance, that the existence of everything he is aware of is holy. And the basic emotion is one of innocent joy, though this joy can include, of course, a reverent dread. . . . So long as the vision lasts the self is 'noughted,' for its attention is completely absorbed in what it contemplates; it makes no judgment and desires nothing, except to continue in communion with what Gerald Manley Hopkins called the inscape of things" (13, 14).

To the familiar idea that, as Gregory of Nyssa expressed it, all things are in the divinity, and the divinity is in all things, we should equally stress the idea of God's transcendence. An important factor of the mystical experience is, Thomas Merton reminds us, the mystic's paradoxical "discovery of God in His immanence and His transcendence. Everything that the soul experiences flows from this central mystery that God is in all things and in the soul, and that He is nevertheless infinitely above the soul and above all things" (219–20). On balance, Vaughan's poems suggest that Vaughan more fully experienced God's immanence than God's transcendence, that he more frequently and deeply enjoyed the Vision of Dame Kind than he did the Vision of God. Perhaps that is another reason why in "The Night," Vaughan, led on by past illuminative visions, so ardently expresses the desire for a unitive Vision of God. That powerful desire for what remains just beyond realization finds vivid expression in the opening lines of "Childe-hood," the poem immediately preceding "The Night":

> I cannot reach it; and my striving eye
> Dazles at it, as at eternity.

Referring to the biblical idea of being born again and becoming like unto a child to enter the kingdom of heaven, the central mystical paradox of regeneration, Vaughan writes "he / Must live twice, that would God's face see;" and he concludes "Childe-hood" by returning to the metaphor of light which opened the poem and then pleading "O for thy Center and mid-day! / For sure that is the *narrow way.*"

The final couplet of the much discussed and highly acclaimed "Regeneration," the first poem of *Silex Scintillans*, which sets in motion and governs the sequence that follows,[15] expresses Vaughan's desire for the mystic death of the first Adam for the sake of rebirth in God:

> Lord, then said I, *On me one breath,*
> And let me dye before my death.

This figurative or spiritual dying which is to precede his actual, literal physical death is the self-noughting which Auden and contemplatives speak of and which precedes or accompanies that spiritual rebirth or regeneration that is the heart of mystical experience. Unlike Donne, who in his divine poems tends to take "death" in its literal sense, as we observed in our discussion of "Hymn to God my God, in my sicknesse," Vaughan sometimes intends the word in its literal and sometimes in its figurative senses. The first two stanzas of "Ascension Hymn," near the beginning of Part II (1655) of *Silex Scintillans* plainly refer to both kinds of death:

> Dust and clay
> Mans antient wear!
> Here you must stay,
> but I elsewhere;
> Souls sojourn here, but may not rest;
> Who will ascend, must be undrest.
>
> And yet some
> That know to die
> Before death come,
> Walk to the skie
> Even in this life; but all such can
> Leave behinde them the old Man.

The dying "Before death . . . Even in this life" clearly refers to mystical death, the death of the first Adam: "but all such can / Leave behinde them the old Man."

The poem "Regeneration," as Stanley Stewart remarks, "represents the three stages—purgative, illuminative, and unitive—of the mystical life" (*The Enclosed Garden*, 109), and, especially, through its last lines, it alerts the reader to the special meaning of death in many of the poems that follow it. Vaughan not only concludes *Silex Scintillans* with a series of eschatological poems, as Herbert concludes "The Church," but so much is death and rebirth or resurrection his primary theme that he also places the closely related eschatological poems "Death," "Resurrection and Immortality," and "Day of Judgment" after "Regeneration." In the first stanza of the next poem, "Religion," expecially in "groves, and leaves," Vaughan in effect locates the setting, or places of self-discovery, of many of his poems: either in the natural world, "groves," or the "leaves" of the Bible or other holy writings, such as Herbert's. The following meditative poem describes "The Search" for the essential self: "all night have I / Spent in a roving Extasie / to find my Saviour." Not at all having the sense it does for Donne, "Extasie" here means a mental wandering or following of the life of Christ from birth through resurrection and apocalypse at various biblically-mentioned places. By the end of the poem, the speaker, who has never actually left his cell or his meditations, "heard one singing," and so learns to "leave thy gadding thoughts" and to "Search well another world," not "The skimme and shell of things" but the inner world and the inward man, as the concluding verse from Acts 17:27–28 indicates: "That they should seek the Lord, if happily they might feel after him, and finde him, though he be not far off from every one of us, for in him we live, and move, and have our being."

Again, in contemplative tradition there are two worlds: the perfect, natural world, including creatures and objects, and created by God and by God in the redeemed person; and the fallen world fabricated by man's conceptualizing ego, an artificial, prideful, and illusory world. The seeming contradiction (in Vaughan and in general) of condemning and enjoying the world is thus resolved by the realization that one must give up the vain, illusory, time-bound world of getting and spending, in which we lay waste our God-given powers, for the sake of (not, as in Donne's resolution, the microcosm of the lovers in a Vision of Eros, but) the natural macrocosm eternally charged with God's grandeur and quickened by Christ playing in ten thousand places or re-created by the last Adam in the redeemed person's imaginative, loving consciousness during a Vision of Dame Kind. These two worlds are conveniently and briefly referred to as the inner and outer worlds of nature, or the world of Eternity and the world of Time, as in Vaughan's famous poem "The World."

Many of Vaughan's poems search well both the world of the inner self and the inner world of nature, which worlds, seemingly two, are one, in that the special unitive relationship between the seeming two is what is most real, and in that Vaughan finds the single reality of divinity, or "my Saviour," at and as the heart of Nature and the inner self.[16] Like "The Night," a large number of Vaughan's poems have both meditative and contemplative elements in them, one typical pattern being for a poem to begin in meditation and end in, or at least move toward, contemplation. This pattern finds one kind of expression in the actual movement of the speaker from indoors to outdoors, as in "Vanity of Spirit":

> Quite spent with thoughts I left my Cell, and lay
> Where a shrill spring tun'd to the early day.
>   I beg'd here long, and gron'd to know
>   Who gave the Clouds so brave a bow,
>   Who bent the spheres, and circled in
>   Corruption with this glorious Ring,
>   What is his name, and how I might
>   Descry some part of his great light.
> I summon'd nature: peirc'd through all her store,
> Broke up some seales, which none had touch'd before,      10
>   Her wombe, her bosome, and her head
>   Where all her secrets lay a bed
>   I rifled quite, and having past
>   Through all the Creatures, came at last
>   To search my selfe, where I did find
>   Traces, and sounds of a strange kind.
> Here of this mighty spring, I found some drills,
> With Ecchoes beaten from th' eternall hills;
>   Weake beames, and fires flash'd to my sight,
>   Like a young East, or Moone-shine night,      20
>   Which shew'd me in a nook cast by
> A peece of much antiquity,
>   With Hyerogliphicks quite dismembred,
>   And broken letters scarce remembred.
> I tooke them up, and (much Joy'd) went about
> T'unite those peeces, hoping to find out
>   The mystery; but this neer done,
>   That little light I had was gone:
>   It griev'd me much. At last, said I,

> *Since in these veyls my Ecclips'd Eye*          30
> *May not approach thee, (for at night*
> *Who can have commerce with the light?)*
> *I'le disapparell, and to buy*
> *But one half glaunce, most gladly dye.*

Leaving behind his cell and his discursive, meditative thoughts, the speaker goes outdoors to a spring, signifying an actual source of water and symbolizing, as in Traherne, pneuma or the essential self,[17] in search of his Saviour, here the Creator. Whereas the typical setting for Donne (at least in the Songs and Sonnets) is the bedroom and for Herbert the church, the setting for Vaughan is often outdoors in nature. Even poems set indoors frequently contain images of nature, particularly what Durr has designated as the major metaphor of the seed and flower. Vaughan is a "nature" poet in the sense that he summons and searches nature to find his God, as Donne and Herbert do not. The vain world (of "Corruption") is "circled . . . with this glorious Ring," imagery echoed in the opening lines of "The World," which distinguish between the worlds of time and eternity. Both positive and negative aspects obtain, as Thomas Merton observes, in "the contemplation of God in nature, which the Greek Fathers called *theoria physica*. On the one hand, *theoria physica* is a positive recognition of God as He is manifested in the essences (*logoi*) of all things. It is not a speculative science of nature but rather a habit of religious awareness which endows the soul with a kind of intuitive perception of God as He is reflected in His creation. . . . The negative aspect of *theoria physica* is an equally instinctive realization of the vanity and illusion of all things as soon as they are considered apart from their right order and reference to God their Creator. Saint Gregory of Nyssa's commentary on *Ecclesiastes*, from which we have quoted, is a tract on the 'contemplation of nature' in its twofold aspect . . ." (27). Vaughan's editors cite the pertinent text from Ecclesiastes 1:14: "I have seen all the works that are done under the sun; and, behold, all *is* vanity and vexation of spirit."

Like "The Night," "Vanity of Spirit" apparently concerns just one occasion but appears to summarize or concentrate into that one occasion many different actual occasions of summoning and searching nature. While other poems present even more certain evidence of successful searchings, lines 9–14 suggest that the quest for finding the Creator in the creation and in creatures fruitfully reveals some secrets. Interestingly, Vaughan's "nature," Dame Kind, is pictured, much as Plato's *Timaeus* pictures the unity of the whole cosmos, as one living creature: "Her wombe, her bosome, and her head . . . ," a point to be returned to later. Moving up the chain of being (see also, for example "I walkt the other day," "The Sap," "The Tempest," and "Man"), "having past / Through all the Creatures," the speaker "came at last / To search my selfe." The search of the created being which is "my selfe" for signs of the Creator reveals something more: "Traces, and sounds of a strange kind." The language of the second half of the poem suggests Neoplatonic emanationism. Teaching that all things are emanations from God, an inevitable overflow of infinite actuality, Plotinus employed not only the metaphor of the sun which radiates light without loss to itself but also the metaphor of the spring from which the stream flows without exhausting its source. The speaker has a Platonic insight into his own nature as partaking of the divine nature, the way small streams emanate from a mighty spring or echoes resound from eternal hills. Reminiscent of "The Night," he finds a dimmed sun within, "Like a young East." The experience is incomplete, broken off, temporary but nevertheless very joyful, a partially successful Vision of Dame Kind continuing on to a partial but illuminative Vision of God within, and the whole experience leads him to wish for that figurative and/or literal death that will give him fuller and more unified vision.

The very next poem, "The Retreat," which word implies a withdrawal from the vain world as well as backward motion, recalls such greater vision from early childhood:

> When on some *gilded Cloud*, or *flowre*
> My gazing soul would dwell an houre,
> And in those weaker glories spy
> Some shadows of eternity;
> Before I taught my tongue to wound
> My Conscience with a sinfull sound,
> Or had the black art to dispence
> A sev'rall sinne to ev'ry sence,
> But felt through all this fleshy dresse
> Bright *shootes* of everlastingnesse.

The theme of childhood is not as primary or pervasive in Vaughan or Herbert as it is in Traherne but it does on occasion, as here, give a varied expression to the overriding archetype of rebirth and to a (past) Vision of Dame Kind. Like Traherne, Vaughan paradoxically regards language, one of man's highest abilities and that which most distinguishes him as a civilized human creature, as a means by which man falls from those felicitous early days. Yet still more paradoxically, by language and intellect, by reading Scripture and by meditating through language on things, man may be led back *toward* eternity and ultimately be truly and fully civilized. Virgil, who stands for reason and language, among other things, can lead Dante through Hell and up Mount Purgatory but not into Eden nor into Paradise. For these last journeys, intuition and revelation, St. Bernard and Beatrice (or, as we shall say in the last chapter, Imagination and Love, the work of poetry) provide guidance. The psyche, the center of the meditating intellect and discursive language, is to a degree instrumental in its own regeneration. What it most critically learns is its own incapacity to effect salvation. He who would save his life shall lose it; he who loses his life, gives up the egoistic struggle, wholly admits, that is, his total dependence on God and discovers God's nearness, attains to wisdom and lives in the mode of eternity.

Whereas "The Retreat" concerns the individual's progress in terms of the theme of childhood, "Corruption" treats mankind's progress in terms of the myth of the Fall, both theme and myth being vehicles for the archetype of death and rebirth and figures for each other:

> Sure, It was so. Man in those early days
>> Was not all stone, and Earth,
> He shin'd a little, and by those weak Rays
>> Had some glimpse of his birth.
> . . . . . . . . . . . . . . . . . . . . . . . . . .
> He sigh'd for *Eden*, and would often say
>> *Ah! What bright days were those?*                          20
> Nor was Heav'n cold unto him; for each day
>> The vally, or the Mountain
> Afforded visits, and still *Paradise* lay
>> In some green shade, or fountain.
> Angels lay *Leiger* here; Each Bush, and Cel,
>> Each Oke, and high-way knew them,
> Walk but the fields, or sit down at some *wel*,
>> And he was sure to view them.
> Almighty *Love!* where art thou now? mad man
>> Sits down, and freezeth on,                                 30
> . . . . . . . . . . . . . . . . . . . . . . . . . .
> All's in deep sleep, and night; Thick darkness lyes
>> And hatcheth o'r thy people;
> But hark! what trumpets that? what Angel cries
>> *Arise! Thrust in thy sickle.*                              40

As the child of "The Retreate" "Shin'd in my Angell-infancy," so also early man in "Corruption" "shin'd a little," "shined" being a word (as it is in "Batter my heart") especially associated with Christ. The spiritual progress of the individual recapitulates that of the human race and vice versa, so that both journey individually and historically from innocence through fallen experience to redemption, as the structure of each poem suggests. Both find paradise or some hint of eternity in the natural world. Both gradually lose sight of divinity and of their own divine origin and nature. And both yearn for or proceed toward, explicitly or implicitly, spiritual rebirth. In "Corruption," filled with biblical allusion and all three major metaphors of regeneration, the seed evidently has been growing secretly and is now ripe for harvest, as the poem concludes with a sudden reversal. Several biblical verses, which express the archetype of death and rebirth in terms of the metaphor of reaping or harvesting, participate in the poem's ending: "So is the Kingdom of God, as if a man should cast seed into the ground: And should sleep, and rise day and night, and the seed should spring and grow up, he knoweth not how . . . he putteth in the sickle, because the harvest is come" (Mark 4:26–27, 29); "Thrust in thy sickle, and reap: for the time is come for thee to reap; for the harvest of the earth is ripe" (Rev. 12:15; see also Joel 3:13).

Appropriately following this poem that recounts the basic biblical myth extending from Creation and the Fall to Redemption and Apocalypse is "H. Scriptures," which in its third stanza alludes to "The Altar" and to "Judgement," poems at the beginning and the end of Herbert's "The Church." "Unprofitablenes" follows "H. Scriptures" and echoes phrases and motifs from a number of Herbert's poems, including "The Flower," with which it shares the themes of spiritual reversal and writing poetry:

> How rich, O Lord! how fresh thy visits are!
> 'Twas but Just now my bleak leaves hopeles hung      10
> · · · · · · · · · · · · · · · · · · · · · · · · · ·
> I smell a dew like *Myrrh,* and all the day
> Wear in my bosome a full Sun; such store
>   Hath one beame from thy Eys.
> But, ah, my God! what fruit hast thou of this?
> What one poor leaf did ever I yet fall
>   To wait upon thy wreath?

The "leaves" are those of the flower which symbolizes the self. They are also associated, here at least by juxtaposition with the preceding "H. Scriptures," with biblical leaves and verses. And "one poor leaf"

seems to suggest a poem, particularly since a few leaves off lies the
self-reflecting "Idle Verse." Both "Idle Verse" and "Unprofitablenes"
contain implicit resolves to turn from matters of lesser to greater im-
port, from profane or secular to divine concerns in both spiritual and
poetic matters. The word "dew" is a familiar symbol of grace and of
Christ's presence, and the frequent seventeenth-century pun on Sun-
Son no doubt obtains, so that the lines reveal that through God's
graces the eternal generation or rebirth of the Son of God takes place
in the hearts of the devout suppliant. "The true and definitely mysti-
cal life does and must open," Evelyn Underhill reminds us, "with
that most actual, though indescribable phenomenon, the coming
forth into consciousness of man's deeper, spiritual self, which . . .
mystical writers of all ages have agreed to call Regeneration or Re-
birth" (*Mysticism*, 122). Given all this and the fact, too, that myrrh
was among the gifts presented by the wise men upon Jesus' birth, it
is appropriate that the next poem is "Christs Nativity," which en-
courages the "glad heart" to awake and sing, and which, given the
recurrent fluctuations of the mystic life, again prays for spiritual
renewal:

> And let once more by mystick birth
> The Lord of life be borne in Earth.

The context of the lines and the second part of the poem, including
the line "Are we all stone, and Earth," ("Man in those early days,"
"Corruption" begins, "Was not all stone, and Earth"), make it very
clear that the prayer is for the birth of Christ also within the indi-
vidual ("in Earth").

Preceding "Unprofitablenes" by fifteen leaves, "The Morning-
watch," like that poem and some of Herbert's poetry (and using some
of the same imagery), opens with one of the many self-renewals
found in Vaughan's poetry. As did Herbert, Vaughan repeatedly ex-
periences the alternations between illuminations and dark nights
of the soul, which are the mark of the mystic. Both Herbert and
Vaughan use the image of the flower to symbolize the reawakened
soul. But unlike Herbert, Vaughan sees nature as more than symbol.
"The Morning-watch" concerns not only the renewal of the self but
also the renewal of nature, and in Vaughan the two are closely re-
lated or at one. After all, divinity graces, animates, and pervades the
self and all creation. As in the poem beginning "And do they so?"
Vaughan sees all of nature filled with a kind of intelligence, a sense,
and a desire for God.

### The Morning-watch

O Joyes! Infinite sweetnes! with what flowres
And shoots of glory, my soul breakes, and buds!
    All the long houres
    Of night, and Rest
    Through the still shrouds
    Of sleep, and Clouds,
  This Dew fell on my Breast;
    O how it *Blouds*,
And *Spirits* all my Earth! heark! In what Rings,
And *Hymning Circulations* the quick world          10
    Awakes, and sings;
    The rising winds,
    And falling springs,
    Birds, beasts, all things
  Adore him in their kinds.
    Thus all is hurl'd
In sacred *Hymnes*, and *Order*, The great *Chime*
And *Symphony* of nature. Prayer is
    The world in tune,
    A spirit-voyce,          20
    And vocall joyes
  Whose *Eccho is* heav'ns blisse.
    O let me climbe
When I lye down! The Pious soul by night
Is like a clouded starre, whose beames though sed
    To shed their light
    Under some Cloud
    Yet are above,
    And shine, and move
  Beyond that mistie shrowd.          30
    So in my Bed
That Curtain'd grave, though sleep, like ashes, hide
My lamp, and life, both shall in thee abide.

Mario Di Cesare rightly notes that *Bloods, Spirits,* and *Circulations* combine the "old notion of blood creating 'spirits' (highly rarefied substance linking soul and body) and Harvey's new theory of circulation of the blood," and he cites Joan Bennett: "The blood begotten vital spirits and the circular movement of the blood represent the revitalizing of the poet and the rest of the created world at dawn" (*George Herbert and the Seventeenth-Century Religious Poets,* 150). We must also consider more fully, as related to yet beyond this significance, two important concepts: the larger doctrine of circulation and the relationship of self to world.

The doctrine of circulation perhaps stems, as so much else does, from Plato, who in his *Timaeus* introduces the theory that the four elements pass into one another "in an unbroken circle of birth" (49c). This idea finds expression in numerous writers, from the ancients Homer, Cleanthes, Cicero, Seneca, and Pliny, to contemporaries of Vaughan, such as the hermetist Robert Fludd, John Milton, who was not a mystic, and Thomas Traherne, who was a mystic. In the later Christian writers it is naturally given a peculiarly Christian significance. In *Paradise Lost* (which of course Vaughan could not have read before publication of *Silex Scintillans*), when Raphael sits down with Adam and Eve to their Edenic feast, which some commentators have taken as a prefiguration of the Eucharistic feast, the Angel explains that "whatever was created, needs / to be sustain'd and fed" and later adds that "one Almighty is, from whom / All things proceed, and up to him return" (V, 414–15, 469–70). In his poetry and prose, Traherne gives the doctrine the particular Christian contemplative significance that we find clearly (though somewhat less fully) in Vaughan's work. Traherne's sequence of six poems from "The Circulation" to "Another" present the doctrine of Circulation in the mystic terms of its relation to the Godhead and to contemplative vision. "All Things to Circulations owe / Themselves; by which alone / They do exist" (*Poems and Thanksgivings*, II, 153). All things are empty and as nothing unless God fills them. "All things do first receive, that give" (154). Throughout this sequence, eating and food metaphors, many with eucharistic connotations, are used to signify that the whole physical-spiritual world is to be regarded as a universal communion feast. All things in the universe are not isolated fragments but interdependent parts of the whole, sustaining one another. All things flow from God and return to Him, Who is the fountain, means, and end. Actually seeing or experiencing all of this requires divine or imaginative vision and is or results in the extrovertive Vision of Dame Kind, seeing the world, as noted in our earlier discussion, with the redeemed heart through the senses. By this contemplative vision, when Christ in us sees, God's infinite gifts are infinitely regarded, loved, and returned. And that all things are circulatory both signalizes and symbolizes the perfection of God's created and ordered world, versus the vanity and illusion of all things considered apart from their right order and reference to God.

Between the Platonic or pagan expression of the doctrine of circulation and Vaughan's work are all the Christian contemplatives who help to give the doctrine the precise significance it has in Vaughan. That significance is succinctly expressed for us by St. Augustine, who writes, "of him, and by him, and in him are all things," in close paraphrase of Romans 11:36.[18] The development of the doctrine from Plato through the contemplatives to Traherne (though again, of course, Vaughan could not have read Traherne before *Silex Scintillans*) should help illuminate Vaughan's work, here particularly, "The Morning-watch" and closely related poems. As in "The Night," night in this poem is a period of "Rest," peace, stillness, silence, the death ("Through the still shrouds / of sleep") of the false self and the rebirth of the true self by means of "This Dew [that] fell on my Breast," dew again being the traditional symbol of transforming grace and Christ's presence. The line "O how it *Blouds*, / And *Spirits* all my Earth," a curious and emphatic use of substantives as verbs, suggests that the self is vitalized, animated, inspired, brought fully to life by "This Dew," which like the Old Testament manna also symbolizes eucharistic food. As in "Corruption" and "Christs Nativity", "Earth" represents the first Adam, of the earth, red clay. "The first man is of the earth, earthy" (1 Cor. 15:47). But "Earth" is also earth, the earth referred to at the beginning of Genesis. That is, the language of these lines, particularly lines 7 to 11, subtly reveals the relationship of the self to the whole of creation to be distinguishable yet indivisible, to be essentially at one, because it is Christ or Wisdom playing in all these places. On a first reading it might seem that Vaughan turns in the middle of line 9 from the self to God's creation, "the quick world," the world of nature. (He does. And he does not.) This interpretation of turning is supported by lines 12 to 15, which refer to "The rising winds, / And falling springs, / Birds, beasts, all things" that "Adore him in their kinds," in their natures, in their true nature. But surely, on a second look, "the quick world" may also be seen to refer to "my Earth" which has been *blooded*, *spirited*, or quickened by the dew, quickened by "the last Adam . . . a quickening spirit" (1 Cor. 15:45), especially because "the quick world / Awakes, and sings" as does the poet's "glad heart," which is encouraged in "Christs Nativity" to "Awake . . . and Sing." Every day is Christ's Nativity whenever "by mystick birth / The Lord of life [is] borne in Earth." The "Earth" of "The Morning-watch" is the first Adam and it is the earth, God's creation, the world of nature, and both have been Christ-quickened. The language of this poem (and other Vaughan poems) and the seeming transition in line 9 from the poet's self to the larger creation rhetorically and poetically suggest that the two are somehow one. They are one in the sense that though distinguishable they yet both in some very real sense are false or dead until they are God-quickened and then they awake and sing, realizing the mystical body of Christ, in the single "great Chime / And *Symphony* of nature." Then "God is in man and God is in everything" and "There is no doer but he" (Julian, 75, 81), in the sense explained in "The Holy Communion":

> Welcome sweet, and sacred feast; welcome life!
>    Dead I was, and deep in trouble;
> But grace, and blessings came with thee so rife,
>    That they have quicken'd even drie stubble;
>    Thus soules their bodies animate,
>    And thus, at first, when things were rude,
>       Dark, void, and Crude
> They, by thy Word, their beauty had, and date;
>    All were by thee,
>    And stil must be,                                    10
>    Nothing that is, or lives,
>    But hath his Quicknings, and reprieves
>       As thy hand opes, or shuts;
>       Healings, and Cuts,
>    Darkness, and day-light, life, and death
>    Are but meer leaves turn'd by thy breath . . .

In the poem "Quickness" (a favored word, which in its various grammatical forms appears repeatedly in Vaughan's work), Vaughan distinguishes between false life and true life and concludes with the characteristic alleged ineffability of the mystic that "life is, what none can express, / *A quickness, which my God hath kist.*" To paraphrase another Welsh poet, the divine force that through the green fuse quickens the flower also quickens the poet's green self. It follows that, as Julian writes, "God's will is that we should greatly value all his works," a sentence which accurately reflects Vaughan's attitude toward all creation, and that "The fullness of joy is to see God in all things," a sentence which characterizes Vaughan's most passionate desire and on occasion, as in "The Morning-watch," its fulfillment (103, 114). This sense of oneness or, more specifically, the sense of a divine presence in all things, which finds expression in other seventeenth-century writers, including Jakob Boehme and Thomas Traherne, is frequently expressed in images of circularity, as in Vaughan's "In what Rings / and *Hymning Circulations* the quick world / Awakes, and sings." We recall also the "glorious Ring" of "Vanity of Spirit." Similarly, "The World" famously begins:

> I saw Eternity the other night
> Like a great *Ring* of pure and endless light,
>> All calm, as it was bright,
> And round beneath it, Time in hours, days, years
>> Driv'n by the spheres
> Like a vast shadow mov'd, In which the world
>> And all her train were hurl'd.

The poem then considers "The doting Lover," "The darksome States-man," "The fearful miser," "The down-right Epicure," and "some who all this while did weep and sing, . . . soar'd up into the *Ring.*" Just as there are two selves or lives, false and true, outward and inward, so there are two worlds, Eternity and Time, the God-quickened and ordered world and the world of vanity and illusion. Those who soared up into the Ring are at one with the Ring, like Dante's doxology of all Paradise, becoming the mystical bride or body of Christ (see Rev. 19 and 21). The others are of and in the world of Time. As Boehme, who considered man "the little spark of light," writes in *The Way To Christ*, "so is man created according to the outward humanity, he is the time, and in the time, and the time is the outward world, and it is also the outward man. The inward man is eternity and the spiritual time and world" (43–44). While the title, "The World," and much of the poem might initially encourage readers to take the glorious first line, "I saw Eternity the other night," as a reference only to the Vision of Dame Kind, the concluding lines confirm through the major metaphor of spiritual marriage that it refers as well to the Vision of God, the other important vision in Vaughan's work:

> But as I did their madnes so discusse
>> One whisper'd thus,
> *This Ring the Bride-groome did for none provide*
>> *But for his bride.*

One kind of vision may lead to another, and, as observed, Vaughan's poetry repeatedly expresses such a pattern. In "I walkt the other day," a poem variously like "The Morning-watch" and "Vanity of Spirit," the speaker again leaves his cell to walk outdoors in a field "to spend my hour" meditating upon "A gallant flowre," such meditation often preceding contemplative vision. Like St. John of the Cross, who also took long walks into the country, Vaughan evidently loved nature in ways which make him, like St. John, akin to St. Francis of Assisi.[19] And while Vaughan is not Blake or Wordsworth, earlier critics perceived important parallels, including so-called nature mysticism, between him and English Romantic Poets.[20] "I walkt the other day" plainly indicates that attentively looking at nature may provide moral instruction and reveal divinity:

### 6.

And yet, how few believe such doctrine springs
    From a poor root
Which all the Winter sleeps here under foot
    And hath no wings
To raise it to the truth and light of things,          40
    But is stil trod
    By ev'ry wandring clod.

### 7.

O thou! whose spirit did at first inflame
    And warm the dead,
And by a sacred Incubation fed
    With life this frame
Which once had neither being, forme, nor name,
    Grant I may so
    Thy steps track here below,

### 8.

That in these Masques and shadows I may see        50
    Thy sacred way,
And by those hid ascents climb to that day
    Which breaks from thee
Who art in all things, though invisibly;
    Shew me thy peace,
    Thy mercy, love, and ease,

### 9.

And from this Care, where dreams and sorrows raign
    Lead me above
Where Light, Joy, Leisure, and true Comforts move
    Without all pain,         60
There, hid in thee, shew me his life again
    At whose dumbe urn
    Thus all the year I mourn.

Alan Rudrum rightly notes that in "Masques and shadows" "there may be . . . a significant pun, involving the notion of mask: concealment and masque; stage representation . . . The idea is that the natural world both reveals and conceals God" (*Henry Vaughan,* 587). The run-on last three stanzas, the protracted quality of which in itself suggests timelessness, lead the speaker from moral instruction (stanza 6), arising from meditation on things (here specifically the flower and its "poor root") to a prayer for a contemplative Vision of Dame Kind, such vision permitting him again to climb from the chain of created being to God, "Who art in all things, though invisibly"; leaving behind the vain world of anxious thought and sorrow, he will be led above to heaven ("Light, Joy, Leisure" interestingly echo Herbert's "Heaven"), where in the final Vision of God he will see too, hid in God, "his life again," his brother (and the flower, and Christ), "For ye are dead and your life is hid with Christ in God" (Col. 3:3).

V

As we have just seen, Vaughan is the only one of the three contemplative poets studied thus far who reads the book of nature, whose poetry contains abundant signs and characteristics of the Vision of Dame Kind. "I walkt the other day" and other poems indicate that Vaughan finds in the creation Christ playing in ten thousand places. But in the passionate desire for union all three poets do seek the Word in the book of Scriptures, and that book has for them the meaning that it had, according to Andrew Louth, for the early Church Father Origen:

> Understanding Scripture is not for Origen simply an academic exercise but a religious experience. The meaning found in the Scripture is received from the Word, and the experience of *discovering* the meaning of Scripture is often expressed in 'mystical' language; he speaks of a 'sudden awakening,' of inspiration, and of illumination. . . . In this engagement with Scripture, Origen enters more and more deeply into communion with God—and leads others into this communion. (64)

So too in differing degrees and ways through their poetry Donne, Herbert, and Vaughan seek, are led, and lead others into this communion, such is the power of the Word. Vaughan's poetry is itself also testimony, as is his 1655 Preface to *Silex Scintillans,* that meditative and contemplative poetry, particularly Herbert's poetry, may, like the Scriptures, lead the self and others to a foretaste of heaven. "Holy writing" has transformative powers. After remarking in his Preface that Herbert's "holy *life* and *verse* gained many pious *Converts,* (of whom I am the least)," Vaughan goes on to suggest the vital connection between the poet's experience and his text:

> It is true indeed, that to give up our thoughts to pious *Themes and Contemplations* (if it be done for pieties sake) is a great *step* towards *perfection*; because it will *refine*, and *dispose* to devotion and sanctity. And further, it will *procure* for us (so easily communicable is that *loving spirit*) some small *prelibation* of those heavenly *refreshments*, which descend but seldom, and then very sparingly, upon *men* of an ordinary or indifferent *holiness*; but he that desires to excel in this kinde of *Hagiography*, or holy writing, must strive (by all means) for *perfection* and true *holiness*, that a *door may be opened to him in heaven*, Rev. 4. I. and then he will be able to write (with *Hierotheus* and holy *Herbert*) A *true Hymn*. (Martin, ed., *The Works of Henry Vaughan*, 391–392)

Vaughan makes plain what Herbert also believed: only to the extent that the writer realizes the Word will he or she be able to write true Hymns, for the life of the Spirit and the life of poetry, inspiration from the gods, are profoundly interrelated. Whereas reading the book of nature leads to the extrovertive Vision of Dame Kind and reading the book of the Soul or Self leads to the introvertive Vision of God, reading the book of Scriptures (or any book of holy writing) may conduce to either extrovertive or introvertive contemplative experiences. In the extrovertive visions, one discovers Christ playing in the places of nature or in the beloved or in other humans; in the introvertive vision, one inwardly discovers one's own Godlike, Christlike nature. Whatever book one reads, it is the Word that is finally apprehended. In this sense and in the sense that ultimately Christ is the only effective writer, speaker, doer, contemplation of God is possible only *per Christum*. The Incarnation is a constantly renewed fact of experience.

Reading the Scriptures may become, as St. Edmund Rich and others point out, a form of contemplation. To the four Visions previously discussed, we might well add a fifth, the Vision of Art, insofar as reading any holy writing (or experiencing non-verbal art work) becomes a religious experience, a matter of entering (as for Origen) "more and more deeply into communion with God." Just as the natural creation and creatures are created by God (or, more exactly, by Christ or the Word as the Second Person, for the First Person), so is all art created by Christ in us (the deific powers of the Imagination. Especially in the modern era, "we say God and the imagination are one," as Wallace Stevens writes.) One may thus experience the presence of divinity in its creations through the Vision of Art as well as through the other Visions. The end or purpose of holy writing is contemplative experience, the realization of one's divine identity. One writes (or Christ, as the only *effective* doer, writes) to bring one's fallen self (and others) to God. Needless to say, this journey is usually a long and arduous one, but then, one should add, the longest way round is paradoxically the shortest way home. Like the other Visions, the Vision of Art, poetry of contemplation, has transformative powers, which will be discussed further in the next chapter, on the modern period.

The central mystical paradox of death and rebirth, the myth of the fall and redemption, is found in all three poets' religious poetry in different degrees. All three poets seek the Vision of God, but actually attain to different stages. Donne's divine poetry seems not to advance beyond Purgation; it is meditative rather than contemplative, pre-mystical rather than precisely mystical. The stages of Illumination and the Dark Night of the Soul appear in Vaughan's religious poetry, as in Herbert's, which is the most spiritually advanced. The sequence of "The Church," exhibiting the contemplative passion for complex unity and interconnections, is a various alternating record of many spriritual conflicts, griefs, and joys, moving in an essentially eucharistic ascent from meditation to contemplation, integrated by the theme of submission to God's will, which helps to effect the transformation of psyche to pneuma, and ending in "Love" (III), a description of the self's perfection in union with Christ, the two Adams or "I"s becoming one. As a lyric sequence, Herbert's "The Church," with its many purgations, illuminations, dark nights, and final union, is the most fully realized poetic expression of a complex *via mystica* in the English language.

Although there are some hints in a few of Vaughan's love poems, such as "To Amoret, Walking in a Starry Evening" and the derivative "To Amoret, of the difference 'twixt him, and other Lovers," the evidence (the characteristics of contemplative experience) is much too insufficient, so that one must conclude that Vaughan's secular poetry, unlike Donne's, reveals no Vision of Eros. Whereas Donne's Group One poems may be said to neglect the soul and Group Three to slight the body, Group Two celebrates the union of the lovers' bodies and souls (a unitary consciousness and a unifying vision) and displays the other distinctive contemplative characteristics. With a view that is both traditional and modern, Donne, like D. H. Lawrence and modern theologians, especially feminist ones, writes of a love that accepts and affirms bodiliness as a valid part of holiness and that re-integrates polymorphously erotic sexuality and spirituality, which have too often been dichotomized. Group Two poems suggest that the mystery of sexual intercourse is a prefiguring realization as well as a symbolic representation of that mystical body of which we are all members. The best poetic expression of the Vision of Eros in the English language, Donne's poems of true love are genuinely mystical and so appropriately expressed in genuinely mystical language.

Understood in "the light of the master revelations," traditional contemplative terms, Herbert enjoyed the Vision of God and, knowing at least intellectually that "all things are in the divinity, and the divinity is in all things," apparently prayed for the Visions of Dame Kind and Philia; and he may have in holy communion, as suggested by "The Invitation" and other poems, confirmed the Jungian insight that in profound ways all humans are connected, one, and one, too, still more deeply with God in the mystical body of Christ. The basis for much utopian thinking and many religious utopian communities, the Vision of Philia, wherein the individual true self is joined by other true selves to form a single choir or Communion of Saints united in God's praise, leads to the City of God, here and hereafter. Augustine writes, "we do worthily approve their [the philosophers'] enjoining a wise man to live in mutual society; for how should our celestial city (the nineteenth book whereof we now have in hand) have ever come to its origin, development, or perfection, unless the saints live all in sociable union?" (*The City of God*, XIX, 5). The mystical theology of many Church Fathers shows a mutual interacting of the mystical and ecclesiastical. And while Donne, Herbert, and Vaughan, like most devout souls, may pursue contemplative ends in predominantly solitary ways, in that love and vision which unites the self to God and to others the contemplative life and the active life eventually come together. The contemplative life may be both essential prelude to and an integral part of the active life. J. Daniélou comments that "the mystical graces have an apostolic purpose. They are all in a sense charismatic graces. To this apostolic aspect of the mystical life there corresponds inversely the mystical aspect of the apostolic life. By that I mean that it is above all in attaining personal sanctity that the soul becomes a source of grace for others. Thus sanctification, far from separating her from the others, is on the contrary that which enables her to serve them. The image which Gregory [of Nyssa] gives us is that of a soul wholly turned towards God, who only draws others to herself for the sake of him" (cited in Louth, 201–202).

There is a Buddhist parable that is pertinent. Three monks, who have searched long and hard for Nirvana, finally find it, eagerly climb over its walls and then luxuriate in paradisal delights. Suddenly, one of them gets up, runs back to the wall and starts to climb back over it. Puzzled, the other two shout at him, "But why are you going?" He answers, "I"m going to tell the others where Nirvana is." Some may end their quest in contemplation; some may follow contemplation with an active life in one form or another. The significance of Donne, Herbert, and Vaughan for the twentieth century, an age literally much more apocalyptic than their own, an age that more than ever needs to learn to live in peaceable and sociable union, is that their contemplative poetry may, like all holy writing, tell us something about where Heaven is and how to get there in this life.

Finally, for all of Herbert's great influence on Vaughan and the many vital similarities between them, including Vaughan's sharing with Herbert the mystic wisdom that weal and woe are equally God's love, as a poem like Vaughan's "Affliction" shows, Vaughan is in some important ways a poet much like Traherne. (It is significant that before Traherne's poetry was properly identified by Bertram Dobell, it was thought to be by Vaughan.) Until the nineteenth century, the poetic expressions of the Vision of Dame Kind by Vaughan and Traherne were unsurpassed in English. The real heirs to the seventeenth-century Metaphysical poets are some of the English Romantics and American Transcendentalists in the sense that some of these latter poets continue the extrovertive Visions of the former, especially the Visions of Dame Kind of Vaughan and Traherne. That Traherne could not have been known to the nineteenth-century writers suggests that such Visions are far more a matter of profound experience rather than literary convention. The discovery of God or a numinous presence in nature by Vaughan, Traherne and later poets was perhaps importantly fostered in part (but only in part) by the Renaissance exaltation of man and the Renaissance's directing of attention and knowledge toward nature, whether in the astronomer's study of stars and planets, the explorer's discovery and exploration of the New World, the physician's study of human anatomy, or the botanist's cataloging of plants and flowers; and so on. Although obviously different enough from the nineteenth-century English Romantic poets and American Transcendentalists and certain soon-to-be-discussed twentieth-century poets, Vaughan and Traherne are very like some of these writers insofar as they all see God in nature or, as Wordsworth and Blake put it, see "every common sight apparelled in celestial light" and "everything as it is, infinite." While Donne,

Herbert, Vaughan and Traherne all seek and variously find an intro-vertive Vision of God (some more, some less), only Vaughan and Traherne truly experience the extrovertive Vision of Dame Kind, a point which significantly helps to account for similarities of subject and style in the two later poets. The two commonplaces that during the sixteenth century men took possession of the book of God and that during the seventeenth century (while the earlier possession continued) they began to decode the book of nature both may help to account, I believe, for important differences between the two ear-lier and the two later seventeenth-century poets. That the rise of sci-ence in the seventeenth and subsequent centuries and the scientific study of nature may be linked to the increasing so-called nature mys-ticism is a consideration of special pertinence to our last chapter, concerned with the modern period, a period when science has be-come significantly different from what it was in the time of Newton and Blake. The modern period has been said to begin with Blake in the age of political revolution and the industrial revolution, much abetted by the then new science which had learned to read so in-sightfully in the book of nature. Space and other considerations do not permit a full discussion of contemplative poetry written be-tween the 17th and 20th centuries, including poems by Christopher Smart, Blake, Wordsworth, Whitman, Francis Thompson, and Hop-kins, among others. But in part to suggest the continuing relevance, indeed the vital necessity, of contemplative tradition and poetry for our apocalyptic modern period, the last chapter discusses some of the twentieth century's holy writing, both literary and scientific. To paraphrase Einstein and Blake, physics and poetry are different paths to the same palace of Wisdom.

# 5

# CONTEMPLATIVE POETRY
# AND THE MODERN PERIOD

The modern physicist is on the brink of Nirvana, the man who follows Einstein right through achieves in the end a state of ecstasy which is the culmination of the way of knowledge. There is a short-cut, through ritual, through yoga practice. And there is the long, long way from Thales and Anaximander down to Einstein. But the final state of consciousness achieved is almost the same, in each case. *And it is the goal*, in each case. The modern physicist is on the brink of the culminating ecstasy, when his search for *knowledge* will consummate itself in the final and inexplicable *experience.* . . . all search for knowledge, *whatever the knowledge*, leads to the same result, the mystic experience of ecstasy in re-birth, the experience of Nirvana, the achievement of the state of Pradhana, one or the other of the ultimate experiences which are all alike, but reached by different roads.

D. H. Lawrence

It is probably true quite generally that in the history of human thinking the most fruitful developments frequently take place at those points where two different lines of thought meet. These lines may have their roots in quite different parts of human culture, in different times or different cultural environments or different religious traditions: hence if they actually meet, that is, if they are at least so much related to each other that a real interaction can take place, then one may hope that new and interesting developments may follow.

Werner Heisenberg

When it comes to atoms, language can be used only as in poetry. The poet too is not nearly so concerned with describing facts as with creating images and establishing mental connections. . . . Quantum theory . . . provides us with a striking illustration of the fact that we *can* fully

understand a connection though we can only speak of it
in images and parables.

Niels Bohr

How can cosmic religious feeling be communicated from
one person to another if it can give rise to no definite no-
tion of a God and no theology? In my view, it is the most
important function of art and science to awaken this feel-
ing and keep it alive in those who are receptive to it.

Albert Einstein

"God is dead!" Nietzsche announced near the end of the nine-
teenth century.[1] He was anticipated by Blake near the begin-
ning of that century:

> God appears and God is light
> To those poor souls who dwell in night,
> But does a human form display
> To those who dwell in realms of day.

These concluding lines from "Auguries of Innocence" express the
preference, to use the terminology of the preceding chapters, for the
Visions of Eros and of Philia instead of the Vision of God. The fam-
ous opening lines of this poem constitute one of the most beautiful
and memorable expressions of the Vision of Dame Kind:

> To see a world in a grain of sand
> And a heaven in a wild flower
> Hold infinity in the palm of your hand
> And eternity in an hour.

As Blake says in "The Marriage of Heaven and Hell," "If the doors
of perception were cleansed, everything would appear to man as
it is, infinite." Presumably, Vaughan, who "saw Eternity the other
night / Like a great *Ring* of pure and endless light," is one of "those
poor souls who dwell in night" in so far as his lines refer to the Vi-
sion of God. (They may of course refer to that Vision or to the Vision
of Dame Kind or both.) In other words, among its many meanings,
Nietzsche's formula suggests that sometime after the seventeenth
century (coincidentally or causally, along with the rise of science
and the increase of nature mysticism in the English Romantics,

American Transcendentalists, and others) the transcendent God descended into nature and into humankind, never to rise again.

At least not for many writers. Some poets, like Gerald Manley Hopkins, T. S. Eliot, and William Everson (Brother Antonius) still continued to seek the Vision of God. But many others see and believe in no transcendent God at all or only in the immanent divinity, thereby *seeming* to belie the old conviction that when the contemplative is aware in mystical experience of God's immanence he is also paradoxically aware of God's transcendence. Most modern poets, from Blake and Whitman on, who continue contemplative tradition do so almost exclusively in its extrovertive aspects only. Has the modern period seen Aristotelianism almost totally triumph over Platonism, so to speak? The Renaissance movement away from certain medieval preoccupations toward a greater interest in man and nature (partially reflected in some of the differences between Donne and Herbert, on the one hand, and Vaughan and Traherne, on the other) has of course variously accelerated in modern times. Whereas seventeenth-century religious poets, like all fully devoted medieval and Renaissance believers, sought the Vision of God, the proper study of mankind, paraphrasing Alexander Pope, seems in more recent times to have become man and kind, to use that old term for nature. So Whitman writes in "Song of Myself,"

> And I say to mankind, Be not curious about God,
> For I who am curious about each am not curious about God . . .

Yet Whitman is a believer in and seer of immanent divinity, giving voice to the extrovertive visions:

> I hear and behold God in every object, yet understand God not
> in the least . . .
> I see something of God each hour of the twenty-four and each
> moment then,
> In the faces of men and women I see God, and in my own face in
> the glass . . .

If God is dead (in whatever sense), many modern and contemporary writers continue, nevertheless, to give brilliant expression in both poetry and prose to key concerns of contemplative tradition. In his essay, "Poetry, Personality and Death," Galway Kinnell, for example, discusses, in ways entirely germane to contemplative tradition, self-absorbed contemporary poetry, the uses of *persona* in poetry, the closed ego of modern man, and poetry's task of transcending this closed ego which neurotically cripples us. By the closed ego of modern man, which is the source of the unshared "I" in self-absorbed contemporary poetry, Kinnell means "that ego which separates us from the life of the planet, which keeps us apart from one another, which makes us feel self-conscious, inadequate, lonely, suspicious, possessive, jealous, awkward, fearful, and hostile; which thwarts our deepest desire, which is to be one with all creation" (Friebert and Young, eds., *A Field Guide to Contemporary Poetry*, 208–209). This conception of the ego or false self as a prideful and painful sense of separate existence, a role one assumes and is assigned to play, an abstraction and convention rather than the concrete, living reality, has, as observed, its roots in biblical and ancient mystical tradition and develops through the centuries in poets and philosophers too numerous to mention, blossoming more recently in such diverse writers as Walt Whitman, D. H. Lawrence, Robert Penn Warren, Theodore Roethke, Robert Bly, and Galway Kinnell. The distinction between the ego and the true self provides vital insights into these and other writers' poetry, which, as Kinnell says of poetry in general, "has taken on itself the task of breaking out of the closed ego" (212).

In his essay, Kinnell considers several contemporary poets whose poems often seem liberated from the self-absorbed ego, among them Robert Bly. In Bly's view, poetry should present a contemplative sense of the world. As an editor, publisher, translator, critic, poet, and friend of other poets, Bly has exerted considerable influence on contemporary poetry. While Bly's techniques have been much affected by modern Spanish surrealists such as Neruda and Lorca, his thought has in turn been influenced by, among others, the seventeenth-century mystic, Jakob Boehme. Bly regards Boehme as "the greatest European genius in the spiritual tradition . . . the tradition in which I find the most nourishment, going from the ancient mystics through the Gnostics, through the people of brotherly love like Boehme, Eckhart, Blake, and St. John of the Cross, to Jung" (69–70). Basic to Boehme's philosophy is his distinction between the outward man, who is as if asleep, and the inner man, who sees as if with a third eye directly into the real nature and mystery of things. Boehme's distinction between outward and inner man is comparable to Kinnell's distinction between false self (ego) and true self, the necessity for the death of the one for the sake of the transfiguring rebirth of the other: in Kinnell's words, "the death of the self I seek, in poetry and out of poetry, is not a drying up or withering. It is a death, yes, but a death out of which one might hope to be reborn more giving, more alive, more related to the natural life" (Friebert and Young, 222).

This archetype of rebirth or regeneration, alternatively designated the myth of the Fall, is a progress and pattern discernible in and central to the work of numerous poets besides the ones discussed in the preceding chapters or mentioned here. Although it does not surprise us that many poets, even those with great stylistic differences, share a similar visionary or mystical philosophy, it is remarkable that such a self- and world-view is increasingly shared by others very different from the likes of Donne, Herbert, Vaughan, Traherne, Blake, Whitman, Lawrence, Warren, Roethke, Bly, or Kinnell. As the physicist Fritjof Capra claims in his *The Tao of Physics*, "the philosophy of mystical traditions, also known as the 'perennial philosophy,' provides the most consistent philosophical background to our modern scientific theories" (Capra, xviii). If in the past science contributed to the death of God, it may also in this century be contributing to a resurrection of God. Indeed, scientists of various disciplines are finally confirming what poets and mystics have intuited and experienced, actually sensed and felt, for centuries. This development and its implications are well worth studying and publicizing. This chapter, then, first describes in sections II, III, and IV essential features of the mystical view of a few modern poets, concentrating on the extrovertive visions of Lawrence, Warren, and Kinnell; then briefly presents in section V recent confirming or pertinent evidence of science, especially of the new physics; and, finally, broadly considers in section VI related matters and consequences, all with particular regard to the central contemplative archetype of rebirth (or myth or the Fall) and to the task of poetry.

## II

In the kinds of experience that underlie and inform modern mystical poems, that part of the world initially presumed to be other is often eventually seen as being at one with the self. Characteristically, there seems to be a movement out of the shell of the smaller self into a certain sense of connection, union or profound relationship with the beloved, another self or some natural object or creature, newly and deeply apprehended, as if its inner mystery were now suddenly revealed. At the least, the persona or unshared "I" somehow breaks out of and exceeds the confines of its usual narrow self; or the closed "I," in exceptional instances, comes to see that all things are inextricably interrelated and that the whole world has become and is one's body. These experiences are frequently accompanied by the clear and vivid certainty that the natural world (or at least certain aspects of it) is so completely right, perfect, or just so, so as to need no justification. Feelings of relief, freedom, joy, rapture, compassion, love for the world usually also accompany such experiences, which historically have variously but not altogether satisfactorily been called *mystical, spiritual, contemplative, unitive,* etc. In one of his frequently anthologized poems, Whitman presents this general vision or mode of awareness, which underlies many of his other works, in this particular way:

> There was a child went forth every day,
> And the first object he look'd upon, that object he became,
> And that object became part of him for the day or a certain part
>     of the day
> Or for many or stretching cycles of years.
>
> (Bradley and Blodgett, 364)

In characteristic fashion, Whitman then lists those "objects," including lilacs, grass, lambs, fish, a staggering drunkard, the schoolmistress, boys, girls, parents, village, river, schooner, clouds, and so on, so that the list or series is in a sense also in apposition with the child. Walt Whitman's friend and biographer, R. M. Bucke, a pioneering psychologist, introduced the useful but also not entirely satisfactory term "cosmic consciousness" for these kinds of mystical experiences, denoting a release from self- or ego-consciousness into not delusions of grandeur but the certain Self-knowledge of one's larger, true identity. As Bucke's friend expressed it, "Walt Whitman, a kosmos, of Manhattan the son." We may change the name, parentage, place of birth and other conventional conveniences of personal identification, but in each instance of cosmic consciousness, the "I," in some real if difficult to explain sense, is at one with the cosmos, or at least with all that he sees or knows of it.

Having said that, one must also say its opposite. The Whitman quotation immediately above is both series and apposition. Walt is paradoxically both separate from and inseparably connected to, even identical with, the cosmos. D. H. Lawrence, who much admired Whitman, considering him "the greatest modern poet," nevertheless chides him for his insistence on "One Identity," for his continuous cry "I am everything and everything is me," for becoming "in his own person the whole world, the whole universe, the whole eternity of time." Lawrence adds a necessary and corrective balance by observing that Whitman's One Identity is enormously important, yes, but only one half of the truth. And so Lawrence insists on irreducible otherness, the other half of the truth, on incomparable uniqueness and distinctiveness: "the quick is the single individual soul, which is never more than itself, though it embrace eternity and infinity, and never *other* than itself, though it include all men" (Bradley and Blodgett, 844–845, 850). A paradox? Yes, but the more paradoxical the more true, paradox being a mode of expressing the miraculous, and a miracle being the point where aspiration and reality meet. So Ursula Brangwen, a major character in both *The Rainbow* and *Woman in Love*, learns by the end of the former novel that the true "self was a oneness with the infinite. To be oneself was a supreme, gleaming triumph of infinity" (397), lines Whitman might have written; and we read in Lawrence's poetry that the true self is "alone and yet reeling with connection" and in "communion with the Godhead" when not "tainted with the ego and the personality" (*The Complete Poems*, 480, 481). In his last work, *Apocalypse*, Lawrence puts the matter plainly and directly: "We and the cosmos are one," but, he adds, "we have lost the cosmos," and "now we have to get [it] back." The Fall, according to Lawrence, occurred when "man felt himself cut off from the cosmos . . . became aware of himself apart, as an apart, fragmentary, unfinished thing. This is the Fall, the fall into knowledge, or self-awareness, the fall into tragedy, and into 'sin'" (23, 24, 150).

For obvious reasons, Eliot would be a likely modern poet to consider in this chapter, following our study of Donne, Herbert and Vaughan, but for the same reasons the study of Lawrence (and Warren and Kinnell) is more challenging and perhaps therefore more rewarding. Whereas the critical charges, particularly formlessness or the fallacy of expressive form, made against Lawrence's poetry by R. P. Blackmur and others have been more than adequately answered by and in the work of critics like V. de S. Pinto (Introduction to Lawrence's *Complete Poems*), Tom Marshall, Sandra Gilbert, and Gail Porter Mandell, it has not yet been sufficiently understood that T. S. Eliot's contention that Lawrence wrote out of no tradition is inaccurate.[2] A knowledge of contemplative tradition enhances understanding of Lawrence's work. Lawrence is a poet in prose as well as a poet in poetry (as Gilbert points out, some of his best poetry is his prose), and the illuminating context of Lawrence's poetry is his own prose as well as the contemplative tradition or the "Perennial Philosophy" of which his friend Aldous Huxley wrote so eloquently in his book of that title. There are several keys to understanding the deep pertinence of contemplative tradition (and, I must add, of Lawrence's own experience) to his writing. The primary key is that, as Mark Spilka, Father Triverton, and other critics have amply demonstrated, Lawrence was first and foremost a religious writer. He himself wrote in a letter to Edward Garnett that "primarily I am a passionately religious man," whose works "must be written from the depths of my religious experience" (*Collected Letters*, 273). Lawrence's letters also show that he knew and approved medieval Christianity though he quarreled vehemently with modern Christianity. Kenneth Rexroth rightly observes that a number of Lawrence's poems are "mystical poems" with "an intense, direct, personal, mystical apprehension of reality" (Introduction to *Selected Poems*, 21). All three extrovertive visions appear in his work, prose as well as poetry, but not the introvertive Vision of God. Like Donne, Lawrence develops a religion of love between man and woman, a Vision of Eros. Unlike Donne's work (but like Vaughan's and Traherne's), Lawrence's writing describes contemplative experiences of nature, Visions of Dame Kind. And other poems of his plainly present Visions of Philia. The key idea of the two selves, ego and true self, or two modes of consciousness, and the related idea of two worlds are central to his work, as is the theme or archetype of death and rebirth, understood in the mystical sense as the metaphorical death of the closed ego and resurrection of the essential self in this life, the phoenix very significantly being Lawrence's totem or special symbol. In this sense, too, his work is apocalyptic, the end of the false self and world coming in this life only, a view very unlike the continuing belief of Donne, Herbert, and Vaughan in the afterlife, even though the works of these seventeenth-century poets also show elements of mystically experienced divinity in this life. Altogether, Lawrence, in effect, "secularizes" contemplative tradition, thereby perhaps making it more pertinent to and meaningful for post-death-of-God, twentieth-century humans.

Many of these and other key mystical elements in Lawrence's work are illustrated in his long apocalyptic poem "New Heaven and Earth," which gives vivid expression to his Vision of Eros and a distinctive individuation of the archetype of death and resurrection or rebirth. The title alludes to the book of Revelation 21:1: "And I saw a new heaven and a new earth: for the first heaven and the first earth were passed away." The poem appears in *Look! We Have Come Through*, which Lawrence himself in the Foreword to the book characterized as a kind of connected sequence: "These poems should not be considered separately, as so many single pieces. They are intended as an essential story, or history, or confession, unfolding one from the other in organic development." (*Complete Poems*, 191). Many of the poems in the subsequent volumes, particularly *Birds, Beasts and Flowers*, *Pansies*, and *Last Poems*, also appear in variously connected groups, exhibiting the mystical writer's tendency to perceive and write in interconnected ways (indeed, the words *connect, connection*, and other grammatical variants are among Lawrence's favorite words.) After the Foreword to *Look!*, Lawrence's Argument clearly points to a special religious or mystical state that is the end of this book of poems: "The conflict of love and hate goes on between the man and woman, and between these two and the world around them, till it reaches some sort of conclusion, they transcend into some condition of blessedness" (*Complete Poems*, 191). On the word "blessedness" (which Warren also uses significantly in his later poetry, as we will see), W. T. Stace remarks: "Whatever may be the root and derivation of this word in common language, it is now a wholly religious and mystical word, and not a part of the common naturalistic vocabulary at all" (*Time and Eternity*, 104). Finally in his brilliant essay on poetics, "Poetry of the Present" (*Complete Poems*, 181–186), which he composed as a Preface to *Look!*, Lawrence asks not for what is fixed, set, or statically infinite or eternal but for "the still white seething, the incandescence and the coldness of the incarnate moment . . . the immediate present, the Now." He distinguishes between "poetry of this immediate present," remarking that "Whitman's is the best poetry of this kind," and "poetry of the infinite past and the infinite future." Ideals are figments and abstractions. "Eternity is only an abstraction from the actual present." Real time is the now-moment, the eternal now-moment. "The quivering nimble hour of the present, this is the quick of Time. This is the immanence. The quick of the universe is the *pulsating, carnal self*, mysterious and palpable. So it is always." In identifying this immediate, carnal self ("The most superb mystery we have hardly recognized") with the quick of the universe, in choosing the flowing over the fixed and the immanent over the transcendent (in effect, Aristotelianism over Platonism), Lawrence aligns himself with extrovertive contemplative tradition and identifies himself as a thoroughly extrovertive mystic.

## New Heaven and Earth

### I

And so I cross into another world
shyly and in homage linger for an invitation
from this unknown that I would trepass on.

I am very glad, and all alone in the world,
all alone, and very glad, in a new world
where I am disembarked at last.

I could cry with joy, because I am in the new world, just ventured in.
I could cry with joy, and quite freely, there is nobody to know.
And whosoever the unknown people of this unknown world may be
they will never understand my weeping for you to be adventuring
    among them
because it will still be a gesture of the old world I am making
which they will not understand, because it is quite, quite foreign
    to them.

### II

I was so weary of the world,
I was so sick of it,
everything was tainted with myself,
skies, trees, flowers, birds, water,
people, houses, streets, vehicles, machines,
nations, armies, war, peace-talking,
work, recreation, governing, anarchy,
it was all tainted with myself, I knew it all to start with
because it was all myself.

When I gathered flowers, I know it was myself plucking my own
    flowering.
When I went in a train, I knew it was myself travelling by my own
    invention.
When I heard the cannon of the war, I listened with my own ears to my
    own destruction.
When I saw the torn dead, I knew it was my own torn dead body.
It was all me, I had done it all in my own flesh.

### III

I shall never forget the maniacal horror of it all in the end
when everything was me, I knew it all already, I anticipated it all in
    my soul.
because I was the author and the result
I was the God and the creation at once;

creator, I looked at my creation;
created, I looked at myself, the creator:
it was a maniacal horror in the end.

I was a lover, I kissed the woman I loved,
and God of horror, I was kissing also myself.
I was a father and a begetter of children,
and oh, oh horror, I was begetting and conceiving in my own body.

## IV

At last came death, sufficiency of death,
and that at last relieved me, I died.
I buried my beloved; it was good, I buried myself and was gone.
War came, and every hand raised to murder;
very good, very good, every hand raised to murder!
Very good, very good, I am a murderer!
It is good, I can murder and murder, and see them fall,
the mutilated, horror-struck youths, a multitude
one on another, and then in clusters together
smashed, all oozing with blood, and burned in heaps
going up in a foetid smoke to get rid of them,
the murdered bodies of youths and men in heaps
and heaps and heaps and horrible reeking heaps
till it is almost enough, till I am reduced perhaps;
thousands and thousands of gaping, hideous foul dead
that are youths and men and me
being burned with oil, and consumed in corrupt thick smoke, that rolls
and taints and blackens the sky, till at last it is dark, dark as night,
    or death, or hell
and I am dead, and trodden to nought in the smoke-sodden tomb;
dead and trodden to nought in the sour black earth
of the tomb; dead and trodden to nought, trodden to nought.

## V

God, but it is good to have died and been trodden out,
trodden to nought in sour, dead earth.
quite to nought,
absolutely to nothing
nothing
nothing
nothing.

For when it is quite, quite nothing, then it is everything.
When I am trodden quite out, quite, quite out,
every vestige gone, then I am here
risen and setting my foot on another world

risen, accomplishing a resurrection
risen, not born again, but risen, body the same as before,
new beyond knowledge of newness, alive beyond life,
proud beyond inkling or furthest conception of pride,
living where life was never yet dreamed of, nor hinted at,
here, in the other world, still terrestial
myself, the same as before, yet unaccountably new.

## VI

I, in the sour black tomb, trodden to absolute death
I put out my hand in the night, one night, and my hand
touched that which was verily not me,
verily it was not me.
Where I had been was a sudden blaze,
a sudden flaring blaze!
So I put my hand out further, a little further
and I felt that which was not I,
it verily was not I,
it was the unknown.

Ha, I was a blaze leaping up!
I was a tiger bursting into sunlight.
I was greedy, I was mad for the unknown.
I, new-risen, resurrected, starved from the tomb,
starved from a life of devouring always myself,
now here was I, new-awakened, with my hand stretching out
and touching the unknown, the real unknown, the unknown unknown.

My God, but I can only say
I touch, I feel the unknown!
I am the first comer!
Cortes, Pisarro, Columbus, Cabot, they are nothing, nothing!
I am the first comer!
I am the discoverer!
I have found the other world!
The unknown, the unknown!
I am thrown upon the shore.
I am covering myself with the sand.
I am filling my mouth with the earth.
I am burrowing my body into the soil.
The unknown, the new world!

## VII

It was the flank of my wife
I touched with my hand, I clutched with my hand,

rising, new-awakened from the tomb!
It was the flank of my wife
whom I married years ago
at whose side I have lain for over a thousand nights
and all that previous while, she was I, she was I;
I touched her, it was I who touched and I who was touched.

Yet rising from the tomb, from the black oblivion
stretching out my hand, my hand flung like a drowned man's hand on
   a rock,
I touched her flank and knew I was carried by the current in death
over to the new world, and was climbing out on the shore,
risen, not to the old world, the old, changeless I, the old life,
wakened not to the old knowledge
but to a new earth, a new I, a new knowledge, a new world of time.
Ah no, I cannot tell you what it is, the new world.
I cannot tell you the mad, astounded rapture of its discovery.
I shall be mad with delight before I have done,
and whosoever comes after will find me in the new world
a madman in rapture.

## VIII

Green streams that flow from the innermost continent of the new
   world,
what are they?
Green and illumined and travelling for ever
dissolved with the mystery of the innermost heart of the continent,
mystery beyond knowledge or endurance, so sumptuous
out of the well-heads of the new world.—

The other, she too has strange green eyes!
White sands and fruits unknown and perfumes that never
can glow across the dark seas to our usual world!
And land that beats with a pulse!
And valleys that draw close in love!
And strange ways where I fall into oblivion of uttermost living!—
Also she who is the other has strange-mounded breasts and strange
sheer slopes, and white levels.
Sightless and strong oblivion in utter life takes possession of me!
The unknown, strong current of life supreme
drowns me and sweeps me away and holds me down
to the sources of mystery, in the depths,
extinguishes there my risen resurrected life
and kindles it further at the core of utter mystery.

In a particularly precise sense, Lawrence is writing poetry of the present or the apocalyptic eternal now-moment in that "New Heaven and Earth," consisting of eight sections, begins and ends in its first and last sections in the present tense; the remaining parts of the poem, sections II through VII, are in the past tense, with the return to present tense occurring in the last stanza of VII. In section I, "I cross into another world," a "new" and "unknown" world that contrasts with the "old world" of II and subsequent sections, the world "I was so weary of" because "everything was tainted with myself . . ., because it was all myself." In Whitmanesque catalogs and long parallel lines, Lawrence develops in a negative sense this variation of the man-cosmos unity and expands it in III to include, also negatively and horribly, the man-God unity: "I shall never forget the maniacal horror of it all in the end / when everything was me . . . / I was the god and creation at once." Why should the unity of self and world, and of self and God, which seems so desirable in *Apocalypse* and elsewhere, seem in this poem so maniacally horrible? We shall see, once again, the answer lies in terms of the two selves, ego and true self.

Section IV, descriptive of World War I in the lines and cumulative repetitions about "the murdered bodies of youths and men," paradoxically affirms the widespread, seemingly universal murder committed by the I-narrator ("Very good, very good! I am a murderer!") and the mutilation, horror, oozing blood, darkness, hellishness, and death, including the burial of the beloved and death of the I-narrator, who is "dead and trodden to nought in the sour black earth / of the tomb." The repetitious rhythms are notably effective, and the affirmations are genuinely ironic, and truly carry double meaning: such universal mayhem and murder is both monstrous and also in some as yet mysterious way actually "very good," marvelously good. The phrase "very good" is exactly the one used by the God of Genesis 1 to describe His creation. Each day after the creation of some part of the universe or some creatures, the creator steps back from his creation, like an artist from his artwork, and pronounces it "good." On the last day of creation, God looks upon the entire creation and judges all of it "very good." By means of effective biblical allusion, the Scriptures being very much a part of Lawrence's learning, tradition, and writing, Lawrence brings both Creation and Apocalypse to bear on his poem, much as Donne frequently conflated various biblical events in his poetry. (This may be an appropriate place to remind ourselves that in his own holy writings, *The Man Who Died* and *Apocalypse* for two examples, Lawrence ambitiously and brilliantly rewrote the Christ story of the gospels and the eschatology of Revelation.)

Through a dialectic of the identity of opposites, section V explains the apparent puzzle of regarding destruction and death as good: "For when it is quite, quite nothing, then it is everything." In other words, Donne's words, "death doth touch the Resurrection." In Lawrence's words, "When I am trodden quite out . . . / then I am here / . . . risen, accomplishing a resurrection." Both creation and destruction are very good. The "I" that is trodden quite out is the self-conscious, closed ego that taints the old world, "everything was tainted with myself," and the "I" that is risen is the true self, the last Adam or Christ, "I, new-risen, resurrected, starved from the tomb," "myself, the same as before, yet unaccountably new," entered into "the other world," the "new world" of section I, a world "still terrestrial." Death and destruction of the ego and the ego-fabricated world of hellishness and murderous horror bring the self out of the past into not the future but the eternal present, the no-time of the only time that truly is. Unlike Donne's, Lawrence's "new heaven and earth" does not come about in the afterlife. The transformation of the self brings about a transformation of this world, or how one sees this world; or, even more precisely, these transformations of self and world are inextricably interconnected, two different expressions of the same visionary experience that radically changes and renews the self and world in this present life.

Sections VI and VII develop the theme of death and resurrection and relate it to touch. In VI, we learn that the narrator's resurrection comes about when "in the sour black tomb, trodden to absolute death" he put out his hand in the night and "touched that which was verily not me." Previously, everything in the world "was tainted with myself," which ego tainting or encapsulation made it all a "maniacal horror." Then he touched the "not me," the other, "the unknown, the real unknown, the unknown unknown." Some critics, evidently unfamiliar with contemplative tradition, regard phrases like "the unknown unknown" as "meaningless or banal," as indications "not that Lawrence was too close to his experience but rather that he was not close enough, that, since the poet's intellect was making no real effort of attention, the whole man was not participating in the utterance of the poems" (Gilbert, 95–96).

Those familiar with apophatic or negative mystical theology will understand that the repeated use of such words as "oblivion," "nothing" and "unknown" by Lawrence in this poem serves the same purpose served by these and similar words in the writings of the anonymous author of *The Cloud of Unknowing*, Augustine, Boehme, Cusanus, Dionysius, Eckhart, Gregory of Nyssa, John of the Cross, and so on through an alphabet of contemplatives: they expound the doctrine of unknowing, of moving toward ultimate reality by negating all predicates for it, for it is beyond the pale of predicating conceptualization, beyond the ken of cerebral consciousness, known only by love and imagination in "blood-consciousness." Putting it otherwise, ultimate reality at last becomes so near as to sweep away ego barriers and intellectual distinctions between us and it, and then we enter into the "unknown," a phrase made very meaningful by centuries of contemplative tradition and by Lawrence's own distinctive uses and poetic context. Far from being "meaningless or banal," Lawrence's "unknown" and similar phrases are precise and essential for indicating that the mystical Vision of Eros cannot be known to the rational intellect, the center of the psyche or first Adam. Lawrence may be considered the foremost modern poet of apophatic theology in the sense that he more than any other modern poet emphasizes that the rational intellect alone cannot know the deepest mysteries.

While Lawrence alleges ineffability ("Ah no, I cannot tell you what it is, the new world"), he continues, as mystics typically do, superbly in both traditional and original terms to try to convey the extraordinary extrovertive contemplative experience at the heart of this poem. In the context of resurrection from the tomb, Lawrence's use of the imagery of light and tiger, an imagery later used by Eliot himself ("Christ the tiger," for example, in "Gerontion"), plainly suggests Christ and the discovery of the speaker's Christlike, new self: "I was a tiger bursting into sunlight." The imagery of geographical exploration, of discovery of a new world, bears comparison to Donne's elegy "To his Mistris going to Bed," which also uses similar imagery to describe the body of the beloved, as well as subtly employing mystical language and ideas,[3] although the two poems appear significantly different in tone. It is not until section VII that we learn that the "not me . . . the unknown, the new world" that the speaker in VI tells us he touched was "the flank of my wife" to whom he was married about three years,

> and all that previous while, she was I, she was I;
> I touched her, it was I who touched and I who was touched.

These lines are related to and further clarify the early parts of the poem "when everything was me": because he was locked into the closed ego, all of the speaker's experiences were limited, tainted, ego-reflecting images. He was never able to break out into the real world. The touching of his wife's flank at this present time, though he must have touched her many times in the past, is inexplicably the speaker's breakthrough to the true self, "a new earth, a new I, a new knowledge, a new world of time," this last phrase indicating again that the new world is eternally present in this life, not the past, not the eternal next life. With its shift of tense from past to present and its allegation of ineffability, the last stanza of VII brings the poem full circle to I. In the typical paradoxical manner of mystic tradition, the speaker, in the very process of telling what this "new heaven and earth" is, claims he cannot tell what the new world is nor "the mad, astounded rapture of its discovery." The stanza then shifts to the future tense, suggesting perhaps the "eternal" or continuing effect of the breakthrough to the epiphanic Now-moment, its lasting or permanent effect on the initiate, who "shall be mad with delight . . . a madman in rapture." Or we may alternatively say the past and future collapse into the eternal now-moment, an infinitely expanded present. From the point of view of the sorry-go-round of getting and spending that is too much with us, the saint is a madman in rapture, experiencing, among other contemplative characteristics, a profound sense of reality and of the holy, feelings of joy and blessedness, and a unifying vision, as the religiously charged and allusive language of the last section especially shows.

Like Donne's saints in "The Canonization," Lawrence's saint, of course, is a secular one, one whose "new heaven and earth" is the body of his wife, as section VIII, echoing the Song of Songs, that highly influential erotic-mystical poetic sequence, makes still clearer. The language of this section has both a religious suggestiveness and specific sexual references, especially good examples being "my risen resurrected life" and "the core of utter mystery," which, among their other meanings, pertain to, respectively, the male and female genitals. Other phrases, like "Sightless and strong oblivion" have precise Lawrentian and mystical significances, implying the non-visual, non-cerebral dark consciousness (Lawrence's short story "The Blind Man" is a telling narrative example) and alluding to the cloud of unknowing or forgetting that must be put upon the merely mental, logical, rational ways of knowing in order to come to the holy incarnate self and "mystery beyond knowledge." After many poems of God in man and woman, the famous and frequently anthologized "The Ship of Death" and the group of poems which follow it and conclude *Last Poems* (716–728) concern death in various senses (including both physical and mystical death), the fall, oblivion, mystery, and renewal in ways directly pertinent to "New Heaven and Earth." Many of these poems travel the *via negativa*. With its references to "autumn and the falling fruit" and "the fallen self," "The Ship of Death," which combines Judaic-Christian, Egyptian, and Etruscan myths, also secularizes or naturalizes the meaning of the Fall. The poem "Forget" reads "To be able to forget is to be able to yield / to God who dwells in deep oblivion. / Only in sheer oblivion are we with God" (725). "Know-All" immediately follows:

> Man knows nothing
> till he knows how not-to-know.
>
> And the greatest teachers will tell you:
> The end of all knowledge is oblivion
> sweet, dark oblivion, when I cease
> even from myself, and am consummated.
>
> (726)

In the last section of "New Heaven and Earth," the "green streams that flow from the innermost continent of the new world," filled with mystery, are the "strange green eyes" of "the other" (Frieda, we might note, had green eyes), of the beloved woman, described largely in terms of landscape. Like Donne's mistress, "my America, my new found lande," she is the new world, the newly discovered shore, the earth, the soil that the speaker burrows his body into. Like Donne's true lovers who give up the fallen macrocosm for the paradoxically greater (that is, more valuable) microcosmic world of the lovers, Lawrence's speaker turns away from the ego-tainted, vain, and self-destructive outer world to find a greater world in his beloved wife. The fallen world is well lost for love because in unitive love a more wonderful world is found. Lawrence has reversed the vehicle and tenor of the biblical simile in Revelation 21:2: "And I John saw the holy city, new Jerusalem coming down from God out of heaven, prepared as a bride adorned for her husband." In the poem it is the bride, the wife who is the holy city, the new Jerusalem, the new heaven and earth. The mystic typically discovers in the Vision of Eros that the beloved is a new world and thereby rediscovers, in a special sense, the human-cosmos unity, just as frequently in the Vision of Dame Kind, the mystic discovers that the world of nature that he is united to is a beloved woman or, putting in otherwise, has a profound polymorphously erotic component. Not surprisingly, one of these extrovertive Visions may lead to the other.

In *The Man Who Died*, for example, using a kind of biblical style in his retelling of the Christ story, Lawrence carefully chooses language to present an instance of a Vision of Eros leading to a Vision of Dame Kind. When the Man and the priestess of Isis, who thinks of him as the lost Osiris (Lawrence is combining and re-fashioning both Christian and pagan myths of the dying and resurrecting god), make love ("I am risen!" the Man says in comic and yet serious erotic play on the meaning of resurrection), the Man refers to the woman as "the heart of the rose" and adds "My mansion is the intricate warm rose, my joy is this blossom!" "So he knew her, and was one with her." When, afterwards, she touches the scars he bears from his crucifixion (he was taken down from the cross too soon and put in the tomb unconscious but not actually physically dead), he refers to them as "my atonement with you" (207). Alone, later, and looking at the world of stars and sea, the Man refers to it also as a "rose" (which, one need hardly say, has acquired rich and powerful religious and erotic symbolism through the centuries) in language that profoundly indicates the unitary consciousness and unifying vision: "How full it is, and great beyond all gods. How it leans around me, and I am part of it, the great rose of Space. I am like a grain of its perfume, and the woman is a grain of its beauty. Now the world is one flower of many petaled darknesses, and I am in its perfume as in a touch" (208). Feeling love and "peace and the delight of being in touch" (among other contemplative characteristics) and playing upon "atonement" as an "at-one-ment," the Man, alone in his cave and previously identified with the invisible or dark sun that symbolizes the reborn man, plainly yet eloquently speaks of the man-cosmos-woman unity: "This is the great atonement, the being in touch. The gray sea and the rain, the wet narcissus and the woman I wait for, the invisible Isis and the unseen sun are all in touch, and at one" (208).

Lawrence is the twentieth-century writer par excellence of all three extrovertive visions. Although detailed discussion of the many descriptions of extrovertive visions in Lawrence's work is beyond the scope and requirements of this book, a few additional examples of such visions deserve attention. Of Lawrence's many descriptions of Visions of Eros, the one found in Chapter 23, "Excurse," of *Women in Love* is especially remarkable, and the following passage may serve as illustration:

They threw off their clothes, and he gathered her to him, and found her, found the pure lambent reality of *her forever invisible flesh*. Quenched, inhuman, his fingers upon her unrevealed nudity were the fingers of silence upon silence, the body of mysterious night upon the body of mysterious night, the night masculine and feminine, never to be seen with the eye, or known with the mind, only known as a palpable revelation of mystic otherness.

She had her desire of him, she touched, she received the maximum of unspeakable communication in touch, dark, subtle, positively silent, a magnificent gift and give again, a perfect acceptance and yielding, a mystery, the reality of that which can never be known, mystic, sensual reality that can never be transmuted into mind content, but remains outside, living body of darkness and silence and subtlety, the mystic body of reality. She had her desire fulfilled, he had his desire fulfilled. For she was to him what he was to her, the immemorial magnificence of mystic, palpable, real otherness.

Given the cultural, religious, philosophical, and intellectual influences of exoteric Christianity, Neoplatonism, Cartesianism, and science (all of which in one way or another have constructed body-mind or body-soul dualities) on Western civilization, it should not be altogether surprising that it took the passage of centuries before erotic love between man and woman could be—greatly through the extraordinary literary genius of D. H. Lawrence—more widely and readily recognized culturally, intellectually and religiously as the wholly (holy) unitive and sacred experience that at its best it is and always has been. Needless to say, Lawrence's work was made somewhat easier and more likely by other extraordinary geniuses, like Donne, Blake, and Whitman, who enjoyed and, in their own distinctive ways, wrote about the Vision of Eros.

In *St. Mawr*, which presents Lou Witt's life-changing Vision of Dame Kind in the magnificent horse, St. Mawr ("Looming like some god out of the darkness,"14), the main characters engage in a discussion of "the Great God Pan" and pantheism (with the proper qualifications we would say "extrovertive mystical theology and experiences"). Recapitulating much that has been said in this book in other words and epitomizing much of Lawrence's own mystical philosophy, the artist Cartwright says that in the old days Pan "was the God that is hidden in everything. . . . If you ever saw the God instead of the thing, you died. If you saw it with the naked eye, that is. But in the night you might see the God. . . . Pan was the hidden mystery—the hidden cause. . . . Pan wasn't *he* at all: not even a Great

God. He was Pan. All: what you see when you see in full. In the day-time you see the thing. But if your third eye is open, which sees only the things that can't be seen, you may see Pan within the thing, hidden: you may see with your third eye, which is darkness" (54–55). When the self breaks out of the restrictive egoistic and merely rationalistic modes of seeing and knowing, the resulting third-eye seeing, depending on circumstances and other considerations, may result in any one of the three kinds of extrovertive vision.

Lawrence frequently uses in poetry and prose the image of containment, encasement, or binding as a symbol of ego and the rational mind, as in the poem "Ego-Bound," which develops the image of the pot-bound plant as a comparison for ego-bound man "enclosed in his own limited mental consciousness"; thus incapable of feelings, "he can only slowly die," unless "he can burst the pot, / shell off his ego / and get his roots in earth again" (*Complete Poems*, 474–475). For Lawrence, it is very much a matter of life and death whether or not one is connected to the beloved and the earth and universe. He apprehended the growing imbalance brought about by the increasing dominance of cerebral consciousness (or of the left brain, as we say nowadays[4]) through the development of logical rationality from the classical time of Socrates and the rise of rationalistic science and Cartesian dualism in the seventeenth century to the reductive Logical Positivism of the early twentieth century. In his view, this growing imbalance, accelerated by intellectual, cultural and scientific developments since the seventeenth century, results in increasing abstraction and disconnection from the earth, increasing mechanism and money madness, leading to universal self-destruction. In *Apocalypse* Lawrence writes that we have lost our vital connections to the cosmos and have substituted a "non-vital universe of forces and mechanistic order . . . and the long slow death of the human being set in. This slow death produced science and machinery"; and although this long slow death, which "parallels the quick death of Jesus and the other dying gods" is, like the fall, in the long view, necessary, it "will end in the annihilation of the human race . . . unless there is a change, a resurrection, and a return to the cosmos" (26). World events since Lawrence's death in 1930 provide all too much grim confirmation of the rightness and continuing relevance of his vision. It is not that he wishes entirely to extirpate the ego and cerebral consciousness, but rather to restore the balance which perhaps better obtained in earlier centuries and at times in the greater love- and God-consciousness of poets/human beings like Donne, Herbert, and Vaughan. In "Climb Down, O Lordly Mind,"

Lawrence puts much of this clearly and plainly in terms parallel to the contemplative tradition's central concept of the two selves:

A man is many things, he is not only a mind.
But in his consciousness, he is two-fold at least:
he is cerebral, intellectual, mental, spiritual,
but also he is instinctive, intuitive, and in touch.

The mind, that needs to know all things
must needs at last come to know its own limits,
even its own nullity, beyond a certain point.

Know thyself, and that thou art mortal,
and therefore, that thou art forever unknowable;
the mind can never reach thee.

Thou art like the moon,
and the white mind shines on one side of thee
but the other side is dark forever,
and the dark moon draws the tides also.

Thou art like the day
but thou art also like the night,
and thy darkness is forever invisible,
for the strongest light throws also the darkest shadow.

The blood knows in darkness, and forever dark,
in touch, by intuition, instinctively.
The blood also knows religiously,
and of this, the mind is incapable.
The mind is non-religious.

To my dark heart, gods *are*.
In my dark heart, love is and is not.
But to my white mind
gods and love alike are but an idea,
a kind of fiction.

Man is an alternating consciousness.
Man is an alternating consciousness.
Only that exists which exists in my own consciousness.
Cogito, ergo sum.
Only that exists which exists dynamically and unmentalised, in my
  blood.

Non cogito, ergo sum.
I am, I do not think I am.

Lawrence would probably be pleased that the new science of the twentieth century has replaced the mechanistic universe of Newtonian physics with a "participatory universe," "a dynamic web of inseparable energy patterns." And he would probably be pleased by the outlook of the distinguished Nobel physicist Wolfgang Pauli: "contrary to the strict division of the activity of the human spirit into separate departments . . . I consider the ambition of overcoming opposites, including also a synthesis embracing both rational understanding and the mystical experience of unity, to be the mythos, spoken or unspoken, of our present day and age" (Wilber, ed., *Quantum Questions: Mystical Writings of the World's Great Physicists*, 163).

Throughout his work, Lawrence often presents the extrovertive Visions and key mystical ideas in plain, explicit, clear terms, especially in his *Pansies* and *More Pansies*, which he described as "a bunch of pensées . . . a handful of thoughts" (*Complete Poems*, 417). Many of these poems are in groups and directly address the mind and ego and the two selves (473–474, 529, 603f, 712f, 480–482, for example) and God or the gods (650f, 671f, 691f, for example). Lawrence writes that "If you will go down into yourself, under your surface personality / you will find . . . the sources . . . What the old people call immediate contact with God. . . . Communion with the Godhead, they used to say in the past" (481). He tells us "There's all sorts of gods" and names them, "Jesus, Buddha, Jehovah, and Ra," among many others, but "Where do you see them?" His answer, like Blake's, Whitman's, Hopkins' and other mystics', is "You see them in glimpses, in the faces and forms of people, in glimpses" (671). "The gods are only ourselves, as we are in our / moments of pure manifestation" (673). This biblical idea (see, e.g., Ps. 82:6) of course finds repeated expression in the Church Fathers: having previously quoted Irenaeus, we may note that Clement of Alexandria writes that those who "have become pure in heart . . . have received the title of 'god'" (Bettenson, *The Early Christian Fathers*, 177; see also 69). Lawrence writes of seeing the gods in the young train-conductor, in the girl taking in her wash from the line, in "the woman who looks for me in the world," in "the broad and thick-set Italian who works in with me" (672) and in many others, many Visions of Philia. He also writes of gods in natural objects, but only as these objects, like the poppies, come into blossom or being and have a body does one see the gods in them, for "Everything that has beauty has a body, and is a body."

## The Body of God

God is the great urge that has not yet found a body
but urges towards incarnation with the great creative urge.

And becomes at last a clove carnation: lo! that is god!
and becomes at last Helen, or Ninon: any lovely and generous woman
at her best and her most beautiful, being god, made manifest,
any clear and fearless man being god, very god.

There is no god
apart from poppies and the flying fish,
men singing songs, and women brushing their hair in the sun.
The lovely things are god that has come to pass, like Jesus came.
The rest, the undiscoverable, is the demi-urge.

(691)

Finally, in *Last Poems* Lawrence prays "Come, holy Silence, reach, reach / from the presence of God, and envelop us" (698), for he knows with Eckhart and other contemplatives that it is in the silence that the word of God is heard. Lawrence believes that "Only men can fall from God" and that the fall is the "abyss of . . . knowledge of the self-apart-from-god" (701). And so, in imagery of the Fall, he prays: "Save me, O God, from falling into the ungodly knowledge / of myself as I am without God. . . . Let me never know myself apart from the living God!" (699), for, expressing the basic and vital contemplative desire, the essence of mysticism, he believes "All that matters is to be at one with the living God" (700).

### III

Although we may speak with accuracy of Lawrence as English heir to as well as admirer of Whitman, the early poetry of Robert Penn Warren, America's first poet laureate, shows more of the influence of the English Metaphysicals as well as reminders of his youthful association with the Fugitives, of the "metaphysical" Ransom and Tate manners, beside his own distinctive poetic signature, which has developed greatly over the years. But like Lawrence and Whitman, Warren has always sought some connection between "my

central and obsessive concern with 'poetry' . . . and the 'real' world."
In an interview published in *Writers at Work*, he describes poetry as
"a vital activity . . . related to ideas and life" (192). His essay on Cole-
ridge records the view that ". . . the truth is implicit in the poetic act
as such . . . the moral concern and the aesthetic concern are aspects
of the same activity, the creative activity, and . . . this activity is ex-
pressive of the whole mind."[5] And in *Democracy and Poetry*, he ob-
serves that the central "fact" of poetry is the concept of the self,
which he defines as "in individuation, the felt principle of signific-
ant unity," *significant* implying both continuity and responsibility:
that is, "the self as a development in time, with a past and a future"
and "the self as a moral identity, recognizing itself as capable of
action worthy of praise or blame . . . What poetry most significantly
celebrates is the capacity of man to face the deep, dark inwardness
of his nature and his fate" (xii–xiii, 31). Thus his expository prose
spells out what we recognize in his fiction and poetry to be his major
twofold theme of self and time, and reveals what for him is the vital
purpose of poetry. Warren's concerns with self and time differ sig-
nificantly from Lawrence's, largely because the sense of original sin
is deeper in Warren than in Lawrence, who is more of a utopian
thinker than his American counterpart. "The deep, dark inwardness
of his nature" has overlapping but significantly different meanings
for these two writers. In "Three Darknesses" from his most recent
work, *Altitudes and Extensions 1980–1984* in *New and Selected
Poems: 1923–1985*, Warren writes of "the darkness of wisdom" ("the
world has been / Trying to tell me something"), of the darkness of
nature and human nature, and the darkness of death, darknesses
that have pervaded his work since the first of his four selected vol-
umes, *Selected Poems: 1923–1943*. Many of Warren's poems have a
decidedly philosophic and religious content, being preoccupied with
his major twofold theme of self and time as well as with darkness
and joy, love and the imagination, death and rebirth. His poetry
moves over the years toward extrovertive "sacramental vision," ex-
pressed increasingly in sequences and in the "principle of inter-
relatedness."

The subject of childhood and Warren's bent for twofoldness are
evident in *Promises: Poems 1954–1956*, which is divided into two
sections and marks a turning point in his poetic achievement. The
first and smaller section, "To a Little Girl, One Year Old, in a Ruined
Fortress," dedicated to his daughter, has a Mediterranean setting in
a season which moves from summer toward autumn. The second,
longer section, "Promises," dedicated to his son, is itself of a twofold

nature: most of these poems draw their material from Warren's recol-
lections of his childhood in Kentucky during the early years of this
century, and other poems are addressed and applicable to his son.
The basic subject matter of childhood helps give thematic con-
tinuity to the book's quest for self-discovery, contemporary child-
hood contrasting and interacting with recollected childhood, and en-
courages a ranging from intense personal feelings to historical and
universal implications, such ranging being a means for transcending
the personal ego.

In his criticism of "The Rime of the Ancient Mariner," Warren
writes that there are two themes, the primary theme of sacramental
vision or of "One Life" and the secondary theme of the imagination;
sacramental vision and the imagination are construed as distinguish-
able aspects of the same reality. He approaches the secondary theme
through the symbol of different kinds of light, discussing the con-
stant contrast between moonlight, symbolizing the deific imagina-
tion, and sunlight, symbolizing the "mere reflective faculty" which,
Coleridge said, partakes of "Death." As in the contemplatives gener-
ally, there are these two modes of consciousness or ways of knowing.
Warren points out that in the poem the good events occur under the
aegis of the moon, and the bad events, under that of the sun. The
issue is a bit more complicated in that the operation and effect of
the imagination can be both joyous and terrifying. In his own poetry,
notably from *Promises* on through his later poetry, Warren makes
similar use of light imagery and the themes of sacramental vision
and imagination, though he often substitutes starlight for moonlight
in his later poetry.

Recollections are present imaginings of the past. In "Court-Mar-
tial," written in short couplets and triplets, the speaker recalls his
grandfather's story of the hangings of bushwhackers during the Civil
War. "I see him now, as once seen." The grandfather and grandson
sit in the shade of an evergreen, "withdrawn from the heat of the
sun," the light of which dapples the objects under the boughs. The
old cavalryman's story is itself a recollection—a history, in one
sense, the significance of which the speaker tries to discover:

> I sought, somehow, to untie
> The knot of History,
> For in our shade I knew
> That only the Truth is true,
> That life is only the act
> To transfigure all fact,

And life is only a story
And death is only the glory
Of the telling of the story,
And the done and the to-be-done
In that timelessness were one
Beyond the poor being done.

While raising questions concerning History, Truth, Time, this poem suggests, like the much later "The Corner of the Eye" from *Rumor Verified: Poems 1979–1980*, that the final reality is somehow involved with the imagination. Just after the old man has concluded his story and before the poem ends, the speaker turns away and sees his grandfather, "not old now— but young," riding out of the sky. This is imagined in detail: the saddle, the cavalry boots, the hanged men with outraged faces taking shape behind the rider. The poem concludes:

The horseman does not look back.
Blank-eyed, he continues his track,
Riding toward me there,
Through the darkening air.

The world is real. It is there.

What, considered in its context, is the world referred to in the last line; what is the referent of "there"? The world external to the mind or the world as transfigured by the deific imagination? The answer may well be both. But internal considerations lead to the conclusion that "world" and "there" refer in a special sense to the world shaped by the speaker's imagination: History, Truth, and Time are functions of the creative imagination, which re-creates and transforms the world and self, and which has a value-giving capacity. The external world or natural order is devoid of values. Taken by itself, there is no one thing in the natural order that is better than any other thing. The poem (and particularly the line, "life is only a story") does not empty reality of its content; it makes it clear that the content is given value and meaning by the imagination, a idea similar to the scientific notion that the very act of observing a phenomenon alters it, for we dwell in a participatory universe.

Just as in this poem of recollection so in "Lullaby: Smile in Sleep" the theme of imagination as a kind of ultimate, transcendental (in Kant's sense) shaping force finds expression. Lulling his infant son, the speaker says "You will dream the world anew." Awake, the boy in years to come will see a violent world, the truth perverted, and love betrayed; thus is his obligation greater to "Dream perfection": the more imperfect the world the greater is the human need for perfection. The image serves to re-create and to perfect imperfect reality and gives "our hope new patent to / Enfranchise the human possibility. / Grace undreamed is grace forgone. / Dream grace, son." The tension of lullaby juxtaposed against images of violence is resolved in the last stanza:

> There's never need to fear
> Violence of the poor world's abstract storm.
> For now you dream Reality.
> Matter groans to touch your hand.
> Toward that cold moon that is your dream's command.
> Dream the power coming on.

The implications are clear: as the moon influences the sea, so the dream or image, which is the working of the imagination, shapes matter. Warren's conception of the imagination is precisely Coleridgean. The imagination organizes what otherwise would be chaotic sensation, and, contrariwise, it anchors the reason in images of sensation, so that the imagination repeats "in the finite mind . . . the eternal act of creation in the infinite I am." The primary imagination creates the world and the self; the secondary imagination is the value-creating capacity; and one knows by creating.

The child as well as the poem is a "promise"; both renew the world. In Warren, childhood has much of the same prominence and significance that it does in Vaughan and Traherne. "The Infant Boy at Midcentury," we read in the poem of that title, enters "our world at scarcely its finest hour . . . in the year when promises are broken," when the need for renewal is great. Thus the poet has attempted to order and set down meaning wrung from early experience as a legacy to the child. It is the illuminative insight into reality, resulting in the silent state of being "blessed past joy or despair" (from "Boy's Will . . .") that Warren's poems, finally, move toward. On the word "blessedness," which in its different grammatical forms appears repeatedly in Warren's later poetry, Walter Stace, as noted in discussing Lawrence, remarks: "Whatever may be the root and derivation of this word in common language, it is now a wholly religious and mystical word, and not a part of the common naturalistic vocabulary at all" (*Time and Eternity*, 104). The ultimate symbolizandum of Warren's poetry, as of all religious language, is the mystical or peak experience. That this is so is clearly evidenced in the sacramental vision and the principle of interrelatedness of Warren's poems from *Promises* on.

Many of Warren's later poems ("later" means after 1960) are remarkable for the quality of unanticipated yet just and engaging, sometimes overwhelmingly effective and memorable last lines. The ring, reason, and rhythm of these last lines remain long in the reader's memory. It will not do to quote only a few lines in illustration. For (and herein lies the principle of interrelatedness), the lines must be taken and understood in context, and by "context" is meant not only the poem of which the last line or lines are a part, but also the sequence of which the poem is a part, the volume of which the sequence is a part, and the total body of Warren's poetry of which any one volume is a part. The principle of interrelatedness functions as the major formal and technical aspect of his later poetry as well as a major semantic dimension of his sacramental vision and the subsumed central themes of time, self, love, death, rebirth, darkness, and joy. And by such integrated means, his poetry deeply reveals the profound contemplative idea that all things are closely interconnected, each part of the world somehow involving every other part.

Since the publication in 1942 of *Eleven Poems On The Same Theme*, Warren has been writing in groups of poems, increasingly so from *Promises* on forward. Not only grouping and repeated subjects and thematic concerns but also full sequences with the recurrence of certain words and images conduce to the sense of continuity, interconnectedness and integration. *Audubon: A Vision* reads as a single long poem composed of shorter poems. And in a foreword, Warren has said exactly that about *Or Else*: "this book is conceived as a single poem composed of a number of shorter poems or sections or chapters." Simplifying slightly, *Or Else*, preoccupied with remembrance of things past ("Time is the mirror into which you stare"), begins in summer, progresses soon thereafter from very frequent images of snow to thaw near the end of the book, from death to rebirth, from parent to self to son and blessedness ("For what blessing may a man hope for but / An immortality in / The loving vigilance of death?"), from uncertainty about the self ("Is this really me?") to rediscovery of the self. The words *dream* and *see* (and their grammatical variations) keep reappearing, often associated with the past, the imagination, and sacramental vision. Images of mountains and especially of stars ("Man lives by images," we read in "Reading Late At Night, Thermometer Falling," a marvelous and moving poem on

Warren's father) abound in this volume. They do also in "Can I See Arcturus From Where I Stand?" which has eight of its ten poems star-lit or night-set and which takes its epigraph, "Is *was* but a word for wisdom, its price?" from a poem in *Or Else*. Warren's own "Afterthought" to *Being Here: Poetry 1977–1980* indicates that the entire book is arranged thematically and narratively: "The thematic order—or better, structure—is played against, or with, a shadowy narrative, a shadowy autobiography" (108). And *Chief Joseph of the Nez Perce* is a single, book-length poem.

Warren employs a number of other means for indicating interrelatedness both within and between sequences and volumes. For example, in the later poetry, he vastly increases the number of run-on lines, not only from line to line but also between stanzas, sections, and even whole poems within a sequence. For another example, *Tale of Time*, which asserts "To know is, always, all," has one poem in the title sequence that ends with the question "What is love?"; the next poem concludes "You have not answered my question." The answer or rather one answer comes two volumes later in *Audubon: A Vision*, in the poem "Love and Knowledge," which tells us about the birds Audubon painted that

> He put them where they are, and there we see them:
> In our imagination.

and then the poem concludes:

> What is love?
> One name for it is knowledge.

Knowledge here is Audubon's loving, creative, imaginative apprehension and rendering of his birds and perhaps also the viewers', "our," imaginative perception.

Added significance and purpose obtain in Warren's poetic sequences because his metaphysic regards reality as relational or interrelated, in a way wholly consistent with the new sciences, as we will see. As *Incarnations* reads, "Truth lives only in relation," and from one of the Arcturus poems: "you are a part / Of everything, and your heart bleeds far / Beyond the outermost pulsar." (It is now an ecological truism that everything is ultimately connected to everything else; science has finally confirmed what poets and mystics have intuited and experienced—actually sensed and felt—for centuries.) Like the world's body, each poem is itself an organic system of relationships, and each poem, as each creature, object, and event in the world, has full meaning, value, and being not just separately in isolation from but especially interdependently in relation to all others; form and content, especially in Warren's later work, are themselves inextricably interwoven, and in the sense of this sentence exhibit a vital aspect of mystical consciousness.

In "Holy Writ," from *Tale of Time*, the biblical Samuel, concerned about his "son," expresses a view of time to be found throughout Warren's poetry and novels too:

> I am the past time, am old, but
> Am, too, the time to come, for I,
> In my knowledge, close my eyes, and am
> The membrane between the past and the future, am thin, and
> That thinness is the present time, the membrane
> Is only my anguish, through which
> The past seeps, penetrates, is absorbed into
> The future, through which
> The future bleeds into, becomes, the past even before
> It ceases to be
> The future.

Earlier in the same volume, Warren had written that "Truth"

> Is all. But
> I must learn to speak it
> Slowly, in a whisper.
> Truth, in the end, can never be spoken aloud,
> For the future is always unpredictable.
> But so is the past . . .
>
>            ("Insomnia")

In *Incarnations* we read that "The world"

> Is fruitful, and I, too,
> In that I am the father
> Of my father's father's father. I,
> Of my father, have set the teeth on edge. But
> By what grape? I have cried out in the night.
>
>            ("The Leaf")

Similarly, in *All the King's Men*, Jack Burden, who comes to realize that "all times are one time" and "nothing is ever lost," says "I eat a persimmon and the teeth of a tinker in Tibet are put on edge." The allusion in both the poetry and prose is of course to the biblical "the fathers have eaten a sour grape and their children's teeth are set on edge" (Jer. 31:290; Ezek. 18:2), which is one succinct formulation of the doctrine of Original Sin. "All times are one time" in the sense that, as Samuel's words suggest, any event in time is meaningful only in relation to past and future events. The past is not separate and completed in itself but an ever-developing part of a changing present and future. Once this knowledge is learned, one's individual life and all life may be seen to fall into coherent and inevitable patterns which give meaning to the past, present, and future. We all have and are a multiplicity of fathers because we inherit all of the past and we bequeath our lifetime.

Warren's conception of the self parallels his view of time: a past self or a past life is never simply over, for the past exists not only as past but simultaneously with the present, in the sense that, being a part of the present self, it influences the present, as it and the present shape the future. Hence the importance and recurrence in Warren's work of history, recollecting the past, childhood, relationships between generations. While Warren's conception of the self emphasizes the past, he understands the self in contemplative terms. As contemplatives generally do, Warren further distinguishes between two selves: a surface, spurious, temporal self and a deeper, essential, and eternal (that is, timeless) self (Warren has used the terms "ideal" and "regenerate" self). As previously noted, the first self or ego is one's conception of oneself, the role one assumes and is assigned to play, the known created object, not the knowing, imaginative, creative Act. As shown, for example, by "Interjection #5: Solipsism and Theology," with its repeated "Wild with ego," Warren also conceives of the ego as a prideful sense of separate existence, a rather abstract and conventional notion of oneself rather than the actual, concrete, living reality. To be in touch with this latter non-temporal real self, which paradoxically develops only in time and in vital relation to community, is to be blessed. Warren writes of Jean Jacques Audubon:

> His life, at the end, seemed—even the anguish— simple.
> Simple, at least, in that it had to be,
> Simply, what it was, as he was,
> In the end, himself and not what
> He had known he ought to be. The blessedness!—
> To wake in some dawn and see,
> As though down a rifle barrel, lined up
> Like sights, the self that was, the self that is, and there,

Far off but in range, completing that alignment, your fate.

Hold your breath, let the trigger-squeeze be slow and steady.

The quarry lifts, in the halo of gold leaves, its noble head.
This is not a dimension of Time.

("The Sign Whereby He Knew")

Various succinct though incomplete expressions of Warren's complex sacramental vision appear throughout his poetry, such as in the problematic, prosy "Interjection #4" from *Or Else*:

If blood

Was shed, it was, in a way, sacramental, redeeming . . .

Dear God, we pray

To be restored to that purity of heart
That sanctifies the shedding of blood.

More clearly and certainly: "we are all one flesh," "The world / Is a parable and we are / The meaning," "do you truly, truly, / Know what flesh is, and if it is . . . really sacred?" from *Incarnations*, one of whose epigraphs is from Nehemiah 5, "Yet now our flesh is as the flesh of our brethren." And "have you . . . eaten the flesh of your own heart?" and "the dream of the eating of human flesh" from *Tale of Time*. The last phrase is from the title poem "Tale of Time," which centrally concerns the death of the speaker's mother, just as many of Warren's later poems dwell or touch upon death. For example, "Grackles, Goodbye," from the "shadowy autobiography," *Being Here: Poetry 1977–1980*, is also a poem about the death of the speaker's mother and presents the archetype of death and redemption or myth of the Fall in various natural, cyclical ways, such as in "sunrise and sunset," the fall of leaves, and the migration of birds, which confirm "the fact that only, only, / In the name of Death do we learn the true name of Love."

"Tale of Time" also provides this fuller "eucharistic" expression of sacramental vision:

But the solution: You
Must eat the dead.
You must eat them completely, bone, blood, flesh, gristle, even
Such hair as can be forced. You

Must undertake this in the dark of the moon, but
At your plenilune of anguish.

Immortality is not impossible,
Even joy.

History, all time, the dead, and the cruel, inescapable fact of death
are to be incorporated in and by the living, in a kind of eucharistic
uniting. Acceptance, indeed sacramental affirmation, of the past and
of change or transience, is essential to knowing one's deep, regener-
ate self, that "unself which was self," "that darkness of sleep which
/ Is the past, and is / The self." Self-knowledge, in turn, gives direc-
tion to the future and induces in one, as in Audubon, a capacity more
fully to love and sympathize. With "stars" referring to the stars in
the sky, to the bright chanterelles or edible mushrooms on "earth,
black as a midnight sky," and to the brain glowing in its "skull sky,"
"Have You Ever Eaten Stars" from *Rumor Verified* ends with a
eucharistic vision that suggests the profound extrovertive correspon-
dence (as it is above, so it is below) and interconnection between
self, earth, and universe:

> Question:  What can you do with stars, or glory?
> I'll tell you, I'll tell you—thereof
> Eat. Swallow. Absorb. Let bone
> Be sustained thereof, let gristle
> Toughen, flesh be more preciously
> Gratified, muscle yearn in
> Its strength. Let brain glow
> In its own midnight of darkness,
> Under its own inverted, bowl-shaped
> Sky, skull-sky, let the heart
> Rejoice.
>        What other need now
> Is possible to you but that
> Of seeing life as glory?

Although there are very important differences between the two
poets, Warren's secularized, eucharistic vision nevertheless bears
some comparison to Herbert's more traditional eucharistic inward
uniting with God, at least in that Herbert seems also to have been
led from it to prayers for, if not realizations of, extrovertive Visions
of Dame Kind and Philia. "You are not you," one of Warren's novels,
*At Heaven's Gate*, reads, "except in terms of relation to other

people." Self-knowledge is difficult because the self is not so much just a knowable object but rather more a series of relations in time and timelessness. Hence the necessity of sacramentally eating the dead, incorporating the past and all time in a kind of communion, to discover one's larger, essential self and thereby attain "Immortality . . . Even joy."

Something of the principle of interrelatedness as method and of an end of sacramental vision appears in *Or Else* in the remarkable "Interjection #2: Caveat":

> Necessarily, we must think of the
> world as continuous, for if it were
> not so I would have told you, for I have
> bled for this knowledge, and every man
> is a sort of Jesus . . .

The poem moves from a prosy "metaphysical" beginning on continuity and discontinuity to contrasting plain, subtle statement, even understatement, describing a highway under construction with miles of crushed rock and recommending that you "fix your eyes firmly on / one fragment of crushed rock," highway and fragment becoming metaphors for continuity and discontinuity. At first the rock "only / glows a little," then it glitters and vibrates, the earth underfoot twitches,

> the bright sun
> jerks like a spastic, and all things seem to
> be spinning away from the univer-
> sal center that the single fragment of
> crushed rock has ineluctably become . . . .
> at last, the object screams
>
> in an ecstasy of
>
> being.

The poem leads suddenly to overwhelming vision, makes us see. In other words, another aspect of Warren's sacramental vision obtains during acts of concentrated attention in the illuminated, imaginative perceptions into reality as joyous and sacred, when "every / Ulcer in love's lazaret may, like a dawn-stung gem, sing—or even burst into whoops of, perhaps, holiness," as we read in "There's A

Grandfather's Clock In The Hall," a poem which attains grace
beyond the reach of art.

At times the divine is seen as incarnate in the world, a Vision of
Dame Kind. In such perfect moments, or epiphanic spots of time, or-
dinary, everyday events and entities appear extraordinary and trans-
cendent, become charged through the creative imagination with
enormous physical, emotional, and spiritual meanings, are more
fully created or brought into fuller being. "All the things of the uni-
verse," as Whitman says, "are seen as perfect miracles." Or as Zen
puts it, "How marvelous, how supernatural, I draw water and carry
wood!" Emerson also, as Warren remarks in his sequence "Homage
to Emerson," "thought that significance shines through every-
thing." Examples abound in Warren's later poetry, often associated
with images of light, such as the exceptionally fine "Two Poems
About Suddenly and a Rose" from the sequence "Delight" in *Tale of
Time*, which lead us to see that "The rose dies laughing, suddenly."
"First Moment of Autumn Recognized" from *Altitudes and Exten-
sions* (in *New and Selected Poems*) presents an epiphanic spot of
time/no-time:

> We know
> This to be no mere moment, however brief,
> However blessèd, for
> Moment means time, and this is no time,
> Only the dream, untimed, between
> Season and season. . . .
> being perfected
> At last, in the instant itself which is unbreathing.

The perfect relationship between self and other, whether the
other is living or not, animate or inanimate, is a reciprocally loving
one. In its best moments, Warren's universe is a living and loving
one. "Trying To Tell You Something" and "Brotherhood in Pain,"
two companion poems, develop the idea that "All things lean at you,
and some are / Trying to tell you something," and conclude that any
chance object you fix your eyes on will "smile shyly, and try to love
you." In *Or Else*, "The mountains lean. They watch. They know"
("Little Boy And Lost Shoe"). In the same volume, the speaker re-
calls the time he looked at the stars and cried out

> "O reality!" The stars
> Love me. I love them. I wish they

Loved God, too. I truly wish that.

("Stargazing")

And he remembers

> How once I, a boy, crouching at creekside,
>> Watched, in the sunlight, a handful of water
>> Drip, drip, from my hand. The drops—they were bright!
>>> ("Blow, West Wind")

Not uncharacteristically, Warren concludes this poem with a balancing ironic tension, "But you believe nothing, with the evidence lost." Nevertheless, sacramental vision exists also in present time without irony or contradiction. From *Incarnations*, we read

> When there is a strong swell, you may, if you surrender to it, experience
> A sense, in the act, of mystic unity with that rhythm. Your peace is the sea's will.

This poem, "Masts at Dawn," indicating that imaginative loving (an act of enlightened loving apprehension) leads to seeing the incarnate divine, concludes "We must try / To love so well the world that we may believe, in the end, in God." And, finally, this instance of "dream"-like or imaginative, illuminated, joyful vision beyond the rational knowing of the "mere reflective faculty," with the consequent "perfect stillness," from *Audubon*:

> The world declares itself. That voice
> Is vaulted in—oh, arch on arch—redundancy of joy, its end
> Is its beginning, necessity
> Blooms like a rose. Why,
>
> Therefore, is truth the only thing that cannot
> Be spoken?
>
> It can only be enacted, and that in dream,
> Or in the dream become, as though unconsciously, action . . .
>
> He walked in the world. He was sometimes seen to stand
> In perfect stillness, when no leaf stirred.
>> ("The Sign Whereby He Knew")

209

If Warren's poetry thus affirms life and its moments of perfect stillness, it does so only after its journey through the valley of the suffering and the dead, only after spending its season in hell. Audubon comes to his vision some time after witnessing the violent death by hanging of a woman and her two sons, described with precise detail. He who "felt the splendor of God . . . , loved the world . . . and wrote: 'in my sleep I continually dream of birds' " knew also that the world "though wicked in all conscience is *perhaps* as good as worlds unknown." Affirmation thus obtains through the tentativeness of the italicized qualifier *perhaps* and after various means of balanced ironic tension. Similarly, *Incarnations* contains both the long poetic sequence "Internal Injuries," which concerns the death by execution of a convict and the death by automobile accident of his mother, and also such balancing *seemingly* contradictory yet all "true" statements as "The world means only itself," "the world is a metaphor," "the world is a parable and we are the meaning," and "only Nothingness is real and is a sea of light," this last being one of several expressions of the mystical *via negativa* to be found in Warren's poetry. A good number of poems in *Or Else* and several poetic sequences in *Tale of Time* likewise centrally involve violence and death, including one death by suicide. And his latest poetic work, *Altitudes and Extensions*, seems to contain more instances of "darkness" than any of his previous volumes. In short, Warren's joyful, interrelated, sacramental vision is not an easy or facilely optimistic one but one gained through judicious qualification and hard, unblinking, recurrent recognition, even a pervasive sense, of pain, darkness, and death. Thus *Incarnations*: "The terror is, all promises are kept. Even happiness"; "and there is no joy without some pain." The rose dies laughing, suddenly.

> All items listed above belong in the world
> In which all things are continuous,
> And are parts of the original dream which
> I am now trying to discover the logic of. This
> Is the process whereby pain of the past in its pastness
> May be converted into the future tense
> Of joy.
> ("I Am Dreaming of a White Christmas . . ." in *Or Else*.)

We may say finally of Warren exactly what he has written of Audubon: "He yearns to be able to frame a definition of joy." And exactly what he has written of Flaubert:

> his heart
> burst with a solemn thanksgiving to God for
> the fact he could perceive the worth of the
> world with such joy.
>
> ("Flaubert in Egypt" in *Or Else*)

For Warren knows, as Yeats has written:

> When such as I cast out remorse
> So great a sweetness flows into the breast
> We must laugh and we must sing,
> We are blest by everything,
> Everything we look upon is blest.

In Warren's later poems, the sense of original sin and human limitations is as strong as in his early poems, but the sense of the possibilities of joy and blessedness is somewhat greater. His poems point to and progress toward the joyous and blessed experience in which lies the perfect repose of silence. "Silence, in timelessness, gives forth / Time, and receives it again" ("The True Nature of Time"). *Incarnations* contains the prayer "Forgive us—oh, give us!—our joy," this one subsequent statement among many on rebirth, "There comes a time for us all when we want to begin a new life," and near the end of the volume these lines, "light rises . . . All, all / Is here, no other where. The heart, in this silence, beats." *Or Else* contains a poem, "Interjection #8," that describes the ubiquitous and "unsleeping principle of delight." *Audubon* concludes with the perfect stillness of Audubon and the petition "Tell me a story of deep delight." And *Tale of Time* ends with a sequence of poems entitled "Delight." Warren's poetry, like much poetry of great or important poets, begins in hellish and purgative pain, makes its progress through darkness to death, including the death of the ego, and then, perfectly aware of the often inexplicable violence and suffering that human flesh is heir to, through its earned and integrated vision may end in rebirth, truth, union, selfhood, even joy. So we read in "Delusion?—No!" from *Altitudes and Extensions*:

> I entered in.
> Was part of all, I knew the
> Glorious light of inner darkness burn
> Like the fundamental discovery. . . .
> Delusion?—No! For Truth has many moments.
> Open your eyes. Who knows! This may be one.

## IV

Kinnell, who admires both Whitman and Lawrence, and whose poetry similarly seeks a recovery of original oneness with the cosmos, recognizes both separateness and identity, insisting like Lawrence on the reality of the former as well: "I don't think things are often really like other things. At some level all things *are* each other, but before that point they are separate entities" (*Walking*, 52). Responding to an interviewer's question about the poem as exploration of the inner self, Kinnell says: "often a poem at least starts out being about oneself, about one's experiences, a fragment of autobiography. But then, if it's really a poem, it goes deeper than personality. It takes on that strange voice, intensely personal yet common to everyone, in which all rituals are spoken. . . . The separate egos vanish . . . when you go deep enough within yourself, deeper than the level of 'personality,' you are suddenly outside yourself, everywhere" (*Walking*, 6). Elsewhere, Kinnell puts the paradox in terms of separation and kinship between the nonhuman and the human: "The nonhuman *is* the 'basic context' of human existence. . . . When in the presence of wind, or the night sky, or the sea, or less spectacular instances of the nonhuman—including its revelation through the human—we are reminded both of the kinship and the separation between ourselves and what is beyond us. If there is one kind of moment from which poetry springs, I would say it's this one" (*Walking*, 88). If paradox must be unravelled and resolved, then Kinnell's phrase "before that point" suggests a resolution in time: at one time things are or are regarded as "separate entitles"; at another time, when the ego shell has been smashed, the very same things are or are regarded as "each other."

Kinnell's style, especially his remarkable syntactic, structural, and semantic skills and poetic strategies, variously helps to transform the isolated persona or the skin-encapsulated ego, seemingly confronted by an alien and hostile universe, into the essential self, particular and real, yet universal and in connection and at peace with the rest of creation. His poetry in its own distinctive ways presents in full or truncated fashion the archetypal movement from the innocent open self to the fallen, closed self and on beyond to the reopened or reborn self. Especially through Visions of Dame Kind and of Art, his poetry offers a sense of transfigured human potentiality. For purposes of illustrating Kinnell's own original individuation of the archetype of rebirth or myth of the Fall, one could hardly choose better than "Fergus Falling," the first poem in *Mortal Acts*,

*Mortal Words.* (Because Kinnell is a regular, almost constant reviser of his poems, the text I use for each poem discussed is the latest, that found in *Selected Poems*.) Although this poem consists of five spatially separated stanzas, its structural division is threefold because the first three stanzas (quoted below) constitute one, very long, complex-compound sentence of some two dozen lines—an admirable syntactic *tour de force*. The last two stanzas, also being the last two structural parts, partly recapitulate the syntax and further develop the significance of the single sentence which is the lengthy structural beginning of "Fergus Falling":

He climbed to the top
of one of those million white pines
set out across the emptying pastures
of the fifties—some program to enrich the rich
and rebuke the forefathers
who cleared it all once with ox and axe—
climbed to the top, probably to get out
of the shadow
not of those forefathers but of this father,
and saw for the first time,
down in its valley, Bruce Pond, giving off
its little steam in the afternoon,

Pond where Clarence Akley came on Sunday mornings to cut down
    the cedars around the shore, I'd sometimes hear the slow spondees
    of his work, he's gone,
where Milton Norway came up behind me while I was fishing and
    stood awhile before I knew he was there, he's the one who put the
    cedar shingles on the house, some have curled or split, a few have
    blown off, he's gone,
where Gus Newland logged in the cold snap of '58, the only man
    willing to go into those woods that never got warmer than ten
    below, he's gone,
Pond where two wards of the state wandered on Halloween, the
    National Guard searched for them in November, in vain, the next
    fall a hunter found their skeletons huddled together, in vain,
    they're gone,
Pond where an old fisherman in a rowboat sits, drowning hooked
    worms, when he goes he's replaced and is never gone,

and when Fergus saw the pond for the first time
in the clear evening, saw its oldness down there
in its old place in the valley, he became heavier suddenly

in his bones
the way fledglings do just before they fly,
and the soft pine cracked . . .

Both the center and end of the poem focus on the pond. Each of
the dependent clauses of the second stanza describes one or another
person's activities at the pond. Each person of each clause, except the
last, shares one thing in common, death: "he's gone" or "they're
gone" concludes every clause but the last. The first three clauses
specifically name individuals; the fourth presents two nameless
"wards of the state"; the last "an old fisherman in a rowboat." What
differs about the old fisherman is that "when he goes he's replaced
and is never gone"; that is, the old fisherman assumes mythic pro-
portions. In a sense, then, before his fall, when Fergus sees the "old-
ness" of the pond, he gazes upon death and also eternal return. At
the literal level, of course, the poem presents a boy who climbs a
white pine, sees a pond, gets excited, and falls out of the tree. Mythi-
cally, the poem is about Fergus's fall from innocence into experience.
It is as if, seeing the pond, Fergus has a vision of all those who were
there and now are gone, dead, so that "he became heavier suddenly
/ in his bones," less angelic, as it were, and more earth-bound. After
his parents reach him on the ground and he exclaims, "Galway, Ines,
I saw a pond!" he experiences a momentary "death": "His face went
gray, his eyes fluttered closed a frightening moment . . . " These lines
signal and seal the death or fall of the innocent Fergus. The fragment
which concludes the poem syntactically and semantically repeats
and then extends the crucial second stanza. Reference is made to the
many who have come and gone to and from the pond, which sym-
bolizes both life and death. At the end of the poem, an old fisherman,
seen only by the pinetops, sits in "his rowboat, waiting for pickerel."
He, who "is never gone," we read earlier, remains a symbol of eternal
return or regeneration.

Structurally, the poem recapitulates the definitive biblical myth
extending from creation in innocence, through the fall, to redemp-
tion or regeneration. The first three stanzas, a single sentence, por-
tray an innocent Fergus who has climbed a tree. The incantatory
rhythms and continuous, almost interminable quality of the ex-
tended sentence—as if it might go on and on forever—generate a
sense of timelessness, a kind of Edenic eternity and immortality.
(Simultaneously, however, this extended sentence, like others in
Kinnell's poetry, encourages an accumulating breathlessness, espe-
cially when read aloud, that perhaps suggests imminent death or

ecstasy.) The second structural part, the fourth stanza, presents the accomplished actual fall of Fergus from a tree and his verbalization of his visionary experience, "I saw a pond," and all that is implied, including a symbolic fall from innocence. The third structural unit, the fifth stanza, syntactically and semantically repeating the second stanza, acknowledges death, but concludes with an image of renewal.

Traditionally, the spiritual progress of a person's life is, or ideally should be, from childhood wonder and innocence through fallen experience to blessed redemption. In biblical and contemplative terms, as we have seen, this spiritual progression, successfully completed, may be spoken of as the regaining of Eden or Paradise, or the death of the fallen Adam, the isolated ego, and the rebirth of that divine, creative, and redemptive image hidden within human beings. This progression, in other words, involves the death of, or, in Kinnell's language, the breaking out of the closed ego and the recovery of the true self, at one with all creation. Kinnell presents the central and definitive biblical myth or archetype of regeneration in the secular, "ordinary," literal terms of a boy's fall from a tree, with suggestive and symbolic resonance, so that the ordinary becomes extraordinary, so that a common event assumes, naturally and without fanfare, mythic meaning. Traditionally, all of nature fell with Adam, and the great atonement includes being again at one with nature and thus more vitally alive. In the words of Kinnell's essay, "Poetry, Personality, and Death": "What do we want more than that oneness which bestows—which is—life? We want only to be more alive, not less. And the standard of what it is to be alive is very high. It was set in our infancy. Not yet divided in mind and body, our mind still a function of our senses, we laughed, we felt joyous connection with the things around us. . . . from here comes our notion of heaven itself. Every experience of happiness in later life is a stirring of that ineradicable memory of once belonging wholly to the life of the planet" (Friebert and Young, 216–217).

Like Lawrence, Warren, and other contemplatives, Kinnell constructs many poems in suites, groups of four, five or seven sections, or composes individual poems which together make a single large poem or sequence. *The Book of Nightmares* is his most striking example of this practice. His structural use of groups or sequences is a technique for revealing the connectedness of all creation and for recovering that self which belonged "wholly to the life of the planet." An illustrating poem, from Kinnell's first published book of poetry, *What a Kingdom It Was*, is "Freedom, New Hampshire." Consisting of four sections, each composed of stanzas differing in number and length, this moving poem, an elegy for Kinnell's brother with elements of both the Vision of Philia and the Vision of Dame Kind, develops in both obvious and subtle ways, largely by means of first-person plural and singular narrative and by means of repetition of certain key images. The young brothers, in a rural setting, enjoying their Edenic summer in Freedom, learn about birth and death and life, with the consequent loss of innocence.

Section 3, the most lyrical part of the poem in six eight-line stanzas, begins with a continuation of moon and birth imagery and concludes with references to a place and time when the sun flashed upon the boys' shining world in and around Freedom and its nearby lakes:

Once I saw the moon
Drift into the sky like a bright
Pregnancy pared
From a goddess doomed
To keep slender to be beautiful—
Cut loose, and drifting up there
To happen by itself—
And waning, in lost labor;

As we lost our labor
Too—afternoons
When we sat on the gate
By the pasture, under the Ledge,
Buzzing and skirling on toilet-
papered combs tunes
To the rumble-seated cars
Taking the Ossipee Road

On Sundays; for
Though dusk would come upon us
Where we sat, and though we had
Skirled out our hearts in the music,
Yet the dandruffed
Harps we skirled it on
Had done not much better than
Flies, which buzzed, when quick

We trapped them in our hands
Which went silent when we

Crushed them, which we bore
Downhill to the meadowlark's
Nest full of throats
Which Derry charmed and combed
With an Arabian air, while I
Chucked crushed flies into

Innards I could not see,
For the night had fallen
And the crickets shrilled on all sides
In waves, as if the grassleaves
Shrieked by hillsides
As they grew, and the stars
Made small flashes in the sky,
Like mica flashing in rocks

On the chokecherried Ledge
Where bees I stepped on once
Hit us from behind like a shotgun,
And where we could see
Windowpanes in Freedom flash
And Loon Lake and Winnipesaukee
Flash in the sun
And the blue world flashing.

This section reverses the progression of the imagery in the preceding section and invokes a Wordsworthian sense of childhood and youth. This reversal underscores the cyclical nature of time, of day and night, paralleling and emphasizing the poem's unfolding revelation of the cyclical and interrelated nature of life and death. In the pasture, the brothers lose their labor, making music by "Buzzing and skirling on toilet-papered combs," not doing "much better than / Flies, which buzzed, when quick / We trapped them in our hands." We recall the simile in *King Lear*: "as flies to wanton boys are we to the gods; they kill us for their sport." But these boys feed the crushed flies (familiar symbols, since the seventeenth century, of mortality and the ephemeral) to the meadowlark's nestlings, associated with the newborn calf of section 2; and thus the flies provide another image of death serving, feeding, life. The third section presents a mixed world of both innocence and experience, "For the night has fallen / And the crickets," like the vitally alive boys and flies also making buzzing music, "shrilled on all sides."

What is most remarkable about this section, the longest in the poem, filled with music and light, is that it is a single sentence. Like "Fergus Falling," by syntax and rhythm as well as semantic meanings, it presents a world of *seemingly* "endless" time, a Romantic sense of prelapsarian childhood when every common sight seemed forever appareled in flashing celestial light. Talking about *The Book of Nightmares*, Kinnell points out that for children "time passes slowly. . . . It hardly exists" (*Walking*, 45). "All Time was Eternity, and a Perpetual Sabbath," as Traherne wrote about his early childhood. On the poetic principle that the sound must echo the sense, the music of this section—its sounds (especially its many long vowels) and rhythms—helps reinforce and, in profound ways, reveals the deeper significance. In "Freedom, New Hampshire," the single sentence of section 3 invokes and conjures up—by means of rhythms, sounds, and considerable length, to say nothing of denotative and connotative meanings—a period of time that is expanded, protracted, languid, the sentence itself mimetically unfolding or going on as childhood seems to unfold and go on almost without end; but through the concomitant rhythmic "breathlessness," through certain harsh sounds and verbs, through the death of the cow and of the short-lived flies, and through the smell of fall in the air and the falling of night, the poem hints at the descending shades that will follow for the boys growing into fallen adult consciousness of time and death, a consciousness in and by which the flashing celestial radiance will dim into the light of common day.

As in a musical suite, the various themes and images of the poem are repeated with variation in the last movement, especially in the first three stanzas of the final section. The poetry of the first stanza also variously suggests an "identity" or interconnection of self and the world that is particularly pertinent to these concluding two stanzas:

> The mind may sort it out and give it names—
> When a man dies he dies trying to say without slurring
> The abruptly decaying sounds. It is true
> That only flesh dies, and spirit flowers without stop
> For men, cows, dung, for all dead things; and it is good, yes—
>
> But an incarnation is in particular flesh
> And the dust that is swirled into a shape
> And crumbles and is swirled again had but one shape
> That was this man. When he is dead the grass
> Heals what he suffered, but he remains dead,
> And the few who loved him know this until they die.

This powerful last stanza, which with its extra line is the only one that violates the poem's stanzaic organization, goes beyond the poem's acceptance and transformation of death, the Whitmanesque transformation of the body into healing grass. In its insistence on the individuality and particularity of incarnate flesh and on the persistence of the felt loss, the stanza, which might serve as a motto for much present-life modern poetry, provides a realistic and tough-minded tension, a credible qualification that precludes the acceptance from being regarded as merely idealistic or facile, with a resulting kind of poetry that Warren has designated "impure." Though one may think that there is a too explicit expression of ideas in these final stanzas as compared to more subtle and indirect techniques used by Kinnell in other poems, the last two stanzas, beyond the poem's use of the first-person *plural*, do emphasize and finally effect the transcending of the merely personal and of the unshared "I"; or, more accurately, they do permit and effectuate the poem's being both personal and universal. In Kinnell's words, "It's only at the very end that the poem 'teaches' in the sense I mean. It stops telling what once happened to this or that person, and turns to the reader and tries to generalize about what happens to us all" (*Walking*, 42; see also 96).

"For Robert Frost," from *Flower Herding on Mount Monadnock*, accomplishes poetry's task of breaking out of the closed ego, moving from the personal to the universal, in yet another way. This myth-opoetic poem breaks out of the closed ego by transforming the poet into the land he walked, worked, and celebrated (now, lamentably, "bulldozed") by transfiguring the personal and transitory through art into the enduring poetic and mythic. "The Porcupine" and "The Bear," in some ways companion poems as well as the last two poems in *Body Rags*, also lend themselves readily to the concerns of this book especially because, as Kinnell has pointed out, in both poems "the one speaking actually becomes the animal" (*Walking*, 56). Since "The Porcupine," unlike "The Bear," does not progress by straightforward narration, it is initially more difficult to determine its structure and the ways it brings about the transcendence of the closed ego. The first four sections of this sequence of seven variously describe the porcupine in third person. In the last three sections, the first-person narrator presents himself in terms resonant with the description of the porcupine in the first half of the poem, so that, rather than just the seven resemblances, simply listed in section 2, between the animal ("he") and human beings ("us"), there appears to be, finally, an identity between the quilled creature and the human narrator. "The Porcupine" achieves this identity of animal and I-narrator through the complex agencies of certain recurrent phrasing and imagery and of the interplay of literal and figurative language. The recurrent imagery of vacancy and emptiness, for example, helps to link the different sections and to effect the transformation of one creature into another apparently, in part, on the principle that he who humbles or empties himself (or is humbled or emptied) will be exalted, transfigured, "suddenly glorified with all my blood." In the ecological vision of this poem, organism and environment, creature and land, if not finally all one, as in "For Robert Frost," appear strikingly similar and profoundly interconnected. "The Porcupine" moves between resemblances and identities. The I-narrator (who suggestively is the poet and represents humankind as well) becomes the porcupine, is in some senses identical with it, thereby breaking out of the closed ego; and both creatures, if not completely at one with the environment through which they move, at least closely resemble it.

Although special complexity is introduced into the second half of "The Bear" by means of the dream device, the structure of this poem is more readily apparent and its meanings seem more immediately accessible than its intricately structured companion poem because "The Bear" develops in a chronologically straightforward first-person narrative. Yet there are complexities of interpretation. Kinnell has referred to the poem's dual character in response to an interviewer's question about "The Bear": "It's easy to grasp, because of its narrative. At the same time there's something raw or uninterpreted about it, and therefore you have to work at it, give something of yourself, if you are to get anything out of it. In that sense it's a hard poem. But maybe if you like it at all, you like it better than poems that require less of you" (*Walking*, 67).

The first four sections of this sequence of seven describe the unusual hunt, a week-long pursuit, and the death of a bear, making abundant use of polysyndeton and repetitions. While some of the poem's conjunctive "and"s join clauses, most link the many verbs of the first half of this active poem, its frequent repetitions helping to establish an incantatory rhythm and to suggest a view of interconnectedness. The most extreme instance and best illustration of polysyndeton occurs at the end of section 4:

> I hack
> a ravine in his thigh, and eat and drink,
> and tear him down his whole length

and open him and climb in
and close him up after me, against the wind,
and sleep.

The most distinctive aspect of the rhythm and syntax of "The Bear"
results from Kinnell's use of conjunctive (not disjunctive or separat-
ing) polysyndeton and other unifying repetitions in the poem. Fur-
thermore, significantly, section 5 begins with no explicit subject for
its main and initial verb, *dream* (which verb, a synonym for imagine,
thereby receives added emphasis), its implied subject being the previ-
ous "I" of the last sentence of 4, quoted above, so that Kinnell's syn-
tax itself in 4 and 5 suggests the loss of "I" or ego, as the hunter
becomes the hunted. Section 5 and 6 read:

5

And dream
of lumbering flatfooted
over the tundra,
stabbed twice from within,
splattering a trail behind me,
splattering it out no matter which way I lurch,
no matter which parabola of bear-transcendence,
which dance of solitude I attempt,
which gravity-clutched leap,
which trudge, which groan.

6

Until one day I totter and fall—
fall on this
stomach that has tried so hard to keep up,
to digest the blood as it leaked in,
to break up
and digest the bone itself: and now the breeze
blows over me, blows off
the hideous belches of ill-digested bear blood
and rotted stomach
and the ordinary, wretched odor of bear,

blows across
my sore, lolled tongue a song
or screech, until I think I must rise up
and dance. And I lie still.

In fact, in spite of the periods ending 4 and 5, the last sentence of 4 and section 5 and 6 syntactically constitute another marvelously accomplished, single extended sentence (at least until the last line of 6, when the second sentence, "And I lie still," occurs). Thus, Kinnell uses syntax to subsume and unify structural sections of the poem at the points most crucial to the central issue of transcending the ego or lesser self, namely those parts of the poem wherein the hunter enters and becomes the bear.

It is apparent that to convey his contemporary contemplative meaning Kinnell skillfully develops sound, rhythm, syntax, and structure as well as the semantic import of his language. The closed ego is transcended in "The Bear" by means of the hunter's, the I-narrator's, becoming the hunted, not only in the familiar and sacramental sense of one's becoming what one eats (death again feeding, serving life, as in "Freedom, New Hampshire") and not only by means of the hunter's literally, actually, physically entering into the bear in order to sleep warmly, but also because in sections 5 and 6 the sleeping hunter dreams he is the wounded bear who lumbers over the tundra until he falls, another fallen creature. That the distinction between waking and dream may be blurred in the second half of the poem serves Kinnell's larger purposes: section 6 continues the dream begun in 5; but, at least on a first reading, it may appear also as a waking reality. "I awaken I think" at the beginning of 7 (compare "I think I prowl" in 7 of "The Porcupine") permits the uncertainty about and blurring or merging of the two states to continue in 7, which concludes with a marvelous ambiguity that further breaks open the closed ego, further expands the persona of the poem:

> the rest of my days I spend
> wandering: wondering
> what, anyway,
> was that sticky infusion, that rank flavor of blood, that
> poetry, by which I lived?

The "sticky infusion" and "rank flavor of blood," both modified by "by which I lived," refer, of course, at one level to the blood-soaked turd that the hunter gnashes down in order to survive and continue the hunt. Much of Kinnell's poetry through the Vision of Art assumes the burden of enhancing vision, opening the reader's third eye. "Saint Francis and the Sow," for example, reveals in one single, long sentence that common objects like the sow have, when rightly apprehended, an uncommon loveliness, fascination, or intrinsic perfection about them, the hidden mystery that Lawrence writes of in *St. Mawr.* So too, when rightly regarded, with dilated or expanded vision, even the conventionally repulsive turd and the conventionally disgusting act of swallowing it for the sake of survival may both be seen, "The Bear" seems to suggest, to have an uncommon loveliness or an inner rightness,

> for everything flowers, from within, of self-blessing;
> though sometimes it is necessary
> to reteach a thing its loveliness.
>
> ("Saint Francis and the Sow")

As a Zen Buddhist might say, everything is uniquely, perfectly itself, just so.

Since the last line of "The Bear," perhaps as perfect a line of "impure" poetry as one might ever see, may be read not just as a cataloging series but as an apposition as well, the conventionally repulsive turd in these extraordinary circumstances is thus seen as a kind of life-giving poetry. (In apposition, "infusions," "flavor," and "poetry" are identical or are different terms with the same referent; and, of course, these terms also refer to the hacked bear—and to "The Bear"—which the "I" eats and drinks and enters and thereby lives.) However humble, lowly, this food or substance is manna in the wilderness, sacramentally sustaining and ultimately allowing and leading to the transfiguration of the eater-hunter into the hunted, eaten, entered bear; therefore, it is spoken of in exalted language: "that poetry, by which I lived." And since, further, it is the poet who lives by poetry, the last line changes the I-narrator into the poet, thereby enlarging the persona by these means also. Because "The Bear" appears as the last poem of *Body Rags,* the last line—especially "that poetry, by which I lived"—includes all the preceding poems in this volume and, indeed, all of Kinnell's previous (and future) books of poetry. Similarly, the last line and the shamanistic hunter-narrator-poet of this poem, who is also imaginatively, eucharistically, and mysteriously the hunted bear, may represent all poetry and every poet, this poem thereby accomplishing in a grand and admirable way poetry's high task of breaking out of the closed ego, opening up and transforming the unshared "I" (particularly in self-absorbed contemporary poetry) into the essential poetic self, personal and universal, and deeply in touch and at peace with the world.

To recapitulate in part, Kinnell's transformative strategies, with examples from his poetry parenthetically given, include: use of first person plural and/or third person to replace first person singular ("For Robert Frost"); the transforming of the I-narrator into another creature, the poet, or representative man ("The Porcupine" and "The Bear"); structuring a poem to move from the personal to mythic and thereby universal dimensions ("For Robert Frost" and "Fergus Falling"); structuring a poem to effect the opening or transcending of the closed fallen ego through repetition and the play of literal against figurative meanings ("The Porcupine"); use of both extended, complex syntax and lengthy poems in sections or sequences to suggest and recreate prelapsarian or regenerated realities and an interconnected, unified cosmos (all of the poems just mentioned, *The Book of Nightmares*, and "Freedom, New Hampshire"). All of these ways give skillful expression to and are an outgrowth of a physically and sensuously rooted contemplative or "ecological" (if one prefers) mode of awareness. In a poem, "Fergus Falling," that structurally recapitulates and otherwise suggests the biblical myth of the Fall, Fergus, before his fall, sees a pond, which symbolizes life, death, and eternal return or regeneration. The syntax and rhythm, particularly of the poem's protracted structural beginning, help to recreate the reality of Edenic timelessness that they ostensibly annotate. Together, structure and syntax (with of course other elements of the poem) construct one image, at least, of the meaning of the cosmically-conscious self. The extended syntax of the third section of "Freedom, New Hampshire" similarly recreates the shining and seemingly endless period of prelapsarian childhood, when the self was united with Nature. One or more of the various falls in this poem and in "The Porcupine" and "The Bear" may be suggestive of and give distinctive individualization to the archetypal Fall. In these last two poems and in "For Robert Frost," the speaker's or a character's body becomes at one with another creature or the land, intimating that the world outside of one's skin is just as much one's true self as the world within.

At this moment in our human history, in a world rampant with ego-consciousness and a seemingly imminent nuclear or ecological armageddon, perhaps we need repeated persuasive reminding that the self and the world, which are abstractly distinguishable though not actually divisible, exist and can exist only in relation to one another, that they are partial glimpses of a unified process. Gestalt theory of perception holds that no figure is ever perceived except in relation to a background. We see but we do not usually fully realize that all elements of the world hold their boundaries in common with the areas that surround them, that the outline of a figure is also the inline of the background. Boundaries, however useful, are largely mental constructs, conventional, artificial, and often arbitrary. As Norman O. Brown observes, "contrary to what is taken for granted in the lunatic state called normalcy or common sense, the distinction between self and external world is not an immutable fact, but an artificial construction. It is a boundary line. . . . The erection of the boundary does not alter the fact that there is, in reality, no boundary. The net-effect is illusion, self-deception; the big lie. Or alienation" (*Love's Body*, 142–144).

# V

In addition to Lawrence, Warren, and Kinnell, there are many other modern and contemporary poets whose work may fruitfully be studied from the point of view of contemplative tradition and concerns, including Gerald Manley Hopkins, William Carlos Williams, Wallace Stevens, T. S. Eliot, Hart Crane, E. E. Cummings, Elizabeth Bishop, Theodore Roethke, Ruth Stone, Robert Bly, Allen Ginsberg, James Wright, Gary Snyder, A. R. Ammons, Mary Oliver, John Logan, and Maria Gillan, among others. But rather than continuing the kind of study previously presented in this chapter, it would perhaps be more valuable at this point to consider briefly and tentatively some of the significance for our subject of the current courtship of metaphysics and physics, of mysticism and the new science, for the world (self) view described in these preceding pages is increasingly shared by scientists of various disciplines.

In the hope that all participants in the enlarged discussion may learn something more about their own and each other's discipline, I should like to introduce into critical literary concerns a relevant dialog and developing relationship that have been ongoing for some years between scientists and mystics. I believe that much of the recent writings on mysticism and the new science may in the long term be useful and clarifying to critical considerations of contemplative literature, and may help to bridge the gap between "the two cultures."

In his Introduction to *The Holographic Paradigm and Other Paradoxes: Exploring the Leading Edge of Science*, Ken Wilber observes that some very respectable and capable researchers in various fields are saying that "the very *facts* of science . . . the actual data (from physics to physiology) seemed to make sense only if we assume some sort of implicit or unifying or transcendental ground underlying the explicit data. . . . Moreover . . . this transcendental ground, whose very existence seemed necessitated by experimental-scientific data, seemed to be identical, at least in description, to the timeless and spaceless ground of being (or 'Godhead') so universally described by the world's great mystics and sages, Hindu, Buddhist, Christian, Taoist" (1, 2). Additionally, biologists, sociologists, and physicists are finding that they cannot say what the organism is doing unless they simultaneously describe the behavior of its surroundings. As noted, it is now an ecological truism that everything is ultimately connected to everything else, that organism and environment are indivisibly interrelated, "define" each other, can only be understood and, indeed, are only real in terms of each other. Similarly, the new physics tells us that "the subatomic world appears as a web of relations between the various parts of a unified whole . . . the concept of a distinct physical entity, like a particle, is an idealization which has no fundamental significance. It can only be defined in terms of its connections to the whole . . ." (Capra, 144). Furthermore, as Gary Zukav points out, "scientists, using the 'in here-out there' distinction, have discovered that the 'in here-out there' distinction may not exist. What is 'out there' apparently depends, in a rigorous mathematical sense as well as a philosophical one, upon what we decide 'in here.' . . . The conceptual framework of quantum mechanics, supported by massive volumes of experimental data, forces contemporary physicists to express themselves in a manner that sounds, even to the uninitiated, like the language of mystics" (92).

The illusion of a solid world "out there" goes hand-in-hand with the illusion that each observer is a separate ego confronted with a reality quite other than himself. According to the new physics, we experience not external reality but our *interaction* with it, and this distinction explains, for example, how the properties of light can seem to be mutually exclusive wave-like and particle-like behaviors. These behaviors are in fact properties of *our interaction with* light. Thus "it appears that light has no properties independent of us. . . . Without us, light does not exist . . . in a similar manner, without light, or, by implication, anything else to interact with, *we do not exist*. As Bohr himself put it: ' . . . an independent reality in the ordinary physical sense can be ascribed neither to the phenomena nor to the agencies of observation' " (Zukav, 95). Since we cannot observe a phenomenon without altering it, as the famous Heisenberg Uncertainty Principle implies, the physical properties which we observe in the "external" world are enmeshed in our own perceptions not only psychologically, but ontologically as well. So important is the role of the "observer" that the physicist John Wheeler suggests replacing that word with the word "participator," and he adds: "Nothing is more important about the quantum principle than this, that it destroys the concept of the world as 'sitting out there,' with the observer safely separated from it. . . . In some strange sense, the universe is a participatory universe" (Mehra, ed., *The Physicist's Conception of Nature*, 244). The recently formulated idea of "participation instead of observation" may be strange to modern physics because it is a new idea that contradicts classical physics' model of the detached observer, but it is an idea very familiar to the student of mysticism.

According to classical physics, the mass of an object has always been associated with an indestructible material substance or ultimate "stuff" of which all things were thought to be made. "Relativity theory showed that mass has nothing to do with any substance, but is a form of energy. Energy, however, is a dynamic quantity associated with activity or processes . . . the relativistic space-time reality is an intrinsically dynamic reality where objects are also processes . . ." (Capra, 66, 134–135), a view wholly consistent with mysticism, as Capra goes on to demonstrate. The external world, then, does not consist of substances, solidly and stolidly each in its own place. Substances, whether construed as material or ideal, are, as boundaries are, fictions, abstract concepts, constructs, if substance be understood as an unperceived, unfelt, unimaginable Lockeian substrate or Kantian *Ding an sich*. The light needs the eye in order to be seen and to come more fully into being, just as the eye needs the light in order to see and fully be. Furthermore, the external reality which one *thinks* of as an object is *in actuality* one with oneself. To the principle *Esse est percipi*, one should add that perceiving, conceiving, imagining is being. To assert all this is not to deny the existence of an external world but rather to affirm that it, like the self, consists in events, activity, energy, as both ancient contemplative tradition and the new physics confirm. "In this world, classical concepts like 'elementary particle,' 'material substance,' or 'isolated object' have lost their meaning; the whole universe appears as a dynamic web of inseparable energy patterns. . . . The basic oneness of the universe is not only the central characteristic of the mystical experience, but is also one of the most important revelations of modern physics" (Capra,, 69, 117).

"The search for the ultimate stuff of the universe ends with the discovery that there *isn't any*. If there is any ultimate stuff of the universe, it is pure energy, but subatomic particles are not 'made of' energy, they *are* energy. . . . At the subatomic level there is no longer a clear distinction between what is and what happens, between the actor and the action" (Zukav, 193). "Ever since the early Greek philosophers," E. M. W. Tillyard writes, "creation had been figured as an act of music; and the notion appealed powerfully to the poetically or the mystically minded." The general world view of Donne's, Herbert's and Vaughan's Renaissance held that "the created universe was itself in a state of music . . . it was one perpetual dance" (94). "Thus all is hurled / In sacred *Hymns*, and *Order*, the great *Chime* / And *Symphony* of nature," we read in Vaughan. The great modern physicist and mathematician Sir James Jeans writes "to my mind, the laws which nature obeys are less suggestive of those which a machine obeys in its motion than of those which a musician obeys in writing a fugue, or a poet in composing a sonnet. The motions of electrons and atoms do not resemble those of the parts of a locomotive so much as those of the dancers in a cotillion" (Wilber, ed., *Quantum Questions: Mystical Writings of the World's Great Physicists*, 137). And the great modern poet William Butler Yeats rhetorically asks "How can we know the dancer from the dance?" Just as the poet implies that (at the supra-atomic level, so to speak) we cannot really separate the two, so the new physics tells us that "at the subatomic level the dancer and the dance are one . . . the world is fundamentally dancing energy. . . . What we have been calling matter (particles) constantly is being created, annihilated and created again" (Zukav, 193–194). Shiva dancing, indeed!

In a comparison of ancient Greek philosophy with the findings of modern experimental science and atomic physics, the Nobel physicist Werner Heisenberg concludes that "Plato was very much nearer to the truth about the structure of matter than Leucippus or Democritus" (Wilber, ed., *Quantum Questions*, 46). In responding to the philosophical dilemma of the "one" and the "many" (essentially the intellectual effort to determine the ultimate single principle that underlies the ever-changing variety of sensuous phenomena), Leucippus and Democritus argued for a material cause, the eternal, indestructible, material atom, the only thing really existing, in their view, since all other things exist only because they are composed of atoms. Plato, on the other hand, took exception to this view that material atoms were the foundation of all existence. He regarded atoms not so much as material things but as geometrical forms, thereby resolving the concept of matter into mathematical forms in a way consistent with his idealist philosophy. This highly important step in philosophical thought has been regarded as "the decisive beginning of the mathematical science of nature," as Heisenberg remarks. "Modern physics has definitely decided for Plato. For the smallest units of matter are, in fact, not physical objects in the ordinary sense of the word; they are forms, structures or—in Plato's sense—Ideas, which can be unambiguously spoken of only in the language of mathematics" (49, 51). The ancient search for the one in the many, for the ultimate principle of all, which "has doubtless played a similar role in the origin of both religion and science" (52), has in modern times apparently become more realizable through mathematics. That ancient quest and Einstein's modern proposal for a unified theory of matter, alternatively designated a grand unified theory (GUT) or, as Stephen W. Hawking has called it, "a theory of everything" (TOE), now seem within the reach of theoretical physics.

Where, philosophically, does modern science's search appear to be leading us? While he notes some limitations imposed by the physical sciences, Sir Arthur Eddington, considered as accomplished a philosopher as Heisenberg and as penetrating a mystic as Erwin Schroedinger, also holds the view that "the idea of a universal Mind or Logos would be, I think, a fairly plausible inference from the present state of scientific theory; at least it is in harmony with it" (Wilber, ed., *Quantum Questions*, 206). Discussing the philosophical outlook of his colleague, Wolfgang Pauli, Heisenberg points out that "the natural science of the modern era involves a Christian elaboration of the 'lucid mysticism' of Plato, in which the unitary ground of spirit and matter is sought in the primeval images, and in which understanding has found its place in its varous degrees and kinds, even to knowledge of the word of God" (Wilber, ed., *Quantum Questions*, 159). And the Oxford physicist Peter Hodgson writes persuasively and informatively about the medieval Christian origin of modern science.

But if science now appears to favor Plato's idealism against Democritus' materialism, as in the nineteenth century it was thought to favor materialism over Christian philosophy, Heisenberg suggests that science's contribution to the philosophical question of the one and the many lies not so much in deciding for one doctrine and against another doctrine but in the cautious, appropriate use of language. "If we wish to appproach the 'one' in the terms of a precise scientific language, we must turn our attention to that center of science described by Plato, in which the fundamental mathematical symmetries are to be found. In the concepts of this language we must be content with the statement that 'God is a mathematician';

for we have freely chosen to confine our vision to that realm of being which can be understood in the mathematical sense of the word 'understanding,' which can be described in rational terms" (Wilber, ed., *Quantum Questions*, 54). But, as Heisenberg points out, Plato, not content with this restriction, employed poetic language, as well.

In *The Republic*, for example, when Glaucon asks for an account of the Good, Socrates, the master of definition, confesses that such an account is beyond his powers. He then uses poetic devices, the analogy of the sun with the Good and the allegory of the cave, in order to give his audience some notion of the Good. (This whole procedure is characteristically contemplative: alleged ineffability followed by a [usually] poetic account of mystical meaning or experience.) In the discussion of the "four stages of cognition," which precedes the allegory of the cave, Socrates distinguishes between the state of mind (*dianoia*) which grasps mathematical objects and the state of mind (*noesis*) which grasps the supreme Form of the Good. As F. M. Cornford explains, "*dianoia* suggests discursive thinking or reasoning from premise to conclusion, whereas *noesis* is constantly compared to the immediate act of vision and suggests rather the direct intuition or apprehension of its object" (*The Republic of Plato*, 223). (The Platonic distinction between *dianoia* and *noesis*, which was widely developed by Christian commentators, is in important respects similar to the distinction between psyche and pneuma.) "Intuition," in its seventeenth-century meaning, is "the immediate knowledge ascribed to angelic and spiritual beings, with whom vision and knowledge are identical" (O.E.D.), and this is one of the meanings of "imagination." It is in this sense for example, that Milton uses the term "Intuitive" in *Paradise Lost* (V, 488).

Heisenberg concludes that the images which are evoked by the language of poetry and which convey understanding different from mathematical understanding "are probably connected with the unconscious mental patterns the psychologists speak of as archetypes, forms of strongly emotional character that, in some way, reflect the internal structures of the world. But whatever the explanation for these other forms of understanding, the language of images and likenesses is probably the only way of approaching the 'one' from more general domains. If the harmony in a society rests on a common interpretation of the 'one,' the unitary principle behind the phenomena, then the language of poetry may be more important here than the language of science" (Wilber, ed., *Quantum Questions*, 54).

Many would agree that in the twentieth century the need to find harmony in society has become greater than at any previous time in human history. It may be, therefore, that contemplative poetry or holy writing (which comes to us through various genres and disciplines) has more than ever before a special contribution to make to human need and aspiration and may provide a progressive revelation of the transcendental ground, a continuous, self-correcting record of divine Self-disclosure. Metaphor or figurative language generally, at the heart of poetry (and of atomic physics, as the epigraph from Niels Bohr suggests), is itself a mode of vision and transformation and may point to the solution of the philosophical problem of the many and the one. The essential nature of metaphor is that two (the many) are one. In other words, it requires the poetic, imaginative, noetic faculty (rather than the rational, logical faculty or dianoia) to perceive the essentially unitive nature of the relationship between self and the universe and God. The feeling of painful separateness is a real and common experience; theologically, it is fallen experience. Contemplative or redeemed experience is the experience of the interrelated or unitive nature of reality. One reads and needs contemplative poetry or holy writing today, or the Vision of Art in general, for the vital reason, among other reasons, that only if a metaphorical apocalypse (transformation of self and world) comes about may we be more confident that a literal ecological or nuclear apocalypse, brought on largely by misuse of science and technology, will not come about.

Another approach to the problem of the one and the many, closely connected with the problem of being and becoming, is through the question of beauty. As Heisenberg points out, from antiquity and on through the Renaissance, there were two definitions of beauty which stood in a certain opposition to one another. "The one describes beauty as the proper conformity of the parts to one another, and to the whole. The other, stemming from Plotinus, describes it, without any reference to parts, as the translucence of the eternal splendor of the 'one' through the material phenomenon" (Wilber, ed., *Quantum Questions*, 56). Because the basis of exact science is found in the responses to these ancient questions, Heisenberg traces in broad outline relevant currents of thought from early Greek philosophy to modern science, remarking that for much of this history "the experience of the beautiful becomes virtually identical with the experience of connections" (58), a point of plain import for mysticism. For our purposes here, it suffices first to observe that simplicity, elegance, and beauty have at all times been recognized as significant in the discovery of both "scientific" and "non-scientific" truth, as expressed, for example, in such mottos as "Simplex sigillum veri" (the simple is the seal of the true) and "Pulchritudo splendor veritatis" (Beauty is the splendor of truth), as well as in, beyond their Platonic import, Keats' famous lines, "Beauty is truth, truth beauty." Secondly, to obtain a somewhat better intellectual understanding of the actual experience of the one in the many we may ask what is the principle which orders the parts in their relation to the whole and what is it that shines forth. No doubt, there actually is the immediate recognition of the beautiful, of which Plato speaks in the *Symposium* and *Phaedrus*, and to which many have since testified. Heisenberg points out that "it seems to have been universally agreed that the immediate recognition is not a consequence of discursive (i.e., rational) thinking," and he goes on to discuss Kepler's and Pauli's ideas that it is the archetypes which shine forth and are received not by a conceptual but rather by an intuitive or noetic process (64f.).

A Christian contemplative, for whom, as often discussed in the preceding chapters, Christ is both Logos, the principle of order, and Light, the eternal splendor of the One shining through material phenomena, might well reformulate a favorite phrase and say that Christ shines and organizes (pun intended) in ten thousand places. The Word, according to Justin, "is called Christ because he was anointed and God ordered all things through him. The name Christ also contains an unknown significance, just as the title 'God' is not a name, but represents the idea, innate in human nature, of an inexpressible reality" (Bettenson, *The Early Christian Fathers*, 63). According to the medieval English mystic, Walter Hilton, Christ implants the desire for beauty (another name for unnameable reality) "within you, and is Himself both the desire and the object of your desire. If you could only understand this, you would see that Jesus is everything and Jesus does everything. You yourself do nothing" (*The Ladder of Perfection*, 162). And according to Marsilio Ficino, the lover "desires the splendour of the divine light shining through bodies, and is amazed and awed by it" (140). Christ as the Logos or principle of order is everywhere doing everything in Herbert's "The Church," and Christ shines in Donne's "Batter my heart" as the unfallen child of Vaughan's "The Retreate" "Shin'd in my Angell-infancy." Turning to modern and contemporary poetry, we find similar epiphanic transforming moments when Warren observes "that significance shines through everything" or Williams writes of the broken green bottle that shines on the cinders between hospital walls or Roethke remarks "all finite things reveal infinitude" or Ammons speaks of "the radiance that . . . pours its abundance without selection into every nook and cranny" or Bishop concludes that "everything was rainbow, rainbow, rainbow," to cite a few of many possible examples. When we see beauty, shining, or order, we (or, rather, Christ, Love, Imagination, in us) see the incarnate God. Whereas the seventeenth-century poets might attach equal significance to the historic figure of Jesus Christ and to Christ understood as pneuma or the shining and ordering principle of the divine-within-nature (human and non-human nature), perhaps the primary importance of Christ (who also was a poet, story-teller, maker of metaphors, analogies, and parables) for the post-death-of-God twentieth century is the mythic latter meaning. And perhaps it is because art and science have in common the quest for beauty, or the apprehension in wonder of the beautiful which is true and "mysterious," that Einstein says "it is the most important function of art and science to awaken this feeling [the cosmic religious feeling] and keep it alive in those who are receptive to it" (Wilber, ed., *Quantum Questions*, 103).

Heisenberg's statement that constitutes one of the epigraphs to this chapter is perhaps nowhere more dramatically illustrated than in the recent work of the neuroscientist Karl Pribram and the physicist David Bohm, highly respected scientists whose studies are related to and have serious implications for other disciplines, such as religion, philosophy, psychology, and literary criticism.[6] To explain the mysteries of human consciousness, Pribram, who was a friend of the late renowned philosopher of mysticism, Alan Watts, has developed a holographic paradigm which has been linked to the theories of Bohm, a former associate of Einstein and close friend of Krishnamurti. Holography is a method of lenless photography by which an object's wave field of light is recorded on a photographic plate, the hologram, as an interference pattern. When the hologram is placed in a coherent light beam like a laser, the original wave pattern is regenerated and a three-dimensional image appears. Any part of the hologram will reconstruct the entire image.

Pribram's research on the brain, like previous research, suggested that memory is not localized but dispersed throughout the brain. Pribram realized that the hologram might serve as a model for how the brain might store memory. Considerable research evidence has accumulated suggesting that the brain's deep structure is essentially holographic, a theory with import for many aspects of human life. When Pribram was led to read Bohm's work, he discovered the physicist was describing a holographic universe. In Bohm's view, as in the view of Plato and many other mystics, "what appears to be a stable, tangible, visible, audible world . . . is an illusion. It is dynamic and kaleidoscopic—not really 'there.' What we normally see is the explicit, or unfolded, order of things, rather like watching a movie. But there is an underlying order that is mother and father to this second-generation reality. [Bohm] called the other order implicate, or enfolded. The enfolded order harbors our reality, much as the DNA in the nucleus of the cell harbors potential life and directs the nature of its unfolding" (Marilyn Ferguson in Wilber, ed., *The Holographic Paradigm*, 21). That is, not only the brain but the universe itself appears to be a hologram, "with each part being in the whole and the whole being in each part," as Ken Wilber puts the matter clearly and essentially: "The brain is a hologram perceiving and participating in a holographic universe. In the explicate or manifest realm of space and time, things and events are indeed separate and discrete. But beneath the surface, as it were, in the implicate or frequency realm, all things and events are spacelessly, timelessly, intrinsically, one and undivided. And, Bohm and Pribram reasoned, the quintessential religious experience, the experience of mystical oneness and 'supreme identity,' might very well be a *genuine* and *legitimate* experience of this implicate and universal ground" (*The Holographic Paradigm*, 2–3). Indeed, the holographic model, which marries brain research to theoretical physics, may help to illuminate many of the paradoxes of mysticism. For example, the explicate realm corresponds to the world of time, and the implicate realm corresponds to the world of eternity, the two worlds recurrently discussed in the preceding chapters.

The idea of a holographic universe and other ideas mentioned above are, by different names, familiar to students of mysticism, as, for example, in Katsaros' and Kaplan's discussion of the mystical philosophy of Nicholas Cusanus: "finite things are related to one another and to the whole so that there is harmony and unity in multiplicity. Like Erigena before him, Nicholas considers the world as a theophany, or manifestation of God: 'God is in all things in such a way that all things are in him. . . . God is in all things by the medium . . . of the universe; so it follows that all is in all, and each in each.' Here Nicholas refers to Anaxagoras' dictum that everything is in everything else. . . . In other words, God is unity in that he contains all things, but he is at the same time the unfolding of all things since all things emanate from him. God is not only transcendent because he is infinite and beyond all things but also immanent in all things because all things compose the theophany" (296).

While many modern poets and mystics from Blake and Whitman continue contemplative tradition mainly in its extrovertive aspects, and while, for this and other reasons, it might seem that in the modern period Aristotelianism has triumphed over Platonism, it is curiously true that theoretical scientists, such as Heisenberg, Jeans, and Eddington, and writers and thinkers in other disciplines, have tended to emphasize the Platonic or transcendental nature of reality. With regard to the complicated issue of immanence and transcendence, not only may we repeat the ancient words of Dionysius the Areopagite, "God is known in all things, and apart from all things," but we may also add the recent wise response of David Bohm: "the ancient tradition includes both immanence and transcendence. . . . the totality can be described as *both* immanence and transcendence in one sense, and *neither* immanence nor transcendence in another, since it is beyond the possibility of description. . . . We call the ultimate heights of mind transcendence; we find in the depths of matter the immanence of the whole of that which is. Both are needed" (Wilber, ed., *The Holographic Paradigm*, 188, 193). Another of Bohm's remarks helps to illustrate further the potentially fruitful relationship between science and mysticism: "mysticism's positive meaning could be that the ground of our existence is a mystery—a statement which Einstein himself accepted. It was he who said that what is most beautiful is the mysterious. To my mind, the word mystic should be applied to a person who has actually had some direct experience of the mystery which transcends the possibility of description. The problem for the rest of us is to know what that may mean. . . . Relativity and, even more important, quantum mechanics have strongly suggested (though not proved) that the world cannot be analyzed into separate and independently existing parts. Moreover, each part somehow involves all the others: contains them or enfolds them. In this sense, a common language may be said to have been established, and a common set of basic concepts, for this is the one point on which all mystics have agreed" (188, 190).

All of our knowledge of the world is a kind of Self-knowledge. We know the world in terms of the body and our consciousness. What we see "out there" is, in an immediate sense, how the inside of our heads look or feel. Everything that we sense is some kind of dancing energy, interacting with our sense organs, nerves, brains, which translate the energy into what we know as light, sound, color, smoothness, heaviness, sweetness, etc. Apart from our bodies, including sense organs and neural system, or somebody's body (such bodies also being substantial as events, activities, or energies rather than as *Lockeian* or *Kantian* substances), all the world's energy would be like the sound of one hand clapping, devoid of all sensuous content and qualities. We could say, as Alan Watts puts it, that the magic of our bodies "is to evoke marvels from the universe, as a harpist evokes melody from the silent strings."[7] And we could conclude with the renown physicist Erwin Schroedinger that "inconceivable as it seems to ordinary reason, you—and all other conscious beings as such—are all in all. Hence this life of yours which you are living is not merely a piece of the entire existence, but is in a certain sense the *whole*; only this whole is not so constituted that it can be surveyed in one single glance. Thus you can throw yourself flat on the ground, stretched out upon Mother Earth, with the certain conviction that you are one with her and she with you" (22).

## VI

This sense of oneness, the so-called "oceanic" feeling or consciousness, long and regularly associated with mystics and certain poets and now shared or confirmed by many scientists, may have its literary origins, as previously observed, in Plato, whose *Timaeus* pictures the unity of the whole cosmos as one living creature; and it finds subsequent varied expression by many writers in different cultures and times. It is not an aberration but rather a genuine, "normal," actual experience given very considerable documentation whether phrased poetically or abstractly. For example, Thomas Traherne, whose central theme was the biblical idea that one must be born again and become like a little child to enter the kingdom of heaven, advises with vivid cosmic images: "You never enjoy the World aright, till the Sea itself floweth in your Veins, till you are Clothed with the Heavens and Crowned with the Stars" (*Centuries*, 15). On the other hand, more abstractly but also unmistakably, Freud writes that "originally the ego includes everything, later it detaches from itself the external world. The ego-feeling we are aware of now is thus only a shrunken vestige of a far more extensive feeling—a feeling which embraced the universe and expressed an inseparable connection of the ego with the external world" (13). Although some analysts regard this expansive feeling as immature and potentially chaotic, others, starting perhaps most notably with the biblical idea just noted, have seen it (re-designated by Neo-Freudians as polymorphous eroticism) as a model or metaphor for the regenerated or reborn state. The possibilities adumbrated in infancy are to be taken not as merely infantile and unnatural but as normative. The aureate and "visionary gleam" which emanates from the visible world in early childhood (or is the gleam conferred upon the object by the observing creative imagination?), as described, for a few among many examples, by Wordsworth in his Intimations Ode, by Kinnell in his "Freedom, New Hampshire," and by Vaughan in "The Retreate," is dimmed and dies away as the child grows into adulthood. Such a diminishing and dying is a central fact of the fall, consciousness of division, boundaries, separation and death supplanting oceanic, polymorphously erotic consciousness. The rule of Thanatos replaces the reign of Eros or Agape. We fall out of the "lovely" and "amorous green" Garden, as Andrew Marvell describes it, into (consciousness of) time and mortality.

But there are two deaths, or, as Kinnell says "death has two aspects—the extinction which we fear, and the flowing away into the universe, which we desire" (*Walking*, 23). And it is through metaphorical death, the death of the ego or lesser self, that one returns to Eden, to cosmic consciousness, recovers an erotic sense of shining reality, the redeemed eroticism of the microcosm of Donne's lovers extended to the whole macrocosm. Poetry conduces to this regeneration—such is the great task of poetry, the great task of the Vision of Art. Kinnell again: "In some great poems, like 'Song of Myself,' a reader is taken through one person into some greater self; there is a continual passing into the 'death of the self,' to use that phrase. . . . In one way or another, consciously or not, all poems try to pass beyond the self" (*Walking*, 22–23). As we have seen, the poetry of many important poets variously presents in full or truncated fashion the archetypal movement from the innocent open self to the fallen, closed self and on beyond to the reopened or reborn self at one with the rest of creation; this poetry also thereby offers a sense of transfigured human potentiality.

As previously observed, the vivid experience and consequent profound transfiguring realization that creatures and things, the "I" and the world, have their meaning, value, and being not simply in isolation from but rather more in relation to one another have in all cultures always been the root and flower of mysticism and of much great poetry. With the world currently seeming to be in a ego-maniacal rage of imminent self-destructiveness, what we need and what poetry and the Vision of Art generally can help to give us is a new consciousness, not of separation and division, of which we have more than enough, but of connections and wholeness. Because the contemplative experience of oneness is unspeakable, in the sense of being beyond the pale of predicating, rational conceptualization and verbalization, to try to describe it satisfactorily in "ordinary" words, rational propositions, has historically been very difficult at best. To convey this experience, the language of poetry, which is the language of imagination and love,[8] is much more appropriate and effective. As art, particularly as a verbal art, poetry is especially suited to make us aware of interrelationships and unity both within and without the poem. The aesthetic and moral functions of poetry are intrinsically and ultimately interwoven. Shelley's position in "A Defense of Poetry" remains true and valid: in conveying a fuller awareness of reality, poetry is formative and moral though not in any didactic, partisan or parochial sense. "The great secret of morals is love . . . a going out of one's own nature," a sympathetic identification with others. The "imagination" is the means for this sympathetic identification with others, and poetry enlarges the range and scope of the imagination, exercises and strengthens this "great instrument of moral good" (*Selected Poetry and Prose*, 502). Similarly, to touch the mystery of the things and creatures on this earth, Kinnell says, "requires . . . love of the things and creatures that surround us: the capacity to go out to them so that they enter us, so that they are transformed within us, and so that our own inner life finds expression through them" (Walking, 52).

Whereas the rational faculties serve our needs for analysis, discrimination and definition, the imagination and love, synthesizing and unifying powers, enable us to see relations, correspondences, identities, wholeness. These two analytical and synthesizing faculties are doubtlessly each at their best not when they function separately but when they interact in mutual enhancement and harmony. As Lawrence powerfully reminds us, we need to recover our balance. With the awareness that poetry can give, the conception of ourselves as skin-encapsulated egos in an alien world can be seen as a sometimes useful illusion, and we can learn to regard and treat the natural world not as foe to be feared and conquered but as beloved.[9] Furthermore, in the consciousness that all things are essentially of one body, the "other" can be imaginatively apprehended, actually seen, as "oneself" and oneself as the other. Imaginative loving leads the incarnate divine to see the incarnate divine. With such awareness and vision, wholesale environmental contamination and widespread modern warfare would clearly be viewed and understood, whatever the short-term outcome, as inevitably suicidal, as indeed they are.[10] "The task of art is enormous," Tolstoy writes. "Art should cause violence to be set aside. And it is only art that can accomplish this"

(286). The great task of poetry is, as always, to reveal our true nature; it should thereby help us replace the divisive, acquisitive, dominating, death-dealing attitude toward reality with an erotic, unitive sense of reality.

The fall is into literal-minded language and the imbalance of the merely rational, discursive, conceptualizing intellect (the center of the ego), which function by means of separation and analysis upon *natura naturata*, nature classified, sorted, murdered for dissection into things, substances. Yet just as implicate or deep reality subsists not in things, but in dancing interplay, interactions (subverting, however useful, imposed rational boundaries), so deep meaning is not in the words but between the words, in the Word, in the silence, beyond the reach of literal-minded explication. In both open-eyed, clear-sighted perception and in genuine poetry, by acts of the deific imagination, we recreate a polymorphously erotic world, *natura naturans*, "nature naturing," nature spontaneous and living, a world that mystics, poets, and physicists, among other enlightened ones, tell us is constantly coming into and going out of being, dancing ecstatically. Like the simple, egoless act of perception, the imaginative poetic achievement, or the Vision of Art, is a divine deed of re-creation of an otherwise joyless, inert world of things. Re-creation is recreation. The living world is the Spirit of God, the imagination, lovingly at play. "By mere playing," as Henry Vaughan said of children, we "go to heaven," once again, in Kinnell's words, "belonging wholly to the life of the planet." The playful, creative words of our best poetry, holy writing, do not just interpret the world but inform and renew it. The fall is into literal language and literal-mindedness; the ascent, recovery of radiant Eden, is by metaphor, symbol, correspondence, connection, identity—imaginative, recreative language, opening the closed ego into cosmic consciousness so that one sees and re-creates the world in sacramental, eucharistic terms: *hoc est corpus meum. Tat Tvam Asi*: You are It.

# APPENDIX A
## *Grouping of the Songs and Sonnets and a General Dating of Poems*

The primary purpose of this Appendix is to indicate clearly which poems are specifically designated by the terms Group One, Group Two, and Group Three as used in Chapter Two. Following Grierson's grouping, basically confirmed by Gardner, I have added a fourth group of poems which, for a variety of reasons, do not with sufficient certainty in my judgment fall into one of the first three groups, or to which the first three groups are not quite applicable.

> *Group One*: poems of inconstant, false, or incomplete love; anti-Petrarchan. Usually, the focus is on physical love.
> *Group Two*: poems of faithful or true love, usually both physical and spiritual.
> *Group Three*: poems of Platonic love (using "Platonic" in the popular sense, "without sexual love"); with Gardner's qualification, also called Petrarchan. Usual focus is on spiritual love.
> *Group Four*: poems which, because of uncertainty or inapplicability, do not readily fall into one of the first three groups.

Songs and Sonnets

1 Song: 'Goe, and catche a falling starre'
1 The Message
2 Song: 'Sweetest love, I do not goe'
4 The Baite
1 Communitie
1 Confined Love
4 Breake of Day

2 The Computation
2 The Expiration
4 Withcraft by a Picture
1 A Jeat Ring Sent
4 The Paradox
4 The Prohibition
1 The Curse
1 The Indifferent
1 Womans Constancy
1 The Apparition
1 Loves Usury
1 Loves Diet
4 Loves Exchange
3 Loves Deitie
4 The Dampe
4 The Legacie
4 The Broken Heart
4 The Triple Foole
1 The Flea
3 The Will
4 Negative Love
3 The Undertaking
2 [Image and Dream]
2 The Exstasie
2 A Feaver
2 A Valediction: forbidding Mourning
2 A Valediction: of my Name in the Window
2 A Valediction: of the Booke
2 A Valediction: of weeping
2 The Good-morrow
2 The Anniversarie
2 The Sunne Rising
2 The Canonization
4 Aire and Angels
2 Loves Growth
2 Loves Infiniteness
2 A Lecture upon the Shadow
4 The Dreame
1 Loves Alchymie
4 Farewell to Love
3 Twickham Garden
2 A Nocturnal upon S. Lucies Day, being the shortest day

2 The Dissolution
3 The Blossome
1 The Primrose
3 The Relique
3 The Funerall

Based on Grierson and Gardner and arranged in the order of Gardner's Table of Contents (xii–xiii), this labeling of these poems in one or another grouping is, nevertheless, finally a matter of my own interpretation of each poem. For example, "Loves Deitie," "The Will," and "A Nocturnall upon S. Lucies Day" are grouped differently by Grierson; and some poems put into Group Two by him, such as "The Dreame," "Breake of Day," "The Baite," and "The Prohibition," I have placed in Group Four. No doubt, other critics interpret some of the Songs and Sonnets differently and so would group them differently. The above table also gives some indication how I would generally interpret each of the Songs and Sonnets, as well as making explicitly clear exactly which poems I include in each Group discussed in the chapter on Donne.

The dating of Donne's poems is in general difficult and uncertain. In her edition of *The Elegies and The Songs and Sonnets*, Helen Gardner divides the Songs and Sonnets into "two sets: poems that I believe to have been written before 1600 and poems that I believe were written after 1602; and within these sets poems that have some connexion in theme, form, or style have been brought together. Even so, the effect of diversity remains" (xxv). With respect to the Holy Sonnets, in her edition of *The Divine Poems*, Gardner dates the first six sonnets of the 1633 edition between February and August 1609; the other six sonnets printed in 1633 are presumed to have been written shortly after the first six. "Batter my heart," fully discussed in this book, appears as sonnet 10 of the first group. Thus the date of its composition would be shortly after the period between February and August 1609. Gardner orders the sonnets into groups of twelve, four, and three, and she analyses the group of twelve sonnets from the 1633 edition into two sequences of six. Including the four sonnets added in 1635 and the three from the Westmoreland MS, we have nineteen sonnets that range, in Gardner's dating, from 1609 to 1620 (see *Divine Poems*, 78–79, 121–127). Other divine poems are also dated according to internal and external evidence.

But various scholars, including Arthur Marotti, David Novarr, and John T. Shawcross, have challenged and corrected Gardner's dating of Donne's poems. Shawcross, for example, writes that "most of the songs and sonnets cannot be dated, but generally they are placed between 1593 and 1601. Perhaps the period of 1593–95 . . . is more appropriate for the witty treatments of love, particularly that which is inconstant. . . . However, these might have been written later, from 1596–98. . . . Gardner's attempt . . . to separate these lyrics into two periods . . . is most unconvincing, except for a few late pieces as here indicated" (*The Complete Poetry of John Donne*, 416–417; see also the "Chronological Schedule of the Poems," 411–416, which designates the "few late pieces," most of which I interpret as Group Two poems.)

The dating of the divine poems has also been much debated (see the Notes to Chapter Two for some of that debate). Yet most scholars would probably agree that most of the divine poems were written after most of the Songs and Sonnets. From my study of Donne's work and the scholarship on it, I would venture to add that most of the Group One poems are earlier and that most of the Group Two poems are later, where "earlier" means before 1599 and "later" means during or after 1599. But even these two broad generalizations are offered very tentatively, especially since the "dating" of Donne's poems in this broad way is merely ancillary but not essential to my main arguments about his work.

If it were indeed true that most of Group One poems were written earlier and most of Group Two later, then it would seem plausible to say that, whatever the reasons, at some point (perhaps in 1599 or somewhat later) Donne found the subject, the Vision of Eros (perhaps because of his own experience), and developed the poetic skill to write a body (Group Two) of the greatest love lyrics in the English language.

In an essay which I have been privileged to read in manuscript, Dennis Flynn questions Gardner's dating, further complicating the matter by closely arguing that some Holy Sonnets may have been written before 1609, perhaps "as early as the 1590s" ("The Dating of Donne's Holy Sonnets"). Such a contention may lend even more support to my general view of spiritual progress in Donne's Group Two and divine poems, of Donne's greater progress in the Vision of Eros than in the Vision of God.

In a recent important essay, Ilona Bell cogently argues that three letters written by Donne and previously assumed to be intended for others may actually have been written by him "to Ann More over a year before their elopement. If so, they are the only known letters Donne wrote to Ann, and they contain the first substantive information about Donne's wooing of Ann . . . enabling us to examine a central moment in Donne's life (and poetry) that has remained unknown and undocumented until now. Beginning with expressions of intense passion and hints of consummated love, Donne in these three letters to Ann responds to a sequence of events that created great stress for them both and made him fear, desperately, that the affair might end" (26–27). Bell's essay sheds light on that crucial period in Donne's life, 1599–1602, and has consequences for the interpretation and grouping of his poems, for, as Bell concludes, "if, as the three Burley letters suggest, John Donne's love affair with Ann entailed a wider range of feelings and experiences than we have assumed, it probably also inspired a larger, more various group of poems than we have considered" ("'Under Ye Rage . . .': John Donne's Love Letters to Ann More," in *The Eagle And The Dove*, eds. Summers and Pebworth, 46). Much remains for scholars to discuss, determine, and clarify in the ongoing critical study of Donne's life and work, especially of the dating of the poems, which may always remain to some extent uncertain.

# APPENDIX B
## A Selected Bibliography of "The Exstasie"

John Roberts' remarks on criticism of "The Exstasie" are so telling and the plea for rescuing Donne is so relevant and important that I quote him at length here at the beginning of this bibliography.

> In fact, one could probably obtain a reasonably good overview of the whole development of modern Donne criticism by simply following out, year by year and step by step, the debate that has been raging over the meaning of "The Exstasie" .... And, if one were to follow out the critical debate on the poem, one might possibly conclude by agreeing, at least in part, with Empson, who, in 1972, reviewing Helen Gardner's edition of the love poems, argued that Donne desperately needs to be rescued (not kidnapped this time) from what he calls "the habitual mean mindedness of modern academic criticism, its moral emptiness combined with incessant moral nagging, and its scrubbed prison-like isolation."
> Although Empson's charge is characteristically too broad and too undiscriminating, I find his rescue plea attractive and perhaps even imperative if Donne criticism is to have much life in the future. . . . I am not suggesting, of course, that we abandon intellectually demanding and highly sophisticated literary approaches to Donne when those approaches are truly helpful in allowing us to appreciate and to understand better and more deeply his poetry, but I would argue for less specialized studies and for more comprehensive studies of his poetry that would enunciate in understandable English the major achievements of Donne's poetry. Donne is not a simple poet, nor is his art simple; but his poems were intended to communicate his particularly brilliant sense of reality to his readers, and I think that it is, therefore, the primary responsibility of critics to make clear, as best they can, what Donne is communicating. . . . I should hope that more critics will give attention to the primary task of making Donne's poetry more, not less accessible to an even wider reading audience than he enjoys at the present time. ("John Donne's Poetry," 65–67)

For annotated listings of some discussions of "The Exstasie," see John R. Roberts, *John Donne: An Annotated Bibliography of Modern Criticism, 1912–1967* and *John Donne: An Annotated Bibliography of Modern Criticism, 1968–1978.*

Andrews, Michael Cameron. "Donne's 'The Exstasy.'" *Explicator,* 39 (1981), 5–6.

Bennett, Joan. "The Love Poetry of John Donne: A Reply to Mr. C. S. Lewis." *Seventeenth Century Studies Presented to Sir Herbert Grierson.* Oxford: Oxford University Press, 1938.

Brooks, Cleanth. *Modern Poetry and the Tradition.* Chapel Hill: University of North Carolina Press, 1939.

————. *The Well Wrought Urn: Studies in the Structure of Poetry.* New York: Harcourt, Brace, 1947.

Cirillo, A. R. "The Fair Hermaphrodite: Love-Union in the Poetry of Donne and Spenser." *Studies in English Literature,* 9 (1969), 81–95.

Coanda, Richard. "Hopkins and Donne: 'Mystic' and Metaphysical." *Renascence,* 9 (1957), 180–187.

Cross, K. Gustav. "'Balm' in Donne and Shakespeare: Ironic Intention in *The Extasie.*" *Modern Language Notes,* 71 (1956), 480–482.

Ellrodt, Robert. *L'inspiration personelle et l'esprit du temps chez les poetes metaphysiques anglais.* Paris: Libraire J. Corti, 1960.

Fausset, Hugh I' Anson. *John Donne: A Study in Discord.* London: Jonathan Cape, Ltd., 1924.

Gardner, Helen. "The Argument about 'The Ecstasy.'" *Elizabethan and Jacobean Studies Presented to Frank Percy Wilson,* eds. Herbert Davis and Helen Gardner. Oxford: Oxford University Press, 1959.

————. "Commentary: 'The Ecstasy'" and "Appendix D: 'The Ecstasy.'" *John Donne: the Elegies and the Songs and Sonnets,* ed. Helen Gardner. London: Oxford University Press, 1965. 183–187 and 259–265.

Garrod, H. W. *John Donne: Poetry and Prose.* Oxford: Clarendon Press, 1946.

Gérard, M. Albert. "Mannerism and the Scholastic Structure of Donne's 'Extasie.'" *Publications de l'Universite de l'Etat a Elizabethville,* 1 (1961), 27–37.

Graziani, René. "John Donne's 'The Extasie' and Ecstasy." *Review of English Studies,* 19 (1968), 121–136.

Grierson, Sir Herbert J. C. "Commentary: 'The Extasie.'" *The*

*Poems of John Donne.* 2 vols. Ed. Sir Herbert Grierson. Oxford: Oxford University Press, 1912. II, 41–45.

_____. *Donne: Poetical Works.* London: Oxford University Press, 1933.

Guss, Donald L. *John Donne, Petrarchist: Italianate Conceits and Love Theory in the 'Songs and Sonnets,'* Detroit: Wayne State University Press, 1966.

Howe, Elizabeth Teresa. "Donne and the Spanish Mystics on Ecstasy." *Notre Dame English Journal,* 13 (1981), 29–44.

Hughes, Merritt Y. "Kidnapping Donne." *University of California Publications in English,* 4 (1934), 61–89.

_____. "The Lineage of 'The Extasie.'" *Modern Language Review,* 27 (1932), 1–5.

_____. "Some of Donne's 'Ecstasies.'" *Publications of the Modern Language Association,* 75 (1960), 509–518.

Hunt, Clay. *Donne's Poetry: Essays in Literary Analysis.* New Haven: Yale University Press, 1954.

Huntington, John. "Philosophical Seduction in Chapman, Davies, and Donne." *ELH,* 44 (1977), 40–59.

Legouis, Pierre. *Donne the Craftsman.* 1928. Reprinted, New York: Russell and Russell, Inc., 1962.

Leishman, J. B. *The Metaphysical Poets: Donne, Herbert, Vaughan, Traherne.* Oxford: Clarendon Press, 1934.

_____. *The Monarch of Wit: An Analytical and Comparative Study of the Poetry of John Donne.* London: Hutchinson University Library Press, 1965.

Lewalski, Barbara K. "A Donnean Perspective on 'The Extasie.'" *English Language Notes,* 10 (1973), 258–62.

Lewis, C. S. "Donne and Love Poetry in the Seventeenth Century." *Seventeenth Century Studies Presented to Sir Herbert Grierson.* Ed. John Purves. Oxford: Oxford University Press, 1938. 64–84.

Louthan, Doniphan. *The Poetry of John Donne: A Study in Explication.* New York: Bookman Associates, 1951.

Marotti, Arthur F. "Donne and 'The Extasie,'" in *The Rhetoric of Renaissance Poetry.* Eds. Thomas O. Sloan and Raymond B. Waddington. Berkeley: University of California Press, 1974.

Martz, Louis. "John Donne: The Meditative Voice." *Massachusetts Review,* 1 (1960), 326–342.

_____. *The Poem of the Mind: Essays on Poetry, English and American.* New York: Oxford University Press, 1966.

McCanles, Michael. "Distinguish in Order to Unite: Donne's 'The

Extasie' ". *Studies in English Literature*, 6 (1966), 59–75.

McCann, Eleanor. "Donne and Saint Teresa on the Ecstasy." *Huntington Library Quarterly*, 17 (1954), 125–132.

Miner, Earl. *The Metaphysical Mode from Donne to Cowley.* Princeton: Princeton University Press, 1969.

Mitchell, Charles. "Donne's 'The Extasie': Love's Sublime Knot." *Studies in English Literature*, 8 (1968), 91–101.

Morris, William E. "Donne's Early Use of the Word 'Concoction.' " *Notes and Queries*, 10 (1963), 414–415.

Mueller, Janel M. " 'The Dialogue of One': A Feminist Reading of Donne's Extasie.' " *ADE Bulletin*, 81 (Fall 1985), 39–42.

Novarr, David. " 'The Exstasie': Donne's Address on the States of Union," in *Just so Much Honor.* Ed. Peter Fiore. University Park: Penn. State University Press, 1972. 219–243. And in Novarr's *The Disinterred Muse.* Ithaca: Cornell University Press, 1980. 17–39.

Paffard, M. K. "Donne's 'The Extasie,' 57–60, 68." *Explicator*, 22 (1963), 13.

Parish, John E. "The Parley in 'The Extasie.' " *Xavier University Studies*, 4 (1965), 188–192.

Parry, Graham. *Seventeenth-Century Poetry: The Social Context.* London: Hutchinson, 1985.

Perry, T. Anthony. *Erotic Spirituality: The Integrative Tradition from Leone Ebreo to John Donne.* University: University of Alabama Press, 1980.

Pinka, Patricia Garland. *This Dialogue of One: The Songs and Sonnets of John Donne.* University: The University of Alabama Press, 1982.

Potter, George R. "Donne's *Extasie*, contra Legouis." *Philological Quarterly*, 15 (1936), 247–253.

Praz, Mario. *Secentisimo e marinismo in Inghilterra: John Donne—Richard Crashaw.* Firenze: La Voce, 1925.

Rugoff, Milton A. *Donne's Imagery: A Study in Creative Sources.* New York: Russell & Russell, 1939.

Sherwood, Terry G. *Fulfilling the Circle: A Study of John Donne's Thought.* Toronto: University of Toronto Press, 1984.

Smith, A. James. "Donne in his Time: A Reading of *The Extasie.*" *Rivista di Letterature Moderne e Comparate*, 10 /19570, 260–275.

———. "The Metaphysic of Love." *Review of English Studies*, n.s. 9 (1958), 352–375.

———. *The Metaphysics of Love.* Cambridge: Cambridge University Press, 1985.

Tillyard, E. M. W. "A Note on Donne's *Extasie.*" *Review of English Studies*, 19 (1943), 61–70.

Thomason, T. Katherine. "Plotinian Metaphysics and Donne's 'Extasie.'" *Studies in English Literature*, 22 (1982), 91–105.

Walker, Julia M. "John Donne's 'The Extasie' as an Alchemical Process." *English Language Notes*, 20 (1982), 18.

Warren, Austin. "Donne's 'Extasie.'" *Studies in Philology*, 55 (1958), 472–480.

Williamson, George. "The Convention of 'The Extasie'" *Seventeenth Century English Poetry*. Ed. William R. Keast. New York: Oxford University Press, 1962. 132–143.

# NOTES

## Chapter 1

1. Although both words are used throughout this book, *contemplative* is preferred over *mystical* because it is the more traditional word, because it does not carry the freight of confused, inaccurate, popular meanings that *mystical* often does, and because it points to more advanced spiritual states as compared to the term referring to beginning spiritual states, *meditative*, the meaning of which term has been made clear and familiar to students of seventeenth-century poetry, particularly by the distinguished work of Louis Martz.

For this present work, I have adapted and incorporated a few paragraphs and sentences from my *The Mystical Poetry of Thomas Traherne*, especially in this chapter.

2. See, for example, Evelyn Underhill, *Mysticism* (New York, 1955); Rufus M. Jones, *Studies in Mystical Religion* (London, 1936); Ray C. Petry, ed., *Late Medieval Mysticism* (Philadelphia, 1957); Charles B. Schmitt, "Perennial Philosophy: From Agostino Steuco to Leibniz," *Journal of the History of Ideas*, 27 (1966), 505–532; Caroline F. E. Spurgeon, *Mysticism in English Literature* (Cambridge, England, 1913); E. Herman, *The Meaning and Value of Mysticism*, 3rd ed. (New York, 1925); Rufus M. Jones, *Spiritual Reformers in the 16th and 17th Centuries* (Boston, 1959); Percy Osmond, *The Mystical Poets of the English Church* (New York, 1919); Gerald Bullet, *The English Mystics* (London, 1950); F. C. Happold, *Mysticism* *(Baltimore, 1964); David Knowles, The English Mystical Tradition* (New York, 1965); E. Cuthbert Butler, *Western Mysticism: The Teachings of Sts. Augustine, Gregory and Bernard on Contemplation and the Contemplative Life* (New York, 1966); Sidney Spencer,

*Mysticism in World Religion* (Baltimore, 1963); Thomas Merton, *Mystics and Zen Masters* (New York, 1967); Thomas Katsaros and Nathaniel Kaplan, *The Western Mystical Tradition* (New Haven: College and University Press, 1969); Henry Bettenson, ed., *The Later Christian Fathers* (Oxford, 1970); Daniel Williams, *The Spirit and the Forms of Love* (Washington, D.C., 1981); Marion Glasscoe, ed., *The Medieval Mystical Tradition in England: Papers read July 1982* (University of Exeter, 1982) and *The Medieval Mystical Tradition in England: Papers read July 1984* (D. S. Brewer, 1984); D. H. Donnelly, *Radical Love* (Minneapolis, 1984); Ken Wilber, ed., *Quantum Questions: Mystical Writings of the World's Great Physicists* (Boston & London, 1985); Andrew Louth, *The Origins of the Christian Mystical Tradition: From Plato to Denys* (Oxford, 1981); Alan Watts, *The Supreme Identity* (New York, 1957), *Myth and Ritual in Christianity* (New York, 1960), and *Beyond Theology* (New York, 1964); and many others.

3. R. C. Zaehner, *Concordant Discord*, 200. I should also mention William Wainwright's *Mysticism: A Study of its Nature, Cognitive Value and Moral Implications* (Brighton: the Harvester Press, 1981), which critically evaluates some of the views of W. T. Stace.

4. Although Auden uses the phrase "Vision of Agape" to denominate this mystical experience, I use "Vision of Philia" because elsewhere in this book the work *agape* refers, as it usually does, to God's sacrificial love. See Auden's "Introduction" to *The Protestant Mystics*, edited by Anne Fremantle. Since the Vision of Philia is of lesser significance in the poetry we will examine by Donne, Herbert, and Vaughan, it is mentioned here mainly for the sake of completeness. The other three Visions will be more fully discussed as they are pertinent to one or another of these poets. "Vision," as employed by Auden and in this book, is used not in the non-mystical sense of "apparition" or "hallucination" or other abnormal psychic phenomena, but in the sense of a profound, usually transforming experience of reality, either sensuous (extrovertive) or non-sensuous (introvertive). I will introduce a fifth Vision, the Vision of Art, where appropriate in Chapters 4 and 5.

In her Preface to *The Protestant Mystics*, Anne Fremantle remarks that the book is a response to "the flat statement by a distinguished philosopher (a Protestant), Dr. W. T. Stace, that 'there are *no* Protestant mystics.'. . . W. H. Auden and I set out to prove there were" (vi). But there are many paths, as the Protestant mystic William Blake wisely observes, to the Palace of Wisdom. Though the goal, contemplation or Wisdom, may be the same, Fremantle goes on to suggest that the means, way, or path of Catholics and Protestants do differ. It is my belief that this is true and that this is probably what Stace intended. That is, just as there is no male or female in heaven, so there is no Catholic or Protestant in contemplation; in other words, regardless of denomination the characteristics of contemplation remain essentially the same. In any case, I am confident that Stace's statement is not to be taken in a merely literal sense, especially since he includes Protestant mystics in his works on mysticism.

5. "The state of progressive unification, in which we receive 'grace upon grace,' as we learn more and more of the 'fulness' of Christ, is called by the evangelist, in the verse just quoted and elsewhere, eternal life. This life is generally spoken of as a present possession rather than a future hope. 'He that believeth on the Son *hath* everlasting life'; 'he *is passed* from death unto life'; 'we *are* in Him that is true, even Jesus Christ. This *is* the true God, and eternal life'" (Inge, *Christian Mysticism*, 52). Eternity is not more and more time but a present timelessness. See also Matt. 19:14 and John 3:3–5.

6. In the Authorized Version of 1611, which I always cite unless otherwise noted, Heb. 4:12 also makes the distinction between soul and spirit. The Old Testament provides important scriptural authority in, for example, Gen. 1:27, Gen. 2:7, and Eccl. 12:17. Rom. 7:22, 2 Cor. 4:16, and Eph. 3:16 similarly refer to the outward and inward or inner man; Col. 3:9,10 to the old and new man.

As well as meaning *soul* and *spirit* respectively in I Cor. 15:45 and other passages, *psyche* and *pneuma*, which after this note will not be italicized, have other biblical significances, including the shared, frequent meaning of *life*. Kittel's and Friedrich's *Theological Dictionary of the New Testament*, which treats only Greek words of theological significance, discusses the New Testament usages of *psyche* as *life* in distinction from *pneuma*: "*psyche* often denotes physical life. *Pneuma* may be used for this too, but whereas the *psyche* can be persecuted and slain, one can only hand back the *pneuma* to God. Only *psyche*, then, can refer to the purely natural life that can reach an end (cf. the contrast in 1 Cor.15:45). . . . Proclamation and edification take place through the *pneuma*. . . . *psyche* is authentic life only as God gives it and one receives it from him . . . *pneuma* . . . tends to be seen as the inner spiritual life that we are given . . . *psyche* . . . tends to be restricted to the physical sphere instead of embracing within this sphere [as *pneuma* does] the gift of

God that transcends death. . . . Paul prefers *pneuma*, which stresses the continuity of the divine activity" (1350–1351).

The Hebrew biblical equivalents of the Greek *psyche* and *pneuma* are respectively *nephesh* and *ruach* (or *rûah*). James Hastings' *Dictionary of the Bible* (revised by Grant and Rowley) points out that "the Biblical concept of soul appears in the Hebrew *nephesh*, which in various contexts may be rendered 'soul,' 'life' or 'self'. . . . In the NT the term *psyche* . . . follows many of the usages of the OT . . ." (932). "The word *rûah* [is] usually represented in the Septuagint by *pneuma*. . ." (389). There are several meanings of the complex terms *psyche, pneuma, nephesh,* and *ruach* which are not strictly germane to our discussion. For a convenient compilation of the many biblical meanings of these terms and their development over time, see the Dictionaries cited above in this note and also see John L. McKenzie, S. J., *Dictionary of the Bible* (Milwaukee: Bruce Publishing, 1965), s.v. soul and spirit, pp. 836–839 and 840–845.

7. Henri Bremond, *Prayer and Poetry*, 108–109; St. Catherine of Genoa is cited in Aldous Huxley, *The Perennial Philosophy*, 18; *Meister Eckhart: A Modern Translation*, tr. Raymond Bernard Blakney, 180; Eckhart variously refers to pneuma as "the little castle," "the tabernacle of the Spirit," "the Light of the Spirit," "a spark" (*fünkelein*); Jan Ruysbroeck, *The Spiritual Espousals*, tr. Eric Colledge (London, 1952), 187–188. For additional examples, see Inge, *Christian Mysticism*, Appendix C, "The Doctrine of Deification"; R. A. Durr's discussion of "The Idea of the Divine Spark, or Seed" in *On the Mystical Poetry of Henry Vaughan*, Appendix A; and Eckhart's "The Nobleman" in Clark, trans., *Meister Eckhart*, 149–159.

8. Blakney, trans., *Meister Eckhart*, 129. See also p. 105: "As I have often said, there is something in the soul so closely akin to God that it is already one with him and need never be united to him." And Julian of Norwich: "Our soul is so deep-grounded in God and so endlessly treasured that we may not come to the knowing thereof till we have first knowing of God. . . . God is nearer to us than our own soul, for He is the ground in whom our soul standeth . . ." Cited in Underhill, *The Essentials of Mysticism*, 193.

9. *The Confessions*, 44. Unless otherwise noted, I cite E. B. Pusey's translation of *The Confessions*. And see *The Life of St. Teresa*: "He seemed to be so near"; and the seventeenth-century *Light on the Candlestick*: "God is nearer unto every man than himself, because He penetrates the most inward and intimate parts of man, and is the Life of the inmost spirit." Both quoted in Sidney Spencer, *Mysticism in World Religion* 243, 279.

# Chapter 2

1. Needless to say, the grouping of these two modern editors of Donne is only one of many possible or valuable classifications, criteria, and approaches, though their grouping certainly deserves careful critical attention. Among the more thoughtful and extended studies of personae, tone, and related matters, see esp. Patricia Garland Pinka's *This Dialogue of One: The Songs and Sonnets of John Donne,* which focuses on seven major types of lovers and also considers a few other speakers. "The fifty-four poems in the Songs and Sonnets have many views on love, that is, statements about love modified by the reader's understanding of the speaker. Seven of these occur in more than one poem; a number of others receive only a single utterance" (14). Our purposes, however, are best served by the Grierson-Gardner grouping. See also Barbara K. Lewalski, "Donne's Epideictic *Personae,*" *The Southern Quarterly,* 14 (1976), 195–202.

2. In his essay, "Poetry, Personal and Impersonal: The Case of Donne," John T. Shawcross rightly argues that "literature should first be viewed as literature—not as biographical statement, even when biography has direct influence; not as philosophy, even when the work propounds strong ideologies." Yet he also rightly defends the efficacy of biographical contexts in helping to determine a writer's point of view in particular works (Summers and Pebworth, eds., *The Eagle And The Dove,* 53–66). Aware that he is "conjecturally assigning a chronology to poems for which solid evidence for dating is difficult or impossible to find," Arthur F. Marotti provides an intelligent, comprehensive rereading of almost all of Donne's poems in order to support his central thesis that "Donne's poetry needs to be read historically as coterie literature," in *John Donne, Coterie Poet,* xiv. See also Richard E. Hughes' attempt to re-create Donne's interior life in *The Progress Of The Soul.*

3. For a fuller discussion of these issues with regard to a single Donne poem see "Harmonized Voices in Donne's 'Songs and Sonnets': 'The Dampe,'" co-authored by Gerald Gallant and A. L. Clements, *Studies in English Literature,* 15 (1975), 71–82, to which the above paragraph is indebted. "The Dampe" is a good example of a poem that so thoroughly deconstructs itself, or so thoroughly overlaps, that it cannot be confidently placed in any one of Grierson's three groups. See also Thomas Docherty's post-structuralist readings in *John Donne, Undone* (London and New York: Methuen, 1986).

4. Elizabeth Howe, for example, in her essay "Donne and the Spanish Mystics on Ecstasy," thoughtfully examines "The Exstasie" in the light of both the poetry and prose mystical works of not only San Juan but also his contemporary, Santa Teresa de Jesús, in order to compare their observations concerning ecstatic union with Donne's." She claims that "both English metaphysical and Spanish mystic may draw inspiration from a common source and, therefore, describe possibly antithetic experiences in analogous terms." She concludes that "fundamental differences of language and interpretation of ecstasy thus exist between Donne's poem and the works of the mystical doctors" (30, 40).

5. Throughout I cite Gardner's *The Elegies and The Songs and Sonnets* and *The Divine Poems*. I have also consulted and found helpful Grierson's work, W. Milgate's *The Satires, Epigrams and Verse Letters* and *The Epithalamions, Anniversaries and Epicedes*, John Shawcross' *The Complete Poetry of John Donne*, Frank Manley's *John Donne: The Anniversaries*, C. A. Patrides' *The Complete English Poems of John Donne*, and my own edition of *John Donne's Poetry*, citing these where necessary.

6. Although these remarks may seem to invoke T. S. Eliot's "dissociation of sensibility," that is not intended. Doubtlessly, in all ages (not just after the middle of the seventeenth century), the sensibility of most people is dissociated, for dissociated sensibility is but another characteristic of the fallen, unredeemed condition. Whatever the validity of Eliot's theory, which he himself later qualified, my point, to be developed in Chapter Five, is that certain ancient, medieval and Renaissance world views allowed and encouraged humans to feel more at home in the universe and at one with the cosmos than certain prevailing modern philosophies.

7. Auden believes that "The Vision of Eros cannot long survive if the parties enter into an actual sexual relation" (20). Other authorities, discussed later in this chapter, believe otherwise and thereby lend support to the view of Donne's poetry presented in this book.

8. Some prefer to translate, "God became man that man might become divine."

9. In the cogent *Fulfilling the Circle: A Study of John Donne's Thought*, Terry G. Sherwood writes "A long view of [Donne's] writings reveals consistent principles that reach fruition in the mature religious prose . . . . the mature works construct one essential context in which to approach troublesome elements in the earlier works . . . . to follow the lines of Donne's development either way, back-

wards or forwards, increases our understanding greatly . . . . Applications to even the more private and secular love poetry can be revealing" (3).

10. Barbara K. Lewalski rightly concludes that in "The Exstasie" Donne suggests "that the Christian mysteries of the Incarnation and of scripture revelation are proper models for these spiritual lovers in their decision to manifest the perfections attained in the realm of the spirit in the less exalted domain of the body." "A Donnean Perspective on 'The Extasie,' " 262. On the meaning of "resurrection" in Donne's work, see the thoughtful study by Kathryn R. Kremen, *The Imagination of the Resurrection: The Poetic Continuity of a Religious Motif in Donne, Blake, and Yeats.* Although Kremen makes many informative observations, her view that "the erotic songs and sonnets present the resurrection of the body in the sexual union of man and woman, while the penitential divine poems portray the resurrection of the soul in the spiritual union of man and Christ; both events take place in history, and their relation is figural" (91) seems somewhat oversimplified, neglecting the timeless aspect of many of the erotic secular poems and insufficiently emphasizing their important spiritual dimensions. See also A. B. Chambers' superb and well-documented study of resurrection in "Glorified Bodies and the 'Valediction: forbidding Mourning,' " *John Donne Journal*, 1 (1982), 1–20.

11. See David Novarr's thoroughly intelligent discussion of " 'The Exstasie': Donne's Address on the States of Union," pp. 17–39 in *The Disinterred Muse*, esp. 37: "The chief stroke of wit in 'The Exstasie' is Donne's tactic of having the 'abler soule' make the case justifying the role of the body in love and educating not 'the layetie' but the refined Neo-Platonist who must be persuaded of the perogatives of the body. This listener has no use for the softnesses of love; he will be persuaded only by the nice speculations of philosophy. In the amorous verses of 'The Exstasie,' Donne affects the metaphysics so that nature may reign."

12. Cf. William J. Rooney, " 'The Canonization'—The Language of Paradox Reconsiderd," *ELH*, 23 (1956), 36–47, reprinted in *Essential Articles for the Study of John Donne's Poetry*, ed. John R. Roberts, pp. 271–278. Rooney asserts that the use of paradox "in the instance of 'The Canonization' is a distinctly poetical one, and from such use nothing can be concluded about whether 'Donne takes both love and religion seriously.' In apprehending this poem, the reader, modern or otherwise, is not faced with the philosophical dilemma, 'Either: Donne does not take love seriously . . . Or:

Donne does not take sainthood seriously,' as Brooks asserts" (278). Nevertheless, not only modern readers but modern critics as well do respond in philosophical and moral terms. In *John Donne's Poetry*, Wilbur Sanders objects that the "canonization conceit" "entails an inflation of sentiment just as grandiose as the Petrarchan hyperboles Donne has already punctured . . . . Donne appears to argue the quasi-divine status of the lovers on the preposterous grounds that they re-enact the resurrection of Christ . . . . He is thus impertinently confounding mere carnality with a prime mystery of religion . . . . this blasphemous witticism . . ." (22). Ably responding "to show how Donne's blend of wit and seriousness in hyperbole has provoked" Sanders, Brian Vickers points out in "The 'Songs and Sonnets' and the Rhetoric of Hyperbole" (*Essays in Celebration*, ed. A. J. Smith) that Sanders falls "back on a kind of puritanical thundering, a moral denunciation in which grace and humor are absent . . . . What he has quite failed to see (and he is evidently not alone) can be summed up in the paradoxical language of Traherne: hyperbole, like love, is 'infinitely Great in all Extremes . . . Excess is its true Moderation: Activity its Rest: and burning Fervency its only Refreshment' " (173–174).

13. See, e.g., Joseph Anthony Mazzeo, "A Critique of Some Modern Theories of Metaphysical Poetry," *Modern Philology*, 50 (1952), 88–92, reprinted in my *John Donne's Poetry*, 134–43, and see also his other articles referred to there on p. 134, n. 1. In *A Lecture in Love's Philosophy: Donne's Vision of the World of Human Love in the Songs and Sonnets*, Denis McKevlin argues that the thematically and structurally unified poems of the Songs and Sonnets may be interpreted as an attempt to establish unity within the individual, the cosmos, and the deity, based on Donne's application of the system of universal correspondences.

14. For these and other details concerning Donne, Ann More, their marriage, and the dating, see R. C. Bald's *John Donne: A Life* and Edward Le Comte's *Grace to a Witty Sinner: A Life of Donne*.

15. See Le Comte's account of the dating of the marriage and the sequence of events leading to it, "Jack Donne: From Rake To Husband" in *Just So Much Honor*, ed. Peter Amadeus Fiore.

16. Another biographer, Derek Parker, writes that "the marriage of John and Ann Donne is on the evidence we have one of the most ideal and complete in the history of the institution; never was a couple more truly one flesh—that was an ideal Donne had always had, in his attitude to love, and it is revealed in the poems written before and after his marriage" (*John Donne And His World*, 39). Ilona

Bell does well "to recall the historical fact that when a Renaissance couple like Donne and Ann More made a private contract of love without parental permission, they were not simply disregarding her father's wishes. They were challenging the patriarchal social structure on which all the country's laws were founded. We can see just how radical and threatening their action seemed by the elaborate moralizing it provoked from Walton . . ." (" 'Under ye rage . . .': John Donne's Love Letters to Ann More" in *The Eagle and The Dove*, ed. Summers and Pebworth, 44).

17. In her *Radical Love: An Approach to Sexual Spirituality*, 1–14, D. H. Donnelly presents a brief history of the bifurcation of sexuality and spirituality, especially in the Christian Church, and in *The Spirit and the Forms of Love*, D. D. Williams similarly discusses "Sex in the Christian Tradition," 215–219.

18. Donne may also have learned from Pico, or another Renaissance Humanist, that "it was a rule among the ancients, in the case of all writers, never to leave unread any commentaries which might be available. Aristotle especially observed this rule so carefully that Plato called him . . . 'the reader' " (*Oration*, 14).

19. Donne's distrust of ordinary reason is apparent in his sermon preached at Whitehall, April 21, 1616 (No. 6 in *XXVI Sermons*), *The Sermons of John Donne*, ed. G. R. Potter and E. M. Simpson, I, 169–170. See also Itrat Husain: "Donne not only distrusted the power of intellect as an absolute entity not liable to err, but he also believed that faith came not through intellectual conviction but through the working of grace . . . Religion in its higher and more spiritual form is thus above reason and rationalism" (*The Mystical Element in the Metaphysical Poets*, 90–91).

20. For a view of the traditions behind Donne's poetry that is somewhat different than the view presented in this section IV, see A. J. Smith, "The Dismissal of Love or, Was Donne a Neoplatonic Lover?" in *John Donne: Essays in Celebration*, 89–131. In this essay, as similarly in his later *The Metaphysics of Love* (195), Smith concludes that the poems show Donne "consciously formalising his experience in a precise scholastic way" and that Donne would "have been chagrined to find people talking of neoplatonic ideas in his verse" (131). Cf. T. Katherine Thomason's article, written partly in response to Smith, "Plotinian Metaphysics and Donne's 'Extasie,' " in *Studies in English Literature*, 1982.

21. Roger B. Rollin sums up critical difficulties with the Holy Sonnets when he observes at the beginning of his essay " 'Fantastique Ague': The Holy Sonnets and Religious Melancholy" that scholars

"continue to be vexed by problems of the sonnets' dating, sequence, possible autobiographical content, and, certainly, interpretation." What he says of his essay applies as well to this section: "such problems shall not be solved here, though they may be rendered somewhat less vexing . . ." (in *The Eagle And The Dove*, ed. Summers and Pebworth, 131). Rollin provides some critical summary of work on the Holy Sonnets. His general contention is that "they constitute powerful dramatizations of how deeply rooted melancholy is in human nature and in the human condition" (146). The meloncholy of the Holy Sonnets is in my view a consequence of a profound belief in and desire for union with God accompanied by an equally profound sense of God's absence. On the ordering of the Holy Sonnets, see esp. Patrick F. O'Connell, "The Successive Arrangements of Donne's 'Holy Sonnets,'" *Philological Quarterly* 60 (1981), 323–342: "My conclusion, then, which is consistent with the evidence of all known manuscripts, supports Gardner's choice of arrangement of Groups I–II (and *1633*) as Donne's definitive ordering of the 'Holy Sonnets,' and rejects her attempt to group the four sonnets added in *1635* as a related group, seeing them instead as sonnets left over from an earlier group of twelve" (334). For the Holy Sonnets and Donne's other poems as well see also John T. Shawcross, "The Arrangement and Order of John Donne's Poems," 119–163 in *Poems in Their Place: The Intertextuality and Order of Poetic Collections*, ed. Neil Fraistat, Chapel Hill: University of North Carolina Press, 1986.

22. I use Gardner's second edition of *John Donne: The Divine Poems*, for all of Donne's divine poems, though again I have also consulted other editions. In this chapter, as in my edition of *John Donne's Poetry*, the numbering (in roman numerals) of the Holy Sonnets in the 1635 to 1669 editions and in Grierson's edition has been retained in brackets, for critics have often referred to the Holy Sonnets conveniently by means of these Roman numerals; but Gardner's renumbering in Arabic numerals of her groups of twelve, four, and three, have also been given, preceding the bracketed Roman numerals.

23. A shorter version of the following analysis of 10 [XIV] was first published as "Donne's Holy Sonnet XIV" in *Modern Language Notes*, 76 (1961), 484–489 and reprinted in my *John Donne's Poetry* (1966), along with several other discussions of the poem. Critics continue to scrutinize this sonnet. See, e.g., John E. Parish, "No. 14 of Donne's *Holy Sonnets*," *College English* (1963), in Clements, ed., *John Donne's Poetry*, 255–259; Willoughby Newton, "A Study of John Donne's Sonnet XIV," *Anglican Theological Review*, 41 (1959), 10–12; William R. Mueller, "Donne's Adulterous Female Town," *Modern Language Notes*, 76 (1961), 312–314; Lucio P. Ruotolo, "The Trinitarian Framework of Donne's Holy Sonnet XIV," *Journal of the*

*History of Ideas*, 60 (1966), 445–446; David K. Cornelius, "Donne's Holy Sonnet XIV," *Explicator*, 24 (1965), 25; Elias Schwartz, "Donne's Holy Sonnets, XIV," *Explicator*, 26 (1967), 27; Mary Wanninger, "Donne's Holy Sonnets, XIV," *Explicator*, 28 (1969/70), 37; John Hagopian, "John Donne: Batter My Heart," *Insight III* (Frankfurt: Hirschgraben–Verlag, 1969), 86–96; Desmond Graham, *Introduction to Poetry* (London: Oxford University Press, 1968), 63–66, 29–30; William W. Heist, "Donne on Divine Grace: Holy Sonnet No. XIV," *Papers of the Michigan Academy of Science, Arts and Letters*, 53 (1968), 311–20; Sister Joan Moorhem, "Two Explications—John Donne's Holy Sonnet XIV and Gerald Manley Hopkins' Sonnet 69," *Insight*, 3 (1971), 62–71; Thomas J. Steele, S.J., "Donne's Holy Sonnets, XIV," *Explicator*, 29 (1971), 74; Michael Steig, "Donne's Divine Rapist: Unconscious Fantasy in Holy Sonnet XIV," *University of Hartford Studies in Literature*, 4 (1972), 52–58; Michael Gregory, "A Theory for Stylistics—Exemplified: Donne's 'Holy Sonnet XIV,'" *Language and Style*, 7 (1974) 108–18; William Kerrigan, "The Fearful Accommodations of John Donne," *English Literary Renaissance*, 4 (1974), 337–63; Reuven Tsur, "Poem, Prayer, and Meditation: An Exercise in Literary Semantics," *Style*, 8 (1974), 404–24; Marvin K. L. Ching, "The Relationship Among the Diverse Senses of a Pun," *The SECOL Bulletin*, 2 (1978), 1–8; Ralph Yarrow, "Admitting the Infinite: John Donne's Poem 'Batter My Heart,'" *Studies in Mystical Literature*, 1 (1981), 210–217; R. D. Bedford, "Donne's Holy Sonnet, 'Batter My Heart,'" *Notes and Queries* 29 (1982), 15–19; Frank McCormick, "Donne, the Pope, and 'Holy Sonnets XIV,'" *CEA Critic*, 45 (1983), 23–24; Tunis Romein, "Donne's 'Holy Sonnet XIV,'" *Explicator*, 42 (1984), 12–14; Terry G. Sherwood, *Fulfilling the Circle: A Study of John Donne's Thought* (Toronto: University of Toronto Press, 1984); R. V. Young, "Donne's Holy Sonnets and the Theology of Grace," in *"Bright Shootes of Everlastingnesse": The Seventeenth-Century Religious Lyric*, eds. Claude J. Summers and Ted-Larry Pebworth (Columbia: University of Missouri Press, 1987).

24. Doniphan Louthan, *The Poetry of John Donne* (New York, 1951), 124; George Herman, "Donne's Holy Sonnets, XIV," *Explicator*, XII (December 1953), 18; George Knox, "Donne's Holy Sonnets, XIV," *Explicator*, XV (October 1956), 2. See also Ruotolo, Cornelius, Schwartz, and Hagopian, cited in n. 23.

25. See also Luke 12:36 and John 14:23. Vaughan, as we shall see in Chapter Four, also makes important use of this marriage metaphor and these pertinent biblical passages.

26. The Lamb-Ram contrast is of course only implicit in this sonnet; but cf. the seventh of the La Corona sonnets, 11. 9–10:

O strong Ramme, which hast batter'd heaven for mee,

Mild Lambe, which with thy blood, hast mark'd the path.

27. Genesis 2:7; see also, e.g., Job 33:4, Isaiah 30:33, 42:5, Acts 17:24–25.

28. *Complete Works*, trans. and ed. E. A. Peers II, 70; for this quotation I am indebted to R. A. Durr.

29. See also 2 Samuel 22:29, Numbers 6:25, Job 41:32, Psalms 18:28, 31:16, 36:9, 67:1, 80:3, 19, 84:11, 119:135, James 1:17.

30. John 14:26, 16:13. See also John 14:16–17, 15:26, 16:7–12, Acts 2:2–11, 19:2–6, 1 John 5:6.

31. See, e.g., Knox: "The triadic division of the sonnet into quatrains follows the extension of the 'knock, breathe, shine,' and the 'break, blow, burn,' alignments. The first quatrain calls on God the Father's omnipotence to batter the heart. The second envisions the admission of God through the medium or agency of Rectified Reason, Reason rectified through love. The third exemplifies the re-born understanding (en*light*ened through the Son). . . ."

32. Cf. 1. 3 of this sonnet, "That I may rise, and stand, o'erthrow mee . . ." with the last line of "Hyme to God, my God, in my Sicknesse": "Therefore that he may raise, the Lord throws down."

33. Perhaps also in the first quatrain, the heart is being compared metaphorically to an alchemical object; note esp. 1. 4 and cf. "Good-friday, 1613. Riding Westward," 11. 40–41: "Burne off my rusts, and my deformity, Restore thine Image. . . ." Or perhaps (see J. C. Levenson, "Donne's Holy Sonnets, XIV," *Explicator*, XI [March 1953], 31, and XII [April 1954], 36) the conceit is that of the heart as a metal object in God's, the metalworker's hands. R. D. Bedford makes a strong case for seeing the imagery of pottery in the first quatrain, *Notes and Queries*, 1982.

34. According to Gardner, the first sequence of six Holy Sonnets more closely follows the pattern of Ignatian meditation than the second, which depends less on the preludes than on the colloquy of the Ignatian meditation. In the second sequence the influence of the meditation is felt not in the structure of the sonnets but in, for one pertinent example, the use of "congruous thoughts," as in "Batter my heart" (*John Donne: The Divine Poems*, xxxvii–lv). Louis Martz confirms the view that some of the Holy Sonnets are by subject and treatment in the tradition of the Ignatian meditation; he shows that several sonnets are developed according to the Ignatian pattern of composition, analysis, colloquy. Martz concludes that the Holy Sonnets "are, in the most specific sense of the term, meditations, Ignatian meditations: providing strong evidence for the profound impact of early Jesuit training upon the later career of John Donne" (*The

*Poetry of Meditation* 43–53, et passim). Taking a more comprehensive approach (including the vocal, meditative, affective, and contemplative modes) to seventeenth-century devotional poetry than previous critics attempted, Anthony Low in *Love's Architecture* rightly concludes "except for relatively minor writers like Alabaster or Southwell, Donne is the most purely meditative of the English devotional poets" (40).

35. Although this poem has usually been attributed to the date given in its title, the discovery in 1974 of a previously unknown manuscript suggests otherwise. While debate about the provenance of the manuscript may continue indefinitely, it has been suggested that the poem may actually have been written in 1610 when Donne traveled to Oxford to receive an honorary M.A.

36. Until Dennis Flynn's argument (see Appendix A) is fully accepted or confirmed, this statement remains true even though Gardner's date of July 1607 or shortly before has been cogently challenged. See David Novarr, "The Dating of Donne's *La Corona*," *Philological Quarterly*, 36 (1957), 259–265, reprinted in *The Disinterred Muse*, from which Novarr's conclusion is quoted: "I suspect that . . . the *La Corona* sonnets . . . were written shortly before the Holy Sonnets, that is, late in 1608 or early in 1609" (93). In " 'La Corona': Donne's *Ars Poetica Sacra*" (in *The Eagle And The Dove*, eds. Summers and Pebworth), Patrick O'Connell concludes: "La Corona" is both a series of meditations on the life of Christ and a record of the personal appropriation of that life through dying and rising with Christ. As such, it provides a paradigm and interpretative key for the entire body of Donne's religious poetry, the principal subject of which is the possibility, and the difficulty, of self-transcendence (that is, prayer) in a world where the self has assumed a degree of independence unknown in previous centuries. Donne's end in the Divine Poems is the traditional one of expressing dependence on and potential union with God; his innovation is in starting from a new point—self-centered individualism, which he identifies with sin and alienation from God and the true self. This autonomous self is 'the God-subverting element in Man,' which must be transcended to discover not only God but also one's own true identity" (130). "The God-subverting element in Man," which in this book is called psyche or ego, is not transcended in Donne's divine poems. See also A. B. Chambers, "*La Corona*: Philosophic, Sacred, and Poetic Uses of Time," in *New Essays on Donne*, 140–72.

37. Walton dated this poem eight days before Donne's death on March 31, 1631, though there is other, more convincing evidence

that the poem was written during his illness in 1623; on the dating of this and other Donne poems see esp. Novarr, *The Disinterred Muse* and Shawcross, *The Complete Poetry*.

38. Studying Donne's thought in his prose writings, Itrat Husain, in *The Mystical Element in the Metaphysical Poets of the Seventeenth Century*, considers Donne a mystic and his philosophical position "essentially that of a mystic" (96). Yet "Donne never seems to have attained the last stage of mystical life, the 'unitive stage' " (103). "Donne, following St. Thomas Aquinas, believed that we cannot behold God in His Essence, though a fleeting vision of God was possible in this life" (110). Evelyn Simpson, in *A Study of the Prose Works of John Donne*, tends to think of Donne "as a good Christian, but not necessarily as a mystic" (94). She points out that Donne was acquainted with mystical writings and could use the language of mysticism, but "this does not, however, necesssarily prove him to have been a mystic, and in the *Sermons* and *Devotions* there is little which can be called mystical in the technical sense of the term" (92). However, she quotes a passage from one of Donne's sermons, "which suggests that Donne has some experience of the ecstasy of mystical contemplation" (94). And she concludes: "Thus it is clear that he regarded the highest state to which a Christian could attain in this life as that of illumination—an experience which involved constant intercourse with God, and which might be raised at moments to a height of transcendental ecstasy, but was nevertheless liable to interruption. It was this lack of absolute continuity that made him, following Aquinas, differentiate mystical experience here, even at its height, from the Beatific Vision. He who has once seen that vision cannot turn away his eyes. Moreover, there is a sense in which flesh and blood cannot inherit the kingdom of God. '*No man ever saw God and liv'd*, and yet, I shall not live till I see God; and when I have seen him I shall never dye.' Yet this life and the next are not violently sundered from one another. The light of glory has its dawn here, though the noon-tide must come hereafter" (96–97). See also Husain, *The Dogmatic and Mystical Theology of John Donne*, 134–143.

## Chapter 3

1. A shorter version of this chapter, titled "Theme, Tone, and Tradition in George Herbert's Poetry" and supported by a Fellowship from the National Endowment for the Humanities, for which I am grate-

ful, was published in *English Literary Renaissance,* 3 (1973), 264–283 and reprinted in John R. Roberts' edition of *Essential Articles For The Study of George Herbert's Poetry,* 1979. Since this essay's original publication, other studies of Herbert's conception of the self, the crucial mine-thine distinction, and/or "Artillerie" have appeared, including William V. Nestrick, "'Mine and Thine' in *The Temple,"* in *"Too Rich to Clothe the Sunne": Essays on George Herbert,* eds. Summers and Pebworth, 1980; Barbara Leah Harman, *Costly Monuments: Representations of the Self in George Herbert's Poetry,* 1982; Diana Benet, *Secretary of Praise: The Poetic Vocation of George Herbert,* 1984; and Sibyl Lutz Severance, "Self-Persistence in *The Temple*: George Herbert's 'Artillerie,'" *University of Hartford Studies in Literature,* 1984. John R. Roberts' very useful *George Herbert: An Annotated Bibliography of Modern Criticism, 1905–1984* shows only a handful of references to "Artillerie" published before 1973. On the "self" in Herbert, see esp. Stanley E. Fish's superb reader-response criticism (or affective stylistics) in "Letting Go: The Dialectic of the Self in Herbert's Poetry" in *Self-Consuming Artifacts: The Experience of Seventeenth-Century Literature,* 1972.

2. Several valuable studies of Herbert's Protestantism and Anglicanism have recently been published. In her *Protestant Poetics and the Seventeenth-Century Religious Lyric* (1979), Barbara Lewalski makes the case that seventeenth-century English poets, including Herbert, owe more to Protestant than to medieval Catholic or Counter-Reformation influences. Like Margaret Bottrall and other critics before her, Heather Asals's purpose in *Equivocal Predication: George Herbert's Way to God* (1981) "is partly to restore Herbert as a specifically Anglican poet" (5), and she points out that Amy Charles' *A Life of George Herbert* (1977) lends support to those who wish to reclaim Herbert as an Anglican, even as a high Anglican. In his thoughtful and informed *Reformation Spirituality: The Religion of George Herbert* (1985), Gene Edward Veith, Jr. stresses that it is misleading and not necessary to contrast "Anglican" and "Protestant" as if they were two separate categories; Veith's study tries "to account for some of the differences evident in seventeenth-century religious verse . . . by stressing the major conceptual shift within Protestantism signaled by the Synod of Dort, in which the emphasis on the action and the will of God, codified by Calvin, was challenged by a new emphasis on the action and will of human beings, codified by Jacobus Arminius" (18). Recently, holding that the emphasis on Herbert's Protestantism and/or Puritanism has become far too pronounced, and taking into account Herbert's Little Gidding audience,

Stanley Stewart restores some balance and makes a valuable contribution to the question of Catholic and Protestant contexts, usefully reminding us, as did Joseph Summers, that "religious categories, Catholic and Protestant among them, were slippery and often weighted with political controversy" (*George Herbert*, 1986, 59), and helpfully suggesting that "in discussing Herbert's art, we deemphasize . . . the polarity between Catholic and Protestant poetic norms" (80). See also the *George Herbert Journal*, 11 (Fall 1987), no. 1, which contains papers by Donald R. Dickson, Daniel W. Doerksen, and Andrew Harnack, and a response by Richard Strier, which were first presented at a Special Session on "George Herbert's Theology: Nearer Rome or Geneva?" at the 1986 MLA convention. And see esp. *A Fine Tuning*, a Festschrift edited by Mary Maleski in honor of Joseph H. Summers, for important essays which pursue the lively debate about Catholic and Protestant influences on Herbert; this book, which I have been privileged to read in manuscript, will be published in 1989 by SUNY-Binghamton's Medieval and Renaissance Texts and Studies. My own view, taking the double perspective of affirming Herbert's Protestant Anglicanism and of regarding it from the Catholic-Protestant lens of ancient-medieval-Renaissance contemplative tradition, is similar to Sister Maria Thekla's *George Herbert: Idea and Image* (1974), which sees a simultaneous double movement in *The Temple* and suggests that, although in one sense Herbert's work can be viewed as an exposition of Anglicanism in poetry, in another sense it is a poetic record of Herbert's mysticism: "It is this double movement which I have tried to lean towards in my exploration of *The Temple*, that is, the reality of Herbert's allegiance to his Church, the Church of England, on earth, with all the consequences, and, then, the reality of the love which can not be contained in the Church on earth, or indeed within the confines of the created world" (14).

3. All quotations of Herbert's poetry and prose are from *The Works of George Herbert*, ed. F. E. Hutchinson (Oxford: Clarendon Press, 1951). I have also consulted and found helpful *The English Poems of George Herbert*, ed. C. A. Patrides, 1974; the Facsimile of *The Temple*, 1633, 1968; the Facsimile of *The Williams Manuscript of George Herbert's Poems*, 1977; the Facsimile of The *Bodleian Manuscript of George Herbert's Poems*, 1984; and *George Herbert and the Seventeenth-Century Religious Poets*, ed. Mario A. Di Cesare, 1978. A number of critics have commented on the crucial lines from "The H. Scriptures, II." For a recent extended commentary on these lines and a thoroughgoing study of the relation of the Bible to *The Temple*,

see Chana Bloch, *Spelling the Word: George Herbert and the Bible*, 1985.

4. In addition to the critical works already mentioned on the unity and structure of or sequences in *The Temple*, numerous other studies have been published. As well as the Bowers' and Charles' essays, John R. Roberts has conveniently collected fine articles on the subject by Elizabeth Stambler, Annabel M. Endicott-Patterson, Stanley Stewart, Valerie Carnes, and Heather Asals in his excellent *Essential Articles: George Herbert's Poetry*. Two important articles not included in the Roberts' collection are John R. Mulder's "George Herbert's *The Temple*: Design and Methodology," Seventeenth-Century Notes, 31 (1973), 37–45, and Sidney Gottlieb's "Linking Techniques in Herbert and Vaughan," *George Herbert Journal*, 2 (1978), 38–53. Joseph Summers' work and Martz's chapter on "The Unity of The Temple" remain seminal. See also Diana Benet's *Secretary of Praise*, ch. 3, and Edmund Miller's *Drudgerie Divine*, ch. 5. Some critics have remarked that *The Temple* may not be Herbert's title and the placement of "The Church Militant" after "The Church" may not be Herbert's arrangement, but that we can be fairly confident that the arrangement of the poems in "The Church" is Herbert's, or very close to it. In *The Living Temple: George Herbert and Catechizing* (1978), Stanley Fish makes a strong argument that *The Temple* was composed and organized on a catechistical model, and in so doing he is able to resolve some previously unresolved critical problems.

5. The works by the authors mentioned are listed under "Works Cited." When so fine a critic as Helen Vendler takes the term "mystical" in an apparently untraditional and misleading sense, it is certain that a rhetorical or definitional problem exists and that greater clarification, explanation, and precision are called for. Writing on his "two poems on Trinity Sunday," Vendler asserts that "Herbert shuns both the apocalyptic and the mystical, nowhere more clearly than here. He is no visionary, and no ecstatic." I completely agree with this last sentence, but although visions (i.e., abnormal psychic phenomena, not Auden's four Visions) and ecstasies may on occasion accompany mystical experience they are neither necessary nor sufficient conditions of it, nor at all definitive of it. (See, e.g., Underhill, *Mysticism*, 266f., 380, 170, and 279–80: "the mystics are all but unanimous in their refusal to attribute importance to any kind of visionary experience.") So it is perhaps not altogether surprising that on the same page Vendler writes of Herbert as if he were a mystic: "for Herbert God . . . is rather, potentially at least, Herbert himself.

The ultimately desirable state of things for Herbert is one in which the self is indistinguishable from God" (152; see also 285 n. 13). I also completely agree with these statements, which clearly suggest, as I understand the term, that Herbert was indeed a mystic.

6. In "Employment" (I), Herbert writes explicitly of this concept:

> I am no link of thy great chain,
>   But all my companie is a weed
> Lord place me in thy consort; give one strain
>   to my poore reed.

7. I am aware of a possible ambiguity in ll. 12–15, particularly l. 14. Rather than stating a conditional argument from which he draws the submissive conclusion of l. 16, Herbert may still be insisting on his own will and way: i.e., "even with blood, I still *do* refuse to wash away my stubborn thought." This reading would see the conflict as continuing right through until the last stanza. However, even though both readings arrive essentially at the same conclusion, I prefer the reading given above in the text for the following reasons: there are no commas before "not" and after "blood" in l. 14; "for" in l. 16 has the force of a conclusive "therefore"; "ought" in l. 16 is "ought" and not "want"; and "but" in l. 17 suggests an exception to, not a continuation of, the meaning of the previous lines.

8. See Hutchinson, 526, on "shooters." The O.E.D. defines "artillery" as "engines for discharging missiles"; the heart is such an engine; cf. "Prayer" wherein prayer is called "Engine against th' Almightie . . . Reversed thunder." The O.E.D. also defines "artillery" as "the science and practice of Gunnery (formerly of Archery)"; hence l. 28, "Shunne not my arrows."

9. Francis Quarles, *Emblems* (London, 1778), 101f. See also Achille Bocchi, *Symbolicarum* . . . (Bologna, 1574), 18, 200; Christopher Harvey, *The School of the Heart* (London, 1778), II, 29; and Mario Praz, *Studies in Seventeenth Century Imagery*, 2nd ed., (Rome, 1964), 94, 97, 103, 105, 107, 111, 150, 152, 155, 229, for additional examples of arrow emblems. For a thoroughgoing recent critical discussion of Herbert and the Emblem, see Charles A. Huttar's "Herbert and Emblematic Tradition" in Miller and DiYanni, eds., *Like Season'd Timber*, which contains important essays in various areas of Herbert studies. And note the similar verbal imagery in ch. 6 of *The Cloud of Unknowing*, (60), with regard to the arrow or dart.

10. The contrast between Donne's anxiety and Herbert's assurance was drawn, as Robert Shaw notes (*The Call of God*, 114), fifty years

ago by Helen White and has since been confirmed by such distinguished scholars as M. M. Mahood, Rosamond Tuve and Louis Martz, among others. As late as 1974, Patrick Grant contrasted Donne's turbulence in the Holy Sonnets with Herbert's assurance (*The Transformation of Sin*, Ch. 3). Shaw also rightly notes that "the most recent trend in Herbert criticism is likely to stress the poet's depiction in *The Temple* of the 'spiritual Conflicts' he suffered before submitting his will to Christ, rather than whatever peace was gained by such a submission," and Shaw mentions the "distinguished examples" of Helen Vendler and Barbara Leah Harman. In *The Living Temple*, Stanley Fish offers a comprehensive account of "Criticism's two Herberts."

11. Cited in *The Poetry of Meditation*, 126–27; see also 128–35. A readily available modern edition of *Spiritual Combat*, including Scupoli's *Path to Paradise* and with an excellent introduction by H. A. Hodges, is *Unseen Warfare*.

12. In his commentary, F. E. Hutchinson observes also the "curiously light, bantering tone" which Herbert brings to the "grave subjects" of "Time," "Death," and "Doomsday" (p. 520). On parody in Herbert, see, e.g., Rosemary Freeman, "Parody as a Literary Form: George Herbert and Wilfred Owen," *Essays in Criticism*, 13 (1963), 307–22.

13. Near the beginning of *A Priest to the Temple*, in discussing "The Parsons Knowledg," Herbert writes that ideally the parson "is full of all knowledg. . . . But the chief and top of his knowledge consists in the book of books . . . the holy Scriptures. There he sucks, and lives." Herbert then describes the four means for understanding what is found in the Bible: "first, a holy Life. . . . The second means is prayer. . . . The third means is a diligent Collation of Scripture with Scripture. . . . The fourth means are Commenters and Fathers." And he adds, "the Countrey Parson hath read the Fathers also, and the Schoolmen, and the later Writers, or a good proportion of all" (pp. 228, 229).

14. In Herbert both "heart" and "mind" may be metaphors for the self. One needs, however, to distinguish between mind and Mind, between the Platonic *dianoia* and *noesis*, between (in modern terms) the rational, logical, discursive mind (allied with the psyche or false self, which must "die") and the intuitive, imaginative, loving Mind (at the center of pneuma or the true self, which must be realized).

15. Writing on Paul as a Christ-Mystic, Adolf Deissman remarks that "even more characteristically Pauline is . . . the Hellenistic-mystical tendency of the experience of Christ: the living Christ is the

Pneuma. As Pneuma, as Spirit the living Christ is not far off, above clouds and stars, but near. . . . The formula 'in the Spirit' . . . he connects with the formula 'in Christ.' . . . Finally there is one characteristically Pauline conviction . . . the conviction of being in Christ raised especially above *suffering*. Paul has here given form to one of the profoundest conceptions that we owe him: since he suffers in Christ, his sufferings are to him the 'sufferings of Christ,' or the 'afflictions of Christ.' It is not the old Paul who suffers, but the new Paul, who is a member of the Body of Christ, and who therefore mystically experiences all that that Body experienced and experiences; . . . a certain fixed measure of 'afflictions of Christ' must according to God's plan be 'filled up' by Paul (Col. 1:24)." This Pauline "mystical contemplation of the passion" is "a subject which cannot yet be properly comprehended by any of us, but whose memorials in written word and drama, in music and pictures often give us a wonderfully sympathetic interpretation of Paul's profoundest meaning" (*Paul* . . . , excerpted in *The Writings of St. Paul*, 376, 377, 386, 387).

16. Edgar Daniels, "Herbert's 'The Quip,' 1. 23: 'say, I am thine,'" *ELN*, 2 (1964), 10–12, argues persuasively for reading the line as a direct quotation.

17. See esp. Martz, *The Poetry of Meditation*, 309–12, and Low, *Love's Architecture*, 103–14.

18. Cf. "Providence": "Thou art in all things one, in each thing many: / For thou art infinite in one and all."

19. In *Love Known*, Richard Strier rightly notes that "A. L. Clements ('Theme, Tone, and Tradition in Herbert's Poetry,' *ELR* 3 [1973], 264–83) reads the lines much as Fish does" (62, n. 3). Stanley Fish's *Self-Consuming Artifacts* (1972) was not available when I prepared the earlier version of this Chapter for publication, and most of this Chapter was written before I read any of Fish's generally brilliant work on Herbert. I do basically agree with many of Fish's views, though I differ in some important details. In his Chapter 3, Strier makes an intelligent but, for me, not convincing counter-argument against viewing Herbert as a mystic. He believes "Fish's reading makes Herbert a 'Manichee,' a mystical pantheist like Servetus or some of the great Eastern and heterodox Western mystics" (63), and he attaches a note to this sentence citing my Herbert essay quoting Eckhart. But one does not have to be a Manichee to be a mystical pantheist (instead of this latter phrase I prefer the more exact and neutral terms "extrovertive mystic" and "Vision of Dame Kind"), and there are of course very orthodox Western mystics who are extrovertive mystics. In any case, Herbert, in my view, is an introvertive not an extrovertive mys-

tic or mystical pantheist; but neither Strier nor Fish distinguishes between extrovertive and introvertive mysticism nor the Vision of Dame Kind and the Vision of God; and Strier's distinction between theology and philosophy seems a more modern than Renaissance distinction.

20. Such embarrassment may help to explain some critics' reluctance to see and say that Herbert and other writers are mystics. It may also help to explain certain differences between Western mentality and Eastern, as illustrated by the following. It is said that in the West when one discovers that "all things are in the divinity, and the divinity is in all things" and expresses (very poorly, to be sure) that wonderful discovery in the formula "I am God" (meaning that his newly-discovered true self, not his false self, is divine) then he is at great risk of being straightjacketed and tossed into a psychiatric ward, whereas in the East when one makes that same discovery and says (loosely) "I am God," he is greeted with the response "Congratulations, what took you so long to realize it?"

21. When in his more recent book, *The Living Temple*, Stanley Fish writes of Herbert's work that the reader is driven "to articulate for himself a deep and dark point of religion," which "is always the same: Christ is everywhere and doing all things" (85), Fish is, though he does not explicitly indicate, placing Herbert squarely within contemplative tradition. (As I see it, it is a "dark" point in the sense of "esoteric," many people, including the faithful, not knowing it.)

22. In his earlier *Self-Consuming Artifacts*, Fish writes "the insight that God's word is all is *self*-destructive, since acquiring it involves abandoning the perceptual and conceptual categories within which the self moves and by means of which it separately exists. To stop saying amiss is not only to stop distinguishing 'this' from 'that,' but to stop distinguishing oneself from God, and finally to stop, to cease to be. Learning to 'spell' in these terms is a self-diminishing action in the course of which the individual lets go, one by one, of all the ways of thinking, seeing, and saying that sustain the illusion of his independence, until finally he is absorbed into the deity whose omnipresence he has acknowledged (thy word is *all*)" (156–57). Although "absorbed into the deity" is imprecise, this statement from his earlier book, insofar as it goes, is excellent, and consistent with contemplative tradition. But it focuses on only one half of the truth. Fish apparently does not see or adequately stress that the record of "The Church" matches Christ's grief and that at some level God and the "I" are finally alike or identical. Barbara Harman similarly attends more to the dissolution of the self: "What I would like to

suggest is that the dissolution of a coherent view of self and sense is indeed Herbert's subject in these poems. In fact, it is *persistently* his subject: neither the self's disappearance into God's word, nor his acquisition of an aesthetic victory, brings the tentative and restless making of distinctions to an end" (*Costly Monuments*, 160–61). The rediscovery and realization of his true self is also persistently Herbert's subject and deserves equal emphasis. (Furthermore, in a very real and practical textual sense, we cannot with any certainty "know too that this tasting of 'the churches mysticall repast' is only preliminary to another siege of doubts and questions" [*The Living Temple*, 136], simply because "Love" (III) is the last poem in "The Church." And if we suppose for the sake of argument that Herbert wanted to end "The Church" without doubt and in perfect rest, we may well conclude that "Love" (III) perfectly completes "The Church.")

23. An important but generally neglected short article on "Love" (III) is James Thorpe, "Herbert's 'Love' (III)," *The Explicator* 24 (1965), 6, which argues persuasively for the four-fold interpretation usual in medieval scriptural exegesis: literally, an invitation to dinner; allegorically, the Eucharistic feast; tropologically, "a dialogue between the soul and love through which a way of psychological and moral action is depicted"; anagogically, the perfection in union with God. "All of them seem essential ways of looking at the poem."

Given the eschatological character of the concluding poems and the fact that "Love" (III) recapitulates "The Church" and the poem's last line refers back to many key moments in the sequence, it might be well also to note the prophetic and apocalyptic mode designated "Recapitulation" in sixteenth-century and earlier biblical exegesis. R. H. Charles observes that "in the sixteenth century . . . the Reformers followed in the main two different methods of interpretation: The first is the Church- or World-Historical, initiated by Petrus Aureolus and adopted by Luther, the second the Recapitulation Method of . . . the eschatological school of Joachim, which was based on a revival of the methods of Irenaeus and Victorinus with borrowings of details from the school of Tyconius [and which] found the events of their own day mystically shadowed forth as well as the impending end of the world" (*Studies in the Apocalypse*, 27, 26). See esp. Irenaeus' *Adversus Haereses*, III and V. Relevant extracts, with notes and introductory commentary, are given in English by Bettenson, who, observing that "Irenaeus may justly be called the first biblical theologian," writes that the second Adam's "redemptive work, by which Christ 'joins the end to the beginning', that is, restores man

to God, is one of the meanings of the famous doctrine of 'recapitula-
tion'. The word is Pauline—or deutero-Pauline—from Ephesians
1.10" (*The Early Christian Fathers*, 13; see also 81–83). Relevant to
"Love" (III), the end of "The Church," Ephesians 1.10 reads "in the
dispensation of the fulness of times he might gather together in one
all things in Christ, both which are in heaven, and which are on
earth; even in him." See also Irenaeus on "The 'Recapitulation' in
Christ" in Bettenson, *Documents of the Christian Church*, 29f. I
have used this book, and Bettenson's *The Early Christian Fathers*
and *The Later Christian Fathers* mainly for their ready availability
and the excellence of the translations.

## Chapter 4

1. The works by the authors mentioned are listed under "Works
Cited." An earlier version of part of this chapter was published as
"Meditation and Contemplation in Henry Vaughan: 'The Night' " in
*Studia Mystica*, 10 (1987), 3–33. Complicating further the already
complex and confused matter of mysticism in Vaughan is the related
question of Hermeticism, which still other critics, like Bain Stewart
and A. W. Rudrum, regard as central or importantly pertinent in
Vaughan. Although I agree with Rudrum "that Vaughan probably did
have a 'mystical' experience . . . and that the experience was such as
to transform his apprehension of the natural world" and that the evi-
dence is in his poetry ("Henry Vaughan and the Theme of Transfig-
uration," 54), I share the view of various scholars that Vaughan's Her-
meticism almost always appears within the context of orthodox
Christian reference (particularly Christian mysticism) and is subor-
dinate to it. Like the word "mysticism," "Hermeticism" has various
meanings. In showing the relevance of some mystical aspects of Her-
meticism to Vaughan, Rudrum and some other scholars have made
well-informed and valuable contributions to Vaughan studies. The
occult, non-mystical dimensions of Hermeticism are in my view
marginally relevant. Rudrum has conveniently collected some of the
important writings on Vaughan and Hermeticism, along with other
essays, in *Essential Articles for the Study of Henry Vaughan*.

2. If a critic does not know what mysticism is or understands it in
inaccurate senses, the critic may nevertheless observe the signs of it
in a poet, even describe them, and yet not be able to identify them
as such. See also, e.g., Post (201, 206, 211); and Seelig, who seems to
deny that Vaughan was a mystic, taking the term mystical in the

very narrow sense of referring "to a quite exceptional ecstatic experience, such as that celebrated by Teresa of Avila" (46), but who sometimes otherwise characterizes Vaughan as if he were a mystic. Ecstasy may be an aspect of mystical experience but it is neither a necessary nor a sufficient characteristic of it. Given the etymological and historical meanings of ecstasy (see O.E.D.), it is not altogether surprising that in certain contexts the term is used, as in the epigraph from Lawrence at the beginning of the next chapter, as a kind of synecdoche for mystical experience or mystical death and rebirth. See Underhill (*Mysticism*, 380, 170) and Stace (*The Teachings of the Mystics*, 175). Other critics (Marilla, e.g.) deny that Vaughan is a mystical poet apparently because they regard mysticism as a phenomenon peripheral rather than central and essential to the Christian religion; carefully compare Durr (*On the Mystical Poetry*, xiii–xv). By so misunderstanding mysticism or misusing the term, critics inadvertently diminish the import and effect of their otherwise valuable work.

3. The purposes of this chapter and my interpretation of "The Night" differ in some important ways from the extended discussions of this poem in the books on Vaughan by Ross Garner (135–144), E. C. Pettet (140–154), Jonathan Post (201–211), and R. A. Durr (113–122), though my view is closest to Durr's. Many critics have written less extensively on the poem. The importance of biblical allusion in it is discussed by Fern Farnham in "The Imagery of Henry Vaughan's 'The Night,' " *Philological Quarterly*, 38 (1959), 425–435 and by Leland H. Chambers in "Henry Vaughan's Allusive Technique: Biblical Allusion in 'The Night.' " *Modern Language Quarterly*, 27 (1966), 371–378. Anthony Low's shorter discussion (201–205) is notably insightful and helpful; he writes, "Vaughan's greatest contemplative poem, perhaps the best evocation of contemplation in English poetry, is 'The Night' " (201). See also Bain Stewart, Seelig (93–102), Melvin E. A. Bradford, "Henry Vaughan's 'The Night': A Consideration of Metaphor and Meditation," *Arlington Quarterly*, 1 (1968), 209–222, A. W. Rudrum, "Vaughan's 'The Night': Some Hermetic Notes," *Modern Language Review*, 64 (1969), 11–19, and Jeffrey S. Johnson, "Images of Christ in Vaughan's 'The Night': An Argument for Unity." *George Herbert Journal*, 7 (1983–84), 99–108. The abundance of comment on "The Night" might well seem to be evidence for what Geoffrey Hartman calls "the drive toward endless interpretation" (149).

4. The text I use for Vaughan's poetry and prose is L. C. Martin's *Vaughan's Works*, 2nd ed. (Oxford: Clarendon Press, 1957). I have

also consulted and found helpful French Fogle's *The Complete Poetry of Henry Vaughan*, 1964; Mario Di Cesare's *George Herbert and the Seventeenth-Century Poets*, 1978; Alan Rudrum's *Henry Vaughan: The Complete Poems*, 1981; and Louis Martz's *George Herbert and Henry Vaughan*, 1986.

5. Although the focus of this book is on the individual's direct and indirect relationship to God as revealed in the poetry, there were of course many historical, political, social and other religious events having significance for seventeenth-century poets, as discussed in numerous critical works. Given the increasing tumult of the times after the deaths of Donne and Herbert, Vaughan may well have been most affected by such events. Recent books which study the historical, social, and political dimensions of Vaughan's poetry include Graham Parry's *Seventeenth-Century Poetry: The Social Context* (which includes Donne and Herbert) and Noel K. Thomas' *Henry Vaughan: Poet of Revelation*. See also Parry's *The Seventeenth Century: The Intellectual Context of English Literature*, 1603–1700 (White Plains: Longman, 1988) and Summers' and Pebworth's essays, "Vaughan's Temple in Nature and the Context of 'Regeneration' " and "Herbert, Vaughan, and Public Concerns in Private Modes."

6. F. E. Hutchinson observes that "a very fine feature of Welsh poetry is *dyfalu*, the piling up of comparisons, sometimes fanciful and even riddling, but all intended to present the object with greater effectiveness. The sixth stanza of 'The Night' is described by Sir H. Idris Bell as 'a perfect example of *dyfalu*; even thus and no otherwise would Vaughan have written, had he been writing in Welsh' " (163). Ruth Preston Lehrman notes that "in his edition of Dafydd's poems, David Bell believes the successive epithets of 'The Night' are the device called *dyfalu* by the Welsh poets" (336). Lehrman adds, however, that "though the epithets in 'The Night' may resemble the Welsh *dyfalu*, they are equally characteristic of English verse" (339). I think it significant, as my text will argue, that Vaughan's fifth and sixth stanzas bear a strong structural similarity to Herbert's "Prayer," which has at least equal claim as a source or influence. Cf. Vaughan's "Son-dayes" (Martin, 447) and see Mario A. Di Cesare's excellent "Image and Allusion in Herbert's "Prayer (I)," *English Literary Renaissance*, 11 (1981), 304–328; for Herbert's use of apposition in the poem, see E. B. Greenwood, "George Herbert's Sonnet 'Prayer': A Stylistic Study," *Essays in Criticism*, 15 (1965), 27–45; for the effectiveness of apposition as a poetic device for expressing mystical consciousness and experiences, see my *The Mystical Poetry of Thomas Traherne*, pp. 75–76, 93, 130–133, 173–174, *et passim*. See also Sid-

ney Gottlieb, "How Shall We Read Herbert? A Look at 'Prayer,'" *George Herbert Journal*, 1 (1977), 26–38.

7. This quotation from *Luke* 21:37 appeared as an epigraph on the title page of the 1652 edition of *The Mount of Olives*, which work begins: "The night . . . was not therefore made, that either we should sleep it out, or passe it away idly. . . . When all the world is asleep, thou shouldst watch, weep and pray . . ." (Martin, 143). Later in the same work, Vaughan writes: "It is an observation of some *spirits*, that *the night is the mother of thoughts.* . . . he that sets forth at *midnight*, will sooner meet the *Sunne*, then he that sleeps it out betwixt his curtains" (169).

8. Cf., e.g., Matt. 2:19ff.; 1:20ff.; 28.2; Luke 1:26ff.; 2:9; 22:43; John 12:29; Acts 5:19; 7:30; 27:23; etc. See also "Religion," 11. 1–16.

9. Cited in Underhill, *Mysticism*, 347. In the same place, Underhill writes: "Of the dim and ineffable contemplation of Unnameable Transcendence, the imageless absorption in the Absolute, Dionysius the Areopagite of course provides the classic example. It was he who gave to it the name of Divine Darkness: and all later mystics of this type borrow their language from him."

10. Although St. John's *Spiritual Works which lead a soul to perfect union with God* was published in 1618 and a Latin edition was published in 1622 and reprinted in 1639, it is not necessary to claim that he directly or indirectly "influenced" Vaughan or that Vaughan was familiar with his *Dark Night of the Soul*. Whether or not Vaughan read other similar texts or St. John's work, the point is that the latter is helpful to the critic for understanding "The Night." And although St. John writes of several nights, there is, strictly speaking, only one night: the mystic consciousness changes throughout the night, and St. John changes terminology in order to characterize this changing consciousness.

11. It is this last dark night or "dazling darkness" of dim contemplation in the stage of Union, not the preceding dark nights, that Itrat Husain actually refers to when he contends that the dark night is absent from Vaughan's writings (*The Mystical Element*, 231, 235). See S. Sandbank's intelligent "Henry Vaughan's Apology for Darkness," *Studies in English Literature*, 7 (1967), 141–152 and Ross Garner's helpful discussion of St. John with respect to Vaughan's "Regeneration" (55–57).

12. I am indebted for this table to E. W. Trueman Dicken and to Mary E. Giles. For a full discussion and comparison of the traditional threefold stages and the stages of spiritual progress in St. John, see

Dicken's *The Crucible of Love*. See also Giles' *The Poetics of Love: Meditations with John of the Cross*.

13. Consider A. J. Smith's wise commentary: "Vaughan's poems attempt nothing less than the defiant grounding of a new life in a myth of sacred love, which accounts for the vitality of the entire universe in terms of a 'continuous commerce' between creatures and their creator, in R. A. Durr's phrase. In essence Vaughan simply tries to live out the doctrine of love drawn from St. Augustine by St. Bernard, St. Bonaventura and the Victorines, which had helped shape Dante's *Divina Commedia*. . . . Vaughan and Milton have in common an understanding of love which sets them against transcendental metaphysicians on the one hand, and empirical scientists on the other. . . . The natural creation of *Silex Scintillans*, as of *Paradise Lost*, is not the universe assumed in mathematical physics, and it controverts the idea of a geometry of nature. To Vaughan, Lockeian empiricists and Cartesian rationalists are alike just dealers in vanity, in as far as they deny that created things have part in an organism of love. . . . Vaughan wrote *Silex Scintillans* partly out of his need to assert the working of providential love within the order of nature, alienating himself not only from a Hobbes but from such pious rationalists as Mersenne, Descartes, and the Anglican divines who would soon express the times, Barrow, Tillotson, South and their like. For Vaughan, the universe of natural philosophy and the universe of rational theology are alike empires of death, a whirl of random atoms. The universe Vaughan inhabits is the antithesis of Newton's because he conceives that it is not inert but essentially alive, not neutral but purposefully animated by loving joy, and providentially disposed for our good" (*The Metaphysics of Love*, 259–262). We shall see in Chapter Five that modern scientists are in some vital ways closer in their complex vision to Dante, Vaughan, and other contemplatives than to, in Blake's phrase, the single vision of Newton.

14. According to Underhill, the true "dark night of the soul" is by St. John called the "night of the spirit" (*Mysticism*, 354 n. 1). Similarly, E. Allison Peers, St. John's translator and editor, writes that "the Passive Night of the Spirit, which is at once more afflictive and more painful than those which have preceded it. . . , is the Dark Night *par excellence*" (*The Complete Works of St. John of the Cross*, 317–318). Rather than the traditional threefold division, Underhill employs a fivefold division to characterize the spiritual life: Awakening; Purgation; Illumination; Dark Night of the Soul; Union. Fol-

lowing illumination, her Dark Night of the Soul corresponds essentially to St. John's passive night of the spirit.

15. See the discussions of "Regeneration" in the previously cited books by R. A. Durr, Ross Garner, E. C. Pettet, William Halewood, and Stanley Stewart, in Alan Rudrum's "Henry Vaughan and the Theme of Transfiguration," and in Louis Martz's *The Paradise Within*. But see especially Thomas O. Calhoun's excellent *Henry Vaughan: The Achievement of Silex Scintillans*, which maintains that the poems of *Silex Scintillans* exist in series, that calendrical, liturgical, and typological sequences function in it, and that Vaughan's book is the last great Renaissance example of the Renaissance lyric sequence. As Calhoun notes, a number of critics have commented on continuity in Vaughan's work (242 n. 11). A. J. Smith regards *Silex Scintillans* as one poem made up of many lyrics in "Henry Vaughan's Ceremony of Innocence," as does Kenneth Friedenreich in his *Henry Vaughan*. See also John Mulder's *The Temple of the Mind*, 147. To the substantial work of some Vaughan critics on the question of sequence in *Silex Scintillans*, the remainder of this chapter tries, beyond its main concerns, to make a small contribution. Again, although writing in sequences is neither a necessary nor a sufficient condition of contemplative expression, it does appear as yet another distinctive inclination or characteristic of mystical consciousness.

16. The engraved title page of 1650 shows a flint in the shape of a heart (which is weeping, bleeding, and flaming while being struck by a steely thunderbolt held by God's arm extended from a cloud). As Martz notes in *The Paradise Within*, "a man [i.e., a face] within can be clearly seen through an opening in the heart's wall" (5).

17. See R. A. Durr, "Vaughan's Spring on the Hill," *Modern Language Notes*, 76 (1961), 704–07.

18. D. W. Robertson, Jr., ed. *On Christian Doctrine*, 10. See also 1 Cor. 8:6. In *The Fountain of Living Waters*, Donald R. Dickson studies "the way Herbert, Vaughan, and Traherne employ the circularity of the waters of life in presenting the Christian paradigm for salvation" (10).

19. See A Benedictine of Stanbrook Abbey, *Mediaeval Mystical Tradition and Saint John of the Cross*, 156.

20. As Alan Rudrum observes in "Henry Vaughan and the Theme of Transfiguration" (50), "It has become fashionable to regard the nineteenth century idea that Vaughan was a nature-mystic as a pleasant naivety good enough for the Victorians but by no means good enough for us. It may be true that the old attitude may have been, as

Kermode says it was, 'part of the romantic conspiracy to redeem the poet from a period cursed with obsolete learning'; it is certainly true that it is very easy to recite the proposition that Vaughan *was* a nature-mystic without having a very clear notion of what one means by this. But one feels that the time has come to assert that the children of the nineteenth century were in their generation wiser than the children of light. Vaughan *was* a nature-mystic; that is, he found God in Nature. His God was not Yahweh thundering on Mount Sinai but a God who is 'in all things, though invisibly.' He was a nature-mystic because his sense of joy in his participation of the phenomena was deepened and strengthened by a philosophy so that it did not degenerate into a mere vague feeling."

## Chapter 5

1. Parts of the following essays have been incorporated in this chapter: "Mysticism, Science, and the Task of Poetry," *Studia Mystica*, 9 (1986), 46–59; "Sacramental Vision: The Poetry of Robert Warren," *South Atlantic Bulletin*, 43 (1978), 47–65; "Syntax, Structure, and Self in Galway Kinnell's Poetry," *Cumberland Poetry Review*, 6 (1987), 56–85.

2. In "Mr. Eliot and Lawrence," the Appendix to his *D. H. Lawrence: Novelist*, F. R. Leavis more than adequately answers in personal and biographical terms the charges that Eliot makes against Lawrence, clearly establishing "that Lawrence *was* brought up in a living and central tradition" (308). My main concern is critically and philosophically to discuss Lawrence's work largely in terms of that living and central contemplative tradition.

3. See Clay Hunt's fine essay on Donne's elegy in his *Donne's Poetry*, reprinted in Clements, ed., *John Donne's Poetry*, 186–201.

4. See especially Julian Jaynes' controversial *The Origin of Consciousness in the Breakdown of the Bicameral Mind*.

5. "A Poem of Pure Imagination: An Experiment in Reading," *The Rime of the Ancient Mariner* (New York: Reynal & Hitchock, 1946), p. 103. See also his "Knowledge and the Image of Man" in *Robert Penn Warren: A Collection of Critical Essays*, ed. John L. Longley, Jr. (New York: New York Univ. Press, 1965), pp. 237–246.

6. For some of these significant implications see *The Holographic Paradigm and other Paradoxes: Exploring the Leading Edge of Science*, ed. Ken Wilber, esp. pp. 9f. My discussion of Pribram and Bohm is largely indebted to this thought-provoking book, which is recom-

mended to the reader seeking more than the highlighting summary that my very brief discussion offers.

7. *The Book*, 91. This paragraph is indebted to Watts.

8. I have in mind particularly the concluding lines from Book XII of Wordsworth *Prelude*:

> This spiritual Love acts not nor can exist
> Without Imagination. . . .
> Imagination having been our theme,
> So also hath that intellectual Love,
> For they are each in each, and cannot stand
> Dividually.

John Gardner writes that "great art celebrates life's potential, offering a vision unmistakably and unsentimentally rooted in love. 'Love' is of course another of those embarrassing words, perhaps a word even more embarrassing than 'morality,' but it's a word no aesthetician ought carelessly to drop from his vocabulary" (*On Moral Fiction*, 83).

9. Cf. Kinnell: "we moderns, who like to see ourselves as victims of life—victims of the so-called "absurd" condition—are in truth its frustrated conquerors. Our alienation is in proportion to our success in subjugating it. The more we conquer nature, the more nature becomes our enemy, and since we are, like it or not, creatures of nature, the more we make an enemy of the very life within us" (Friebert and Young, 209).

10. Many of the themes of this book are developed in Matthew Fox's excellent *The Coming of the Cosmic Christ: The Healing of Mother Earth and the Birth of a Global Renaissance*, San Francisco: Harper and Row, 1988. The purpose of Fox's highly recommended book is "to explore the meaning behind the term and the tradition of the Cosmic Christ [what we have been calling the mythic sense of Christ, pneuma, essential Self, the incarnate divine, etc.] in the West and to offer that meaning as a common ground for understanding and responding to the challenges of our time" (243).

# WORKS CITED

Works which are cited *fully and only once* in the Notes and works which are cited *only* in Appendix B, "Selected Bibliography of 'The Exstasie,'" are not repeated here.

## Editions used for the works of Donne, Herbert and Vaughan

*John Donne: The Divine Poems.* 2nd ed. Ed. Helen Gardner. Oxford: The Clarendon Press, 1978.

*John Donne: The Elegies and The Songs and Sonnets.* Ed. Helen Gardner. Oxford: The Clarendon Press, 1965.

*John Donne: Pseudo-Martyr.* Facsimile. Introd. Francis Jacques Sypher. Delmar, N. Y.: Scholars' Facsimiles and Reprints, 1974.

*John Donne: Selected Prose.* Chosen by Evelyn Simpson. Ed. Helen Gardner and Timothy Healy. Oxford: The Clarendon Press, 1967.

*The Sermons of John Donne.* Ed. George R. Potter and Evelyn Simpson. 10 vols. Berkeley: University of California Press, 1953–62.

*The Works of George Herbert.* Ed. F. E. Hutchinson. Oxford: Clarendon Press, 1951.

*The Works of Henry Vaughan.* 2nd ed. Ed. L. C. Martin. Oxford: Clarendon Press, 1957.

## Other editions of Donne, Herbert, and Vaughan which were consulted and cited

*The Bodleian Manuscript of George Herbert's Poems: A Facsimile of Tanner 307.* Introd. Amy M. Charles and Mario A. Di Cesare. Delmar, N. Y.: Scholars' Facsimiles and Reprints, 1984.

*The Complete English Poems of John Donne.* Ed. C. A. Patrides. London: J. M. Dent, 1985.

*The Complete Poetry of John Donne.* Ed. John T. Shawcross. Garden City: Doubleday, 1967.

*The Complete Poetry of Henry Vaughan.* Ed. French Fogle. New York: Doubleday, 1964.

*The English Poems of George Herbert.* Ed. C. A. Patrides. London: Dent, 1974.

*George Herbert and Henry Vaughan.* Ed. Louis Martz. Oxford: Oxford University Press, 1986.

*George Herbert and the Seventeenth-Century Poets: Authoritative Texts, Criticism.* Ed. Mario Di Cesare. New York: W. W. Norton, 1978.

*Henry Vaughan: The Complete Poems.* Ed. Alan Rudrum. New Haven: Yale University Press, 1981.

*John Donne: The Anniversaries.* Ed. Frank Manley. Baltimore: Johns Hopkins Press, 1963.

*John Donne: The Epithalamions, Anniversaries and Epicedes.* Ed. W. Milgate. Oxford: The Clarendon Press, 1978.

*John Donne's Poetry: Authoritative Texts, Criticism.* Ed. A. L. Clements. New York: W. W. Norton, 1966.

*John Donne: The Satires, Epigrams and Verse Letters.* Ed. W. Milgate. Oxford: The Clarendon Press, 1967.

*The Poems of John Donne.* 2 vols. Ed. Herbert J. C. Grierson. Oxford: Oxford University Press, 1912.

*The Temple, 1633.* Introd. M. C. Bradbrook. London: Scolar Press, 1968.

*The Williams Manuscript of George Herbert's Poems.* Introd. Amy M. Charles. Delmar, N. Y.: Scholars' Facsimiles and Reprints, 1977.

## Other Works

A Benedictine of Stanbrook Abbey. *Mediaeval Mystical Tradition and Saint John of the Cross.* London: Burnes and Oates, 1954.

Andreason, N. J. C. *John Donne: Conservative Revolutionary.* Princeton: Princeton University, 1967.

Anon. *Contemplations of the Dread and Love of God.* 1916.

Anon. *The Cloud of Unknowing.* Trans. Clifton Wolters. Baltimore: Penguin, 1961.

*Anselm of Canterbury.* Vol. 3. Ed. and trans. J. Hopkins and H. Richardson. Toronto: Edwin Mellen Press, 1976.

Aquinas, Thomas. *Basic Writings of St. Thomas Aquinas.* Trans. Anton C. Pegis. New York: Random House, 1945.

_____ . *Summa Theologica: Latin Text and English Translation.* 5 vols. New York: McGraw Hill, 1964.

Aristotle. *The Complete Works of Aristotle.* 2 vols. Ed. Jonathan Barnes. Princeton: Princeton University Press, 1984.

Asals, Heather A. R. *Equivocal Predication: George Herbert's Way to God.* Toronto: University of Toronto Press, 1981.

Auden, W. H. "Introduction" to *The Protestant Mystics.* Ed. Anne Fremantle. London: Weidenfeld and Nicolson, 1964.

Augustine. *The City of God.* 2 vols. Trans. John Healey, 1610. Ed. and revised Ernest Barker. London: J. M. Dent, 1945.

_____ . *The City of God.* Trans. Gerald B. Walsh et al. New York: Doubleday, 1958.

_____ . *The Confessions.* Trans. Edward B. Pusey. New York: Random House, 1949.

_____ . *The Confessions.* Trans. F. J. Sheed. London: Sheed and Ward, 1944.

_____ . *On Christian Doctrine.* Trans. D. W. Robertson, Jr. Indianapolis: Bobbs-Merrill Company, 1958.

Aulén, Gustaf. *Christus Victor: An Historical Study of the Three Main Types of the Idea of Atonement.* Trans. A. G. Hebert. New York: MacMillan, 1961.

Bald, R. C. *John Donne: A Life.* Oxford: Oxford University Press, 1970.

Bedford, R. D. "Donne's Holy Sonnet, 'Batter My Heart.' " *Notes and Queries,* 29 (1982), 15–19.

Bell, Ilona. " 'Under Ye Rage Of A Hott Sonn & Yr Eyes': John Donne's Love Letters to Ann More." *The Eagle and the Dove.* Ed. Claude J. Summers and Ted-Larry Pebworth. Columbia: University of Missouri Press, 1986.

Benet, Diana. *Secretary of Praise: The Poetic Vocation of George Herbert.* Columbia: University of Missouri Press, 1984.

Bettenson, Henry, ed. and trans. *Documents of the Christian Church.* 2nd ed. Oxford: Oxford University Press, 1963.

_____ , ed. and trans. *The Early Christian Fathers: A Selection from the Writings of the Fathers from St. Clement of Rome to St. Athanasius.* Oxford: Oxford University Press, 1956.

_____ , ed. and trans. *The Later Christian Fathers: A Selection from the Writings of the Fathers from St. Cyril of Jerusalem to St. Leo the Great.* Oxford: Oxford University Press, 1970.

Blackmur, R. P. *Language as Gesture.* New York: Harcourt, Brace, 1954.

Blake, William. *The Poems of William Blake.* Ed. W. H. Stevenson. Text by David V. Erdman. London: Longman, 1971.

Bloch, Chana. *Spelling the Word: George Herbert and the Bible.* Berkeley: University of California Press, 1985.

Bly, Robert. "Interview" by Kevin Power. *American Poetry Observed: Poets on Their Work.* Ed. Joe David Bellamy. Urbana: University of Illinois Press, 1984.

Boehme, Jakob. *The Way to Christ* and *The Confessions* in *The Protestant Mystics.* Ed. Anne Fremantle. London: Weidenfeld and Nicolson, 1964.

Boenig, Robert. "George Herbert and Mysticism." *Studia Mystica,* 5 (1982), 64–72.

Bonaventura, *The Mind's Road to God.* Trans. George Boas. Indianapolis: Bobbs-Merrill, 1953.

Bottrall, Margaret. *George Herbert.* London: John Murray, 1954.

Bowers, Fredson. "Herbert's Sequential Imagery: 'The Temper.'" *Modern Philology,* 59 (1962), 202–13. *Essential Articles: George Herbert's Poetry.* Ed. John R. Roberts. Hamden: Archon Books, 1979. 231–48.

Bradley, Sculley, and Harold W. Blodgett, eds. *Walt Whitman, Leaves of Grass: Texts and Criticism.* New York: W. W. Norton, 1973.

Bremond, Henri. *Prayer and Poetry.* Tr. Algar Thorold. London: J. M. Dent, 1927.

Brooks, Cleanth. "Henry Vaughan: Quietism and Mysticism." *Essays in Honor of Esmond Linworth Marilla.* Ed. Thomas Austin Kirby and William John Olive. Baton Rouge: Louisiana State University Press, 1970.

Brown, Norman O. *Love's Body.* New York: Random House, 1966.

Calhoun, Thomas O. *Henry Vaughan: The Achievement of Silex Scintillans.* London and Toronto: Associated University Presses, 1981.

Capra, Fritjof. *The Tao of Physics.* 2nd ed. New York: Bantam Books, 1983.

Chambers, A. B. "Glorified Bodies and the 'Valediction: forbidding Mourning.'" *John Donne Journal,* 1 (1982), 1–20.

———. "La Corona: Philosophic, Sacred, and Poetic Uses of Time." *New Essays on Donne.* Ed. Gary A. Stringer. Salzburg: Universität Salzburg, 1977. 140–72.

————. "The Fly in Donne's 'Canonization.'" Journal of English and German Philology, 65 (1966), 252–59.

Charles, Amy M. *A Life of George Herbert*. Ithaca: Cornell University Press, 1977.

————. "The Williams Manuscript and *The Temple*." *Renaissance Papers* (1972), 59–77. *Essential Articles: George Herbert's Poetry*. Ed. John R. Roberts. Hamden: Archon Books, 1979. 416–32.

Charles, R. H. *Studies in the Apocalypse*. New York: Scribner's, 1913.

Clark, Ira. *Christ Revealed: The History of the Neotypological Lyric in the English Renaissance*. Gainesville: University Presses of Florida, 1982.

Clements, Arthur L. "Donne's Holy Sonnet XIV." *Modern Language Notes*, 76 (1961), 484–89. *John Donne's Poetry*. Ed. A. L. Clements. New York: Norton, 1966. 251–55.

————. "Harmonized Voices in Donne's 'Song and Sonnets': 'The Dampe.'" *Studies in English Literature*, 15 (1975), 71–82. Co-authored with Gerald Gallant.

————. "Meditation and Contemplation in Henry Vaughan: 'The Night.'" *Studia Mystica*, 10 (1987), 3–33.

————. *The Mystical Poetry of Thomas Traherne*. Cambridge: Harvard University Press, 1969.

————. "Mysticism, Science, and the Task of Poetry." *Studia Mystica*, 9 (Winter 1986), 46–59.

————. "Sacramental Vision: The Poetry of Robert Penn Warren." *South Atlantic Bulletin*, 43 (1978), 47–65. Reprinted in *Robert Penn Warren*, ed. W. B. Clark, Boston: Hall and Co., 1981, and in *Robert Penn Warren: Critical Considerations*, ed. N. Nakadate, Lexington: University of Kentucky Press, 1981.

————. "Syntax, Structure, and Self in Galway Kinnell's Poetry." *Cumberland Poetry Review*, 6 (1987), 56–85.

————. "Theme, Tone and Tradition in George Herbert's Poetry." *English Literary Renaissance*, 3 (1973), 264–83. *Essential Articles: George Herbert's Poetry*. Ed. John R. Roberts. Hamden: Archon Books, 1979. 33–51.

Dante. *The Divine Comedy*. Trans. H. R. Huse. New York: Holt, Rinehart, and Winston, 1954.

————. *The New Life*. Trans. William Anderson. Baltimore: Penguin, 1964.

Deissmann, Adolf. *Paul, A Study in Social and Religious History*. Trans. William E. Wilson. Excerpted in *The Writings of St. Paul: Annotated Text, Criticism*, ed. Wayne A. Meeks. New York: Norton, 1972.

Descartes, René. *A Discourse on Method and Selected Writings.* Trans. John Veitch. New York: E. P. Dutton, 1951.

Dicken, E. W. Trueman. *The Crucible of Love: A Study of the Mysticism of St. Teresa of Jesus and St. John of the Cross.* London: Darton, Longman and Todd, 1963.

Dickson, Donald R. *The Fountain of Living Waters: The Typology of the Waters of Life in Herbert, Vaughan, and Traherne.* Columbia: University of Missouri Press, 1987.

Dionysius. *Dionysius the Areopagite on the Divine Names and the Mystical Theology.* Trans. C. E. Rolt. New York: The Macmillan Company, 1957.

Donnelly, D. H. *Radical Love: An Approach to Sexual Spirituality.* Minneapolis: Winston Press, 1984.

_____. "The Sexual Mystic: Embodied Spirituality." *The Feminist Mystic.* Ed. Mary E. Giles. New York: The Crossroad Publishing Company, 1982.

Durr, R. A. "Donne's 'The Primrose.'" *John Donne's Poetry.* Ed. A. L. Clements. New York: W. W. Norton and Company, 1966. 212–16.

_____. *On the Mystical Poetry of Henry Vaughan.* Cambridge: Harvard University Press, 1962.

Eckhart, Meister. *Meister Eckhart: A Modern Translation.* Trans. R. B. Blakney. New York: Harper, 1941.

_____. *Meister Eckhart: Selected Treatises and Sermons.* Trans. James M. Clark and John V. Skinner. London: Faber and Faber, 1958.

Eliot, T. S. *George Herbert.* London: Longmans, Green and Company, 1962.

Ferguson, George. *Signs and Symbols in Christian Art.* Oxford: Oxford University Press, 1966.

Ficino, Marsilio. *Commentary on the Symposium of Plato.* Trans. Sears Jayne. Columbia: University of Missouri Press, 1944.

Fiore, Peter Amadeus, ed. *Just So Much Honor: Essays Commemorating the Four-Hundredth Anniversary of the Birth of John Donne.* University Park: The Pennsylvania State University, 1972.

Fish, Stanley. "Letting Go: The Dialectic of the Self in Herbert's Poetry." *Self-Consuming Artifacts: The Experience of Seventeenth-Century Literature.* Berkeley: University of California Press, 1972. 156–223.

_____. *The Living Temple: George Herbert and Catechizing.* Berkeley: University of California Press, 1978.

Flynn, Dennis. "The Dating of Donne's Holy Sonnets." *A Fine Tuning*. An unpublished collection of essays in honor of Joseph H. Summers. Ed. Mary A. Maleski. 238–63.

Freud, Sigmund. *Civilization and Its Discontents*. Tr. J. Riviere. London: Methuen, 1930.

Friebert, Stuart, and David Young, eds. *A Field Guide to Contemporary Poetry and Poetics*. New York: Longman, 1980.

Friedenreich, Kenneth. *Henry Vaughan*. Boston: Twayne Publishers, 1978.

Gardner, John. *On Moral Fiction*. New York: Basic Books, 1978.

Garner, Ross. *Henry Vaughan: Experience and the Tradition*. Chicago: University of Chicago Press, 1959.

Gilbert, Sandra. *Acts of Attention: The Poems of D. H. Lawrence*. Ithaca: Cornell University Press, 1972.

Giles, Mary E. *The Poetics of Love: Meditations with John of the Cross*. New York: Peter Lang, 1986.

Grant, Patrick. *The Transformation of Sin: Studies in Donne, Herbert, Vaughan, and Traherne*. Montreal: McGill-Queen's University Press, 1974.

Gregory of Nyssa. *From Glory to Glory: Texts from Mystical Writings*. Trans. H. Musurillo, London: St. Vladimir's Seminary Press, 1962.

_____ . *The Life of Moses*. Trans. E. Ferguson and A. J. Malherbe. London: Society for Promoting Christian Knowledge, 1979.

_____ . *The Lord's Prayer; The Beatitudes*. Trans. Hilda C. Graef. London: Longmans, Green and Co., 1954.

Halewood, William. *The Poetry of Grace: Reformation Themes and Structures in English Seventeenth-Century Poetry*. New Haven: Yale University Press, 1970.

Happold, F. C. *Mysticism: A Study and an Anthology*. Baltimore: Penguin, 1964.

Harman, Barbara Leah. *Costly Monuments: Representations of the Self in George Herbert's Poetry*. Cambridge: Harvard University Press, 1982.

Harpur, Tom. *For Christ's Sake*. Toronto: Oxford University Press, 1986.

Hartman, Geoffrey. *Saving the Text*. Baltimore: Johns Hopkins University Press, 1981.

Hastings, James, ed. *Dictionary of the Bible*. Rev. ed. Frederick C. Grant and H. H. Rowley. New York: Scribner's, 1963.

Hilton, Walter, *The Goad of Love*. Ed. Clare Kirchberger. London: Faber and Faber, 1952.

_____ . *The Ladder of Perfection*. Trans., with an Introduction by Leo Sherley-Price. Baltimore: Penguin Books, 1957.

Hodgson, Peter E. "The Christian Origin of Modern Science." *The World and I*, (July 1988), 198–203.

Hopkins, Gerard Manley. *Poems of Gerard Manley Hopkins*. Ed. W. H. Gardner. New York and London: Oxford University Press, 1948.

Howe, Elizabeth Teresa. "Donne and the Spanish Mystics on Ecstasy." *Notre Dame English Journal*, 13 (1981), 29–44.

Hughes, Richard E. "George Herbert and the Incarnation." *Cithera*, 4 (1964), 22–32. *Essential Articles: George Herbert*. Ed. John R. Roberts. Hamden: Archon Books, 1979. 52–62.

_____ . *The Progress of the Soul: The Interior Career of John Donne*. New York: William Morrow & Co., 1968.

Huntley, Frank Livingstone. *Bishop Joseph Hall and Protestant Meditation in Seventeenth-Century England: A Study with the texts of the Art of Divine Meditation (1606) and Occasional Meditations (1633)*. Binghamton: Medieval & Renaissance Texts and Studies, 1981.

Husain, Itrat. *The Dogmatic and Mystical Theology of John Donne*. New York: Haskell House Publishers, 1938.

_____ . *The Mystical Element in the Metaphysical Poets of the Seventeenth Century*. Edinburgh: Oliver and Boyd, 1948.

Hutchinson, F. E. *Henry Vaughan*. Oxford: The Clarendon Press, 1947.

Huxley, Aldous. *The Perennial Philosophy*. London: Chatto and Windus, 1946.

_____ . *Texts and Pretexts*. New York: Harper and Brothers, 1933.

Inge, William, Dean. *Christian Mysticism*. London: Methuen, 1948.

Jaynes, Julian. *The Origin of Consciousness in the Breakdown of the Bicameral Mind*. Boston: Houghton Mifflin, 1976.

John of the Cross. *The Complete Works of Saint John of the Cross*. Trans. and ed. E. Allison Peers. Westminster, Md.: The Newman Press, 1964.

Jones, Rufus M. *Spiritual Reformers in the 16th and 17th Centuries*. Boston: Beacon Press, 1959.

Julian of Norwich. *Revelations of Divine Love*. _rans. into Modern English, with an Introduction by Clifton Wolters. Baltimore: Penguin Books, 1966.

Katsaros, Thomas and Nathaniel Kaplan. *The Western Mystical Tradition: An Intellectual History of Western Civilization*. Vol I. New Haven: College and University Press, 1969.

Kermode, Frank. "The Private Imagery of Henry Vaughan." *Review of English Studies*, 1 (1950), 206–225.

Kinnell, Galway. *The Avenue Bearing the Initial of Christ into the New World: Poems 1946–64*. Boston: Houghton Mifflin, 1974. Collects *First Poems 1946–1954, What a Kingdom It Was* and *Flower Herding on Mount Monadnock*.

———. *Body Rags*. Boston: Houghton Mifflin, 1968.

———. *The Book of Nightmares*. Boston: Houghton Mifflin, 1971.

———. *Mortal Acts, Mortal Words*. Boston: Houghton Mifflin, 1980.

———. *Selected Poems*. Boston: Houghton Mifflin, 1982.

———. *Walking Down The Stairs: Selections from Interviews*. Ann Arbor: The University of Michigan, 1978.

Kittel, Gerhard and Gerhard Friedrich, eds. *Theological Dictionary of the New Testament*. Trans. Geoffery W. Bromiley. Grand Rapids: William B. Eerdmans Publishing, 1985.

Knox, George. "Donne's Holy Sonnets, XIV." *Explicator*, 15 (October 1956), 2.

Kremen, Kathryn R. *The Imagination of the Resurrection: The Poetic Continuity of a Religious Motif in Donne, Blake, and Yeats*. Lewisburg: Bucknell University Press, 1972.

Lawrence, D. H. *Apocalypse*. Ed. Mara Kalnins. London: Granada, 1981.

———. *The Collected Letters of D. H. Lawrence*. Ed. Harry T. Moore. 2 vols. New York: Viking, 1962.

———. *The Complete Poems*. Eds. Vivian de Sola Pinto and Warren Roberts. 2 vols. New York: Viking, 1964.

———. *The Rainbow*. New York: Avon, 1943.

———. *Selected Poems*. Introduction by Kenneth Rexroth. New York: Viking, 1956.

———. *St. Mawr* and *The Man Who Died*. New York: Random House, 1953.

———. *Women in Love*. New York: Random House, 1950.

Leavis, F. R. *D. H. Lawrence: Novelist*. New York: Simon and Schuster, 1955.

LeComte, Edward. *Grace to a Witty Sinner: A Life of Donne*. New York: Walker and Company, 1965.

———. "Jack Donne: From Rake to Husband." *Just So Much Honor*. Ed. Peter Amadeus Fiore. University Park: The Pennsylvania State University Press, 1972. 9–32.

Lehrman, Ruth Preston. "Henry Vaughan and Welsh Poetry: A Contrast." *Philological Quarterly*, 24 (1945), 329–342.

Lewalski, Barbara K. "A Donnean Perspective on 'The Extasie.'" *English Language Notes*, 10 (1973), 258–62.

_____. *Protestant Poetics and the Seventeenth-Century Religious Lyric*. Princeton: Princeton University Press, 1979.

Louth, Andrew. *The Origins of the Christian Mystical Tradition: From Plato to Denys*. Oxford: Clarendon Press, 1981.

Low, Anthony. *Love's Architecture: Devotional Modes in Seventeenth-Century English Poetry*. New York: New York University Press, 1978.

Mahood, M. M. *Poetry and Humanism*. London: Century, 1950.

Maleski, Mary A., ed. *A Fine Tuning: Studies of the Religious Poetry of Herbert and Milton*. An unpublished collection of essays in honor of Joseph H. Summers, to be published by SUNY-Binghamton's Medieval and Renaissance Texts and Studies, 1989.

Mandell, Gail Porter. *The Phoenix Paradox: A Study of Renewal Through Change in the Collected Poems and Last Poems of D. H. Lawrence*. Carbondale: Southern Illinois University Press, 1984.

Marilla, E. L. "The Mysticism of Henry Vaughan: Some Observations." *Review of English Studies*, 18 (1967), 164–166.

Marotti, Arthur F. *John Donne, Coterie Poet*. Madison: The University of Wisconsin Press, 1986.

Marshall, Tom. *The Psychic Mariner: A Reading of the Poems of D. H. Lawrence*. New York: The Viking Press, 1970.

Martz, Louis. *The Paradise Within*. New Haven: Yale University Press, 1964.

_____. *The Poetry of Meditation*. 2nd ed. New Haven: Yale University Press, 1962.

Mazzeo, Joseph Anthony. "A Critique of Some Modern Theories of Metaphysical Poetry." *John Donne's Poetry*. Ed. A. L. Clements. New York: W. W. Norton and Company, 1966. 134–43.

McKevlin, Dennis. *A Lecture in Love's Philosophy: Donne's Vision of the World of Human Love in the Songs and Sonnets*. Lanham, MD: University Press of America, 1984.

*The Mediaeval Mystics of England*. Ed. Eric Colledge. New York: Scribner's, 1961.

Mehra, J., ed. *The Physicist's Conception of Nature*. Dordrecht, Holland: D. Reidel, 1973.

Merton, Thomas. *The Ascent to Truth*. New York: Harcourt, Brace, and Company, 1951.

Meyer, Marvin W., trans. *The Secret Teachings of Jesus: Four Gnostic Gospels*. New York: Random House, 1984.

Miller, Edmund and Robert DiYanni, eds. *Like Season'd Timber: New Essays on George Herbert.* New York: Peter Lang, 1987.

Miller, Edmund. *Drudgerie Divine: The Rhetoric of God and Man in George Herbert.* Salzberg: Institüt für Anglistik und Amerikanistik, Univerität Salzburg, 1979.

Milton, John. *Complete Poems and Major Prose.* Ed. Merritt Y. Hughes. New York: Odyssey Press, 1957.

Mulder, John. *The Temple of the Mind: Education and Literary Taste in Seventeenth-Century England.* New York: Pegasus, 1969.

Nestrick, William V. " 'Mine and Thine' in *The Temple.*" *"Too Rich to Clothe the Sunne": Essays on George Herbert.* Eds. Claude J. Summers and Ted-Larry Pebworth. Pittsburgh: University of Pittsburgh Press, 1980. 115–127.

Novarr, David. *The Disinterred Muse: Donne's Texts and Contexts.* Ithaca: Cornell University Press, 1980.

———. *The Making of Walton's "Lives."* Ithaca: Cornell University Press, 1958.

Nygren, Anders. *Agape and Eros.* Trans. Philip S. Watson. London: Society for Promoting Christian Knowledge, 1953.

O'Connell, Patrick F. " 'La Corona': Donne's Ars Poetica Sacra." *The Eagle and the Dove.* Eds. Claude J. Summers and Ted-Larry Pebworth. Columbia: University of Missouri Press, 1986.

Oliver, H. J. "The Mysticism of Henry Vaughan: A Reply." *Journal of English and Germanic Philology,* 53 (1954), 352–360.

Origen. *On First Principles.* Trans. G. W. Butterworth. London: Society for Promoting Christian Knowledge, 1936.

———. *The Song of Songs: Commentary and Homilies.* Trans. R. P. Lawson. London: Longmans, Green and Co., 1957.

Palmer, George H., ed. *The English Works of George Herbert.* Boston: Houghton, Mifflin, 1905.

Parker, Derek. *John Donne and His World.* London: Thames and Hudson, 1975.

Parry, Graham, *Seventeenth-Century Poetry: The Social Context.* London: Hutchinson, 1985.

Pettet, E. C. *Of Paradise and Light: A Study of Vaughan's Silex Scintillans.* Cambridge, England: University Press, 1960.

Pico Della Mirandola, Giovanni. *Oration on the Dignity of Man.* Trans. A. Robert Caponigri. Chicago: Henry Regnery Company, 1956.

Pinka, Patricia Garland. *This Dialogue of One: The Songs and Sonnets of John Donne.* University, Alabama: The University of Alabama Press, 1982.

Plato. *The Republic*. Trans. Francis Macdonald Cornford. Oxford: Oxford University Press, 1941.

———. *The Symposium*. Trans. W. Hamilton. Baltimore: Penguin, 1951.

———. *The Works of Plato*. Ed. Irwin Edman. New York: Random House, 1928.

Plotinus. *The Enneads*. 3rd ed. Trans. Stephen McKenna and B. S. Page. London: Faber and Faber, 1962.

Pollock, John J. "The Divided Consciousness of Henry Vaughan." *Papers on Language and Literature*, 10 (1974), 422–424.

Post, Jonathan F. S. *Henry Vaughan: The Unfolding Vision*. Princeton: Princeton University Press, 1982.

Rickey, Mary Ellen. *Utmost Art: Complexity in the Verse of George Herbert*. Louisville: University of Kentucky Press, 1966.

Roberts, John R., ed. *Essential Articles: George Herbert's Poetry*. Hamden, Conn.: Archon Books, 1979.

———., ed. *Essential Articles: John Donne's Poetry*. Hamden, Conn.: Archon Books, 1975.

———., ed. *George Herbert: An Annotated Bibliography of Modern Criticism, 1905–1984*. Rev. ed. Columbia: University of Missouri Press, 1988.

———., ed, *John Donne: An Annotated Bibliography of Modern Criticism, 1912–1967*. Columbia: University of Missouri Press, 1973.

———., ed. *John Donne: An Annotated Bibliography of Modern Criticism, 1968–1978*. Columbia: University of Missouri Press, 1982.

———. "John Donne's Poetry: An Assessment of Modern Criticism." *John Donne Journal*, 1 (1982), 55–67.

Rolle, Richard. *The Form of Perfect Living and Other Prose Treatises*. London: T. Baker, 1910.

Rollin, Roger B. " 'Fantastique Ague': The Holy Sonnets and Religious Melancholy." *The Eagle and the Dove*. Eds. Claude J. Summers and Ted-Larry Pebworth. Columbia: University of Missouri Press, 1986.

Rooney, William J. " 'The Canonization': The Language of Paradox Reconsidered." *ELH*, 23 (1956), 36–47. *Essential Articles: John Donne's Poetry*. Ed. John R. Roberts. Hamden, Conn.: Archon Books, 1975. 271–78.

Rudrum, A. W., ed. *Essential Articles for the Study of Henry Vaughan*. Hamden, Conn.: Archon Books, 1987.

———. "Henry Vaughan and the Theme of Transfiguration." *Southern Review: Australian Journal of Literary Studies*, 1 (1963), 54–68.

Ruysbroeck, John. *The Adornment of the Spiritual Marriage. The Sparkling Stone. The Book of Supreme Truth.* Trans. C. A. Wynschenk, Dom.; ed. Evelyn Underhill. London: John M. Watkins, 1951.

Sanders, Wilbur. *John Donne's Poetry.* Cambridge: Cambridge University Press, 1971.

Schroedinger, Erwin. *My View of the World.* Cambridge: University Press, 1964.

Scupoli, Lorenzo. *Unseen Warfare: being the SPIRITUAL COMBAT and PATH TO PARADISE.* Trans. E. Kadloubovsky and G. E. H. Palmer. London: Faber and Faber, 1952.

Seelig, Sharon Cadman. *The Shadow of Eternity: Belief and Structure in Herbert, Vaughan, and Traherne.* Lexington: University Press of Kentucky, 1981.

Sexton, Anne. *The Complete Poems.* Ed. Linda Gray Sexton. Boston: Houghton Mifflin, 1981.

Severance, Sibyl Lutz. "Self-Persistence in *The Temple*: George Herbert's 'Artillerie.'" University of Hartford *Studies in Literature*, 16 (1984), 108–117.

Shaw, Robert B. *The Call of God: The Theme of Vocation in the Poetry of Donne and Herbert.* No City: Cowley Publications, 1981.

Shawcross, John T. "Poetry, Personal and Impersonal: The Case of Donne." *The Eagle and the Dove.* Eds. Claude J. Summers and Ted-Larry Pebworth. Columbia: University of Missouri Press, 1986.

Shelley, Percy Bysshe. *The Selected Poetry and Prose.* Ed. Carlos Baker. New York: Random House, 1951.

Sherwood, Terry G. *Fulfilling the Circle: A Study of John Donne's Thought.* Toronto: University of Toronto Press, 1984.

Simmonds, James D. *Masques of God: Form and Theme in the Poetry of Henry Vaughan.* Pittsburgh: University of Pittsburgh Press, 1972.

Simpson, Evelyn. *A Study of the Prose Works of John Donne.* 2nd ed. Oxford: The Clarendon Press, 1948.

Smith, A. J., ed. *John Donne: Essays in Celebration.* London: Methuen & Co., 1972.

———. "The Dismissal of Love or, Was Donne a Neoplatonic

Lover?" in the above *John Donne: Essays in Celebration,* 89–131.

———. *John Donne: The Songs and Sonets.* London: Edward Arnold, 1964.

———. "Henry Vaughan's Ceremony of Innocence." *Essays and Studies,* 26 (1973), 35–52.

———. *The Metaphysics of Love: Studies in Renaissance love poetry from Dante to Milton.* Cambridge: Cambridge University Press, 1985.

Spencer, Sidney. *Mysticism in World Religion.* Baltimore: Penguin Books, 1963.

Spilka, Mark. *The Love Ethic of D. H. Lawrence.* Bloomington: Indiana University Press, 1955.

Stace, W. T. *Mysticism and Philosophy.* New York: Lippincott, 1960.

———. *The Teachings of the Mystics.* New York: The New American Library, 1960.

———. *Time and Eternity.* Princeton: Princeton University Press, 1952.

Stewart, Bain Tate. "Hermetic Symbolism in Henry Vaughan's 'The Night.'" *Philological Quarterly,* 29 (1950), 417–422.

Stewart, Stanley. *The Enclosed Garden: The Tradition and the Image in Seventeenth-Century Poetry.* Madison: The University of Wisconsin Press, 1966.

———. *George Herbert.* Boston: Twayne Publishers, 1986.

Strier, Richard. *Love Known: Theology and Experience in George Herbert's Poetry.* Chicago: The University of Chicago Press, 1983.

Summers, Claude J. and Ted-Larry Pebworth, eds. *The Eagle and the Dove: Reassessing John Donne.* Columbia: University of Missouri Press, 1986.

———., eds. *"Bright Shootes of Everlastingnesse": The Seventeenth-Century Religious Lyric.* Columbia: University of Missouri Press, 1987.

———., eds. *"Too Rich to Clothe the Sunne": Essays on George Herbert.* Pittsburgh: University of Pittsburgh Press, 1980.

———. "Herbert, Vaughan, and Public Concerns in Private Modes." *The George Herbert Journal,* 3 (1979–80), 1–21.

———. "Vaughan's Temple in Nature and the Context of 'Regeneration.'" *Journal of English and Germanic Philology,* 74 (1975), 351–60. Reprinted in Rudrum's *Essential Articles: Henry Vaughan,* 215–225.

Summers, Joseph H. *George Herbert: His Religion and Art.* Cambridge: Harvard University Press, 1954.

Suzuki, D. T. *Mysticism: Christian and Buddhist.* New York: Collier Books, 1962.

Thekla, Sister Maria. *George Herbert: Idea and Image.* Buckinghamshire: Newport Pagnell, 1974.

Thomas, Noel Kennedy. *Henry Vaughan: Poet of Revelation.* Worthing: Churchman Publishing, 1986.

Thomason, T. Katherine. "Plotinian Metaphysics and Donne's 'Extasie.'" *Studies in English Literature,* 22 (1982), 91–105.

Tillyard, E. M. W. *The Elizabethan World Picture.* London: Chatto & Windus, 1960.

Tolstoy, Leo. *What is Art? and Essays On Art.* Trans. Aylmer Maude. Oxford: University Press, 1969.

Traherne, Thomas. *Centuries, Poems, and Thanksgivings.* 2 vols. Ed. H. M. Margoliouth. Oxford: University Press, 1958.

Triverton, William (Martin Jarrett-Kerr). Foreword by T. S. Eliot. *D. H. Lawrence and Human Existence.* London: Rockliff, 1951.

Tuve, Rosemond. *A Reading of George Herbert.* Chicago: University of Chicago Press, 1952.

Underhill, Evelyn. *The Essentials of Mysticism.* New York: E. P. Dutton, 1960. (Originally published in 1920.)

————. *Mysticism.* New York: Meridian Books, 1955. (Originally published in 1911, revised twelfth edition in 1930.)

Veith, Jr., Gene Edward. *Reformation Spirituality: The Religion of George Herbert,* London and Toronto: Associated University Presses, 1985.

Vendler, Helen. *The Poetry of George Herbert.* Cambridge: Harvard University Press, 1975.

Walton, Izaak. *Lives.* Oxford: Oxford World Classics, 1927.

Warren, Austin. "Donne's Extasie.'" *Studies in Philology,* 55 (1958), 472–480.

Warren, Robert Penn. *All the King's Men.* New York: Harcourt, Brace, 1946.

————. *At Heaven's Gate.* New York: Random House, 1943.

————. *Audubon: A Vision.* New York: Random House, 1969.

————. *Being Here: Poetry 1977–1980.* New York: Random House, 1980.

————. *Chief Joseph of the Nez Perce.* New York: Random House, 1983.

————. *Democracy and Poetry.* Cambridge: Harvard University Press, 1975.

————. *Eleven Poems On The Same Theme.* Norfolk, Conn.: New Directions, 1942.

_____ . *Incarnations: Poems 1966–1968*. New York: Random House, 1968.

_____ . Interview in *Writers at Work*. Ed. Malcolm Cowley. New York: Viking, 1959.

_____ . *New and Selected Poems: 1923–1985*. New York: Random House, 1985.

_____ . *Or Else: Poem/Poems 1968–1974*. New York: Random House, 1974.

_____ . *Promises: Poems 1954–1956*. New York: Random House, 1957.

_____ . *Rumor Verified: Poems 1979–1980*. New York: Random House, 1981.

_____ . *Selected Poems: 1923–1943*. New York: Harcourt, Brace, 1944.

_____ . *Selected Poems: 1923–1975*. New York: Random House, 1976.

_____ . *Tale of Time: New Poems 1960–1966 in Selected Poems: New and Old, 1923–1966*. New York: Random House, 1966.

Watts, Alan. *Behold the Spirit: A Study in the Necessity of Mystical Religion*. New York: Vintage, 1971.

_____ . *The Book*. New York: Pantheon, 1966.

Weiner, Andrew. *Sir Philip Sidney and the Poetics of Protestanism: A Study of Contexts*. Minneapolis: University of Minnesota Press, 1978.

White, Helen C. *The Metaphysical Poets*. New York: Macmillan, 1936.

Wilber, Ken, ed. *The Holographic Paradigm and Other Paradoxes: Exploring the Leading Edge of Science*. Boston and London: New Science Library, 1985.

_____ . *Quantum Questions: Mystical Writings of the World's Great Physicists*. Boston: New Science Library, 1985.

Williams, Daniel Day. *The Spirit and the Forms of Love*. Washington, D.C.: University Press of America, 1981.

Wordsworth, William. *The Prelude, Selected Poems and Sonnets*. Ed. Carlos Baker. New York: Holt, Rinehart and Winston, 1954.

Young, R. V. "Donne's Holy Sonnets and the Theology of Grace," in *"Bright Shootes of Everlastingnesse": The Seventeenth-Century Religious Lyric*. Eds. Claude J. Summers and Ted-Larry Pebworth. Columbia: University of Missouri Press, 1987.

Zaehner, R. C. *Concordant Discord: The Interdependence of Faiths*. Oxford: Clarendon Press, 1970.

Zukav, Gary. *The Dancing Wu Li Masters: An Overview of the New Physics*. New York: Bantam Books, 1980.

# INDEX

group two, 20–23, 31–32, 43, 51, 59,
62–63, 65, 69, 77–78, 241, 244;
group three, 20–23, 42–43, 48, 57,
65, 241; group four, 241, 243
"A Feaver", 242
"A Jeat Ring Sent", 242
"A Lecture upon the Shadow", 31,
242
"A Nocturnal upon S.Lucies Day,
being the shortest day, 242, 244
"A Valediction: Forbidding
Mourning", 19, 32, 53, 242
"A Valediction: of my Name in the
Window", 53, 242
"A Valediction: of the Book", 242
"A Valediction: of Weeping", 68,
242
"Aire and Angels", 41, 242
"Breake of Day", 241, 243
"Communitie", 241
"Confined Love", 241
"Farewell to Love", 242
"Image and Dream", 242
"Loves Alchymie", 56, 242
"Loves Diet", 19, 242–243
"Loves Exchange", 242
"Loves Growth", 242
"Loves Infiniteness", 54, 242
"Loves Usury", 19, 55, 242
"Negative Love", 32, 242
"Song: 'Goe, and catche a falling
starre'", 19, 56, 241
"Song: 'Sweetest love, I do not
goe'", 241
"The Anniversarie", 55, 242
"The Apparition", 242
"The Baite", 241, 243
"The Blossome", 20, 243
"The Broken Heart", 242
"The Canonization", 19, 45–53,
59, 61, 242
"The Computation", 242
"The Curse", 56, 242
"The Dampe", 242, 255
"The Dissolution", 243
"The Dream", 242, 243
"The Expiration", 242
"The Exstasie", 19, 22–46, 52–53,
61, 65, 132, 242, 246

"The Flea", 242
"The Funerall", 20, 243
"The Good-morrow", 54–55, 242
"The Indifferent", 19, 242
"The Legacie", 242
"The Message", 241
"The Paradox", 242
"The Primrose", 243
"The Prohibition", 242–243
"The Relique", 29, 243
"The Sunne Rising", 54–55, 242
"The Triple Foole", 242
"The Undertaking", 242
"The Will", 242, 243
"Twickham Garden", 20, 242
"Witchcraft by a Picture", 242
"Womans Constancy," 19, 242
*Biathanotos*, 39
*Pseudo–Martyr*, 39
*Sermons*, 40–41
Donnelly, Dorothy, 60, 259
Durr, R.A., 62, 129, 143, 156, 254, 262,
274, 278

Eckhart, Meister, and Contemplative
Tradition, 1, 16, 181, 176, 254; and
Donne, 29, 30, 32; and Herbert, 83, 119,
126; and Lawrence, 196; and Modern
Poetry, 176; and Vaughan, 143–144
Eddington, Sir Arthur, 229, 235
Endicott–Patterson, Annabel M., 267
Egerton, Sir Thomas, 57
Ego, 95, 236–238; and Blake, 122; and
Donne, 38; and Kinnell, 212, 215, 220,
222–224; and Lawrence, 180, 186–187,
193, 195; and Traherne, 45. *See also*
False Self; Pneuma; Psyche; True Self;
Two Selves
Einstein, Albert, 172, 174, 229, 233, 235
Eliot, T.S., 97, 175, 179, 188, 225, 256, 279
Emerson, Ralph Waldo, 208
Erigena, 234
Everson, William, 175

Fall, the, 13, 36, 177, 239; and Donne, 52,
70; and Herbert, 103, 122; and
Illumination, 169; and Kinnell, 212,
214–215, 224, 237; and Lawrence, 179,
190, 196; and Purgation, 16; and